Ushering Civil Rights into Law

USHERING CIVIL RIGHTS INTO LAW

Judge Richard T. Rives and Desegregation in the Public Sphere

PAT ARNESON

THE UNIVERSITY OF ALABAMA PRESS
Tuscaloosa

The University of Alabama Press
Tuscaloosa, Alabama 35487-0380
uapress.ua.edu

Typeface: Adobe Caslon Pro

Cover image: Richard T. Rives, ca. 1925. Photograph courtesy of Ginny Granade
Cover design: Terrell Harris

Cataloging-in-Publication data is available from the Library of Congress.
ISBN: 978-0-8173-2259-5 (cloth)
ISBN: 978-0-8173-6241-6 (paper)
E-ISBN: 978-0-8173-9589-6

Contents

Acknowledgements

During the past decade, this project has recursively shifted from the foreground to the background in my life. Many people have helped me in ways large and small that have made all the difference in realizing this book.

To Ginny Granade goes my deepest gratitude. She generously allowed me access to Judge Rives's papers. I cannot thank her enough for allowing me to gain insight into her grandfather's life and remarkable accomplishments. Special thanks also to J. Mills Thornton III for offering his encouragement of this first book-length project about Judge Rives. I truly value the gift of his discernment and patience.

I am indebted to a number of Judge Rives's clerks who have helped me gain a better understanding the time, the man, and the law: Neil T. Bradley, Norman L. Blumenfeld, George E. Dix, Howard M. Feuerstein, Jonathan R. Harkavy, Lawrence R. Levin, John Daniel Reaves, Craig E. Smith, Charles C. Stebbins, E. Lloyd Sutter, and several sources who wished to remain anonymous.

In addition, people have generously offered to share their personal knowledge and professional resources, sending articles and references, and sharing their life experiences: Kathleen Blee, Butler Browder, Anne Sodini Emanuel, Jonathan R. Harkavy, Ray Jenkins, Lawrence R. Levin, Joe McDonald, Bobby Segall, and John M. Spivack.

I am grateful to the Alabama Department of Archives and History, Stephen E. Cotton of the *Southern Courier*, and Ginny Granade for allowing the use of their photographs in this book. For those orphan images whose sources or creators could not be identified, I apologize for the omission and welcome any information that would help me properly acknowledge them. Thank you to the librarians who aided my "nothing ventured, nothing gained" questions with patience and provided valuable research: Norwood A. Kerr, Meredith

McDonough, Haley Aaron, and Amelia Chase of the Alabama Department of Archives and History; Jim Baggett of the Birmingham Public Library; Jane Bahnson of the Goodson Law Library at Duke University School of Law; Marcia Rapchak of the Gumberg Library at Duquesne University; Jake Kobrick of the Federal Judicial Center; Jeff Flannery of the Library of Congress; Megan Garton of the Tulane University Law Library; Mon Yin Lung and Spencer L. Simons of the University of Houston Law Library; Connie L. Phelps of the University of New Orleans Earl K. Long Library; and Marian Drey of the US Court of Appeals for the Fifth Circuit Library.

Thank you to my research assistants at Duquesne University: Tyler Bowen, Justin Bonanno, Mark Gardner, Kristen Haldeman, Jack Hickly, Lindsey Laverty, Erin Lionberger, Rachel Morrell, Katherine Rogers, and Alexis Scott. This book is better because of your able assistance. I also appreciate those who agreed to read early drafts of this project, including Todd Allen, Nichole Brazelton, Dave Dewberry, David Errera, and Lawrence R. Levin. Your thoughtful questions and comments were invaluable to me. To Jillion Benion: this project would never have seen the light of day without your kind encouragement.

The preparation of this book was made possible, in part, through the National Endowment for the Humanities Summer Stipend Program, a Duquesne University Severino A. Russo Endowed Faculty Development Award, a Duquesne University Presidential Scholarship Award, and a sabbatical leave from Duquesne University. That financial support allowed me to access sites to conduct the research needed to complete this project.

I extend my deep gratitude to Dan Waterman, editor in chief of the University of Alabama Press, for his continuing interest in this project. The staff have been most helpful throughout the publication process, including Tyler Arnold, Jon Berry, Carol Connell, Samantha Huff-Robertson, and others. I wish to offer my heartfelt appreciation to Joanna Jacobs and Irina du Quenoy for their keen attention to detail. I would also like to acknowledge several anonymous reviewers who offered many useful comments. Any flaws in this work remain mine alone.

I am also grateful to my friends for emboldening me, especially Spiff, Mrs. Snow, Emily, and Nichole. You helped me maintain perspective, laugh until my sides hurt, and pursue things in life that are truly important. And to Algis Mickūnas and Žilvinas Svigaris, ačiū už mano intelektualinio gyvenimo puoselėjimą.

Words can't describe my appreciation for my family—always, you're my heart.

Ushering Civil Rights into Law

Introduction

A Southern Judge at the Forefront of Legal and Social Change

Judge Richard Taylor Rives (1895–1982) wrote significant Civil Rights decisions on behalf of three-judge panels between 1955–1966 as a member of the US Court of Appeals for the Fifth Circuit. Hugo Black Jr., whose father was a US Supreme Court justice during that time, said of Rives, "Never was a federal circuit judge more respected by the members of the one Court that could reverse him. . . . Rives was the most influential and powerful federal judge below the Supreme Court level during the period between *Brown v. Board of Education* and, at least, his taking senior status, in 1966."[1] The implications of Rives's Civil Rights rulings continue to resonate throughout society.

Judge Rives's record as a member of the Fifth Circuit establishes him as a pivotal figure in Civil Rights jurisprudence. Althea T. L. Simmons, a lawyer for the National Association for the Advancement of Colored People (NAACP) for over thirty-five years, explained that during the Civil Rights era, the Fifth Circuit came to be seen by Black citizens and members of other minority groups as a "citadel in the civil rights arena."[2] Though he was prominent in his time and well-regarded as a member of the Fifth Circuit, history has yet to remember Rives (rhymes with "leaves") and his exigent judicial legacy with adequate regard, given the significance of his decisions related to racial equality in the public sphere. This monograph addresses the formation of Rives's judicial philosophy and his Civil Rights decisions from the mid-1950s through the 1960s that justify his place as one of the nation's great judges.

Following Reconstruction (1865–1874), the Jim Crow South installed state laws sanctioning injustices against Black citizens. In opposition to these injustices, the Legal Defense and Education Fund (LDF) Civil Rights law practice, originally an arm of the NAACP, was incorporated in 1940. The LDF was first led by the NAACP Legal Department's director-counsel, Charles Hamilton

Houston, and then by his protégé Thurgood Marshall. Lawyers associated with the LDF relied, in part, on the US Constitution's Fourteenth Amendment, which prohibits states from abridging the rights of any citizen, giving all citizens equal protection under the law.[3]

One of the LDF's notable cases, *Brown v. Board of Education of Topeka I* (1954, hereafter *Brown I*), desegregated public educational facilities. The following year, in *Brown v. Board of Education of Topeka II* (1955, hereafter *Brown II*), US Supreme Court justices mandated that public education be racially desegregated "with all deliberate speed."[4] The justices allotted this task to judges in the Southern states, primarily the seven federal judges of the Fifth Circuit. At that time, the circuit included the Gulf states of Texas, Louisiana, Mississippi, Alabama, and Florida; the state of Georgia; and the Panama Canal Zone. After the *Brown* decisions, numerous legal cases were filed to contest conflicting federal, state, and municipal laws and policies related to the Civil Rights of Black citizens. For Judge Rives, who joined the Fifth Circuit in May 1951, *Brown* marked a significant turning point in society. He heard numerous district court trials and Fifth Circuit appeals addressing racial desegregation. Rives, a man who prioritized equality, applied *Brown* across the public sphere—in areas of public transportation, elementary and secondary schools, higher education, reapportionment of state legislatures, voter registration (including the use of poll taxes and literacy tests), and jury pools.

During the 1950s and 1960s, judges rarely discussed their judicial philosophy. In *Boeing Co. v. Shipman* (1969), a personal injury lawsuit that addressed the standard for evidence required to submit a case to a jury, Judge Rives identified himself as a "common-law lawyer . . . armed with the Constitution." American legal scholar David A. Strauss explained that in the common-law approach, democracy develops "through the accumulation and evolution of precedents, shaped to some degree by notions of fairness and good policy." A "living Constitution" metaphor allows interpretations of the US Constitution to adapt to shifting social needs. This judicial philosophy maintains that the Constitution was written using broad language that permits concepts to evolve over time and allows the fundamental tenets of the Constitution to remain current. Strauss expanded, "A common law Constitution is a 'living' Constitution, but it is also one that can protect fundamental principles against transient public opinion, and it is not one that judges (or anyone else) can simply manipulate to fit their own ideas." Judicial interpretations may continue an evolution of the law, but "not by ignoring what exists and starting anew."[5] Common-law judges interpret the Constitution by relying on the law as developed in legislation and as tested in judicial decisions. Rives's judicial philosophy was guided by fairness and common sense and undergirded by the principle of equality. That approach led him to equally apply the law to each citizen, regardless of race. The phrase "We the People," designated in the preamble to the Constitution, influenced his thinking about the evolution of democracy. On that basis, he interpreted that *Brown I* should be expanded throughout the public sphere.

As discussed in greater detail in the coming chapters, Judge Rives has been considered by some people to be an activist—a trailblazer and advocate for Civil Rights.[6] Rives was a man who worked humbly in his position and did not identify himself as an activist. He believed that the US Constitution demands that all citizens be treated equally under the law. He did not have a perfect record in support of Civil Rights throughout his judgeship, which a strict judicial activist would have. Rives's view on race was undoubtedly shaped while he was a child in the South and shifted while he was a lawyer—having conversations with his son about race and contesting the Boswell amendment to the Alabama Constitution, which was crafted to prohibit Black citizens from registering to vote. Rives embraced education and over time developed his common-law judicial philosophy.

My argument is structured as follows. Each chapter serves as a case study that validates the importance of Rives's judicial contribution to democracy, which is little known in Civil Rights history. Relying on evidence presented throughout, the book concludes that Rives's Civil Rights legacy is significant and warrants further attention.

Chapter 1, "Making the Man: Deep-Rooted Relationships and Political Initiations," provides background on Judge Rives's early life as it shaped his judicial philosophy. The chapter documents the influence of his family, education, and entrance into legal practice. His military experience included service in the Mexican Border War (1910–1919) and World War I (1914–1918). In Alabama politics, Rives supported liberal-leaning Democrats against the conservative Democrats who dominated the state. Each of these experiences would influence his approach to the law.

Chapter 2, "A Foray into Racial Desegregation: A Judicial Interpretation of Public Law in Transportation," examines the circumstances surrounding Judge Rives's *Browder v. Gayle* (1956) majority decision on behalf of himself and his protégé Judge Frank M. Johnson Jr. *Browder*, a Montgomery bus transportation case, directly addressed a conflict between state and federal laws regarding the racial segregation of public facilities. In the decision, which refuted *Plessy v. Ferguson*'s (1896) acceptance of state-mandated segregation, Rives publicly documented his interpretation of *Brown I*. When he did so, the *New York Times* quoted Euel Screws Jr., a clerk for Rives, who declared that Rives "crossed the Rubicon," ripping apart the segregated social fabric and becoming an enemy of many white citizens and organizations across the Southern states.[7]

Chapter 3, "Fighting for Commensurate Access: Allegations of Court-Packing to Desegregate Primary and Secondary Public Education," addresses Judge Rives's involvement in desegregating public educational facilities. Law professors Frank T. Read and Lucy S. McGough reported that from 1956 to 1966, Rives participated in more educational desegregation decisions than any other Fifth Circuit judge. He ruled on behalf of the court in *Borders v. Rippy* (1957), wherein the judges required public schools to create and implement student placement plans. He confirmed in *Shuttlesworth v. Birmingham Board of Education* (1958) and *Gibson v. Board of Public Instruction of Dade County, Florida* (1959) that a constitutional school placement plan, when proven to be applied in an inequitable manner, is unconstitutional. When Rives recognized that educational administrators would not voluntarily obey court orders even if given the time to do so, he began to act more decisively. His decision in *Armstrong v. Birmingham Board of Education* (1963) prompted Fifth Circuit Judge Benjamin F. Cameron, a segregationist from Mississippi, to write a dissent charging that court-packing was occurring in the Fifth Circuit. That accusation prompted the Fifth Circuit's Houston Conference, which brought the judges' divided opinions on racial segregation into the public sphere. Rives's involvement in the *Lee v. Macon County Board of Education* (1967) decision brought a close to over a decade of education decisions.[8]

Chapter 4, "Demanding that the Executive Branch of Government Intervene: The Desegregation of Public Higher Education," examines Judge Rives's entry into the desegregation of higher education in *Board of Supervisors of Louisiana State University and Agricultural and Mechanical College v. Tureaud* (1953), which addressed the admission decision concerning a Black applicant into an all-white university. He informally encouraged Judge Harlan H. Grooms of the Northern District of Alabama Court to support gradualism in *Lucy v. University of Alabama* (1955). The US Supreme Court justices overruled Grooms, which stimulated Rives to shift his approach to the law. He was also involved with *Meredith v. Fair* (1962), a series of racial desegregation lawsuits brought by James Meredith against the University of Mississippi. Rives was an experienced judge by the early 1960s and behind-the-scenes confrontations emerged between him, President John F. Kennedy, Mississippi governor Ross Barnett, and Attorney General Robert F. Kennedy. A telephone conversation between Rives and the president resulted in Kennedy shifting his public stance on Civil Rights. In addition, Rives was instrumental in *United States v. Barnett* (1965) addressing Barnett's unwillingness to submit to the judicial branch of government.[9]

Chapter 5, "Adjudicating Representation in State Legislatures: Making Strides in Reapportionment," addresses the reapportionment revolution of the 1960s. Judge Rives's understanding of state politics was a significant advantage to the judiciary in addressing the Alabama legislature's refusal to reapportion citizens' representation in government. The state legislature had not been reapportioned since 1901, and lawsuits were prompted, in part, by *Gomillion v. Lightfoot* (1960), a gerrymandering case that required the court to redraw electoral district boundaries. Rives led a three-judge panel in ruling on several interrelated cases to require equity in the apportionment of legislators representing voting districts. He was involved in *Sims v. Frink* (1962), which became linked to *Reynolds v. Sims* (1964), *Sims v. Baggett* (1965), and *Sims v. Amos* (1972).[10] At that time, Rives and his colleagues could not have foreseen that their ruling to redistrict and reapportion the Alabama State Legislature would be expanded into a nationwide decree by the US Supreme Court.

Chapter 6, "Addressing State-Sanctioned White Supremacy in Elections: Refuting Discrimination against Black Voters," examines several cases in which Judge Rives participated to stop discrimination against Black citizens who tried to register to vote. *Smith v. Allwright* (1942), a US Supreme Court case ruling that state political parties could not prohibit Black citizens from voting in primary elections, provoked members of the Alabama legislature to propose the Boswell amendment, which Rives campaigned against as a lawyer. On the bench, Judge Johnson made three voting registration decisions during 1961 and 1962 that became known as the "freezing doctrine." However, Rives thought Johnson's decisions violated the law by allowing voting registrars to continue to use illegal procedures when registering some white voters. In 1963, Rives wrote an opinion in *United States v. Atkins* overruling Johnson's doctrine. Among other Civil Rights lawsuits, Rives wrote the majority decisions in *Dent v. Duncan* (1966) and *United States v. Alabama* (1966), which eliminated the use of literacy tests and forbade the use of poll taxes to qualify a person to register to vote.[11]

Chapter 7, "Ordering Conditions That Allow for an Impartial Jury: Desegregating Juror Selection Processes," recognizes that although the US Supreme Court ruled in *Norris v. Alabama* (1935) that excluding Black citizens from jury service is unconstitutional, lawyers continued into the 1960s to identify ways to include only white citizens on Southern juries. In *United States ex rel. Goldsby v. Harpole* (1959), Judge Rives ordered judges and lawyers to alter illegal juror selection processes to act in accordance with the law. He reiterated that decision in *United States ex rel. Seals v. Wiman* (1962) and *Rabinowitz v. United States* (1966).[12] He did so on the basis that excluding people from a jury pool due to their race violates the rights of the accused person and the rights of citizens who are not allowed to potentially participate on juries. Portions of Rives's *Rabinowitz* decision were subsequently replicated in the 1968 Jury Selection and Service Act.

Chapter 8, "Judge Richard T. Rives: A Civil Rights Legacy," acknowledges the influence Rives had on Civil Rights in the United States during his time as a federal judge. Judge Rives's Southern familial heritage, as well as his temporal and physical proximity to the Civil War, influenced how he thought about race. In making legal decisions, he relied on lessons learned during his Alabama childhood, information gained while reading law as an apprentice to Wiley Hill Sr., knowledge of the law gained in his years as a lawyer, social knowledge gained in his military and political experience, and wisdom masked as common sense that he acquired in everyday life. These personal experiences, along with the US Supreme Court *Brown* (1954, 1955) decisions, uniquely situated him to advance democratic change. Rives's jurisprudence was guided in large part by the first three words in the preamble to the US Constitution: "We the People."[13] His common-law interpretation of justice was guided by the Charters of Freedom—the Declaration of Independence, the US Constitution, and the Bill of Rights—along with federal legislation and legal precedent.

In each of these chapters, Rives's decisions on behalf of three-judge panels in district and circuit courts established legal precedents that continue to be relevant. Remnants of Jim Crow laws continue to resonate in American society. In this book, I want to impart an understanding of the intellectual evolution of Rives as a man and as a judge who sought equality for all citizens. Despite momentous opposition from some white citizens, Rives stood firm in his position to legally abolish Jim Crow and in so doing, forever changed the United States.

1

Making the Man

Deep-Rooted Relationships and Political Initiations

Richard Taylor Rives was born in Montgomery, Alabama, on January 15, 1895, a time when citizens in the South observed strict racial lines. His family heritage was deeply rooted in Southern culture. Before the Civil War, his grandfather William H. Rives Sr. owned two large plantations, enslaved people valued at the time to be worth $90,000, and other personal property.[1] Rives's father, William H. Rives Jr., was born in 1854 and witnessed the war as a boy. When Rives was young, he was surrounded by conflicting messages about racial differences. As he matured, his view would shift from thinking that slavery and Jim Crow laws were the norm to recognizing that systemic inequality was constitutionally wrong and personally unjust. The whole of Rives's life experiences contributed to shape his judicial philosophy.

Rives's parents, William H. Rives Jr. and Alice Bloodworth Taylor Rives, were married on December 3, 1879. Both the Rives and Taylor families were pioneers in the state, settling in Alabama to work in agriculture.[2] Alice and William were both born before the Civil War, yet following the war each adhered to a different cultural narrative about race.

Like many Southerners, Rives's mother continued to accept the narrative of an idealized antebellum American South. She supported the idea of white racial superiority. Throughout her life, she remained opposed to Civil Rights for Black citizens. Religion was a vital part of Southern life in the late 1800s, and Alice grew up in the Baptist church. James Rives Childs, the Rives family genealogist, documented that Alice's maternal grandfather, James McLemore, founded the first Baptist Church in Montgomery County, whose membership before the Civil War included some of Montgomery's "wealthiest and most influential families." After the war, she continued to see herself as a member of the Southern aristocracy, despite her reduced economic condition. Rives recalled to historian John M. Spivack that his mother's political leaning was that of a "dyed-in-the-wool rebel" who remained "unReconstructed" her entire life.[3]

In contrast to his wife, William held a more liberal view regarding race relations. The Civil War had destabilized the social, political, and economic hierarchies that undergirded the dominant narrative of white supremacy. Rives told political scientist Tinsley E. Yarbrough that his father matured "in the difficult period right after the War between the States, but he felt that Blacks should be given opportunities at least to go as far as they could." Rives's father thought that all people had the potential to advance their standing. He told his sons that "he thought perhaps it was a good thing for the Yankees to win the war, for the slaves to be free, [and] for the Union to be preserved." Given his mother's opinions, Rives confessed to Yarbrough that his father's teaching was "imparted to us discreetly, man to man."[4]

The complexities of his parents' views toward Black citizens held lessons that would develop in Rives an ability to interpret a situation from multiple perspectives. Taylor, which was Rives's middle name and how his family members and close friends referred to him, told Spivack that he spent his free time doing the "things most young boys do," such as playing sports, reading for pleasure, and spending time outdoors. Ray Jenkins reported in the *Alabama Journal* that Rives "fished from the banks of the Alabama River and hunted field larks in the woods that lay beyond Montgomery's southernmost boundary, Fairview [Avenue]."[5] His life was also guided by the morality imparted by religious teachings and biblical principles. Montgomery was then a town of forty thousand people; as Rives matured, his father introduced him to business and politics. Rives learned to hold aspects of different views in tension with one another as his understanding of justice and equality evolved.

During his early life, Rives learned that education, work, and success are connected. He also learned the importance of honesty, personal responsibility, and the law, as well as the need to be self-reliant and responsible for his affairs. Rives was, as he told Spivack, "always improving, always trying to make . . . [himself] better." An aspirational impulse "to live up to . . . [his] potential" drove Rives. He understood that there were rules that children were expected to follow and that parents were expected to enforce those rules with discipline. An aristocratic morality of "right or wrong," shaped by the Presbyterian Church, his parents, and his friends, complemented these expectations. Living in the South at the turn of the twentieth century, Rives was exposed to and adopted the biases typical of his family's standing—in short, he embodied a genteel view toward race.[6]

Rives learned to think critically and negotiate different viewpoints as he considered the varying information he received at home and at school. Lawyer Deborah J. Barrow and political scientist Thomas G. Walker note that the majority of Rives's education occurred in a "one-room schoolhouse" for white boys with his brother, Thomas, who was two years older than him. In 1910 the construction of Sidney Lanier High School—the first white coeducational public high school in Montgomery—was completed. Rives would enter Lanier as a senior, in the first graduating class. Although the class initially had twenty-five students, Rives informed Spivack that nine boys had to drop out of school during the academic year to help support their families. However, his parents' dedication to education kept Rives in school.[7]

In the spring of 1911, at the age of sixteen, Rives was named valedictorian of the first graduating class of Lanier High School and was awarded a one-year scholarship to Tulane University in New Orleans, Louisiana. Although Rives's scholarship covered the cost of tuition, he told Joe Simmons of the *Montgomery Advertiser* that "money was hard to come by in those days."[8] Despite his parents' encouragement and emotional support, they could not afford to pay for Rives's living expenses. Nevertheless, he was interested in ideas and determined to attend classes at the university.

Preparing to attend Tulane University for the 1911–1912 academic year, Rives borrowed $400 from his sister Janie, a teacher at Capitol Hill School, to cover books and other living expenses for his first year. The amount was a large sum at the time, but she believed education was fundamental to achieving one's full potential. During that time, Rives was interested in mathematics and the physical sciences. He explained to Peggy Roberson of the *Birmingham News* that he thought he "could solve all the mysteries of life through science." Rives wanted to work in biological chemistry but soon enough recognized that pursuing a career in the exact sciences was only possible with an advanced degree, and he could only continue at Tulane with additional funding. Rives revealed to Simmons that he was afraid that if he borrowed more money from his sister, he would not be able to pay her back, which went against his principles.[9] Rives did not return to the university after his first year but retained those life lessons as he returned to Montgomery.

Rives learned the importance of earning one's way in life from his parents. Jenkins reported that after attending Tulane for a year, Rives "worked at odd jobs." In early 1912, he and another young man worked "in a relative's laundry," running a small pants-pressing business. The enterprise was formally known as the Flower-Rives Pressing Company, but the two young men called their venture The Pressing Club. The shop was located in an upstairs room on Dexter Avenue, where they pressed garments in the summer heat. Rives told William H. McDonald of the *Southern School News* that the young men had "a devil of a time" between contending with the heat and the challenges of starting a new business. Rives shared with Spivack that after working for a time in the business, his father helped him realize that he was not living up to his potential. William contacted his very good friend Wiley Croom Hill Sr., whose family's plantation bordered the Rives plantation before the Civil War, to assist his son.[10]

Wiley Hill Sr. was a prominent common-law lawyer in the Montgomery firm of Hill, Hill, and Whiting, which he opened around 1897. According to legal scholar David A. Strauss, a common-law approach to legal issues presupposes that lawyers and judges "should build on previous decisions . . . and that innovation should be justified based on what has gone before." As a lawyer, the elder Hill was known to make very persuasive legal arguments. Although he was shy, Rives remarked to Spivack that his mentor "became a lion in the courtroom." Rives thought Hill was a genius in court, "a magnificent lawyer, the best lawyer . . . [Rives had] ever known." Virginia Durr, whose husband Clifford Durr was also a Montgomery lawyer and a friend of the Rives family, described the Hills as "hard-boiled, ruthless people," which may have also described their legal approach on behalf of their clients.[11] When William called on his friend, Wiley Hill Sr. agreed to take Rives on as an apprentice in his firm.

Rives told Spivack that his apprenticeship was initiated when Hill sent him a short note. Rives recalled the message to McDonald: "If you would like to study law, I'll show you what books to read." A legal apprenticeship (often called "reading the law") was the dominant educational model for lawyers in the early 1900s, despite the emergence of law schools across the country in the 1870s. Rives described his situation to Spivack: as an incentive to bolster his career prospects, William urged him to "study a month" with Hill, and in the meantime, Rives would be permitted some personal freedom and could "grow sideburns" if he chose to do so. Although Rives had little idea what it meant to be a lawyer, he told McDonald that he "jumped at the chance to get out of the pressing business" to try something new.[12]

In late 1912, Rives set out to learn the common-law system. This approach, according to Strauss, rests on three principles. First, a lawyer must acknowledge the limitations of human reason. Humility about one's thought processes is fundamental to the system. This humility includes appropriate hesitation about the significance of legal precedent, which includes laws that legislators passed potentially years before the event under consideration. The second principle requires a lawyer to consider how an action will or will not work empirically in a specific situation. A lawyer cannot draw a conclusion to an everyday problem strictly based on abstract ideas about "how the world should be." In addition, personal experience is a helpful guide in understanding how an abstract concept, such as justice, can be successfully implemented. Third, lawyers must recognize the evolution of the law. Innovation is needed "for reasons of what we would call justice, or fairness, or good policy—'right reason' in the language of an earlier era." The principle of innovation is responsive to "the limitations of abstract reasoning" and "the value of experience." A common-law approach "cautions against change but does not preclude changes" that would bring about a fairer, more just society.[13] This legal orientation was consistent with the principle of fairness that had by this point come to characterize Rives's own life.

Still living with his family, Rives followed his father's initial encouragement and began to read the law with Wiley Hill Sr. Rives recalled to Spivack that Hill and other lawyers in the firm mentored him for two years in keeping with the apprenticeship model. A profile of Rives that appeared in the *Montgomery Advertiser* quoted him as saying, "Wiley Hill, especially, would take an hour or so off every week to teach me law." Rives told Spivack that he thought Hill "had a splendid, logical mind," and would encourage him when he saw that Rives was "trying to study." Rives created a small commonplace book to aid him in identifying legal trends and deriving basic principles of law from decisions in various cases.[14] A vast body of legal decisions and statutes make up the common law, and Hill's educational and professional experience were undoubtedly invaluable to Rives in learning his craft.

During Rives's youth, he explained to Spivack, he learned the importance of history. His judicial decisions reveal that he also had a strong background in English, political science, and economics. His interest in the exact sciences increased his sharp critical thinking skills. As a result of his education, Rives learned how to express himself clearly in writing and how to recognize different perspectives and use these to inform his thinking on various matters. He relied on his knowledge of the law and accompanying legal precedent, along with an understanding of legal principles that may apply in cases.[15] Rives's reading across various academic disciplines and use of the case study method honed his intellectual dexterity, upon which he relied when constructing legal arguments.

Rives also learned everyday courtroom practices and strategies from Wiley Hill Sr. This included interpreting the cultural and social context in which a case takes place from multiple perspectives. Making an oral argument in court requires a lawyer to present claims that advocate a particular outcome—one that, as Strauss explained, "makes sense as a matter of policy or fairness . . . [and as] a matter of common sense." Rives explained to Spivack that Hill's reputable skills as a trial lawyer demonstrated "how to make facts live" in the courtroom.[16] Hill would introduce the facts of a case along with legal precedents and regional understandings that would exhibit how the law does, or could, operate in practice. In the end, Rives's one-month investment in the legal profession turned into a two-year apprenticeship.

After his apprenticeship, Rives sat for the Alabama bar exam, which was a three-day test. He had turned nineteen years old only two months before. Rives later commented to one of his clerks that he had gained a great deal of knowledge in his apprenticeship regarding the types of law that the Hill firm handled, which were primarily civil and criminal cases. However, upon reaching a question about riparian rights (landowner rights attached to waterfront property where the property meets a shoreline) on the exam, namely, "What is the general rule of water law?," Rives was stumped. Recalling the incident, Rives said he simply wrote, "Water flows downhill." Even with this playful response, Rives was admitted to the bar on March 13, 1914, after which the Hill firm employed him in a salaried position. His job was to write case briefs, which he told McDonald "paid $65, $75 a month," a steady and substantial income for a young single man.[17]

The Hill firm was the only large law firm in Montgomery that handled criminal cases; however, Rives told Spivack that he preferred to take civil lawsuits. He liked working in a firm that did not represent large corporations and allowed him the freedom and independence to select clients. He often represented Black citizens as plaintiffs in cases that were unpopular in the white legal community. As lawyers Dan Abrams and Fred D. Gray explained, at that time Black lawyers "rarely attracted white clients, and many Black people needing representation often preferred hiring a white lawyer to do battle in white offices and courtrooms."[18] The Hill firm had several lawyers who supported one another on case strategy.

Rives would work throughout the week, and on Sunday afternoons he would meet with colleagues in the office to review cases and discuss how to best represent their clients in court. Rives explained his approach in his *Alabama Lawyer* article titled "Trying a Case." He addressed, in part, the need to establish a "reputation for hard work." Rives's style included letting the client talk, speaking plainly, and carefully attending to one's duty. The lawyer's job, Rives wrote, is fundamentally "to secure a judgment that can be enforced, and . . . therefore, he must avoid every possibility of error and of having the case reversed." Rives advocated that a plaintiff's lawyer argue a case truthfully and use commonsense to seek justice—while also recognizing that lawyers for the defense could appeal to prejudice and fear to sway members of a jury.[19] Members of Hill's firm aided Rives as he continued to hone his practice of the law.

While working at Hill's law firm, in November 1914 Rives signed a three-year contract, enlisting in the Alabama National Guard. The Mexican Border War had commenced in November 1910, and Rives was ready to serve his country as his forefathers had. He soon received a call to service and was mustered into the National Guard on June 27, 1916. His rank was first class sergeant in the First Field Company of the Signal Corps out of Montgomery. Signal Corps units delivered messages, patrolled the border, and went on reconnaissance missions. Rives was assigned to serve in the cavalry unit, which allowed soldiers to patrol the extensive Mexican border more easily. His knowledge of horses came, in part, from working with them as a boy. Rives told Spivack that before being activated, his unit was more of "a social outfit," but they soon understood they had "real responsibilities" to defend the United States.[20]

Rives served with his unit in New Mexico and Arizona. He explained to Spivack that the Signal Corps had "one wire telephone company along with the radio company." Rives's older brother, Thomas, left Alabama Polytechnic to go with him into military service. Alluding to the difference between officers and enlisted personnel, Rives told Spivack, "Tom was a captain of the company. He was First Lieutenant there; I was First Sergeant." Rives pointed out that being a first sergeant, lower in rank than a first lieutenant, "was a harder job." Rives was released from his assignment on March 6, 1917. World War I had been under way in Europe since before Rives returned from the border, and he reenlisted. He returned to Montgomery to practice law while awaiting his next military assignment.[21]

When Rives returned home he learned that the lawyer for the City of Montgomery, Warren Andrews, wanted him to apply for the position of assistant city lawyer. Rives disclosed to Spivack that he approached his mentor, Wiley Hill Sr., who recommended that Rives take the position—assuring him that he could return to the Hill firm after learning what he could from Andrews. Rives met with Andrews in mid-March 1917 and accepted the position. Even with a substantial salary, earning approximately $125 each week, Rives shared, "That was the worst time I believe I had . . . in an office where you're not doing much business." Rives was used to being busy in the military and enjoyed the feeling of accomplishment that work brings. He only worked in the city office about three months; on June 18, 1917, he was again called up to serve.[22]

The military mobilized Rives's National Guard unit to support US Army combat missions in Europe during World War I. His first stop was Camp Wheeler, six miles east of Macon, Georgia, a training camp for Army and National Guard units in federal service. Rives was stationed there for over a year, and during that time he met Jessie Hall Dougherty. They obtained a marriage license on July 23, 1918, and were married in Georgia. Less than two weeks later, on August 5, Rives shipped out to serve in France with Company A, 106th Field Signal Battalion of the American Expeditionary Forces. Meanwhile, Jessie relocated from Georgia to live with his parents in Montgomery. Soon after she arrived in Alabama she received a Red Cross postcard from France with a preprinted message: "The ship on which I sailed has arrived safely overseas." Rives landed in Europe less than a month before the armistice and told Spivack that his radio company "never actually got up to the front."[23] The horrific war, which had resulted in the loss of millions of lives, was over.

Rives and his brother, Thomas, returned to Montgomery on May 10, 1919, and were formally discharged two weeks later. Upon returning home, Rives resumed his legal practice at what had then become Hill, Hill, Whiting, and

Stern. He and his wife moved into their own house and on December 4, 1920, Jessie gave birth to their first child, a daughter who was born premature and lived for only one day.[24] Even in his grief, Rives continued to practice law, focusing on becoming a well-respected lawyer in Montgomery and across the state of Alabama. He pursued that goal, in part, by becoming involved in political activities.

Generations of Rives men had been politically active in their communities. Rives's father was a member of the Central Council of the Democratic and Conservative Party in Montgomery. Noted Southern historian J. Mills Thornton III described the Democratic Party in Alabama as generally divided into two different factions. The Black Belt conservative-leaning wealthy planters and Big Mule industrialists were at odds against the more liberal-minded small farmers whom Rives supported. Democratic politics in Montgomery had long been a two-party system, as represented in two of the city's well-established families—the Gunters and the Hills. The Gunters were members of the conservative wing of the Democratic Party, supported by Alabama's Big Mules (a nickname for the state's business leaders and large agriculturalists). William A. Gunter Jr. led the political machine as mayor of Montgomery from 1910 to 1915 and from 1919 until he died in 1940. The Gunters were against the Ku Klux Klan (also known as the KKK or the Klan) and rejected the prohibition amendment. For their part, the Hills were members of the liberal wing of the Democratic Party, upholding "a strong New Deal Roosevelt-Truman tradition." Judge William Wallace Hill was repeatedly elected as Montgomery County's probate judge and led the Hill faction in Montgomery County. The Hills' state political support lay in the rural areas of the state. The Hills supported the Eighteenth Amendment to the US Constitution, the prohibition amendment, passed in January 1919. In the 1920s the Hills saw the rise of the KKK as an organized mechanism for, they hoped, eventually defeating the Gunter machine.[25] The division between the Hill faction and the Gunter faction of the Democratic Party was evident in the two Montgomery newspapers.

Information published in the *Montgomery Advertiser* aligned with the Gunters on political matters. Thornton explained that the newspaper's editor, Grover C. Hall Sr., was one of Gunter's "closest advisers." The *Montgomery Advertiser*, a morning newspaper, supported Alabama's Big Mules, while the *Alabama Journal*, Montgomery's afternoon paper, was generally aligned with the Hills and supported white, working-class Alabamians who aligned with the views of Franklin Delano Roosevelt and the New Deal.[26] During Gunter's political reign, Rives would find himself helping Richard F. Hudson purchase the *Montgomery Advertiser*, a primary vehicle for his opponent's political rhetoric.

In 1903 Hudson joined the *Montgomery Advertiser*'s newspaper staff as the city circulation manager. Over time, he began to advance in the company even as the newspaper underwent several changes in editors and owners. Then, in December 1927 Franklin P. Glass became the newspaper publisher with Grover C. Hall Sr. as editor of the publication. According to the *Montgomery Advertiser*, while Hudson was working as Glass's assistant, Glass "fraternally conveyed" the purchase of the newspaper to Hudson. Upon Glass's death in 1934, his heirs arranged to sell the newspaper at auction. Representatives of a Texas newspaper company determined that they would bid for the Alabama newspaper. Rives assisted Hudson and may have introduced him to William A. Bellingrath; both Rives and Bellingrath were members of Presbyterian churches in Montgomery. The day before the newspaper was to be auctioned, Bellingrath—an early pioneer in the Coca-Cola bottling industry, whom businessman Jesse B. Hearn described as a "leader in the civic and social welfare of Montgomery and the State of Alabama," and "quiet philanthropist"—offered to loan Hudson whatever capital he would need to purchase the newspaper. At the auction, Rives laid the document from Glass to Hudson, "together with a check for $200,000, on the bench and said, 'Here's our money on the barrel head.'" Hudson purchased the newspaper, benefiting from Rives's legal and political connections. The Hills perhaps hoped that Rives's assistance to Hudson might garner support from the newspaper. However, five years later Hudson also bought the *Alabama Journal* and combined the two papers. The newspaper merger resulted in support for the Gunter faction, causing the Hills to lose their political voice, but they retained the support of the Klan.[27]

The Hills, Thornton wrote, were "allied closely" with the second iteration of the KKK. The first iteration of the Klan, established after the Civil War, sought to reimpose a segregated racial system after the end of slavery. The members used lynchings, torture, and terrorism to intimidate anyone who might challenge white supremacy. The first Klan disbanded in the 1870s, and a second Klan emerged in 1915. The second Klan was noticeably different from the first, even as members continued to support white racial superiority. Thornton explained that the second Klan was driven by "the belief that American morality was in a marked decline, that the republic itself was threatened by that decline and by the alien forces which played upon it, and the preservation of all that the United States had come to mean in the world depended upon the restoration of the faith, attitudes, and modes of behavior" of the nation's founders. Millions of Americans across the country embraced the values of the second era Klan, even though many of them were not members of the organization. The Alabama Klan, Thornton wrote, became a "protest movement of poorer and more marginalized whites, whether urban, small town, or rural." Historian Linda Gordon explained that the group "seemed ordinary and respectable" to the general public. The organization's leaders celebrated American-ness: they did not gather in secret but "operated in daylight and organized mass public events" at which politicians frequently spoke.[28]

Members of the KKK became more involved in politics as divisions within the Democratic Party became more pronounced. As Klan membership grew, so did their national voting base and political influence. The Klan's strategic placement of some of its members within the political structure was indicative of how they saw themselves—as a benevolent society seeking to provide protection and security to white citizens through government intervention. The Klan's political influence reached its height in the 1920s, coinciding with the rise of liberalism, which emphasized a limited government that placed restrictions on the powers of its officials, support for a free market economics based on marketplace competition with little government regulation, and freedom of religion. In some areas of Alabama, Klan membership was nearly a requirement for a person seeking employment as a policeman, a judge, or a local official.[29]

As stated earlier, the liberal branch of the Democratic Party, which included the Hills and the Alabama Klan, supported prohibition. Thornton wrote that supporters of "the prohibition movement sought to compel the universal adoption of its principles of private moral conduct through legal and constitutional mechanisms." Klan members believed that people who were against the prohibition amendment corrupted public morals. The Klan was strongly fundamentalist in its religious and moral approach to the world. Thornton recalled that Rives supported prohibition and working men, and despised corporate wealth. Rives grew up poor, was not anti-Catholic or anti-Jewish, and "certainly thought of the Klan as an organized voice for the common man." Most members of the new Alabama KKK were not interested in violence; they were seeking reassurance that their livelihoods were secure in the face of the uncertainties of the mid-1920s.[30]

The Hills were politically active, which provided them with opportunities to influence government decisions in Montgomery and across the state. Rives told Spivack that he became involved in Alabama politics alongside Hill's older brother, Will. Together they worked to gain votes for Democratic political candidates and talked with people who might become potential clients. As political candidates often did, Will and Rives would likely trade stories with farmers on their front porches, in churches, and at general stores. Traveling throughout the state gave Rives a broader awareness of people's situations and the challenges they faced in everyday life.[31]

Around this time, Rives befriended Hugo Black, a Birmingham lawyer, and was influenced by Black's and the Hills' connections to the KKK. Lawyer and historian Tony A. Freyer wrote that Black and Rives attended a rally together in 1923, where Rives paid his $10 membership dues with the prospect of developing alliances that would prove helpful in his career.[32] At the time, the Klan had a powerful influence on juries—on which Rives's clients and his practice depended. Ambitious men such as politician Bibb Graves and Hill, Rives, and Black could reap political and economic benefits from such associations. Rives surrounded himself with men who were active in the Klan and, for a time, was himself involved with the organization.

Rives told Jenkins that during the 1920s he "was briefly a member" of the Klan. As Jenkins noted, "at that time, any young man with political ambitions joined the Klan more or less as perfunctorily as they joined the American Legion." Rives told one of his clerks, E. Lloyd Sutter, a lifelong Southerner, that Black served as general counsel for the Alabama chapters of the KKK, providing legal advice to the organization. Freyer wrote that when Black was preparing to campaign for a seat in the US Senate, he acknowledged an inconsistency between his political aspirations and the Klan's public stance of political noninvolvement: "Ala

bama Klan leaders did not allow their followers seeking elected office to campaign formally as Klansman." After a few years of formal affiliation with the Klan, Black quietly left the organization. As long as he "retained the leadership's good will, Black received Klan support, while he could nonetheless publicly disclaim membership." Sutter recalled that after Black became a US senator, Rives became the organization's legal counsel. As to Rives's succession, Sutter explained, "He was Hugo Black's friend. And Lister Hill's friend. End of discussion." Membership in the Klan placed Rives in a precarious position, given that he was a lawyer in a firm that represented white and Black clients. KKK members who served on juries in cases Rives argued before the court would see him present the law in ways that supported Black clients. However, Rives could plausibly stave off Klan criticism by claiming that each Black client, as an individual, was not disruptive in the community. Rives was aligned with the liberal wing of the Democratic Party, which Barrow and Walker wrote, "often engaged in political battle with those Democrats who held fiercely to states' rights and segregationist views."[33] Rives recognized the political support the Klan could provide.

As a constitutional lawyer, Rives supported the law; as a Klan member, he publicly associated with men who advocated prejudice and racial division. Rives commented to author and journalist Jack Bass that he "dropped out" of the organization when "it became clear the Klan was no American Legion"—for whom Rives would later serve as the Montgomery post commander and judge advocate of the state organization. Rives thus fell away from the Klan, although at that time he remained supportive of the organization's values.[34]

Klan leaders likely saw a benefit in not making a negative fuss about his departure, and he, as had Black, remained in their good graces.

Rives was beginning to thrive as a lawyer. One of his clerks remarked that Rives had built a reputation as a considerate man in his interactions with everyone, regardless of race. For Rives, the virtue of fairness as well as common sense—which A. G. Danish wrote involves "ethical, empathic, and rational choices"—was intertwined with justice. As a young lawyer, he and Jessie were moving through the grief of losing their first child in 1920 and they continued to establish their family. They became parents to a son, Richard T. Rives Jr., born on October 16, 1922, not long after the passing of Rives's father in May 1922. Rives's third child, daughter Callie Dougherty Rives, was born on March 20, 1924. As his family grew, Rives continued to hone his legal skills, and in 1925 he was named a partner in the Hill, Hill, Whiting, Thomas, and Rives firm. Then on July 26, 1926, Rives's fourth child and second son, Jesse Dougherty Rives, was born. Unfortunately, he only lived to be two months old.[35] Within six years, Rives had experienced the loss of his daughter, son, and father—while also gaining a son and daughter. All the while, his professional reputation steadily rose, even as he navigated personal sorrow and racial incongruities in the law.

One of Rives's early cases reveals his difficulty accepting racial inequalities while holding fast to his ideas of fairness and justice. Rives recalled the case in an interview with law professor Frank T. Read. Shortly after joining the Hill firm, Rives represented the estate of a pregnant woman who died after falling down a faulty elevator shaft that lacked a guard rail in a new office building. The accident almost decapitated the woman. Rives told Read, "A casualty insurance adjuster came to me and said, 'I'll pay you a thousand dollars.'" The adjuster was ready to dispense with the case quickly, providing a fixed $1,000 payout designated for the death of a Black person regardless of the circumstances. Rives's interpretation of the law is evident in his response. According to Read, he stated, "Now, that's ridiculous. I wouldn't think of such a thing." For Rives, justice required equality for white and Black citizens. In response, the insurance adjuster replied, "Well, you must know that no verdict has been obtained over here for a Negro death for more than that." Rives continued, "I almost ran him out of my office . . . because the liability was perfect. The elevator operators under the law then were common carriers and subject to the highest degree of care." Ultimately, as the insurance adjuster first offered, the jury awarded $1,000 to the complainant, to which Rives said, "That's just typical of where Negroes stood."[36] This early confrontation with injustice chafed Rives to the extent that over fifty years later, he was able to provide a detailed account of the case to Read.

Another early case that stayed with Rives was *Parke v. Dennard* (1928).

Rives recounted the lawsuit to his granddaughter, United States District Court for the Southern District of Alabama Senior Judge Ginny Granade. In 1928, Myrtle Dennard, who was married to Randolph Dennard, drove approximately fifty miles from Selma to meet Rives at his office in Montgomery. Rives, then a partner in the Hill law firm, told Granade, "I thought I had acquired quite a reputation." Randolph Dennard's sister had married Clifford W. Parke, and Rives said Parke "treated her just like a chattel." Randolph went to confront Parke about his behavior. When Parke saw him coming, Parke loaded his shotgun and after a brief interaction, killed Randolph. Parke was tried for murder in Selma, found "not guilty by reason of insanity," and sent to Bryce Hospital in Tuscaloosa. After six weeks, the superintendent in charge of Parke at Bryce Hospital discharged him. According to Parke's doctor, the man did not have a mental illness, he was "just mean as a devil." Parke returned to Selma, yet Myrtle Dennard wanted to hold Parke responsible for killing her husband. Rives said that since he "did a good deal of damage suit work, [and] it seemed to be an excellent case," he drafted the complaint and filed the lawsuit.[37]

After receiving notice, Parke replied to the Hill law firm in a letter, stating that he wanted to know the person responsible for filing the lawsuit. After reading the letter, Rives returned to Bryce Hospital to inquire further about Parke. Rives recalled for Granade one piece of advice from Dr. William Partlow: "Don't ever turn your back on him," and "don't ever let him see you're the least bit scared of him . . . he'd kill you in a minute. He's the meanest man I ever came in contact with." With that information, Rives returned to working on the case: "All I wanted was getting the woman compensated for the loss of her husband." In Rives's research, he uncovered an Alabama statute that allowed the court to impose a levy on "property, without any bond whatsoever" if a lawyer could prove that a person evaded service of the legal process. Rives returned to Selma with a levy attachment signed by Assistant Attorney General Thomas E. Knight Jr., and the sheriff served the court summons to Parke.[38]

In anticipation of meeting Parke, Rives recalled for Granade that he strapped his Army pistol to the side of his office chair. One morning when Rives arrived early at the office, as was his custom, he found Parke seated by his desk. As Rives explained to Granade, "there was no danger of recognizing him at all." Parke met the description that Partlow had given him: he was a man of six feet, four or five inches tall, developed in muscular proportion, who "could break you in two with his bare hands." Rives asked Parke to have a seat, and Rives took the chair behind his desk to face him. He reached to put his hand on the pistol, but there "wasn't any gun there." When Parke asked which lawyer from the firm brought the lawsuit against him, Rives replied, "I brought the suit and I'm going to see it through. Now, Mr. Parke, it seems to me that a man of your intelligence and your material worth would want to see these children taken care of and Miss Dennard taken care of." Parke accused Rives of only being "interested in the contingent fee . . . [he was] going to get." Rives replied, "'Well, there's some truth in what you say. She's got no way to pay a fee except to pay a contingent fee. . . . but I'm also interested in the crime and in the children. And I think she's got a just case.' He said, 'That's a non-truth, sir.' That fellow telling me I was lying. Oh, well, I did get mad then. . . . I said, 'Mr. Parke, you may kill me, and I guess you can. But if you repeat that one more time, I'm going to do my best to knock your damn teeth down your throat.' . . . I was so cock-eyed mad when he called me a liar." After they exchanged a few more words, Parke left. Ultimately, Rives won the case for Myrtle Dennard. Hearing about the case from the judge, his clerk Neil T. Bradley reflected, "You can do a lot of things, but if you call him a liar, those are fighting words to him."[39] Rives's word was his bond, and he would not have his character questioned.

Rives's integrity helped him become a well-known lawyer and political leader aligned with the Hill faction of Democrats. In 1926 he managed Graves's successful campaign for the office of governor of Alabama. Rives directed Graves's Speakers' Bureau, aligning speakers with groups and organizations around the state. He simultaneously directed Black's winning campaign for the US Senate from Alabama. Democratic candidates backed by the Alabama KKK won the positions of governor (Graves), US senator (Black), state attorney general (Charlie McCall), and Alabama Supreme Court (Joel Bascom Brown). Thornton wrote that, ironically, both Black and Brown—and later Rives—would come "to espouse from the bench attitudes . . . sympathetic to civil liberties and civil rights."[40] The Klan and its political candidates benefited from tensions within the conservative and moderate wings of the Democratic Party.

After Graves served his initial term as governor (1927–1931), Alabama law prohibited him from seeking a second consecutive term. He ran for governor again in 1934 and Rives again served as his statewide campaign manager. Rives worked with county managers and coordinated fundraising, polling, and getting out the vote. Graves won the election, and during his second term as governor (1935–1939), pursued practices similar to those of his first term. He skillfully used the patronage of his office. For example, the *Anniston Star* reported that the state of Alabama paid fees and salaries to more than one hundred lawyers. This included lawyers who worked for the attorney general and those who worked for other governmental departments on a fee or percentage basis. Rives was one of the men tapped to do some legal work for the state. A newspaper article in Hudson's *Montgomery Advertiser* identified lawyers and law firms that profited from doing legal work for the state of Alabama during

Graves's four-year administration. Rives earned $4,391, while Hill, Hill, Whiting, and Rives gained $11,500, approximately 2 percent of the entire amount spent on legal work and special tax collections for the state.[41] Federal judgeships are another, more prestigious, type of political patronage.

In May 1938, the US Congress added a seat to the Fifth Circuit to assist with the growing number of appeals that challenged decisions from the lower courts. Speaking at a meeting of the Atlanta Bar Club, Rives explained that the function of an appellate court, such as the Fifth Circuit, is to review the decision made by a judge or judicial panel in a district court—the trial courts of the federal government—or another designated federal court or administrative agency. Circuit courts do not retry a case or hear new evidence; instead, judges review the lower court's procedures to ensure fairness in the proceedings and to confirm that the proper law was correctly applied to warrant the decision.[42] As a form of patronage, Rives's name was identified as a possible candidate for the circuit position.

Lister Hill, whom Governor Graves had appointed to fill a temporary US Senate vacancy from Alabama, first approached Rives about the judgeship while Rives was working at the Hill law firm. Hill was the nephew of Wiley Hill Sr., with whom Rives had apprenticed as a lawyer. He talked with Rives about the vacancy, who in turn discussed it with his son. Rives later told Bass that his son "thought that on the beliefs we had and things that mattered to us, I would have a much wider effect as a judge."[43] But the time was not yet right. Rives declined to have his name put forward, and instead, Leon Clarence McCord, another lawyer in private practice in Montgomery, was selected. Rives would continue his legal work and involvement in the liberal wing of the Democratic Party.

Liberalism reached its peak during the height of New Deal. Historian Virginia Van der Veer Hamilton explained that alliances in the US Congress were no longer divided along Democratic-Republican lines, as they had been at the beginning of the New Deal. Instead, the division held the more liberal New Dealer Democrats on one side and a coalition of the more conservative anti-New Dealer Democrats and Republicans on the other.[44]

Rives was an avid New Dealer. He was attracted to politics but only ran for one office, Alabama's delegation to the July 1940 Democratic National Convention. Rives mentioned to Peggy Roberson of the *Birmingham News* that to win the post, he "had to campaign like . . . [he] was going to Congress." He subsequently received more than 90 percent of the votes cast in Montgomery. The convention delegates nominated Franklin D. Roosevelt for an unprecedented third time to represent Democrats on the fall presidential ballot. Roosevelt would remain president from 1933–1945, through most of the Great Depression and during most of World War II, implementing his New Deal agenda.[45] In addition to his political involvement, Rives was an industrious lawyer and was active in numerous professional and community organizations.

Rives reported on the 1940 census that he worked approximately sixty-six hours each week. He was involved in the Montgomery County Bar Association, serving as president in 1923 and again in 1934. Rives was elected by his peers to serve as president of the Alabama State Bar Association from 1939–1940. Lawyer Pat Boyd Rumore recorded that during Rives's term, he helped create the state bar journal, the *Alabama Lawyer*. He also initiated "a law institute for the Young Lawyers Section of the association, which held discussions around the state on legal subjects"; created "a legislative reference service to aid the Alabama legislature" called the Judicial Council; and established "an organized legal aid service" for poor people in the state. Spivack wrote that as president, Rives also "became involved with problems of professional standards."[46] Rives felt strongly about lawyers exhibiting ethics when working with the law.

In 1887, members of the Alabama Bar Association voted to endorse a code of ethics for the organization, written by future Alabama governor Thomas Goode Jones, who would also serve as a federal judge in a joint appointment to the Middle and Northern Districts of Alabama. The code directed lawyers to "deal honestly and courteously with each other, to seek no advantages with judges, to defend the poor and friendless, and above all to refrain from encouraging litigation." However, Rives was aware that since the code had been adopted, professional ethics among members of the association had declined. Therefore, in his annual report to the membership in 1940, Rives spoke on "standards of ethics and decorum among lawyers." He wanted the association to oversee the conduct of members of the Alabama bar and remove what he called the "unscrupulous scoundrels among us." Rives's call to ethics was met with widespread resistance from members of the group. He explained to Spivack that the collective opposition to ethical practice disturbed him.[47] Afterward, he allowed other interests to absorb the time he had previously dedicated to leadership responsibilities in the Alabama Bar Association.

Rives continued to focus on his law practice, spending time in the community providing public service and strengthening his reputation as a leader in Montgomery. Law professor Harvey C. Couch described Rives as "a deeply religious man" and a member of Trinity Presbyterian Church. An aristocrat in the region, Rives belonged to most of white society's exclusive clubs and, as one of his law clerks shared, he seemed to "derive great pleasure from the social life of Montgomery society." At various times his community involvement included being a member of the Kiwanis, Masons, and Shriners organizations. He was also a director of the Montgomery Chamber of Commerce. In addition, he was appointed as a member of the Armory Commission of

Alabama, twice served as chairman of the Montgomery chapter of the Red Cross, and served as post commander of the local American Legion and judge advocate of the State Legion. After the bombing of Pearl Harbor, he would chair the Alien Enemy Hearing Board for the Middle District of Alabama.[48] Rives was a recognized and influential member of Montgomery's elite citizens. As such, he was helpful to Graves in his third bid to return to the Alabama governor's seat.

The 1942 gubernatorial primary continued the contest between the liberal and the conservative wings of the Democratic Party in Alabama. Graves led the political field as the representative of the liberal wing of the party. During his first two terms, he worked with representatives in the state legislature to accomplish numerous initiatives. Two important endeavors for Rives and for working-class citizens were an improved highway system and enhanced educational opportunities for children. As Graves's campaign chairman, Rives made plans to kick off the campaign in Montgomery. Graves was recuperating in Florida from a kidney operation earlier in the year, and a family genealogy site recorded Graves as saying he was "in fine condition" to campaign across Alabama. Rives and other campaign planners suggested that because of Graves's recovering health and status as the frontrunner in the race, delivering five speeches should be sufficient. Soon after returning to Montgomery, Rives and others learned that Graves had died of kidney failure.[49]

Graves's death reduced the field of gubernatorial candidates to five men and, as historian George E. Sims wrote, "confounded the clear-cut alignment of Democratic factions." People close to Graves acknowledged that, as Rumore documented, Rives was a "heavy hitter" in politics and could have been elected governor despite his egalitarian stance on race. Historian William D. Barnard states that Rives's supporters investigated the possibility that Rives could replace Graves and learned that he could still potentially "enter the race if the Democratic Executive Committee would reopen the eligibility list." However, the Democratic State chairman, Gessner McCorvey of Mobile, was "anti-Graves and refused to call the committee into session."[50] With the prospect of Rives's candidacy closed, the remaining five candidates would run for governor of Alabama.

One of the candidates, Jim Folsom, submitted his candidacy papers several weeks after the other four contenders. Sims suggested that Folsom may have known about Graves's illness. Folsom submitted his name as a candidate "on the chance that Graves might withdraw," which Folsom thought would "leave him as the logical leader of progressive Alabama Democrats." However, as Freyer recognized, "Rives's business was politics, and he had a [sharp] perception of the shifting political winds." Barnard recorded that Rives declared two of the contenders, Folsom and Christopher J. Sherlock, "'self-styled liberals' and it would be 'a sad day for the true liberals in Alabama'" if either were elected. Folsom, who was unaware of Rives's views, sought out Rives to ask for his endorsement.[51]

On the day of Graves's funeral, "Big Jim" Folsom visited the Rives home. Rives told Bradley that "he went to the funeral, and he came back to the house and his wife told him that Jim Folsom was upstairs and wanted to see him. . . . And he said he went up there and Folsom was stretched out on a bed fast asleep. And so he just let him sleep for a while and finally woke him up." Folsom said to Rives, "You know, with your support, I can be Governor." Rives was a major figure in Alabama campaigns and had the credibility to influence citizens' votes by endorsing specific candidates. According to Rives's clerk, Rives responded, "I don't know that I have that kind of influence, but I sure wouldn't want to take responsibility for doing that—for making you Governor." At the time, Sims wrote, Folsom had never won an election and had yet to prove himself as a candidate. The most widely known candidate from the conservative wing of the Democratic Party was Chauncey Sparks, who was relatively moderate. Given Sparks's popularity, Sims continued, "the majority of the Graves organization decided to ignore Sparks's conservative legislation record and give him support," even though his "conversion to liberalism" was questionable. Barnard characterized Rives's efforts to depict Sparks as a genuine liberal in the race as unconvincing to the general public.[52] Nevertheless, Sparks won the gubernatorial election for the 1942–1945 term by a slight majority.

World War II came to an end in 1945. Black soldiers returned to the racially segregated United States after experiencing equality overseas, and many of them engaged in Civil Rights activism to secure the rights guaranteed to them in the US Constitution. Black activism led to the nationwide Civil Rights campaign of the 1950s and 1960s, effectively buoyed by the news media. However, less recognized instances of activism occurred even before the media began covering the movement.

In September 1943, Arthur Madison, a native of Montgomery and a lawyer who became legal counsel for the Montgomery chapter of the NAACP, started a voter registration drive in Montgomery County. The campaign's purpose was specifically to register residents of Madison Park to vote, a prerequisite to casting a ballot in Alabama. Residents of Madison Park, a small all-Black community in northern Montgomery County, wanted to create a municipal government. To do so, the state of Alabama required that the geographic area contain a minimum number of registered voters. When Black citizens went to register, the county registrars rejected every application. Madison then filed a lawsuit against the Montgomery Board of Registrars in Montgomery County Circuit Court on behalf of sixteen citizens.[53]

While Madison was out of town, six of the plaintiffs went to court on

February 8, 1944, to withdraw their case. They claimed Madison did not ask their permission to represent them in the lawsuit. For example, Thornton explained that Mildred Hardy, Madison's niece, was told by white supremacists that she would be fired as a teacher unless she claimed Madison represented her without her permission. This terrorism led Hardy to testify that Madison represented her without her consent. That allowed white authorities to document that Madison had committed a crime in misrepresenting Hardy. If found guilty, Madison would be disbarred.[54]

In April 1944, the *Montgomery Advertiser* reported that Hill, Hill, Whiting, and Rives offered pro bono assistance to the Montgomery Board of Registrars. During the trial, Rives assisted County Solicitor Temple Seibels. The Circuit Court of Montgomery County heard Madison's trial and he was convicted, fined $2,500, and his Alabama law license was withdrawn.[55] Rives had legally supported the Montgomery County Board of Registrars in limiting Black citizens' development of a municipal government.

Rives also supported the Montgomery registrars in another instance. He described the interaction to Read. Black citizens were lined up to register to vote and the line extended "all the way around the park." Board members asked, "'What shall we do?' I said, 'Well, the only thing to do is to go on and let them come in, take their application, let them sign up and you all pass on it after they leave.' Of course, I didn't tell them how to pass on it; they didn't need any advice on that. They did and they soon got rid of the line. They turned them all down later."[56] Early in his professional career, Rives relied on contradictions within the law and fluidity within language to adapt his advice to the client's needs.

As Rives conducted his legal work, he contemplated a future in which he and his son Richard T. Rives Jr. would practice law together in Montgomery. Rives provided his son with access to the type of education he desired but never had for himself. Richard Jr. received his primary education at the Barnes School for Boys in Montgomery and his secondary education at Phillips Exeter Academy in New Hampshire. After graduating from high school, he attended Harvard University and earned his degree in June 1944.[57] He then entered the military to serve his country, as his father had done.

Rives recalled to Yarbrough that Richard Jr. enlisted in the Navy as a lieutenant and served in the Pacific during World War II. While on active duty, he became seriously ill and spent weeks recuperating in a military hospital. During that time, Black soldiers, who were also recovering from injuries or illnesses, lay in beds beside him. Richard Jr. would later tell his father that while he was in the hospital, he began to consider the racial differences he had witnessed while traveling and living in different parts of the United States and around the world. He was released from the military due to his illness and then returned to racially segregated Montgomery. The senior Rives shared with Yarbrough that upon his son's return from the Pacific, they talked together about race. During World War I, Rives likely also served with some Black servicemen who worked in limited positions. Bass wrote that Richard Jr. told his father of "the valiance with which African American soldiers fought," shared that Black soldiers were doing the same job as he was, and thought they deserved to exercise their constitutional rights in the same manner as white citizens. Rives recalled to Yarbrough that on numerous occasions he and his son "discussed the propriety of southern racial norms, with [the younger Rives] invariably urging reform."[58] Studying the law would be a necessary precursor to pursuing the social changes Richard Jr. wished to make.

Discharged from the Navy, Richard Jr. began studying at the University of Michigan Law School in the fall of 1947. Meanwhile, in Montgomery, Rives continued his public political support for liberal Democratic candidates. He was a gradualist on the issue of race, what Bass called "a man of his time," adhering to sentiments common to his race and class. However, American historian Frye Gaillard wrote that in private, Rives "had begun to brood about the issue [of racial segregation] more and more." Rives's son, in law school at Ann Arbor, "concluded from his studies that something was terribly wrong in the South." He recommended that his father read Swedish economist Gunnar Myrdal's 1944 study of race relations, *An American Dilemma: The Negro Problem and Modern Democracy.*[59]

Law professor Anne S. Emanuel reported that Rives read the two-volume study and "was deeply influenced by Myrdal's work and by the progressive views of his own son." Myrdal wrote that "political and social interaction in the United States" should be shaped by a "democracy [that] would triumph over racism and . . . an 'American Creed, one that emphasizes the ideals of liberty, equality, justice, and fair treatment of all people.'" Rives and his son agreed, Gaillard wrote, that Myrdal's work was "a remarkable piece of scholarship" addressing questions about the nature of race relations. Hugo Black Jr. explained that the younger Rives "had developed a strong sense of racial justice" and was "the person who contributed most to . . . [Rives's] own profound commitment to racial justice."[60] Their conversations about race strongly influenced the evolution of Rives's gradually increasing liberal views.

Rives began to struggle between ideas toward race advocated respectively by the conservative and liberal wings of the Democratic Party. He was a proponent of fundamental justice for all citizens and relied on core principles such as equality, while recognizing fairness as central to justice and the development of society. Rives wrote that he sought to understand the "intense popular interest and feeling" of bureaucracy in politics. While political documents, such as the US Constitution, proclaimed that all citizens are free and equal, many politicians used bureaucratic structures to sustain a social contract that benefited white citizens. For Rives, the moral basis of human equality was more fundamental to realizing justice than the influence of politicians strategically operating within a bureaucratic system.[61] He determined that justice as fairness requires treating all people without bias, in conformity with an egalitarian application of the law.

In August 1947, in anticipation of his son's future graduation from University of Michigan, Rives dissolved his decades-long association with Hill, Hill, Whiting, and Rives to establish a law firm of his own. Aside from his tours of duty in the military, Rives had been associated with the Hill firm continuously since 1911, and leaving would mean ending his well-known partnership in the courtroom with John Blue Hill. Despite feeling what Rives told Spivack was "some trepidation about starting out anew in his mid-fifties," Rives enjoyed the idea of working with his son. Rives decided to work independently until his son graduated from law school and returned from clerking for Rives's good friend, US Supreme Court Justice Black. Until then, Rives kept busy with what he told legal scholar Roger K. Newman was "a heavy volume of work, primarily plaintiffs' work and criminal cases" in his firm.[62]

By this time, Judge McCord had served on the US Court of Appeals for the Fifth Circuit for nearly a decade and was preparing to retire. McCord was aware that he had been identified as a candidate for the bench only after Rives declined to be nominated for the judgeship. He approached Rives to discuss the possibility of him taking Alabama's informal seat on the Court of Appeals. This was Rives's second invitation to be potentially nominated as a federal judge. However, he looked forward to developing a private practice with his son and again declined the opportunity.

As Richard Jr. continued in law school, his father kept up with political developments. Across the country, change was occurring that would impel social movement toward greater racial justice. Transformations were appearing at the highest level of government. Governors of Southern states were astounded at President Harry S Truman's audacity in liberalizing the Democratic Party. At the July 1948 national Democratic convention, the inclusion of a Civil Rights plank in the party platform led Southern delegates to form a political bloc. Delegates who supported state rights and racial segregation vowed to break away from the Democratic Party if Truman was renominated as the 1948 presidential candidate. When Truman won the nomination, thirty-five Southern delegates walked out of the convention. After their departure, traditional conservative Southerners formed the States' Rights Democratic Party, also known as the Dixiecrats. On July 17, 1948, they convened in Birmingham with over six thousand delegates from thirteen states in attendance.[63] The Dixiecrats intended to elect Strom Thurmond as their candidate for president in 1948.

A motion was made to endorse Thurmond's candidacy for president at the September 1948 convention of the Alabama Bar Association. Rives, described by Rumore as "esteemed in liberal circles as a political tactician," was in attendance and spoke against the motion for about thirty minutes.[64] His genuineness and persuasion ultimately prevailed, and the association did not endorse Thurmond. In public, Rives was often able to use his persuasive skills to affect change; in his private life, Rives realized that he could not control the outcome of some events.

On Friday, April 1, 1949, Rives was called out of a zoning hearing before the Montgomery City Commission to learn that his son had been involved in a terrible automobile accident. Richard Jr. was a front-seat passenger in a car of friends traveling from Ann Arbor to Miami, Florida, for spring break. A rainstorm had cropped up near the city limits of Jacksonville. The car skidded, the driver crossed into the wrong lane, and the vehicle was involved in a head-on collision with two other cars. The *Alabama Journal* reported that the young man "was thrown from the car, his skull crushed, and he was rushed to a Jacksonville hospital for brain surgery." Rives and Jessie departed immediately for Jacksonville. They were stopped in Ozark, Alabama, by a highway patrol officer who told them their son had died earlier that afternoon.[65]

Rives was despondent following the death of his son, whom Gaillard called "a young man of sensitivity and promise." Rives's normal pace as a lawyer slowed, and he ultimately took time away from his practice. Three months later, Rives asked John C. Godbold, a native of Alabama and recent graduate of Harvard Law School, to join his firm. He renamed the practice Rives and Godbold and "helped Godbold establish a successful law practice" with an introduction to the influential Hill firm. One of Rives's clerks recalled that for nearly a year after his son's death, Rives sat for long stretches on his porch in a rocking chair, trying to come to terms with his loss. He likely reflected on life, God, and discussions he and his son had about race and equality. The clerk conveyed that Rives visited his son's grave every day at lunchtime for many years trying to contend with his grief. Rives told Spivack nearly thirty years later that he "never completely recovered from this loss" and said he continued to mourn his son.[66] Yet, in his anguish Rives was transformed.

Rives told Hugo Black Jr. that his commitment to racial justice "resulted in part from the most severe tragedy of his life." After his son died, Rives may have felt he had nothing else to lose, which may have contributed to his courage to pursue racial justice. Rives decided that if he was ever approached for a federal judicial appointment again, he would agree to become a candidate. Bass quoted Douglass Cater, a close personal friend of Richard Jr. who stated that becoming a judge would allow Rives to honor his son's legacy and help establish the egalitarian New South the two men discussed. A judgeship would allow Rives, Bass wrote, to "have more influence on establishing racial equality" than he could as a lawyer in private practice.[67]

Rives recognized that his son's perspective on race complemented his own common-law training at the Hill firm. Strauss explained that the common-law approach, "the oldest tradition in Anglo-American law," allows lawyers and judges to adapt and transform laws that no longer work in society. A common-law lawyer considers legal precedent and policies, and how philosophy, history, tradition, and sociology provide coherence and a direction to thinking about the law. Judicial decisions, in common law, should be supported not just by a judge's views about good policy but also by a history of the law that may demonstrate a prior practice to be no longer viable. Lawyer and jurist Benjamin N. Cardozo, writing in 1921 about *The Nature of the Judicial Process*, addressed the importance of legal innovation: "What really matters is this, that the judge is under a duty, within the limits of his power of innovation, to maintain a relation between law and morals, between the precepts of jurisprudence, and those of reason and good conscience." During the 1940s and 1950s, Strauss explained, courts were "gravitating to a new rule" regarding racial segregation.[68]

The NAACP's legal department under the leadership of Charles Hamilton Houston had begun to implement an attack on segregated educational facilities, following recommendations in the 1930 Margold Report. In 1940 Thurgood Marshall founded the LDF, an associated entity separate from the NAACP. Marshall was lead counsel and worked with other lawyers to successfully desegregate a state law school in *Sipuel v. Board of Regents of the University of Oklahoma* (1948) and to argue against public school segregation in *Briggs v. Elliott* (1951, 1952), a lawsuit that began in 1947.[69] Yet the law, as a framing mechanism for society, moved slowly toward greater racial equality. Rives gradually began to return to a more active social life, steadfast in his determination to pay tribute to his son by pursuing the constitutional values and ideas they had discussed together.

Alabama lawyers prepared to address challenges to racial laws at the 1949 Alabama Bar Association meeting in Mobile, which Rives attended. Rumore recounted the meeting, which included an agenda item to make a recommendation to the American Bar Association regarding state rights. A subcommittee of the association offered three resolutions in the business meeting. The first and second resolutions involved opposing the US ratification of "The Convention on the Prevention and Punishment of the Crime of Genocide" and "the International Covenant on Human Rights," based on the United Nations' 1948 Universal Declaration of Human Rights.[70] Admitting that there was "a considerable lack of information" about the convention and about the international covenant, Judge Logan Martin, the subcommittee chair and Alabama delegate to the American Bar Association House of Delegates, explained the two resolutions.

Rumore documented Martin's claim that the US ratification of such ideas "would impose international obligations that might interfere with US constitutional rights and responsibilities and the operation of both federal and state governments." The delegates moved the resolutions for adoption, and then Rives moved to table the resolutions until members could further study the matters. Discussion continued, during which time someone "pointed out that the meeting schedule called for the members to proceed to a fish fry." Before adjourning, Rives again spoke, addressing the lack of information available to the association members before the resolutions came up for a vote: "I . . . don't know whether I will stand alone on this matter or not. . . . We are in a Bar Association every man is a member of. In controversial matters, they have a right to study those controversial matters; they have got a right to express themselves on those controversial matters. . . . I have been railroaded enough into this kind of thing; and I am not going to be railroaded into adopting a thing I don't know anything about any more. . . . I don't propose to have Logan Martin, Borden Burr, or anybody else dictate to me. I haven't studied the subject. I didn't read it or study it; but I say that it has got no part in our deliberations when we know nothing about it." The meeting minutes recorded applause following Rives's remarks, but after the votes were counted, both resolutions against human rights were passed.[71]

The third resolution, Rumore wrote, "called upon the State Senate 'to adopt and submit to the people the proposal now pending in the Senate known as the Voter Qualification Amendment.'" She recalled that Rives again spoke against the resolution. He stated, "I have studied the Boswell Amendment which was declared unconstitutional. This amendment—it is a proposed substitute for the Boswell Amendment—in my opinion is just as unconstitutional as the Boswell Amendment. . . . I came here not to be railroaded into this kind of resolution. It has got nothing to do with our Bar Association. And I submit to you that the opinion of the Federal Court of Appeals, on which certiorari was denied by the Supreme Court, says we must have reasonable and definite rules for determining the right to vote . . . that will make this a government of laws and not men." At this point, Rumore continued, Ben Turner asked Rives, "Didn't you appear before the Committee charged with the enactment of the resolution?" To which Rives responded, "I appear before everybody I know." Turner probed, "Did you tell them your thought?" Rives replied, "Yes, sir." Turner pushed, "Did they adopt your thought?" "No, sir," Rives answered. Turner then announced, "It ought to be closed." Rives stated, "I appear before everybody I know to oppose an amendment . . . [that is] in my opinion unconstitutional, when I have sworn to support the Constitution. This proposed amendment imposes two additional tests for the right to vote, any one of which could be interpreted by registrars in different ways."[72] Rives had stated his case, and he was on record in the meeting minutes, but there would be no time to study the resolution. The Alabama Bar Association deemed the vote to be urgent, and the motion to support the voter qualification amendment carried.

These examples from the Alabama Law Association business meeting, which occurred two years before Rives was named a federal judge, provide a glimpse into his political position and foreshadows his philosophy as a judge. He would later reflect on his changing views toward race, telling Read that "experience is some indication that people change their views as they go along." The shift in Rives's thinking was not simply one of chronological age but an amalgamation of his personal and professional experiences—the meanings of which continued to deepen as they accumulated.[73]

In September 1949, Rives spoke at a Montgomery Labor Day event, introduced by his friend Senator Hill. According to Jonathan R. Harkavy, one of Rives's law clerks, Rives was inclined toward enforcing the National Labor Relations Act, which was not always a popular position in the anti-union South. Referring to the importance of workers being able to take collective action under labor laws, Rives said, "continued prosperity in this nation rest[s] in fair dealing and recognition of the legitimate rights and interests of each other."[74] His comments could have easily referred to his shifting view on issues of race and the law, politics, and society at large.

Rives was soon approached for a third time about a possible judgeship on the US Court of Appeals for the Fifth Circuit. Judge McCord had put off his retirement for over a year until Rives began to participate in public life once again. McCord considered Rives the best person to succeed him on the Fifth Circuit. Ray Jenkins of the *Alabama Journal* shared McCord's sentiment: "Anyone else was simply unacceptable." Hamilton wrote that Rives was known to be a "quiet but effective tactician" as a lawyer in the courtroom, and McCord thought a good federal judge was worth the wait. Rives told Spivack that McCord shared with him that he was interested in running for governor of the state. McCord asked Rives "if he wanted the seat" that he would be vacating on the Fifth Circuit. Rives recalled, "I sure did."[75] Rives saw an opportunity to influence racial equality as laid out in the US Constitution under the rule of law.

Rives shared with Read that he had not been "pure on this question of bigotry," and his outlook was evolving toward individual equality under the law. Rives was fifty-six years old, young enough to effect change yet mature enough to understand the cultural nuances and the political and economic history of the South. His dreams of working in a law practice with his son had evaporated. Over the past thirty-five years Rives had become what McDonald called "a gifted Montgomery lawyer." If the US Senate confirmed his nomination, he would need to give up his private law practice worth, according to Geoffrey Birt of the *Montgomery Advertiser*, "$50,000 a year" in 1951. As a circuit court judge with a lifetime appointment, Rives would start at $17,500 a year.[76] His willingness to decrease his annual income reveals that he thought public service was more important than financial gain, and he agreed to be nominated for the judicial position.

A prospective federal judge's candidacy is generally championed by US senators from the state in which there is a vacancy. Judge McCord recommended to Senators Hill and John Sparkman that Rives be nominated to succeed him on the bench. Since Rives had a close relationship with Hill, McCord encouraged Rives to talk with Hill regarding his possible appointment. Rives drafted a letter addressed to the senators, requesting their consideration in support of his nomination. He then went to see Hill in Washington, DC, at which time Hill assured Rives that he fully supported his nomination to the Fifth Circuit. Hill then sent Rives to see Sparkman. Though Rives knew Sparkman, they were not close associates. In *Unlikely Heroes*, Bass reported that Sparkman told Rives "he would make a fine judge, was well qualified, and that he would give him 'every consideration.'"[77] After Rives left Sparkman's office, he returned to Hill's office.

According to Bass, Rives shared with Senator Hill the conversation that had taken place between himself and Senator Sparkman. Hill asked Rives if he had ever walked down the foot trail that runs beside the Alabama River in Montgomery. After Rives indicated he had, Hill told him, "I made that trail walking back from being sold down the river so many times." The nature of political relationships is very tenuous. On the one hand, politics is a game of building and maintaining relationships; on the other hand, politics is about seeking gain from those relationships to accomplish one's personal objectives. Hill seemed to suggest that Sparkman was a politician whose words were carefully chosen and could contain several meanings. Hill pressed Rives to secure an explicit endorsement from Sparkman rather than being satisfied with a potentially obscure response. Rives returned to Sparkman's office and repeated Hill's words to Sparkman. Sparkman denied having any intentions other than his support of Rives. Senators Hill and Sparkman subsequently submitted Rives's name to President Truman. Hamilton wrote that US Supreme Court Justice Black, whose circuit assignment was the Fifth Circuit, "quietly added his endorsement."[78] The process to nominate Rives for a potential judgeship on the Fifth Circuit was under way.

The news of Rives's potential nomination to succeed Judge McCord soon hit the newspapers. The *Montgomery Examiner* wrote that Rives was one of "Alabama's most distinguished legal minds." People mailed unsolicited letters and telegrams supporting Rives to US Attorney General J. Howard McGrath and to Senators Hill and Sparkman. Rives received numerous letters of support from lawyers, district judges, and Fifth Circuit Court judges, all wishing him a smooth nomination and encouraging him to fill the nation's need for "steady hands and stout hearts," as Daniel H. Thomas (a staunch conservative from Alabama who was also nominated by President Truman for a federal judicial position) put it.[79] Rives replied to their letters, adding comments about newspaper clippings people sent to him and thanking them for their good wishes. Over the next six weeks, he continued to work in his law practice in Montgomery, waiting to hear more about his nomination.

On February 27–28, 1951, Rives was in Washington, DC, to argue his only case as a lawyer before the US Supreme Court, *Alabama Public Service Commission v. Southern Railway Company* (1951). While Rives was in Washington, he formally received word that President Truman had supported his nomination for a federal judgeship. Rives told Spivack that he was notified, without any specifics, "that the announcement of his appointment was going to be made in a rather novel way." As he argued *Alabama Commission*, "in the middle of his presentation, he received a note from Judge McCord indicating that everything had been cleared." Rives shared with Spivack that he nearly collapsed upon reading the note. After recovering, he "looked up and saw Justice Felix Frankfurter smiling and nodding" at him. Even though the nomination process was moving along, Rives's sincerity brought to the surface some reservations he had about serving as a judge for the Fifth Circuit.[80]

Rives completed his argument before the Court and then stopped by Justice Black's chambers to ask his friend for advice about whether to accept the nomination. Rives told Spivack he had concerns about his lack of formal education and how that gap would affect his ability to make informed decisions. Recalling the situation to Bass, Rives recalled that he reminded Black that he had never been to law school. Rives said, "I don't know the difference between an admiralty case and a case of some other kind that I have never heard of; I have never tried a patent case; I don't know anything about all these various types of cases—Labor Board matters are beyond my conception." Rives continued, "I'm pretty happy in my law practice. I just wonder if I am competent to fill this job and really ought to accept it or ought to stay in my law practice." Spivack shared that Rives wondered aloud with Black "if he wasn't stepping in over his head." According to Rives, Black thought he was "pulling his leg." Bass wrote that Black was sure Rives would do the job well. Black told Rives, "When the cases reach the Supreme Court, and it's almost true when they reach the Circuit Court of Appeals, they are so extremely close they could be decided either way." Black was confident that Rives was fully capable of fulfilling the judicial responsibilities. One of Rives's clerks, John Daniel Reaves, recalled that Black facetiously stated that Rives "could not do any real harm." When Rives recounted the exchange for Bradley, the clerk asked Rives if he believed Black. Rives replied, "No."[81] Rives's response demonstrates his awareness of the position's importance in a time of increasing racial turmoil, as well as his humble character.

Rives formally accepted the nomination, and President Truman forwarded Rives's name to the US Senate for confirmation on April 12, 1951. The majority of senators were Democratic. The *Congressional Record* documents that when the Senate met on May 1, the chief clerk read Rives's nomination in executive session. The process for appointing federal judges during the 1950s and 1960s was brief. The Federal Bureau of Investigation and the American Bar Association submitted reports addressing a candidate's qualifications. Generally, few senators were present and, as legal historians Tony Freyer and Timothy Dixon explained, "after a few routine questions, confirmation was automatic." Rives was confirmed, the *Congressional Record* reported, "without objection." Rives later shared with Spivack that he was told that the support of Senators Hill and Sparkman, Attorney General J. Howard McGrath, and the president assured his appointment.[82]

On May 7, 1951, Rives took the oath of office in the courtroom of the Fifteenth Judicial Circuit of Alabama in Montgomery at 12:00 noon. Over five hundred friends and professional colleagues, including state and county leaders, attended the event. Many people believed Rives accepted the judgeship because he would not be practicing law with his son. Ralph Kennamer wrote in the *Alabama Lawyer* that those people also knew that Rives had "the ability, the energy, and the character, to make a great appellate judge."[83] After his investiture, Rives took office in Room 430 of the Federal Building in downtown Montgomery. His life—and the lives of millions of people in the South—would never again be the same.

During the early 1950s, judges in Southern states generally followed legal precedents that supported the status quo of racial segregation. Rives, as has already been discussed, held a common-law judicial philosophy and took a gradualist view toward racial desegregation. His thoughts were still evolving in 1951, becoming more liberal for the time. He negotiated Southern history and tradition with legal precedent and his interpretation of the US Constitution, which he viewed as a living document. As a member of the Fifth Circuit when the US Supreme Court decided *Brown I* and *II* (1954, 1955), Rives continued to witness societal change. Five years after Rives assumed the bench, with a firm understanding of how the judicial system functioned and the force of a number of prior decisions, he relied on *Brown I* to leave his mark on Civil Rights in *Browder v. Gayle* (1956), the landmark Montgomery bus desegregation decision.[84]

2

A Foray into Racial Desegregation

A Judicial Interpretation of Public Law in Transportation

Richard T. Rives was sworn into office as a judge on the US Court of Appeals for the Fifth Circuit in Montgomery, Alabama, on May 7, 1951. As he settled into his judicial position—hearing cases, writing decisions, and completing administrative work—lawsuits related to the racial desegregation of the public sphere became more frequent. The accepted legal precedent for racial segregation at that time was *Plessy v. Ferguson* (1896), a transportation case. In *Plessy*, the US Supreme Court justices ruled that state laws governing racial segregation did not violate the Fourteenth Amendment to the US Constitution as long as "separate but equal" accommodations were available for white and Black citizens.[1]

Black citizens had long resisted the inequities of racial segregation. The legal department of the NAACP began to formally strategize desegregation with the 1930 Margold Report. They initially directed their attention to racially desegregating higher education. The organization's first counsel, Charles Hamilton Houston, wisely selected cases that, as lawyers Dan Abrams and Fred D. Gray wrote, would have "greater national impact" and allow them to establish a series of legal precedents to attack the "separate but equal" doctrine established in *Plessy*. He relied on the Fourteenth Amendment, which requires, in part, that no state shall "deprive any person of life, liberty, or property, without due process of law; nor deny to any person within its jurisdiction the equal protection of the laws." Finding success in desegregating higher education, one of Houston's protégés, Thurgood Marshall, created the Legal Defense and Education Fund as a separate entity from the NAACP. The LDF turned its attention in the 1950s to desegregating public primary and secondary schools. Within Judge Rives's first year on the bench, educational desegregation cases were filed in federal courts in Kansas, South Carolina, Virginia, Delaware, and the District of Columbia. In each case, racial segregation in public schools was upheld. This led the LDF to appeal several cases to the US Supreme Court, which would be combined in *Brown I*.[2]

Brown I was a class action lawsuit that focused on a conflict between state and federal laws regarding the separation of white and Black students into different educational facilities. The US Supreme Court heard the *Brown I* appeal on December 9–11, 1952. After the hearing, the nine justices could not agree on several issues in the case, so they compiled a list of questions and asked lawyers to prepare their responses. In the interim, Dwight D. Eisenhower was sworn in as president in January 1953, and Earl Warren joined the Supreme Court as chief justice in October of that year. Warren and Judge Rives took a similar approach to the law. *Oyez* described Warren's decisions as "rooted in Progressive beliefs supported by the rule of common law," while Rives described himself as "a common-law lawyer" on the bench.[3] Members of the legal community, including Rives, closely followed developments in the case. Racial tensions were escalating in the South, and he would undoubtedly be involved in adjudicating Civil Rights cases.

Alabama legislators viewed the US Supreme Court's decision to hear the *Brown I* appeal as judicial overreach; they thought the Supreme Court was interfering in issues under the purview of state legislatures. Protected by the Tenth Amendment, which guarantees that powers not delegated to the US Constitution are reserved to the state, members of the Alabama Legislature passed Act no. 894, a Senate Joint Resolution, on September 21, 1953. The act formed a committee that was charged with drafting legislation to "protect the interests of the State and its [white] citizens" if the Supreme Court ordered the racial desegregation of public schools.[4]

The US Supreme Court justices considered the lawyers' responses to their questions and on May 17, 1954, they decided *Brown I*, ordering that racial segregation in public schools violates the Fourteenth Amendment. However, the judicial order did not spell out exactly when or how states were to begin their desegregation efforts. Without a deadline, the implementation of the Court's order lay fallow.

The public's unwillingness to desegregate public schools led the justices to issue a second ruling in *Brown*. On May 31, 1955, in *Brown II*, the US Supreme Court handed down its decree for implementing *Brown I*. Even then, ambiguous phrasing in the *Brown II* decision, which stated that desegregation should occur "with all deliberate speed," and the justices' acknowledgment of the inevitable difficulties of transitioning to desegregated education, allowed plenty of room for state defiance. Judge Rives told historian John M. Spivack that he thought the *Brown II* decision was clear. Rives was surprised "only by the deliberate speed language" in the Court's order. He thought a person's constitutional rights should be immediately available.[5] However, outside the courtroom, legislators and citizens across the South escalated their fight to retain racial segregation based on state rights.

White supremacists were outraged and reacted to the *Brown* decisions with open defiance and violence. Sociologist David Cunningham wrote that the decisions gave the KKK a "new impetus" for their message of Christian morality, which was interwoven in an ideology of white supremacy and implemented with violence. White supremacists also formed other organizations, including the White Citizens Council (WCC), to quash Black citizens' Civil Rights. The WCC established chapters across the Southern states. The Central Alabama WCC chapter was one of the largest groups, registering twelve thousand members. The WCC's message paralleled that of the KKK; however, the WCC was a public organization consisting primarily of middle- and upper-class white citizens. Abrams and Gray recalled that the Montgomery Chapter of the WCC "resorted to violence and threats," although as historian James W. Silver wrote, most Southern chapters declared their "respectability" through using economic reprisals and social pressure to maintain racial segregation. For example, Southern historian J. Mills Thornton III explained, their members agreed that all white business owners would deny employment and refuse credit to Black citizens who exercised their right "to attend white schools or to use other white facilities." WCC members also exerted pressure on political candidates to support the council's principles. They were also alert to any judicial action that would change their way of life.[6]

As legislators prepared to respond against the US Supreme Court order, a change occurred in the federal judiciary. In June 1955, Judge Charles B. Kennamer of the US District Court for the Middle District of Alabama died, leaving a vacancy. Kennamer's office was located two floors beneath Judge Rives's Circuit Court office in the Montgomery federal building. Kennamer, nominated by Republican president Herbert Hoover, had been a district judge since 1931.[7] President Eisenhower needed to nominate a candidate to replace him. People began to express an interest in the judgeship and to speculate about Kennamer's potential successor.

As is tradition, President Eisenhower sought to appoint a person from his own political party for the seat. Frank M. Johnson Jr., a Republican from northern Winston County, worked for Eisenhower's 1952 presidential campaign. In an act of political patronage, Johnson was appointed in 1953 to be the US attorney for the Northern District of Alabama. Robert F. Kennedy Jr. noted that by custom in Alabama, the judge for the Middle District "was and always had been" a resident of that district. Since Johnson did not live in the Middle District, the Montgomery Republican Committee and the *Montgomery Advertiser* refused to endorse him. Ultimately, the Alabama Republican

Party found none of the candidates for the federal judgeship to be satisfactory. With no nominee, Johnson and his father began to campaign for the judgeship. The looming question was whether Democratic senators Lister Hill and John Sparkman would support a judicial candidate from the Republican Party.[8]

Johnson recounted the situation surrounding his judicial candidacy and appointment to Lawrence R. Levin, a law clerk for Judge Rives. Johnson told Levin that he and Rives knew each other professionally, so Johnson went to see Rives to solicit his advice. Although Rives was now a judge, he still had considerable political power and influence in the Democratic Party. Johnson asked Rives whether he thought Democrats Hill and Sparkman would oppose his nomination for the judgeship. Rives told Johnson that he perceived him to be a fine US attorney, and that thanks to his astute legal abilities he deserved to be a judge. Johnson recalled that Rives said he knew Hill and Sparkman and would talk with them about Johnson's potential candidacy. Rives mentioned that although Hill and Sparkman were members of the Democratic Party and the president was a Republican, "it would be inappropriate" for the senators to oppose the president's nomination. Rives thought the circumstances did not require either Alabama senator to speak against or even comment publicly on Johnson's candidacy.[9]

The US Senate confirmed Johnson on January 31, 1956, and he received his commission on February 1, 1956, at age thirty-seven.[10] He began working the same day in the federal building two floors below Rives's office. Johnson was seated on the Middle District Court shortly after Judges John R. Brown and Elbert P. Tuttle were seated on the Fifth Circuit with Judge Rives.

Judge Brown was a man, law professor David S. Caudill wrote, who "enjoyed the law and 'getting it right.'" When Brown joined the court in 1955, he sought suggestions from Judge Rives about work habits that might increase his efficiency. Judge Johnson recalled in a conversation with lawyer Stephen J. Rowe that Rives went into the office very early in the mornings, generally before seven o'clock. He usually began working before other employees arrived, researching and drafting decisions and managing the requirements of his office. Judge Ginny Granade described Rives's work habits as "steady" and "rarely varied." After working all morning, he would walk or drive home for dinner, the largest meal of the day, rest for twenty minutes, and then return to the office in the afternoon. Rives explained to Granade that arriving early at work and working steadily throughout the day allowed him to leave "early, as I always have," meaning he was generally home before 6:00 p.m., sometimes bringing work with him if he had reading or writing to do.[11]

Judge Rives wrote to Judge Brown that his "method of studying the cases before argument varies somewhat with each case, but in general it is to read the pleadings, the findings of fact and conclusions of law, and the judgment appealed from. I do not usually try to read the entire record, as the number of cases makes that impossible. I do read all of the briefs before argument and check the record references from the briefs." Rives continued that he usually made no notes or the bare minimum of notes "before argument for fear that I will get my views too settled before hearing from the lawyers on oral argument." Instead, he relied on his clerk's memorandum to summarize the content of the case. Rives mentioned that his initial thoughts did not always agree with that of his clerk—"Sometimes I come around to his views, and sometimes I do not." After the hearings, "I usually spend the rest of that day studying the four cases heard that day in preparation for the conference the following morning before Court. Our conferences are usually very brief, I think too brief. When the cases are assigned for opinion, it is, of course, necessary for the judge preparing the opinion to read and study the entire record and all briefs."[12] Rives reinforced that Fifth Circuit judges faced a large workload.

Judge Rives admitted to Judge Brown, "I have a difficult job getting through with the tremendous volume of them by any method." During 1954–1955, Rives wrote seventy-five majority opinions, "in addition to . . . about fifteen dissenting opinions, and about six special concurrences." He confessed, "The enormous volume of work simply has not permitted us to devote as much study to the cases as we should. It had been my dream of a judge's life that I would be able to catch up on all of the reading I had to forego while practicing law, but I have barely had time to read the newspapers the last four years." Rives dedicated himself to his work, and most important to him was that the decisions be correct. Rives wrote to Brown that he "always welcome[s] . . . the most searching criticisms of my opinions, so that when published they may be right." Rives took his duty as a judge very seriously, declaring "we must get them decided right."[13]

Granade shared that during the summers Judge Rives and his family would vacation in Mary Esther, Florida, for about six weeks. The family cook, Minnie Crystal, and their part-time maid, Clarrie Hodge, also joined them in Florida. When Rives's son and daughter were young, he bought them a boat to use at the Mary Esther house. The boat was christened *The Feud.* Rives would generally work while others would go boating and swimming. Granade recalled, "The original garage to the house was converted into an office and he had a full set of *Reporters* there." Rives's law clerk at the time would accompany the family to Florida to work as Rives adhered to his regular routine.[14] When working in Montgomery, Rives's office was segregated from sections of the city in which Black citizens resided, although city buses traveled on the streets below his window.

Montgomery is well-known for the bus protest of 1955–1956. However, Black citizens had begun to call for the racial desegregation of public transportation in the city over five decades earlier. *Hawkins Rails* reported that a city ordinance, first adopted in 1900, required racial "segregation on public conveyances," including electric streetcars. The ordinance provoked a protest of Montgomery's Capital City Street Railway (also called the "Lightning Route" by Black citizens) later that year. At that time, there were no formal meetings with officials about the segregation ordinance. Civil Rights activist Butler Browder explained that the protest was led from the pulpits. Reverend Joshua Jimmy Shine, his mother's grandfather, was one of the organizers. Thornton wrote that Black citizens who had refused to ride the streetcar ended their protest "when the City Council agreed to amend the new ordinance to forbid compelling anyone to vacate his seat unless there was another seat to which he could move. This proviso remained a part of the city code." With the rise of automobiles and buses, the streetcar line ended operation in 1936 and the city began to use buses.[15] Black riders would load the bus from the rear; white riders would load the bus from the front. Problems often arose when the two groups would meet in the middle and no seats were available. Often in those cases the ordinance to not relocate a Black rider unless another seat was available seemed to pass by the wayside, and a Black rider was told to move to the back of the bus.

As time passed, Black civic leaders in Montgomery hoped to achieve racial progress through political activity. Educator Jo Anne Robinson recorded that Mary Fair Burks established the Women's Political Council (WPC) in 1949, which in the 1950s became "the most active and assertive black civic group in Montgomery." Robinson became president of the WPC in the early 1950s and readied to make the political influence of Black citizens known. In her memoir, *The Montgomery Bus Boycott and the Women Who Started It*, Robinson said that the organization's leaders (three WPC chapter presidents led by Robinson), met intermittently for what she characterized as "several years" with the Montgomery city commissioners (the mayor, police commissioner, and city commissioner) to improve conditions for Black citizens living in Montgomery. In November 1953 a special election was held to fill the vacant seat of city commissioner. Dave Birmingham, whom historian David J. Garrow called "a genuine racial liberal," won the election.[16]

Birmingham met with community leaders Robinson and Rufus A. Lewis. Thornton explained that Birmingham encouraged Robinson and Lewis "to seek redress from the city government for long-standing grievances: the lack of black policemen, the inadequacy of parks and playgrounds in black sections of the city, and the conditions on city buses." White citizens pushed back against the city's liberal commissioner. Black leaders then began to use other means, Thornton wrote, to influence Montgomery's city commissioners "outside the context of politics." The first organized large-scale protest of segregated municipal buses occurred in 1953 in Baton Rouge, Louisiana. The Baton Rouge protest was prompted by two issues: requiring Black riders to change their seats even though seats in the white section were empty, and an increase in bus fare. The protest was ultimately successful in making some changes in the seating arrangement, which historian Samuel Momodu wrote demonstrated that "peaceful, well-organized and supported grassroots protests could be effective in the Deep South." That protest provided a model for the Alabama bus protest.[17] Conditions would soon come together to make that model a reality in Montgomery.

On December 1, 1954, Rosa Parks, secretary of the Montgomery Chapter of the NAACP, was arrested on a crowded bus for refusing to relinquish her seat to a white patron. Parks's arrest provided an opportunity to publicly unify members of the Black community in demanding their Civil Rights. Her arrest stimulated mass meetings of Black citizens in Montgomery, which resulted in a citywide protest designed to continue until conditions changed on buses. She appealed her quasi-criminal violation to the Alabama Court of Civil Appeals in *Parks v. City of Montgomery* (1957). However, as a case against the city, any appeals would have to go through the state criminal appeals process before a federal appeal could be filed, which could take years. The *African American Registry* reported that even then, Montgomery lawyer Clifford Durr "believed it was possible that the outcome would merely have been that the conviction of Parks would be vacated with no changes in segregation laws." Abrams and Gray stated that she entered a plea of not guilty and "was convicted and fined $10, plus $4 in court costs." Unable to use Parks's arrest as a test case to desegregate city buses, lawyers Gray, Charles Langford, Arthur Shores, and other colleagues, including Durr, began to prepare a different lawsuit against bus desegregation.[18]

Although Black citizens did not yet trust the federal court system, Abrams and Gray observed that Black lawyers in the South began to pursue racial equality by "us[ing] the law to change the law."[19] The LDF had found success in desegregating public education, and Montgomery lawyers reasoned that the same legal strategy should be transferrable to other public facilities. The lawsuit listed five plaintiffs—Aurelia Browder, Claudette Colvin, Susie McDonald, Jeanetta Reese, and Mary Louise Smith. Each woman had previously experienced racial discrimination on city buses.

On February 1, 1956, Judge Johnson's first day in office, Gray filed the *Browder v. Gayle* complaint in the federal court for the Middle District of Alabama against city and state officials.[20] Lawyers identified the defendants as Montgomery Mayor William Armistead ("Tacky") Gayle, members of the

Board of Commissioners of the City of Montgomery, Montgomery's Chief of Police, the bus company, two bus drivers, and the three members of the Alabama Public Service Commission. In Alabama, when enforcing racial segregation on a city bus, the bus driver acted as an agent of the state, which also implicated the Alabama Public Service Commission in the lawsuit.

When lawyers for *Browder* submitted their pretrial brief, they cited federal statutes and supporting court decisions upon which they would argue their case during the trial. In writing their petition, the men relied on a 1908 US Supreme Court decision in *Ex Parte Young*, which permits lawsuits to be filed in federal court against state officials to prohibit them from enforcing a state law deemed unconstitutional. The statutes were alleged to deny Black citizens, Abrams and Gray asserted, "those rights, privileges and immunities as Citizens of the United States and equal protection of the laws." Relying, in part, on an analogy between public education and public transportation, the plaintiffs' lawyers argued that principles in *Brown I* substantiated their case. In *Brown I*, US Supreme Court justices decided "segregated public schools are not 'equal' and cannot be made 'equal,' and that hence . . . [Black children] are deprived of the equal protection of the laws."[21] The attorney general for the state of Alabama, John M. Patterson, represented the defendants and did not file an answer to the complaint. Instead, he filed a motion to dismiss the case based on established city and state laws requiring racial segregation on public buses.

Word of the bus desegregation case spread quickly through the Montgomery community. Alabama state legislators immediately responded—as they did when passing Act 894. Historian George E. Sims documented that the day after Gray filed the complaint, Representative Charles McKay of Talladega County introduced a resolution in the Alabama legislature. Representatives quickly passed Act no. 42, which declared, "The decisions and orders of the Supreme Court of the United States relating to separation of races in the public schools are, as a matter of right, null, void, and of no effect; and the Legislature of Alabama declares to all men that as a matter of right, this State is not bound to abide thereby." State officials passed this plan of nullification, relying on the Tenth Amendment to interpose the state legislature between the US Supreme Court and citizens of Alabama.[22] State and federal governments were at odds with one another, leading Judge Johnson to further his judicial protégé/mentor relationship with Judge Rives.

Judge Johnson shared with Levin that after studying the lawsuit filed in his court, he privately contacted Judge Rives to explain that he perceived the case would require a special three-judge panel as required by the US Code to restrain the enforcement of a state statute. At that time, generally a judge from the higher circuit court and two district judges from the state in which lawyers filed the lawsuit would try the case. That method, law professor Michael E. Solimine wrote, related to geographical convenience and to the assumption (generally supported by the US Supreme Court justices in Civil Rights cases appealed from the Fifth Circuit) that "local judges presumably would be more knowledgeable about the facts." For example, if Fifth Circuit Chief Judge Joseph C. Hutcheson Jr. called a three-judge panel in a case that emerged from the state of Alabama, Rives would likely serve as the circuit judge, along with the district judge filing the request and one other district or circuit judge. Although lawyers filed *Browder* in Johnson's district court, Rives, representing the circuit court, would provide what the New Orleans *Times-Picayune/The States-Item* newspaper called a "guiding spirit" for the case.[23]

With Judge Rives's support, Judge Johnson followed protocol and on his first day as a judge, February 1, 1956, he wrote a letter to Chief Judge Hutcheson, whose office was in Houston, Texas. Johnson's letter petitioned Hutcheson to assign a panel of three judges to hear *Browder*. Hutcheson wasted no time in responding and wrote a terse reply to Johnson dated February 3, 1956. Hutcheson indicated his frustration with Johnson, who he perceived to be an inexperienced judge seeking to use judicial resources for a case in which they were not necessary. Hutcheson wrote, "The suit is against local instead of state officers, and, while it does refer to a state statute, it really seeks relief from a city ordinance." He informed Johnson that "it doesn't take a three judge panel to hear a matter of local law." Hutcheson forwarded a confidential copy of the correspondence to Judge Rives, typing a note at the bottom of the letter: "Memo to Judge Rives: Johnson, speaking as one having authority and trying to get some business for you, writes me [on his first day as a judge that] this case is one for three judges. Humble and ignorant as I am [after nearly thirty-seven years on the court], I have presumed to differ with him and to deprive you of the business."[24] Rives, however, agreed with Johnson that the case interlinked city, state, and federal law.

On February 21, 1956, Judge Johnson again sought out Judge Rives to talk about the case. Following their meeting, Rives wrote a letter to Johnson identifying "applicable law" and "such thoughts as I have" in advocating for a three-judge panel. Rives cited the US Supreme Court decision in *Cleveland v. United States* (1945), in which city officials were "enforcing state laws embodying a state-wide concern and in the state's interest, and in such a case Section 266 [of the Judicial Code, requiring a three-judge panel] is applicable." Emboldened by Rives's letter, the next day Johnson sent a second letter to Chief Judge Hutcheson, citing long passages verbatim from Rives's letter to Johnson, including references to the 1940 Code of Alabama and legal precedent. Johnson contended that Alabama's state segregation laws prevailed over Montgomery's city bus segregation ordinance. He laid out the argument, noting that city employees acted as officers of the State in their capacity as bus drivers for Montgomery City Lines, Inc. He reiterated that the US Code required a three-judge district court panel to restrain the enforcement of a state statute. The argument was concise yet detailed. Near the end of the letter, Johnson acknowledged Rives's assistance: "Our mutual friend, Judge Rives, has been kind enough to discuss this matter with me to a limited extent," and he may be able to "make the matter clearer than I."[25] Rives likely expected Hutcheson to call him to discuss the lawsuit, and Hutcheson did.

On February 28, 1956, Chief Judge Hutcheson replied by letter to Judge Johnson that he had "discussed . . . [the case] fully with Judge Rives." Hutcheson reasoned that assigning a three-judge court would turn a local matter into an unnecessary statewide matter. Nevertheless, Rives had persuaded Hutcheson that a substantial Constitutional issue existed and he should let the lawyers make their case. Hutcheson's letter to Johnson continued, "I am still of the opinion that the complaint does not state a case for three judges. This does not mean that the petition could not state such a case. It means that it does not do so." Hutcheson explained to Johnson what the lawsuit needed to say to meet Johnson's interpretation. Johnson again contacted Hutcheson on March 8, indicating that Gray had adjusted his pretrial pleading. On March 12, 1956, Hutcheson issued an order constituting a three-judge court to hear *Browder*.[26]

The three-judge panel assigned by Chief Judge Hutcheson to hear *Browder* included Judge Johnson of the Middle District of Alabama, Judge Seybourn Lynne of the Northern District of Alabama, and Judge Rives of the Fifth Circuit. Freyer and Dixon described Rives as the eldest of the three men on the *Browder* panel. He was, they wrote, a "tradition-minded" Southern National Democrat. The National Democratic Party was a short-lived (1896–1900) liberal splinter group of the Democratic Party that emerged, in part, in response to the free silver economic platform advocated at the 1896 Democratic Convention by Populist Democrats. *The Campaign Text-Book of the National Democratic Party, 1896* characterized a "true Democrat" as one who, in part, stands for "Individual Liberty," which includes a belief in "the rule of an impartial law" and "strict observance of the mandates of the Federal Constitution." Rives had, Freyer and Dixon wrote, "an overriding faith in fundamental fairness." His perspective stemmed from his early life, including the convictions he gained from family members and working as a lawyer in an "atypical jury trial practice" that represented white and Black clients, people who were down on their luck, and potential social outcasts. He was a "quintessential political and social insider from Montgomery" who had developed a reputation as a fair man. American historian Frye Gaillard wrote that politicians and judges generally regarded Rives as "an Old South lawyer, aristocratic, reflective, not a boat-rocker on the issue of race."[27] Instead of publicly embracing racial desegregation, Rives took the stance that each individual citizen, regardless of race, must be protected equally by the US Constitution. If desegregation was a byproduct of that protection, then citizens must accept that. Rives took seriously his sworn duty to the judicial oath of office and provided a behavioral example for the newly appointed Johnson.

Judge Johnson, the youngest federal judge in the country at that time, hailed from northern Alabama near the Tennessee border where Republicans outnumbered Democrats. Republicans in Winston County, Gaillard explained, "were holdovers from the party of Lincoln, fiercely independent and proud of their history of being out of step. Just before the Civil War, when the state of Alabama seceded from the Union, the county of Winston seceded from the state. . . . Most of Winston County's young men fought for the Union." Gaillard characterized Johnson as "a maverick, . . . in many ways, a hillbilly to the bone. He liked to fish and chew tobacco . . . and he was always partial to a good country song." The *New York Times* reported that Johnson's approach was to "follow the law and the facts without regard to the consequences."[28] He had yet to reveal his thinking on race cases.

In contrast to Johnson and Judge Rives, Judge Lynne had long established his reputation as a racial segregationist. Judge Lynne, Gaillard wrote, "was more conservative than either of his colleagues" on the panel. President Harry S Truman appointed Lynne in 1946. While Lynne's seniority on the federal bench surpassed Rives's by five years, Rives held a position in a higher court. Yarbrough referred to Lynne as a descendant of an old northern Alabama family "with impeccable confederate credentials." His ancestors fought in the Civil War, and Lynne continued to support racial segregation. Thornton added that Lynne was a "paternalist segregationist," whose motives to restrict the freedoms of Black citizens was, Lynne perceived, in their best interests. Historian Joseph Mark Bagley wrote that Lynne "established himself as openly hostile to plaintiffs' causes in civil rights cases and became infamous for letting such actions wither on his docket." Lynne's orientation toward Civil Rights cases was summarized by political scientist Richard C. Courtner. Lynne consistently found "no merit in Negroes' civil rights complaints" and believed in the "separate but equal" structure of public life.[29]

Judges Rives and Lynne, before they joined the federal judiciary, were Democrats, while Judge Johnson was previously a Republican. Freyer and Dixon noted that although Rives and Johnson were from different political parties, they "shared economic and political values and associations inherent in the national liberal consensus." In their law practices, both men usually won cases representing poor and minority clients before "all-white, middle-class male juries."[30] Their success in the courtroom reinforced their fundamental belief in fairness.

Although Judges Rives and Lynne were both appointed by President Truman, they applied the law differently. Lynne equated justice with the rule of law, which American legal scholar David A. Strauss explained "is in substantial part about following precedent and otherwise maintaining continuity with the past."[31] As previously noted, Rives's common-law approach to justice accepted that justice requires the law to be steady yet also malleable enough to be responsive to conditions within a particular historical moment. The three judges were familiar with one another and recognized that they agreed in some areas and disagreed in others.

Judges Rives had received his *Browder* assignment by Chief Judge Hutcheson and prepared to hear arguments presented by each side. Jonathan R. Harkavy, a law clerk for Rives, explained that he and his co-clerk were required to do legal research and write a memorandum for each of Rives's cases. While some judges relied heavily on clerk memoranda, Rives was also compulsive about doing his own legal research. This parallel review of the law reassured Rives of having complete and accurate information, which surely added to his confidence as a judge.[32]

The US Supreme Court had already decided a number of racial desegregation cases. The justices decided a cluster of appeals on June 5, 1950, ruling in three desegregation cases. Two of the lawsuits resulted in the desegregation of higher education facilities (*Sweatt v. Painter* and *McLaurin v. Oklahoma State Regents*). An additional lawsuit resulted in the desegregation of dining cars on passenger trains that traveled across state lines (*Henderson v. United States*). Then, on May 17, 1954, the US Supreme Court justices declared in *Brown I* that segregation of the lower levels of public education "is a denial of the equal protection of the laws." That same day, the justices desegregated public schools in the District of Columbia in *Bolling v. Sharpe*. Other decisions to desegregate the public sphere soon followed. On May 24, one week after their *Brown I* decision, the Supreme Court ordered the racial desegregation of city parks in *Muir v. Louisville Park Theatrical Association*. The theatrical association was a "privately operated enterprise that leased the amphitheater from the city" that barred Black citizens. The justices were building a record that made clear the *Brown I* ruling was not limited to education. In *Muir*, the justices vacated the lower court ruling that upheld racial segregation, and the case was remanded back to the lower court "for consideration in the light of . . . [*Brown I*], and conditions that now prevail." In 1955, additional US Supreme Court decisions reinforced their earlier rulings. On November 7, the justices affirmed *Dawson v. Mayor and City Council of Baltimore*, a Fourth Circuit decision that desegregated public beaches and bathhouses.

Justices heard appeals in *Rice v. Arnold* and *Holmes v. City of Atlanta* that same day. This time they desegregated municipal golf courses.[33] Collectively, these Supreme Court decisions racially desegregated a variety of institutions in the public sphere—including educational facilities, city parks, public beaches and bathhouses, and municipal golf courses.

Judge Rives, who pushed Chief Judge Hutcheson to have *Browder* heard, wrote to Judges Lynne and Johnson on May 5, 1956. In his letter, Rives inquired as to how the other judges were thinking about the lawsuit. Rives offered his perspective: "our approach to this case is most important. Should we take the position that we have no real responsibility because the Supreme Court has already decided the issue [in *Plessy v. Ferguson*], or is it our duty to consider and decide the important constitutional question presented? From my study thus far, I am firmly convinced that the latter is our only true course." Rives perceived that a doctrinal trend, defined by the Legal Information Institute as a "widely followed" principle that provides "a comprehensive way to resolve" legal disputes, to desegregate public spaces had begun even before *Brown.*[34]

As the circuit judge on the *Browder* panel, Rives had the all-important power to assign which judge would write the court opinion. He added a postscript in his May 5, 1956, letter to Judges Lynne and Johnson, "PS Incidentally, if in our final consideration we find ourselves in agreement, and if you two approve, I would like to write the opinion in this case." On May 7, Judge Lynne replied to Rives. In anticipation of following *Plessy*, which justified "separate but equal" facilities in transportation, he wrote, "Enclosed is a proposed draft of opinion in our three-judge case." Lynne continued, "While I shall hear the arguments with an open mind, I must confess that . . . I perceive no 'new doctrinal trend' which indicates that *Plessy v. Ferguson* would no longer be followed by . . . [the US Supreme Court] in an intrastate transportation case." Johnson had argued numerous cases in Lynne's courtroom as a US attorney, and Lynne had already contacted Johnson to persuade him to either support Alabama attorney general Patterson's motion to dismiss *Browder*, or to hold that *Plessy* controlled the outcome of the case.[35]

Judge Lynne told political scientist Tinsley E. Yarbrough that he thought highly of Johnson's "legal skill, tenacity, and conscientiousness." Lynne also commented that he respected Judge Rives as "a great lawyer and judge" but realized, too, that "no earthly power could shake" Rives once he had reasoned through an issue. Assuming from Rives's letter that he would write an extensive dissent if he was not in the majority, Lynne ribbed him, "I shall bring the record with me on Friday and you may have one of your friends return it in a pick-up truck when it has served your purpose" in writing a dissent. Lynne hoped the three judges would find themselves in agreement, but he also agreed that if they were not unanimous and he was in the minority, Rives should write the decision in the case. Rives continued to refine his logic in a May 9 letter to Lynne and Johnson, working to clarify his interpretation of the law.[36]

Then, on May 18, 1956, Judge Rives, a descendant of ancestors who owned enslaved people, wrote to Judge Johnson that he was engaged in "much soul searching and labor" related to *Browder*. In his contemplation, Rives likely reflected on conversations with his mother, which writers Donnie Williams and Wayne Greenhaw explained would have included hearing "stories, handed down from generation to generation, about the Cause of the Confederacy." He likely also considered his father's more liberal ideas, religious teachings, talks with his son, work in the community as a lawyer, and his personal experiences—including his relationships with his childhood friends, his family's cook, their part-time maid, and other Black citizens. His labor included a careful review of areas within the law. Harkavy commented that Rives had a "keen sense of both justice and the supremacy of the rule of law." Although justice and the law are related constructs, the principle of justice is not the same as the law. As Abrams and Gray explained, "The law is simply a body of rules and regulations" that govern citizens' behavior. The law "does not guarantee justice or even fairness" and is, in short, "what the judicial system says it is."[37] However, the law can be written to provide justice. Rives began to work on a potential *Browder* dissent, drawing from thoughts he had shared in letters to Judges Lynne and Johnson.

The language in *Brown I* provided room for an interpretation that allowed Judge Rives to conclude that *Plessy* was no longer valid. Legal scholar and later Seventh Circuit Judge Richard A. Posner explained that the "vagueness of the text" in *Plessy* "permitted reexamination of the decision in light of half a century of social and political change." By addressing the question of law (the legal principle guiding the case) in *Brown*, the US Supreme Court justices had moved the issue of racial segregation to a more abstract level.[38] Judges could then potentially interpret the legal principle of equality as desegregating all areas of society, especially when considering Supreme Court decisions that racially desegregated other areas of the public sphere.

Judge Johnson told Levin that while he was thinking about *Browder*, he went upstairs to Rives's chambers to talk with him about the case. Johnson told Rives that he understood that the US Supreme Court decision in *Plessy* technically appeared to be the controlling decision for *Browder*. However, Johnson did not believe that the *Plessy* segregation decision was "still good law" and did not know whether the Supreme Court would uphold it. Johnson had only been a judge for a few months and recognized how unpopular a dissenting vote could be so early in his career. Johnson had practiced law extensively in Judge Lynne's courtroom and referred to Lynne as his "mentor" on courtroom management.[39] Johnson respected Lynne but thought *Plessy* was contrary to the US Constitution and out of sync with the global and national events of the time.

Judge Johnson shared with Levin that he told Judge Rives that he did not know what to do. At that point, Rives looked at him and said, "Well then, if I were you, I would just join the majority opinion that I am writing, and we'll declare the ordinance unconstitutional." Johnson said that he was relieved that both men had reached the same tentative conclusion. Johnson recalled the same incident to Yarbrough, explaining that he and Rives agreed that *Plessy* had been decided incorrectly, while also agreeing that they should wait until after the briefings and arguments to determine whether *Plessy* should be considered controlling in *Browder* or whether *Brown* changed the legal landscape.[40] They did so in a context where many lawyers, judges, US congressmen, and citizens from the Deep South refused to accept the US Supreme Court justices' racial desegregation orders.

Southern legislators in the US Congress, led by Virginia Senator Harry Byrd, issued the Declaration of Constitutional Principles, better known as the Southern Manifesto, on March 12, 1956—the same day Chief Judge Hutcheson assigned a panel of three judges to hear *Browder*. The manifesto denounced *Brown*, asserted "the right of states to ignore the decision," and directly challenged "the practice of judicial review." The document characterized the Court order as "unwarranted" and "a clear abuse of judicial power." The final section of the manifesto included a series of provocative statements, including a denunciation of "the Supreme Court's encroachments on rights reserved to the States and to the people, contrary to established law." In short, the declaration called on leaders of Southern states to prevent the enforcement of *Brown*. One hundred and one of the 128 members of Congress from the eleven former Confederate states signed the official declaration. Political historian Tony Badger wrote that even Alabama senators Hill and Sparkman signed the manifesto, despite each man's reputation as an established moderate who preferred to avoid engaging in the politics of race.[41]

After the manifesto and list of signatories was made public, Judge Rives visited the Montgomery office of his longtime friend, Senator Hill. In that meeting they discussed the manifesto. As reported by author and journalist Jack Bass, Hill reluctantly explained to Rives that because of "changed political realities," he and Senator Sparkman were forced to go along with the manifesto. Rives listened carefully before responding and replied, "Well, Lister, I think I understand it now. You fellas have just risen above principle." A quiet and thoughtful man, Rives held a deep respect for the US Constitution. He interpreted Hill as unwilling to stand for what was right, putting personal political aspirations above the principles of justice and fairness. As a result of that meeting, historian Virginia Van der Veer Hamilton noted that years would go by before the two men would renew their friendship.[42] Hill was not the only individual with whom Rives regularly interacted who refused to accept racial desegregation.

Judge Lynne arrived in Montgomery the day before the *Browder* trial, and Judge Johnson told Levin that the three judges met at a restaurant. The judges happened to see a copy of the May 10, 1956, issue of the *Alabama Journal* newspaper. On the front page an article reported that Alabama's Fifteenth Judicial Circuit Court Judge Walter B. Jones, a segregationist, had upheld state and local laws requiring segregated busing in *City of Montgomery v. Montgomery City Lines*. In his decision, Jones included a comment about a recent Fourth Circuit ruling in *Flemming v. South Carolina Electric and Gas Co.* In that case, Flemming sued a bus company for monetary damages rather than for injunctive relief (an order that requires a person to do or stop doing a specific action). Flemming claimed the South Carolina Code requiring racial segregation violated her rights under the Fourteenth Amendment. The newspaper article quoted Jones's criticism of "the unsound reasoning, or rather lack of reasoning" by the federal judges in that case.

Jones did not acknowledge that over two weeks earlier, on April 23, 1956, the US Supreme Court decided not to review the Fourth Circuit Court's ruling, given that the case had not yet been heard by a jury and a decision on monetary damages had not yet been made. The justices remanded the case back to the Eastern District of South Carolina Court for trial. A reporter for the *Alabama Journal*, paraphrasing Jones's court order in *City of Montgomery*, wrote, "There is no straight out decision of the Supreme Court of the United States holding that a state or city may not require the separation of the races on buses where carriage of passengers is solely intrastate."[43] Alabama laws requiring bus segregation would remain in effect. The day before the *Browder* trial in district court, federal Judges Rives, Johnson, and Lynne were placed in the position of potentially contradicting a state court decision.

The *Browder* trial was scheduled to begin at 9:00 a.m. on Friday, May 11, 1956. Abrams and Gray described people gathering in front of the courthouse before 8:00 a.m. As the time neared for the trial to begin, spectators took seats segregating themselves into their respective areas. Black citizens, including Reverend Martin Luther King Jr., were in attendance. Lawyers and their clients settled into their seats. Shortly after 9:00 a.m., Judges Rives, Johnson, and Lynne were escorted by a security official from Johnson's chambers to the courtroom. Rives, who presided over the court proceedings, took a seat in the center of the twenty-foot-long oak bench, which Gaillard wrote was "polished to a shine." Frank Sikora, a journalist for the *Birmingham News*, observed that

Johnson sat to Rives's left and Lynne to his right.[44] The formality of the setting signaled serious implications for cases tried in the courtroom.

Abrams and Gray commented that seven Black men and women sat at the plaintiffs' tables and over fifteen white men sat at the defendants' tables. The plaintiffs were one fewer than when Gray filed the case. He recalled that one plaintiff, Reese, was employed "in the home of a high-ranking Montgomery police official." She had been challenged by her employer and others about her involvement in the lawsuit. After her participation "was reported in the newspapers, she received several threatening phone calls" warning of "economic retaliation and violence" toward her and her husband. Under severe pressure, she claimed no involvement in the case. The warnings to Black citizens in Montgomery were real, and foreshadowed what would happen if protests for desegregation in the city did not stop.[45] Four of the five women remained to testify—Browder, Colvin, McDonald, and Smith.

Each of the four women had been arrested prior to December 5, 1955, when the bus protest began. As mentioned earlier, beginning in November 1953, Robinson and other WPC representatives started to meet with city commissioners and bus officials about conditions on city buses. Abrams and Gray wrote that the requests in over twenty meetings were the same: "courtesy, equity in seating, and hiring colored drivers." Negotiations with city commissioners and bus officials prior to the lawsuit stemmed from the idea that "before we filed a lawsuit to desegregate the buses we ought to try to get the city to agree to something less than that." However, in the *Browder* lawsuit, the plaintiffs' lawyers "directly attacked Montgomery's segregated transit system." While there were originally three demands, those goals "had long been dismissed."[46] The legal goal had shifted to complete desegregation after the Montgomery city commissioners were unresponsive to Black citizens' demand for respect and the US Supreme Court issued its orders in *Brown I* and *II*. the March 8, 1956, filing, the Montgomery Improvement Association (MIA) lawyers' objective was to present testimony that the lawsuit resulted from racial segregation on city vehicles. If the judges eliminated segregation, Black citizens would ride the buses again.

The court reporter's transcript reveals that lawyers for the defendants advanced the argument that at the time the women were arrested, the city "enforced the laws" as they were written. Further, the city and bus company had no authority to override state segregation law. Relying on dated information from earlier meetings between representatives of the MIA, city commissioners, and the bus company, defense lawyers set out to prove that the three demands initially proposed by Robinson and others could be met without desegregating the buses: Black riders "wanted better treatment," Black drivers, and seating on a "first come, first served" basis. (Black citizens could currently sit where they wanted to on buses—as long as they sat in the section designated for their use.) Defense lawyers contended that these outcomes did not require changing bus segregation laws. The *Alabama Journal* reported that Black citizens "didn't ask an end to segregation but rather proposed a new seating arrangement within the segregation laws." That interpretation would allow the women's arrests to stand and, as Judge Jones ruled in state court, segregation would remain a part of city and state law. As Thornton observed, white citizens "simply did not reflect carefully on the legal points" raised by Black lawyers.[47]

Judge Rives managed the trial. As the trial began, he read the complaint aloud. He asked Gray, one of the plaintiffs' lawyers, to call his first witness. Gray called the lead plaintiff, Browder, to the stand. Her son recalled that her long-standing involvement in Civil Rights advocacy in Montgomery meant she was the least likely of the four women to be shaken by intimidation under cross-examination. She had been working with Robinson in the WPC, and they had become close friends. Browder's arrest in April 1955 was at least the second time she had been charged for not allowing a white passenger to take her seat on a bus.[48]

Browder knew that historically there were few benefits to publicly contesting the status quo. As Abrams and Gray wrote, if she "fought the system, the system would fight back." She knew that the tires on her car may be slashed, her family would surely receive threatening telephone calls and letters, and the "normal" racial slurs and insults would escalate. But she had "lost patience waiting for equality." As her son explained, his mother "refused to bow down" to the constant intimidation from bus drivers. His mother and Robinson talked constantly about the problems riding city buses. Browder agreed with Robinson to be named in the lawsuit if her name was listed first. Robinson then conveyed that information to Gray.[49] Gray addressed her request by listing the litigants alphabetically. As she expected, the system fought back.

Browder's residence was in Centennial Hill, identified by Civil Rights historian Mark Hilton as "once Montgomery's most prestigious black community." Browder's son explained that eggs, flour, and sugar were thrown on the front porch. The combination of ingredients, readily available in kitchens, was difficult to remove after it dried. White supremacists twice placed bombs around the Browder home. Abrams and Gray explained that on one occasion the device was "actual dynamite." While explosions occurred outside of other houses in Montgomery, the bomb at her house did not explode. Her son recalled that another time broomsticks were wrapped up like dynamite. Racist extremists commonly stage attacks that portray the possibility of serious outcomes but do not actually result in physical damage. This form of terrorism sends a clear message of violence but does not put the extremists in legal jeopardy resulting from an actual explosion. On the witness stand, Browder recounted her experience, saying she would begin riding the city bus again if she could sit any place she wanted.[50] After Browder's initial testimony, Judge Rives called for cross-examination by the defense lawyers.

The defense lawyer's questioning quickly proved to be ineffective. The trial transcript reveals that when Browder did not respond as the lawyer expected, he stated, "You didn't understand my question." In their cross-examination of each plaintiff, lawyers for the city used various strategies to try to confuse the women. Lawyers focused on the role of King ("Did Negro King ask three certain things at that time, did he not."), asked questions in the negative ("—is it not true"), and downplayed whether the witness was "*injured* in being subjected to segregation" on city buses.[51] Lawyers also engaged in wordplay, challenging the plaintiffs' testimony.

Each of the four women took the witness stand in turn, testifying to their mistreatment on city buses. The defense lawyers argued that the women were not interested in desegregating buses at the time of their arrests, but only after Reverend King moved to Montgomery. Butler Browder, along with lawyers Jonathan L. Entin and Robert O. White II, wrote that the plaintiffs' "motivation was that of frustration to a common condition and not a staged or fabricated effort. The people were acting as one unit and the various classes and factions of the community were at once on the same page." Lawyers continued to press witnesses about demands that Abrams and Gray explained had been "long ago" discarded by the MIA.[52]

One of the keys to the complaint was to link the city ordinance with state law (both supported racial segregation), which would then be subject to the US Constitution's Fourteenth Amendment. Abrams and Gray recalled that after a brief recess, Gray requested "to amend our complaint," including "and the due process of laws, as secured to them by the Fourteenth Amendment to the Constitution of the United States." Lawyers for the city and bus company objected to the plaintiff's motion but the court stated, "so amended."[53]

After the plaintiffs' lawyers presented their witnesses, the defense presented their side of the case. Defense lawyers first called C. C. ("Jack") Owen, president of the Alabama Public Service Commission, as a witness. Thornton explained that under examination Owen was asked about the responsibilities of his position and the connection between city and state laws. He "flatly denied that his agency had any jurisdiction over municipal bus systems," reinforcing his view that the case was a local lawsuit rather than statewide case. Steve Lesher of the *Montgomery Advertiser* reported that Rives then introduced a portion from the General Acts of Alabama, passed in July 1945, giving the Public Service Commission "authority to oversee interstate or intrastate transportation." Rives read the state statute, which a US Senate Subcommittee on

Constitutional Rights reported, "expressly imposes on the Alabama Public Service Commission the duty of administering and enforcing its requirements as to segregation of the races." According to the court transcript, Rives asked Owen if he interpreted the act to exclude "common carriers such as busses in the City of Montgomery?" Owen responded, "That refers to the 1939 Motor Carriers Act, which does not put such companies as the Montgomery City Lines directly under our supervision." Rives countered, "This was passed after the 1939 Motor Carriers Act, I am just asking you what your construction of it is, you are testifying under oath, and I am asking what you construction of those words is." Owen replied, "I had never thought of it in that particular line of thinking. This is the first time that point has ever been brought up. It seems to me like that means segregation as far as segregation is concerned."[54] Rives was attentive to how words could be used strategically to bypass certain meanings.

As the trial progressed, Judge Rives sustained objections and reminded the defense that Gray filed the lawsuit primarily to determine "a question of law," in which judges would examine the legal principles that apply to the facts in the case. The plaintiffs' lawyer addressed the *Flemming* case, insisting that although the case was for monetary compensation for damages suffered by the rider, the decision could be interpreted as ruling bus segregation to be unconstitutional. Judge Lynne interrupted the lawyer to note that the *Flemming* decision was written at the circuit court of appeals level, not in an order by the US Supreme Court. As such, Lynne asserted that *Flemming* did not change *Plessy* as controlling public transportation throughout the nation. Abrams and Gray recalled that during the trial Rives and Lynne agreed that they "did not believe" that outlawing segregation across the public sphere "was the intention of the [US Supreme Court]" in denying certiorari in *Flemming*. In the *Birmingham News*, Hugh W. Sparrow reported that Rives and Lynne "declared several times . . . during arguments" that the US Supreme Court had not ruled with finality regarding bus segregation laws.[55]

At another point in the trial, Sparrow recorded that Judge Lynne reminded the courtroom that the US Supreme Court ban on segregation in schools in *Brown I* invalidated segregation in public educational facilities. He reported that Rives expressed that he held "a similar opinion" to Lynne when interpreting *Brown I*.[56] Both Judges Rives and Lynne agreed that *Brown I* required the racial desegregation of public educational institutions. Their disagreement lay in how they interpreted the language within the ruling. As addressed earlier, Rives perceived that the US Supreme Court rulings exhibited the trend toward a doctrine of racial desegregation. He emphasized principles of equality in *public* facilities, including but not limited to schools, which made the desegregation of public space a constitutional issue. Lynne read *Brown I* as pointing only to public *educational* facilities. From that vantage point, Lynne reasoned that the Supreme Court's ruling in *Plessy* would stand in the *Browder* case. The three judges continued to listen as both sides argued their case.

Defense lawyers called witnesses to the stand to speak about the possible violent consequences of a desegregation ruling. Recent events had aroused public anxiety, including the US Supreme Court's *Brown* decisions, the justices' decision in *Lucy v. Adams* (1955) to admit Autherine Lucy and Pollie Anne Myers to the University of Alabama, and the US Congress's announcement of the Southern Manifesto.[57] Abrams and Gray wrote that after listening to witnesses "threaten that ending segregation would rip apart the city," Rives had heard all he needed to. According to Steve Lesher of the *Montgomery Advertiser*, in response to defense witnesses' statements about violence, Judge Rives asked a defense lawyer, "Can you command one man to surrender his constitutional rights, if they are his constitutional rights, to prevent another man from committing a crime?" Rives's question echoed the words of Thomas Jefferson's anti-slavery clause, which appeared in an early draft of the US Declaration of Independence. Jefferson accused King George, who supported slavery, of paying off crimes he committed against one group (colonists) with crimes he wanted them to commit toward another group (enslaved people).[58] Whether violence would erupt was legally immaterial for Rives in deciding *Browder*. His view was that justice requires no citizen to surrender one's constitutional rights.

The *Alabama Journal* announced that both sides finished presenting their argument before the 12:00 noon recess. The court reconvened at 1:30 p.m. to hear final arguments, which lasted until about 3:00 p.m. In Robert Carter's closing argument for the plaintiffs, Abram and Gray recalled he made a "dramatic, direct attack on segregation" in which he cited numerous US Supreme Court decisions to assert "the doctrine of separate but equal has been so weakened as to be without any remaining legal substance." Bass wrote that when the hearing ended, Judge Rives announced there would be no immediate decision because the three judges would need to "study and deliberate on the evidence, because this is an important case." At that time, there was no roadmap for how to dismantle legal segregation. Judge Lynne shared with Yarbrough that several newspaper reporters speculated that he and Rives might uphold segregation on city buses but none were certain of the outcome after the trial.[59]

After the trial concluded, the judges gathered for a judicial conference in Judge Johnson's private chambers. Johnson relayed to Frank Sikora, a journalist for the *Birmingham News*, that the three men sat in silence for several minutes. Then Judge Rives said to Johnson, " you're the junior judge here. You vote first. What do you think?" The practice of voting in the order of least seniority is a judicial practice used to prevent junior members from being influenced by senior members' votes. Johnson replied, "Judge . . . as far as I'm concerned state-imposed segregation on public facilities violates the Constitution. I'm going to rule with the plaintiffs here." Johnson recalled that Judge Lynne shook his head in disapproval while Johnson was speaking.[60]

Judge Lynne, also a district judge from Alabama, voted next. Judge Johnson told Sikora that Lynne asserted, "I don't reach it that way. . . . The (Supreme) Court has already spoken on this issue in Plessy. It's the law and we're bound by it until it's changed." Lynne, an astute technician of the law, took the position that only US Supreme Court justices can overrule precedent decided by the Supreme Court. The vote was tied, one vote to racially desegregate city buses and one vote to retain segregation on city buses. Judge Rives would cast the deciding vote. According to one of Rives's clerks, Rives looked at Johnson, nodded, and said, "You know, I feel the same way as you." Johnson recalled to Sikora that the post-hearing conference in Johnson's chambers was brief, taking "only ten minutes."[61] Yet, stating one's preliminary conclusions in a post-hearing conference is different than documenting an argument as a published decision. Writing and announcing the court's order would take several weeks.

Abrams and Gray identified two questions that Judge Rives had to address in writing for the majority in *Browder*. Rives needed to tackle whether the district court "had jurisdiction to make any kind of ruling" in the lawsuit, as well as "whether the boycott initially had been intended to attack segregation or had it been limited to a protest against specific regulations." Rives worked from his letters and other legal documents to address the fundamental question of whether the "separate but equal" doctrine validly applied to intrastate transportation in *Browder*. A week after the trial, on May 18, 1956, Rives sent a draft decision to Judge Johnson, who had voted with him in the majority. Drawing from his experience as a law clerk to Rives, Norman L. Blumenfeld explained that when Rives wrote decisions, he tried to word sentences specifically "so his opinions would not be open to three or four interpretations." The argument Rives made in the draft decision was thorough and careful—and would undoubtedly cause him to be exiled from his community, friends, and potentially even his family members. The US Supreme Court's *Brown* decisions, legal scholar Louis Michael Seidman wrote, "generated a backlash that . . . affected the political alignment of the country."[62] *Browder* would likely be no less significant.

In drafting an opinion for the majority, Judge Rives relied on his common-law approach. He stated, "There is . . . a constitutional difference, between voluntary adherence to custom and the perpetuation and enforcement of that custom by law. . . . We cannot, in good conscience, perform our duty as judges by blindly following the precedent of *Plessy v. Ferguson*." He continued, "We hold that the statutes and ordinances requiring segregation of the white and colored races on the motor buses of a common carrier of passengers within the city of Montgomery and its police jurisdiction violate the due process and equal protection of the law clauses of the Fourteenth Amendment to the Constitution of the United States." Rives supported his interpretation by quoting the insight of US Supreme Court Justice Oliver Wendell Holmes Jr. in *Perkins v. Endicott Johnson Corporation* (1942): "'The life of the law,' as Mr. Justice Holmes said, 'has been experience.'" Holmes recognized that logic alone could stultify the law, and he respected the intuition that judges gained as a result of their experience on the bench and in life. Rives continued quoting Holmes, "Legal doctrines, as first enunciated, often prove to be inadequate under the impact of ensuing experience in their practical application. And when a lower court perceived a pronounced new doctrinal trend in Supreme Court decisions, it is its duty, cautiously to be sure, to follow [and] not to resist it."[63] Rives responded to inequities between state and federal law by embracing the equality requirement of the Fourteenth Amendment.

John Daniel Reaves, one of Rives's clerks, shared that Rives was "not progressive" on racial issues in the sense of a judicial activist, but he adamantly supported the equality of individuals under the law. Rives recognized that *Brown I* was more than simply a "school" case; the US Supreme Court's decision completely dismantled the racial caste system operating within the United States. The Supreme Court had taken a stand and, as Spivack wrote, Rives would "follow the law." Strauss explained that in a common-law judicial philosophy, democracy develops through "the accumulation and evolution of precedents, shaped to some degree by [common sense] notions of fairness and good policy." The Warren Court concluded in *Brown I* that what is separate can never be equal, thereby extending the progression of desegregation law and individual equality under the US Constitution.[64] Rives understood that a federal court order in favor of the plaintiffs in *Browder* could precipitate an already impending culture war. However, if the court ruled in favor of the defendants, justice would not be served.

Judge Lynne received the draft decision with Judge Johnson's revisions and reviewed the material. He replied by letter to Judge Rives on May 29, 1956, writing, "I agree with your opinion in the Browder case down to its rejection of the 'separate but equal' doctrine in a transportation case." Lynne rejected Rives's reasoning that the *Brown I* decision, buttressed by the *Flemming* decision out of the Fourth Circuit, applied to *Browder*, given that the Court refused to hear the *Flemming* appeal. He insisted that the judges were overreaching their jurisdiction. He offered some wording suggestions to the decision and added his dissent. In the letter, Lynne characterized his dissent as "a short, restrained opinion," writing that he felt "a profound philosophical disagreement" with Rives and Johnson.[65]

In response to Judges Rives's and Johnson's reference to their "good conscience" in the draft decision, Judge Lynne noted in his letter of May 29, 1956, that his "conscience dictated" that he apply *Plessy* as established precedent. Lynne defended his logic, writing that he did not engage in "blind obedience to a legalistic formula embodied in the rule of stare decisis." (Stare decisis refers to a doctrine guiding courts to follow established precedent when an issue has been previously introduced in court and a ruling has been made.) As such, Lynne held that his disagreement "was the result of a simple belief that the laws . . . should evidence not only the appearance but also the spirit of stability." For Lynne, stability in the law would yield stability in society. He continued, "judges of trial courts frequently find themselves in disagreement with the rationale of an old, but clearly controlling precedent. . . . [But the district court is] neither designed nor equipped to perform the legislative function of putting off the old and putting on the new." A judicial decision, Lynne asserted, cannot reflect the majority judges' impulse simply because precedent does not coincide with their thinking at the time a case is decided.[66] He illustrated his point by citing a recent decision from Rives.

In his reply, Judge Lynne quoted Judge Rives's April 20, 1956, decision for the majority of Fifth Circuit judges in *Howard v. United States*. In that case, the question arose of "the proper test of criminal responsibility where insanity is asserted." Rives reasoned that the US Supreme Court's decision in *Davis v. United States* (1897) should be followed. A more recent decision—*Durham v. United States* (1954), decided in the District of Columbia Circuit Court—required only that the defendant establish a defense of insanity "beyond a reasonable doubt." In *Howard*, Rives relied on the earlier Supreme Court ruling in *Davis* rather than the more recent Circuit Court ruling in *Durham*. Lynne quoted Rives: "In the face of such recognition by the Supreme Court of a test of criminal responsibility, we do not feel at liberty to consider and decide whether in our opinion the recent modification of such test in the District of Columbia is sound or unsound, nor whether some other test should be adopted. This Circuit follows the law as stated by the Supreme Court and leaves any need for modification thereof to that Court." Lynne wrote that Rives "stated my position [in *Browder*], clearly and concisely" in *Howard*.[67]

Judge Lynne also addressed Judge Rives's reference to *Flemming* in his *Browder* dissent. *Flemming* held persuasive authority for Rives and Judge Johnson. Persuasive authority, defined by the Legal Information Institute, refers to a decision written by another court that carries "authoritative weight," which the judges may choose to follow, but do not have to follow. While Rives and Johnson perceived a new doctrinal trend, Lynne did "not at all agree." In the draft opinion Rives explicitly stated, "the separate but equal doctrine can no longer be safely followed as a correct statement of the law."[68] Having prepared their comments, the judges let the decision rest a few weeks.

In early June 1956, the three judges met in New Orleans, Louisiana, to finalize the *Browder* decision. During that meeting, a paragraph was added relating to procedures to be followed if the defense chose to appeal the district court decision to the US Supreme Court. On behalf of himself and Judge Johnson, Judge Rives added, "In fact, we think that *Plessy v. Ferguson* (1896) has been impliedly, though not explicitly, overruled" by the Supreme Court's decisions augmenting desegregation in public areas.[69] The *Browder* decision was retyped, running only one and a half double-spaced legal pages, and was filed with the district court clerk on June 5, 1956, six months after the bus protest had begun. The historical record exhibits that Rives's decision on behalf of the court in *Browder* was the first judicial decision holding racial segregation on public buses unconstitutional. The defendants' lawyers appealed the ruling to the Supreme Court. Either the justices would overrule Rives and Johnson or *Browder* would stand.

Judge Rives "crossed the Rubicon" in *Browder*, explained Euel Screws Jr., one of Rives's clerks. Rives had taken an irrevocable step that brought to the public eye his interpretation of the US Constitution and legal precedent regarding inequities based on race. The published decision would cement the case in history and label Rives a "desegregationist." His family had lived in the Montgomery area for generations; his grandfather had owned one of the largest plantations in the state before the Civil War. Now Rives was going against Southern tradition, against many people in the community of Montgomery and the state of Alabama, and against the thinking of some of his family members. Rives's good friend Clifford Durr shared with Bass that Rives's "mother must have turned in her grave." Although the language of the majority decision in *Browder* now seems mild, the ruling sparked fury in Montgomery where, for the first time, a state judge and two federal judges in the same city had issued contradictory rulings on the same issue. Until that point, white Southerners lived in a society that did not publicly question racial segregation. Abrams and Gray quoted Joseph B. Sadler, a Montgomery City Lines bus driver. Sadler described the "mindset of the white population" toward Black citizens: "Negroes were treated 'right.' They were not entitled to equality but rather they were treated right, as defined by the white establishment."[70] The *Browder* decision, which would unsettle societal norms, was perceived by some white citizens as threatening their entire way of life.

The federal judiciary's recent racial desegregation rulings, legal scholar Louis Michael Seidman wrote, signified a redistribution of power and resources, increasing some white citizens' anger and resentfulness toward the courts, judges, and Black citizens. The judiciary was seen by some citizens as engaging in "judicial legislation," which Seidman explained as the court interfering in issues that were under the purview of elected representatives in the state legislature. The general public had begun to view Judges Rives and Johnson as "activist judges," accused of introducing their ideas into the law, wreaking havoc with the doctrine of stare decisis, and overturning legal segregation, which had been working reliably to maintain white supremacy. Reaves shared an example where members of the Montgomery County Bar Association made clear their thoughts on Rives's decision. At the time, members of the association held regular open breakfast meetings. Upon arriving at the usual location, Rives discovered the lawyers had moved the location of the meetings so he would not know where they would be held.[71] Letters against and in support of the *Browder* decision arrived for Rives from citizens all over the South, especially from those in his home state.

Judge Rives told law professor Frank T. Read that nearly 95 percent of the "deluge of mail" he received in response to *Browder* was disparaging. Across the South, many white citizens were disgusted with the decision, but the reaction of some of his fellow Montgomerians was vicious. People who were familiar with Rives, or thought they knew him as a friend, indicated that they felt personally affronted by the decision. Rives's actions enraged segregationists because they had considered him to be what Barrow and Walker referred to as "a friend of the people of Alabama," coming from a white family with limited financial resources as he did. McDonald wrote that Rives responded to his vulnerability to violence by sardonically calling the hate mail "fan letters." One writer referred to the *Browder* decision as "unfair to the Fine People of Alabama." Another writer asserted that Rives's conscience was "warped." Writing as a "former friend," the critic chided, "You can slap your friends in the face, but you can't make them like it." People turned on Rives with the force of history. One woman asked, "What is to become of the SOUTH, when it's [*sic*] native son, such as you, will betray it?" She was possibly alluding to Richard Wright's 1940 novel *Native Son*—simultaneously calling Rives an ethnic slur and suggesting that Black citizens cannot escape their natural destiny as subordinate to white citizens. Another woman claimed that Rives and Judge Johnson had "made a mess of affairs for no reason at all."[72] The *Browder* decision would require a sea change in some white citizens' views on race; however, not all citizens resisted the prospect of a racially desegregated public sphere.

Indeed, some citizens supported the *Browder* decision. One person wrote to praise Judge Rives "on the strength and convictions of . . . [his] legal and moral principals [*sic*]." Another writer was gratified by Rives's and Judge Johnson's "forthright stand on this issue which has caused so much inconvenience and humiliation by a minority people." Rives replied to one woman who complimented him on the decision, "I am receiving many more critical letters, and even abusive ones, than I am letters like yours, I can only say that I am deciding to the best of my ability and conscience."[73] Supporters urged him to be careful, hoping (but not sure if) he would live a long time to continue his work as a judge.

The bus protest continued during the summer and fall of 1956 while defense lawyers appealed *Browder* to the US Supreme Court. Judge Rives recalled to Read, "There were talks of the Klan burning crosses. I remember when the police called me. I said, 'Don't be guarding my house. I've got my old shotgun and my old pistol; I'll take care of myself out there.' . . . [I had a] little bit too much braggadocio. 'If anybody starts burning a cross in front of my house, I'm going to pepper them up with bird shot.' Next, I heard they had burned a cross in front of [Judge] Johnson's house. The FBI finally traced down the two high school boys who had perpetrated the act." Rives said that both he and Johnson perceived that the boys, coming from "an old, old family" in Montgomery, acted in a way that was "culturally misguided."[74] As a judge, Rives's employment was protected by lifelong tenure, and he knew that hatred would be forthcoming from individuals and groups in Alabama and states throughout the Fifth Circuit.

The *Alabama Journal*'s headline on June 5, 1956, declared, "City Bus Segregation Doomed in Ruling by Federal Court." Two weeks later, on June 19, 1956, a Montgomery labor newspaper, *Alabama Labor News*, wrote a front-page article titled "Quislings in the South." The reporter defined a "quisling," as "one who betrays his country to the enemy and is then given political power by the conquerors." The writer noted that Judge Rives "should denounce the Cradle of the Confederacy as his home and move above the Mason-Dixon line." He was called "a turn-coat" and upon his death, "former friends . . . would not like to have the hallowed soil of the Cradle of the Confederacy contaminated" by his burial in Montgomery. Sparrow, of the *Birmingham News*, branded Rives as an "agitator" and predicted that his effort "to destroy long established Southern customs" would work against him. Rives told Spivack that his ex-communication from Montgomery society was reinforced by "an editorial in a local paper that instructed people to shun him completely." One of Rives's law clerks shared that some of Rives's longtime friends refused to be seen with him, crossing the street to avoid any personal contact. Spivack wrote that Rives "was treated as a pariah" and the ostracism extended to his family members.[75]

One of Judge Rives's law clerks recalled that Rives's wife, Jessie, loved children. She taught piano lessons to Montgomery's young, upper-middle-class white children for many years. The clerk shared that after the *Browder* decision her pupils withdrew from her and no new requests for lessons were forthcoming. She finally had to stop giving piano lessons for lack of students. The clerk explained that segregationists sought to terrorize Rives at every turn, including his workplace. The FBI had installed a small buzzer under Rives's desk in his chambers. If at any time he felt threatened, he could push the button and the FBI would be there almost immediately. The clerk said that no one recalled Rives ever pressing the button.[76] Rives had a deep knowledge of the territory and families in the area and may not have felt as threatened as segregationists might have hoped because of his deep familial lineage in Montgomery and his experience with the law.

Many lawyers held the same point of view as segregationist Judge Lynne. Judge Rives made a note in the margin of a letter he received from one lawyer, as if to respond to the writer's criticism: "See also *S. Car. vs. US* 199 US 437 decided in 1905." In that decision, Justice David Brewer wrote that the "vital question . . . is one of far-reaching significance. We have in this republic a dual system of government—national and state—each operating within the same territory and upon the same persons, and yet working without collision because their functions are different. There are certain matters over which the national government has absolute control, and no action of the state can interfere therewith, and there are others in which the state is supreme and in respect to them the national government is powerless. To preserve the even balance between these two governments and hold each in its separate sphere is the peculiar duty of all courts . . . a duty oftentimes of great delicacy and difficulty."[77] The Tenth Amendment, in support of state rights, was a confounding factor in the coexistence between state and federal governments. Nevertheless, Rives was confident about the rationale for his stance in *Browder*, although not all Fifth Circuit judges agreed with him on the issue of individual equality for all citizens. One of those judges was his colleague Benjamin F. Cameron.

Judge Cameron was commissioned to the Fifth Circuit in March 1955. A lawyer from Mississippi, Cameron was a staunch advocate of the Tenth Amendment and a man whom *The Mississippi Encyclopedia* called "an unabashed defender of Old South ways." Cameron adhered to a states' rights approach to cases involving the US Constitution to restrict the jurisdiction of the federal government, rejected the US Supreme Court's *Brown I* decision as applicable to individual states, and consistently voted against desegregation during his nine-year tenure on the Fifth Circuit. Spivack wrote that during Judge Rives's early years as a lawyer, he and Judge Cameron shared some of the same attitudes.[78] However, on the federal bench, Rives's and Cameron's views on some parts of the US Constitution differed.

Shortly after the *Browder* case was tried in district court, Judge Cameron was a member of a three-judge Fifth Circuit panel, along with Chief Judge

Hutcheson and Judge Brown, hearing the appeal of *Denton v. City of Carrollton* (1956), a case filed against the city of Carrollton, Georgia, by a worker who sought to unionize labor without a license. *Denton* was unrelated to either transportation or racial segregation and Cameron dissented from the majority opinion. For Cameron, state rights were not simply an intellectual justification for a political system based on white supremacy. In his dissent, he positioned state rights as "the axis upon which our entire constitutional system revolves." He reasoned that the Tenth Amendment gave citizens of each state the right to decide whether to adopt a policy of racial segregation. Cameron wrote, "what is here done [by the majority] seems to be but another step in a series of decisions in this Circuit demonstrating a dangerous tendency to exalt the federal judiciary and debase the states in their efforts at [the] performance of their legitimate and important function of local self-government." He identified the *Browder* decision as "another recent instance of disregard for the rights of the states" and pointedly criticized the federal district court for ruling in that case while "identical questions" were pending in Judge Jones's state court.[79] Cameron's dissent revealed to the public a discord between himself and some other members of the Fifth Circuit, including Rives.

Judge Rives, whom Bass described as a "patient" man, was angered over what he perceived to be an unwarranted attack from Judge Cameron in *Denton*, a case unrelated to *Browder*. On July 23, 1956, Rives wrote a letter to Judge Cameron in which he referred to "more than a page of gratuitous" criticism toward the federal courts in Cameron's *Denton* dissent. Rives wanted Cameron to correct his comments about how the judicial system worked, asserting that there are "certain facts of which you were either ignorant, or which you chose to ignore." Rives forwarded his draft letter to Edward W. Wadsworth, his former law clerk who was at the time serving as the Fifth Circuit Clerk of Court, and asked him to show Cameron's dissent and Rives's reply to Judge Johnson.[80] Johnson supported Rives's comments, and Rives's letter of rebuke was mailed to Cameron.

On July 25, 1956, Judge Cameron replied to Judge Rives, writing, "What I wrote concerning Browder v. Gayle was not based upon ignorance or indifference with respect to the facts of that case, but upon my conviction that the law and respect for the states required that the federal case be held reasonably in abeyance pending [the] outcome of the state case." Rives then asked Wadsworth to write a memo about the relationship between state and federal courts. Rives was already aware of this information but as was his practice, he likely wanted confirmation from authoritative sources before replying to Cameron. On July 31, Wadsworth submitted his summary to Rives. In a note that accompanied his report, Wadsworth summarized his finding: "Federal courts have jurisdiction over US Constitutional issues."[81] This removed any judicial discretion on issuing a stay in *Browder* until the state court had concluded the *City of Montgomery* case.

As Judges Rives and Cameron struggled behind the scenes, lawyers for the state of Alabama appealed the *Browder* ruling to the US Supreme Court. Rives wrote to Cameron again on August 2, 1956, with an intensity in his tone: "Your Denton Case and our Browder Case were considered almost simultaneously. Your case was argued on April 25, while ours was argued on May 11th. I must confess, therefore, that I was surprised to find our decision treated as a precedent and criticized in your opinion." Rives continued, "I had been the successful champion for state rights before the Supreme Court in Alabama Public Service Commission v. Southern Railway Company, 341 US 341 [1951], and I had hoped that my convictions on that score had carried over into my functions as a judge."[82] However, Rives interpreted state rights differently than did Cameron.

Judges Rives and Cameron each relied on credible sources for their understanding of the relationship between state and federal courts. However, a legal source used by Rives contained information that contradicted the primary source used by Cameron. Rives referenced the US Code in *Browder*, which at the time required a federal three-judge court to cease "the enforcement, operation or execution of any State statute" found to be inconsistent with the US Constitution. Cameron's dissent in *Denton* referenced a US Supreme Court case, *Douglas v. City of Jeannette* (1943, hereafter *Jeannette*), on that subject. *Jeannette* was filed by petitioners who were charged with violating "a city ordinance which prohibits the solicitation of orders for merchandise without first procuring a license from the city authorities and paying a license tax." Cameron relied on Chief Justice Harlan F. Stone's decision: "Where the threatened prosecution is by state officers for alleged violations of a state law, the state courts are the final arbiters of its meaning and application, subject only to review by this Court on federal grounds appropriately asserted."[83] The US Code and the Supreme Court's *Jeannette* decision provided inconsistent guidance about the responsibilities of state and federal courts.

Several days later, Judge Rives wrote a third time to Judge Cameron. Rives was apologetic for taking a professional disagreement personally. On August 7, 1956, he wrote, "Here I am writing after stating so positively that I was going to stop writing and get to work on the cases I have left. . . . I feel badly about the obvious ill-humor displayed in my previous letter as contrasted with the courtesy of yours of the 25th." In his letter, Rives acknowledged that *Jeanette* could weaken the *Browder* decision: "I hope not, but Browder may be reversed on the point of the Jeannette case. While the second reason prompted me to write again, the first [collegiality] is more important."[84] Rives's relationships with his brethren on the court were important to him, and he wanted to keep Chief Judge Hutcheson informed of his correspondence with Cameron.

Judge Rives copied Chief Judge Hutcheson on his August 7, 1956, letter to Judge Cameron, attaching the previous letters. Hutcheson replied by returning Rives's letter with a handwritten note on the bottom of the page, advising, "I have received copies of your letters to Cameron and copies of his replies. . . . I am sorry that you keep writing to him. I would recommend the scriptural advice 'Ephraim is wedded to his idols, leave him alone.' . . . [L]et our erring brother go in peace." Although Rives did not write to Cameron again about his *Denton* dissent, Cameron did reply to Rives on August 10, 1956. His letter read, "I appreciate very much the tone and content of your letter of August 7th." Cameron continued, "I think we are in the midst of one of the great constitutional crises of the Republic. For many years I, in common with . . . practically all of the thinking people with whom I have come in contact, have felt that the Supreme Court was re-making the Constitution according to the ideas of the current judges."[85] Cameron thought the US Supreme Court consisted of a majority of liberal activist judges, led by Chief Justice Warren, who were driven by interests other than those written into the original US Constitution. Rives and Cameron would professionally disagree with one another on a number of legal issues over the years.

While the *Gayle v. Browder* appeal was under review by the US Supreme Court, Judge Rives replied to a letter from Judge Joe E. Estes of the Northern District of Texas. Perhaps reflecting on his experiences the previous few months, Rives recognized that Southern history and the deep-seated opinions about racial segregation would pose significant challenges for federal judges. The South was, he wrote, in a "near state of rebellion . . . actively fomented by some groups." Regardless, Rives conveyed to Estes that he was determined to act by "being right in taking one step at a time."[86] *Browder* (1956) would be Rives's first right step related to the desegregation of the public sphere.

The US Supreme Court justices reviewed Judge Rives's decision to desegregate public transportation in *Browder*. In their *Brown II* decision, the justices essentially delegated racial desegregation decisions to the lower courts when they "remanded to the District Courts to take such proceedings and enter such orders and decrees consistent with this opinion as are necessary and proper." At that time, Reaves explained, the justices "really didn't get into" racial desegregation cases. He continued, the "Supreme Court was not in the forefront of civil rights." On November 13, 1956, six months after the district court's ruling, the justices issued a one-sentence decision in *Gayle*: "The motion to affirm is granted and the judgment is affirmed." The appeals process was completed on December 17, 1956, when the justices rejected appeals by the city and state to reconsider their decision.[87] Rives's decision in *Browder* was the first federal court order stating that racial segregation on public buses was unconstitutional.

During the 1930s, as Freyer and Dixon explained, the general public had begun to recognize that the courts were inconsistent on the status of individual rights. The defense of economic liberty, which had been the historically dominant position of federal judges, was being overtaken by "a new presumption favoring civil rights and liberties" of the individual.[88] *Brown I* was one of the first significant cases that brought the issue of individual equality in the public sphere to the foreground in the courts. Federal court decisions had pointed to the logical extension of *Brown I* beyond education, a doctrinal trend prompting Judge Rives to recognize individual rights at a time when the courts were slowly moving in that direction.

Given that US Supreme Court justices and federal judges from the Fourth Circuit had recently issued racial desegregation orders, Circuit Judge Rives and District Judge Johnson were not alone in their thinking. However, Rives would be the first judge to author a decision explicitly stating that the doctrine of "separate but equal" in public transportation was unconstitutional, and he would do so in the Deep South. *Browder* would provide the legal precedent on which many judges would rely in extending the Supreme Court's *Brown* decisions beyond education to other areas of public life. Yet not all members of the Fifth Circuit would agree on the legal applications of *Brown I* and *II*.

3

Fighting for Commensurate Access

Allegations of Court-Packing to Desegregate Primary and Secondary Public Education

One year after Richard T. Rives was born, the US Supreme Court decided *Plessy v. Ferguson* (1896), a case that concerned racial segregation in public transportation. In *Plessy*, the justices declared that the purpose of the Fourteenth Amendment "was undoubtedly to enforce the absolute equality of the two races before the law" but was not intended "to enforce social, as distinguished from political, equality." In that ruling, racial segregation of public schools—from primary school to higher education—was identified by the justices as "a valid exercise" of state political power that did not conflict with the Fourteenth Amendment.[1] During his youth, Rives was educated under the law of "separate but equal," attending public school with other white boys and socializing within racial constraints. Nearly sixty years later, the Supreme Court reversed *Plessy* in *Brown I*, a landmark decision handed down three years into Rives's tenure as a judge on the US Court of Appeals for the Fifth Circuit.

The US Supreme Court ruling in *Brown I* ordered the racial desegregation of public schools nationwide. While school desegregation cases had been filed in the United States as early as 1849 (*Roberts v. The City of Boston*), such cases generally occurred outside the Fifth Circuit. Some white Alabamians saw the judiciary's decision in *Brown I* as a direct attack by the Supreme Court on the South. They interpreted the Court's decision as usurping white citizens' political power to shape their culture and way of life as they saw fit. In response to *Brown*, white citizens pressured their state legislators to support the Tenth Amendment, which assured states' rights.[2] Representatives in the Alabama State Legislature pushed back against racial desegregation, as did representatives in other Southern state legislatures. Political strategies were quickly implemented to continue the segregation of public schools, and legal cases were filed both by supporters of segregation and by supporters of desegregation.

When Judge Rives joined the Fifth Circuit in 1951, LDF lawyers had made inroads in racially desegregating higher education and were beginning to file lawsuits related to desegregating primary and secondary schools across the country. In the wake of the *Brown II* decision, wherein the justices decreed that Black students must be admitted to public schools "on a racially nondiscriminatory basis with all deliberate speed," the task of desegregating the public school system fell squarely on the shoulders of Southern federal court judges.[3]

Law professors Frank T. Read and Lucy S. McGough recorded that from 1955 to 1966, Judge Rives participated in more educational desegregation decisions than any other Fifth Circuit judge. He authored decisions on behalf of three-judge panels to require public schools to create and implement student placement plans (*Borders v. Rippy*, 1957) and confirmed that an unfair application of a constitutional student placement law is illegal (*Shuttlesworth v. Birmingham Board of Education*, 1958; *Gibson v. Board of Public Instruction of Dade County, Florida*, 1959). Rives also signed the decision ruling that school officials were responsible for initiating students' application processes for admittance to schools that they indicated they wanted to attend (*Armstrong v. Birmingham Board of Education*, 1963). After hearing school desegregation lawsuits piecemeal from many of the school districts in Alabama, Senior Judge Rives contributed to a per curiam decision to require the uniform statewide desegregation of Alabama public schools (*Lee v. Macon County*, 1967). A per curiam ruling, historian John M. Spivack explained, is "prepared by the Court as a whole rather than by a single judge speaking for the Court. They are often used when the law is clear, there is little dispute over facts, and/or when judges want to make a statement to the public and lower courts."[4] In the Fifth Circuit, per curiam decisions were often used to reinforce the need to align state laws with the US Constitution.

The US Supreme Court's decision in *Brown II* reiterated that racial discrimination in public schools is unconstitutional and declared that no federal, state, or local law could evade this legal principle. In response, the Alabama legislature worked to safeguard racial segregation in the public sphere by passing several acts of legislation. Alabama's Pupil Placement Law: Act 201 and Amendment 111 to the Alabama Constitution, both passed in 1956, played a significant role in statewide school desegregation discussions.[5]

Alabama's Pupil Placement Law came to be when Birmingham lawyer J. Paul Meeks initiated a proposal to Alabama governor Seth Gordon Persons. Lawyer Pat Boyd Rumore wrote that Meeks suggested that the law could resemble one already put in place by the North Carolina legislature in response to the *Brown* decisions. He recommended that while the law would not identify race as a consideration when placing students in a particular school, race could continue to be used to quietly maintain segregation. Following Meeks's advice, Albert Boutwell, an Alabama state senator and chair of the Senate Education Committee described by historian Joseph Mark Bagley as a "moderate segregationist," coauthored the bill. *Time* magazine reported that the law would permit school boards to manage applications using "seventeen separate standards for assigning pupils to public schools." Criteria identified in Act 201 included, among others, "the psychological qualification of the pupil for the type of teaching and associates involved," "the possibility of threat or friction or disorder," "the possibility of breaches of the peace or ill will or economic retaliation within the community," and "the maintenance or severance of established social and psychological relationships with other pupils and with teachers."[6] Passage of the Pupil Placement Law provided academic administrators a means to maintain racially segregated schools.

In addition to the Placement law, Boutwell also sponsored Amendment 111, a "freedom of choice law" often referred to as the Boutwell amendment. The amendment thus construed public education as conferring a right to choose whether or not to seek an education, not as a civil right per se. Political historian Gordon Harvey explained that parents who wanted their child to "attend schools provided for their own race" could make that preference known. Most significantly, the Boutwell amendment included a clause stating that nothing in the state constitution "should be construed as creating or recognizing [that students have] any right to education or training at public expense." Voters approved the amendment in September 1956.[7] Alabama legislators and segregationist voters relied on these measures to provide a barrier against implementing the *Brown* decisions while the *Browder v. Gayle* (1956) bus desegregation decision was under appeal to the US Supreme Court.

Even as members of the Alabama Legislature worked against federal judicial decisions ordering educational desegregation, Judge Rives continued his measured pace in dealing with the Fifth Circuit workload. Letters reveal that in June 1957, Rives's only surviving child, Callie, called him from Louisville, Kentucky. She recently had a cancerous melanoma removed from her back. Rives and his daughter traveled to New York for an operation to ensure her melanoma would not return.

All the Fifth Circuit judges had a heavy workload, and Judge John R. Brown wrote to Rives reassuring him that he asked Rives's clerk to aid in the judge's professional responsibilities (doing "record searching, briefing, and drafting") while Rives was away. In a second letter, Brown acknowledged to Rives and his wife that they had "suffered already so much tragedy" and expressed his admiration that their "faith might have, but has not, been shaken." A profoundly religious man, Rives replied to Brown that he and his wife were greatly relieved and "truly thankful . . . most of all to God and our

Savior." Rives was away from the office for a week and, while he was gone, segregationists across the South continued their massive resistance against racial desegregation.[8] School administrators preparing for the fall term in Southern cities like Little Rock, Norfolk, Nashville, and other locations continued their fight to keep public schools white.

Federal judges for US district and circuit courts affirm in their oath of office that they will administer justice in conformity with the US Constitution and laws of the United States. However, during the 1950s, some segregationist federal judges worked against Rives's and other judges' interpretation of the US Supreme Court's *Brown* orders. Not long after *Brown II*, Judge Rives found himself hearing an appeal in *Borders v. Rippy* (1957, hereafter *Rippy*), a case that extended over six years, involved multiple plaintiffs, and revealed differences in judicial philosophies between Judges Glen H. Davidson and William Hawley Atwell of the US District Court for the Northern District of Texas and several judges on the Fifth Circuit Court of Appeals. Specifically, Davidson and Atwell refused, as long as possible, to interpret *Brown* in a way that allowed racial desegregation to occur.[9]

Law professor Betsy Levin documented that from September 1955 through June 1961, Edwin L. Rippy, the president of the board of trustees of the Dallas Independent School District of Dallas County, Texas, was a party in over fifteen court actions regarding the desegregation of Dallas public schools. The first complaint was brought by the LDF on behalf of parents of twenty-eight Black students. Judge Rives would write the *Rippy* decision on behalf of the court's majority requiring the US District Court for the Northern District of Texas to comply with the US Constitution. Rives wrote that when the district court first dismissed the case by asserting that plaintiffs had not exhausted their administrative remedies, the students were "deprived of their constitutional rights." The Fifth Circuit majority ruled that "so long as . . . [students] are excluded from any public school of their choice solely because of their race or color the plaintiffs are being denied their constitutional rights. It is not a sufficient answer to say that the school board has made a 'prompt and reasonable start' and is proceeding to 'good faith compliance.'" Rives continued, echoing James 2:26 without direct reference to the Bible, "Faith by itself, however, without works, is not enough. There must be 'compliance' at the earliest practicable date."[10] Rives advocated a pupil placement plan that, if implemented in good faith, could manage the desegregation of public educational facilities. Judges in the Fifth Circuit and elsewhere relied on that decision in early school desegregation cases.

While the *Rippy* lawsuit continued, Fred Shuttlesworth and the parents of three other children residing in Alabama filed a lawsuit in the Northern District of Alabama Court on May 9, 1958, captioned *Shuttlesworth v.*

Birmingham Board of Education. Shuttlesworth's lawyers charged that Birmingham's board of education failed to comply with the US Supreme Court's *Brown II* desegregation ruling ordered three years earlier. In response, the board of education asserted that Alabama's Pupil Placement Law permitted administrators to exercise discretion in assigning students to schools. Judge Rives authored the decision on behalf of a three-judge panel that included himself and District Judges Seybourn Lynne and Harlan H. Grooms, both from the Northern District of Alabama.[11]

The question at hand was whether the Pupil Placement Law was constitutional. Judge Rives recognized that the purpose of the Alabama placement law was to perpetuate segregated schools, assigning Black students to Black schools. The wording of the law allowed school administrators to intentionally misinterpret the legislation. Rives wrote on behalf of the court in *Shuttlesworth*, "All that has been said in this present opinion must be limited to the constitutionality of the law *upon its face*." Rives ordered school administrators in Alabama to implement the Pupil Placement Law "in a constitutional manner by the admission of qualified pupils upon a basis of individual merit without regard to their race or color." He speculated that the school administrators' segregationist behavior may continue, stating that if school administrators did not follow the Pupil Placement Law in good faith, then "in some future proceeding it is possible that it may be declared unconstitutional in its application." The *Shuttlesworth* decision allowed school authorities additional time to exercise "deliberate speed," while also providing them with an opportunity to be honest. Upon the school board's appeal to the US Supreme Court, legal historians Tony Freyer and Timothy Dixon wrote, the justices affirmed Rives's "moderate approach" to racial desegregation. The Supreme Court's decision in *Shuttlesworth* rested on "limited grounds"—the decision concentrated specifically on the law itself, not applications of the law.[12]

During the 1950s, school officials across the South generally employed some form of pupil assignment law, as upheld by both Judge Rives and the US Supreme Court in *Shuttlesworth*. In the early years following the *Brown* decisions, Rives initially followed Judge John J. Parker's decision on behalf of the Fourth Circuit in *Carson v. Warlick* (1956), which favored pupil placement plans decided by local school boards. Parker hoped that if given an opportunity by the courts, school board members would exercise "good faith" in assigning students to various schools.[13] Operating under this assumption, Rives continued to serve on three-judge school desegregation panels across the circuit.

Over two years after *Brown II*, the guardians of six Black children petitioned the court to declare that a section of the Florida state constitution violated the Fourteenth Amendment by requiring racial segregation of public schools in Florida. They filed *Gibson v. Board of Public Instruction of Dade County, Florida* in the Southern District of Florida Court. On December 22, 1958, District Judge Joseph Patrick Lieb ruled that the plaintiffs already had a remedy for attending a desegregated school in the Florida Pupil Assignment Law of 1956. His decision followed Circuit Judge Rives's ruling in *Shuttlesworth*.[14] The decision required plaintiffs to first pursue all administrative remedies available to them to manage desegregation of the public schools. If a child was denied relief after exploring administrative channels, they could turn to the court system.

Lawyers for Gibson appealed Judge Lieb's decision to the Fifth Circuit, and Judges Rives and Brown were assigned to the case along with Judge John Minor Wisdom, who had recently joined the court. Read and McGough explained that Wisdom was building a "liberal record on civil rights." The three judges denied the Dade County school board's contention that the students were not entitled to relief because they had failed to exhaust administrative remedies. Writing for the panel, Rives ordered in *Gibson* that no "law can justify a violation of the Constitution of the United States by the requirement of racial segregation in the public schools." Rives emphasized that in school choice, students cannot be required to attend racially segregated schools, just as they cannot be required to attend racially desegregated schools. His constitutional approach was to use racial desegregation as a means to eliminate educational discrimination—not as a means for "mixing" Black and white students in a classroom.[15] The Fifth Circuit reversed the district court's judgment and sent the case back to the lower court for action.

After the Fifth Circuit order, Judge Lieb once again ruled in *Gibson* that the plaintiffs were provided "adequate remedies under the Pupil Assignment Law for any of their grievances" and should pursue them to exercise their rights. Gibson's lawyers petitioned the Fifth Circuit for a rehearing of the original appeal. On August 23, 1957, Judge Rives wrote to Judges Warren L. Jones and Brown, who were assigned to the appeal with Rives. He disclosed, "sometimes I think we should understand the other judge's feeling and thinking in cases of this kind, though probably the briefer our opinions are the better." In his letter Rives continue to think through his position on school desegregation:

> It has always seemed to me that these pupil assignment laws have a field for legitimate operation and that so long as we cannot say that they are being used for an evil purpose or are obviously enacted for such purpose, they should be allowed to operate within their legitimate scope. . . . To my mind the school desegregation decisions do not affirmatively require integration,

> but simply forbid enforced segregation. Though the Supreme Court has been bitterly criticized for going that far, I thoroughly agree with them, both because I think it is fundamental that all men stand equal before the law and that enforced segregation necessarily signifies the inferiority of the minority race, and because the classification according to race is not a reasonable classification. The Elder Justice Harlan, in his dissent in Plessy v. Ferguson, expressed what I think the law should be, namely, "color blind."[16]

In short, Rives supported racial desegregation as an issue of equality, but his position did not extend to requiring racial integration.

As *Gibson* continued, lawyers for the Board of Public Instruction in Miami persisted in supporting a position outside the law by arguing that an unfair application of the Pupil Placement Law was legal. Judge Rives enclosed a draft per curiam order with his August 23, 1957, letter to Judges Jones and Brown denying the rehearing of *Gibson*. He commented, "after examining the petition for rehearing and the basis of it, I am somewhat shocked that responsible counsel should be guilty of such half-truths, if not entire misrepresentations."[17] Rives held higher expectations of lawyers. His morals had not changed since he was president of the Alabama Bar Association; he believed lawyers should engage in ethical professional practices.

Although the Fifth Circuit judges refused to rehear *Gibson* in 1957, after additional legal proceedings Gibson's lawyers once again appealed the case to the Fifth Circuit in November 1959. Judges Rives, Brown, and Wisdom heard the appeal, which centered around what Gibson's lawyers perceived as an unfair assignment of pupils to schools. Plaintiffs petitioned the court to order that the Board of Public Instruction desegregate public schools without requiring students "to attend or not to attend particular public schools because of their race." Judge Rives wrote the opinion, which was handed down on November 24, 1959. He relied on Census records and other school board forms to document that a formally segregated, dual school system was unconstitutionally still in place in Florida.[18]

In the 1959 *Gibson* decision, Judge Rives discussed the difference between the *Gibson* and the *Shuttlesworth* cases. He pointed out that in *Shuttlesworth*, the plaintiffs had confined their assault on segregation to the constitutionality of the law. In *Gibson*, the plaintiffs argued that the school board had unfairly applied the pupil placement law. The court required the school board to submit a desegregation proposal to the district court. If the court approved the proposal, a transition period would be allowed to desegregate the school system. Spivack clarified that Rives did not order the school board to speed up the desegregation process and did not rule on Gibson's request for immediate desegregation.[19]

During the 1950s, Rives maintained a judicial philosophy of moderate racial desegregation. According to Spivack, at that time white citizens from rural areas and those who were working-class tended to be segregationists; white citizens in larger towns and cities were "somewhat more moderate." While they did not support school desegregation, most people who were moderate "believed in obedience to the law." Their interest in economic progress surpassed their interest in racial segregation. Moderates argued that "segregationists were creating turmoil in the South and discouraging national business leaders" from exploring the region's possibilities for economic development. They urged calmness in society and supported keeping the public schools open to advance education and potentially attract industry. Judge Rives granted school boards and district judges "time and discretion" to generate and implement desegregation plans. However, as Spivack noted, "any evidence of delay for its own sake or of less than good faith compliance with the Supreme Court's directions, brought his swift rebuke." Rives was not an activist on the court—but as he told Spivack, he "stretch[ed] equitable remedies" to ensure that Black citizens' rights were available to them. Rives admitted that he was not comfortable doing so and preferred plans that allowed freedom of choice in education during the transition years after *Brown*.[20]

In October 1959, Judge Rives was elevated to the position of chief judge of the Fifth Circuit, a commission established, in part, by seniority on the bench. The transition occurred when Chief Judge Joseph C. Hutcheson Jr. advanced to senior status. As required by the US Code, when a judge reaches the age of seventy, he moves to senior status. The next most-senior judge then becomes the chief judge, and the judge taking senior status receives a reduced workload. As chief judge, Rives's responsibilities shifted and he took on additional juridical and administrative duties instead of hearing as many district cases and circuit appeals. The new responsibilities included, for example, dismissing frivolous appeals without merit, deciding some appeals without oral argument, and determining which appeals require limited oral argument. Law professor Anne S. Emanuel wrote that the addition of Civil Rights cases to the Fifth Circuit Court's regular caseload had greatly increased the administrative tasks that Rives, at age sixty-four, found "burdensome." The judges were required to appropriately respond to the demands of all cases throughout the circuit, and the workload continued to increase. Although Rives continued to hear some appeals as chief judge, he was not able to spend as much time in the courtroom as he would prefer. He decided that he would relinquish his position as chief judge in December 1960, allowing the court to begin 1961 with a new chief judge.[21]

Chief Judge Rives recommended to his colleagues that Judge Tuttle, next in seniority to Rives, become the new chief judge. Emanuel wrote that Rives thought Tuttle was "ideal" for the position. She described Tuttle as a judge who "carefully applied precedent to precise facts" and had a liberal approach to Civil Rights. Tuttle had been on President Eisenhower's short list for the US Supreme Court on more than one occasion and "had an opportunity of getting on the Supreme Court if Nixon were elected President." Emanuel explained that as a result of their working relationship, Rives was "one of Tuttle's most steadfast allies and one of his closest friends." In addition to relieving himself of the position's responsibilities, Rives wanted to help Tuttle advance in his career.[22]

Chief Judge Rives confessed to Judge Brown, another close associate, that he was resigning from the chief judge position partly because he did not think he could devote the time needed to do the job as well as he would like. He explained that he relinquished the office "out of a conscientious concern" for his judicial responsibilities. The administrative work led Rives to feel he was "behind in his cases," but he assured Brown that after stepping away from the position he would soon catch up; in the future, he did not wish to sit on fewer cases than the other judges. Rives wrote to all judges of the Fifth Circuit on December 2, 1960, "During my fifteen months as Chief Judge, even though I have worked practically without vacation, I have been unable to devote to the cases under consideration as much time, study and deliberation as I feel they deserve." In addition, the Fifth Circuit, headquartered in New Orleans, made extensive travel demands on Rives despite the convenience of traveling by train from Montgomery to other cities in the circuit; there were direct routes to New Orleans and to Atlanta. Judge Ginny Granade wrote that Mrs. Rives traveled with the judge to court sittings until the late 1950s, when she became too unwell to travel. She preferred that her husband travel by train instead of an airplane when he traveled alone. Ray Jenkins interviewed Rives for the *Alabama Journal*. Rives said that he would get his own train compartment and accomplish "a great deal of work en route" to keep up with the very heavy workload.[23] Rives returned to a position as judge after his voluntary separation from the chief judge position, beginning his second decade on the court in a job that he felt better suited his situation at the time.

After Judge Rives had served the Fifth Circuit for ten years, Jenkins wrote a series of articles about him for the *Alabama Journal*. While Jenkins was working on the articles, Rives found himself in the hospital. Elaine Fowler, the Fifth Circuit secretary, wrote to Judges Jones and Brown on May 3, 1961, that Rives "look[ed] fine" following a surgery and was "in excellent shape." Jenkins wrote that Rives "was hardly out of the recovery room before his law clerk was beating a path between the library and the hospital. His bed was piled high with law books. Rives, sick or not, approached 'work as usual.'" Rives returned to the office the following week.[24]

Jenkins's articles were published on May 8, 9, and 10, 1961. The general public in Southern states had grown increasingly distrustful of the courts, and Judge Rives asked Jenkins about any feedback he may have received on the articles. Jenkins wrote to Rives on May 18, 1961, sharing that he received only one letter, which arrived from a woman "known to us as a pathological letter-writer." While written feedback was scarce, the articles did generate some informal comments. At the *Alabama Journal*, the news department and editorial page operated independently of one another. Jenkins wrote to Rives that the newspaper editor, C. M. Stanley, complained to Jenkins after his first article was published. Stanley had criticized Rives in many editorials, and Stanley thought Jenkins was undermining his viewpoint. One day, while Jenkins was discussing the news stories with his supervisor, managing editor John Hamner, "Bill Mahoney poked his head in the door, and observed with a chortle, 'I see where you're making a hero out of the most unpopular man in Montgomery.' To which Hamner, a plain-spoken man, responded: 'If you don't like it, cancel your subscription.'" Some newspaper employees were positive and "generous in their praise" over the articles, while other employees received "a storm of protest" from readers. Jenkins summarized the feedback: "All in all, I suspect the articles had a good reception among those who read them, and from all I can gather, they were widely read. The chief complaints came from those who didn't read them."[25] The series of articles did not seem to affect the number or kind of messages Rives received from citizens about his racial desegregation decisions.

The majority of communication that Judge Rives received from the general public was hate mail written by citizens who disagreed with the court's decisions to racially desegregate public schools and other areas of the public sphere. Missives included unsigned postcards and letters, as well as anonymous telephone calls, many of which included death threats. Spivack recalled Rives as saying that late-night calls referred to Mrs. Rives as "Soon to be Widow Rives." Bagley recounted an interview with the judge, in which Rives shared that a letter writer demanded, "The order you issued must—I mean MUST be rescinded—reversed—done away with altogether or you or your families will pay a mighty big price for it." Another letter recorded in Read and McGough was signed by "Armed Service men" who had spent "two years in Vietnam killing, sniping, and going through hell." They incorrectly claimed that Rives, along with Judges Johnson of the Middle District of Alabama and Grooms of the Northern District of Alabama, had served on the *Shuttlesworth* case together, and each received the warning: "If you, by this order[,] force the schools and teachers against their will to mix in the Alabama schools you will not live to see the end of the year—Your families will also suffer severe punishment—possibly death due to your efforts. . . . Judge Rives, YOU OLD SOB had better get ready also, you don't have much longer to live and the sooner we get rid of you the better it will be. . . . GET READY TO GO OUT LIKE A LIGHT." In addition, a headshot of Rives had been cut out of a newspaper and glued to the back of an unsigned postcard with a similar message, "OLD SOB," written on it.[26] In addition to private messages, public warnings were also aimed at Rives and other judges on the court.

Seymour Trammel, who ran George Wallace's 1962 gubernatorial campaign, was quoted in the *Southern School News* as telling an audience at the Dallas County Citizens' Council in Selma, Alabama, that "Southerners should ostracize federal judges, their families, and friends. . . . 'How can a white man in the South perform in the manner they (federal judges) are conducting themselves? These federal judges should be scorned . . . by responsible Southerners.'" Judge Rives enjoyed socializing and participating in his community, and Trammel's advocacy that Rives be treated as a pariah was a severe blow. White segregationists increasingly showed the judge their true character. Read and McGough warned, "The threats were not isolated and they were not idle." They suggested that the "judicial office is a lonely one and perhaps self-sustaining men can best handle its pressures in difficult times."[27] As the number of school desegregation cases moved through the courts, Rives adapted his behavior, relying on his family, a few friends, and judicial colleagues for companionship.

In January 1963, George Wallace took office as the governor of Alabama for the first of his three four-year terms. The website BlackPast reported that by electing Wallace, "who had emerged as the leading opponent to the growing civil rights movement," the majority of white citizens in Alabama expressed that they were still determined to live in a segregated society. As winter turned to spring, Birmingham had become what legal scholar Tomiko Brown-Nagin described as a "flashpoint" in the Civil Rights Movement. The Southern Christian Leadership Conference had begun to engage in nonviolent demonstrations designed to racially desegregate department store facilities in Birmingham, which historian Robert J. Cook described as a "rigidly segregated city."[28]

Nearly eight years after *Brown II*, the city of Birmingham again made newspaper headlines with *Armstrong v. Birmingham Board of Education* (1963), another school desegregation lawsuit. In 1960, James Armstrong, a Black citizen, sought to enroll his two sons in an all-white public elementary school across the street from his home. Three years would pass before the case was finally decided, and Fifth Circuit Judge Benjamin F. Cameron's rage at his colleagues who relied on *Brown* in racial desegregation decisions would become public.[29]

Lawyers first filed *Armstrong* in the Northern District of Alabama Court. Judge Seybourn Lynne, who dissented from Rives's majority decision on behalf of the three-judge panel in the *Browder* bus transportation case, presided over the trial. Lynne, an obstructionist in racial desegregation litigation, delayed any action and allowed Armstrong's complaint to sit in his Court for three years without any development on the case, attempting to maintain the structure of segregated schools in Alabama as long as possible.[30]

On May 27, 1963, liberal US Supreme Court Justice Arthur J. Goldberg wrote in *Watson v. City of Memphis* that the justices "never contemplated that the concept of 'deliberate speed' [articulated in the 1956 *Brown II* decision], would countenance indefinite delay in [the] elimination of racial barriers in public schools, let alone other public facilities not involving the same physical problems or comparable conditions." To expedite justice, the Court further decreed that the "basic guarantees of our constitution are warrants for the here and now." The next day, May 28, Judge Lynne issued a ruling in *Armstrong*. He denied Armstrong's petition to allow his sons to attend a white school. He relied on Judge Rives's judgment in *Shuttlesworth* (rather than the later *Gibson* decision) to argue that the plaintiffs in *Armstrong* needed to properly exhaust their administrative remedies as provided in the Alabama School Placement Law.[31] Armstrong's lawyers appealed the district court's decision to the Fifth Circuit.

While *Armstrong* was waiting to be heard in the Fifth Circuit, a desegregation case from the Southern District of Alabama Court, *Davis v. Board of School Commissioners of Mobile County* (1963) was also on the Fifth Circuit docket. In *Davis*, Bagley observed that District Judge Daniel Holcombe Thomas was "clearly on the side of the segregationists." Thomas decided that the local school system should have "ample time for consideration and discussion of alternatives. The arbitrary, hasty, and premature imposition of a plan would defeat the intended purpose and would create confusion, and impair the educational process for all pupils." Thomas interpreted "deliberate speed" to mean as slowly as possible.[32]

Davis's lawyers appealed Judge Thomas's decision to the Fifth Circuit and the case was assigned to Judges Brown, Wisdom, and Griffin B. Bell for a hearing on July 8, 1963. The three judges filed a per curiam decision reversing the lower court decision. Their ruling cited *Stell v. Savannah-Chatham County Board of Education*, a recent school desegregation appeal from Savannah, Georgia, heard by a three-judge panel of Chief Judge Tuttle, and Judges Rives and Bell. Chief Judge Tuttle wrote the *Stell* decision, ordering the board of education to submit a desegregation plan that would "make an immediate start" to racially desegregate the public schools. The plan, to be submitted to the Fifth Circuit no later than July 1, 1963, was to "include a statement that the maintenance of separate schools" for Black and white children in Savannah-Chatham County "shall be completely ended with respect to at least one grade during the school year commencing September, 1963, and with respect to at least one additional grade each school year thereafter."[33] The Savannah-Chatham County Board of Education was required to begin to desegregate immediately using a grade-a-year plan. Tuttle agreed with Rives that appellants should no longer be required to exhaust the Alabama Pupil Placement Law administrative remedies. The differences between Rives's and Tuttle's judicial philosophies toward educational desegregation were becoming clear. While Rives disagreed with Tuttle's *Stell* decision implementing school desegregation on a grade-a-year plan, he did not file a dissent. Their difference of opinion would become more apparent in *Armstrong*.

On June 26, 1963, the *Armstrong* appeal was heard in an emergency session of the Fifth Circuit by Chief Judge Tuttle and Judges Rives and Walter P. Gewin. Tuttle declared six cases, including *Armstrong*, as urgent appeals that needed to be heard quickly because of the academic deadlines and the appeals process timeline. The school year would begin within three months, and Tuttle recognized that any meaningful desegregation of public schools for 1963–1964 academic year would require immediate action by the court.[34] After the hearing, Tuttle, Rives, and Gewin took the appeal under advisement, carefully considering the volatile Birmingham situation.

In the lower court ruling on *Armstrong*, Judge Lynne required that the plaintiffs should first exhaust their administrative responsibilities. In the *Armstrong* appeal to the Fifth Circuit, Judge Rives addressed Lynne's judgment by quoting from *Brown II*, "School authorities have the primary responsibility" for managing desegregation, not Black students. Citing his *Rippy* (1957) decision, Rives continued, "The long-standing order of responsibility is 'first the school authorities, then the local district court, and lastly the appellate courts.'" Regarding Lynne's comment about the timeframe for desegregation, Rives quoted *Davis*: "The time available for the transition from segregated to desegregated school systems is, with the passage of years since the *Brown* decisions, becoming more sharply limited." This time lag, he wrote, had to be balanced with "the concept of 'deliberate speed' to the extent of not causing undue or unnecessary confusion." Following a procedure Rives identified in July 1962 for the *Augustus v. Board of Public Instruction of Escambia County, Florida* school desegregation case, the *Armstrong* decision required the Birmingham Board of Education to submit a desegregation plan "as to all school grades without racial discrimination" before August 19, 1963, for the 1963–1964 academic year.[35] Rives's order required Lynne to reverse his decision and ordered the Birmingham school system to provide a full desegregation plan to the Fifth Circuit by the aforementioned date of August 19.

Judges Rives and Tuttle agreed that Armstrong did not need to exhaust potential remedies under state law before seeking relief in the federal courts. However, as to pupil placement, Tuttle wrote a special concurrence in *Armstrong*, indicating that he preferred the "immediate" approach that he laid out in *Stell* rather than implementing the plan Judge Rives identified in *Augustus*, which allowed the county one additional year to design and implement a full plan. Tuttle thought that the Birmingham Board of Education should be required to begin to move more quickly than the deadline set by Rives, which would be possible with Tuttle's grade-a-year plan. Tuttle wanted school authorities to take immediate responsibility for "putting an end to racially segregated schools" by arranging at least "one grade of the public schools of that city be completely desegregated . . . pending the appeal of this case."[36] Although Rives's and Tuttle's perspectives differed regarding implementation of school desegregation, following *Brown* they both advocated racial desegregation in schools. Judge Gewin dissented from the majority decision, blasting Rives and Tuttle.

In Judge Gewin's conservative *Armstrong* dissent, he asserted that District Judge Lynne's opinion, which required Armstrong to exhaust administrative channels before moving to the court system, should have been affirmed. Gewin stated that Judges Rives and Tuttle's ruling signaled "*a clear abuse of discretion* or *usurpation of judicial power*." In his dissent, Gewin wrote that Armstrong must follow administrative application procedures for school transfers. He accused his colleagues of perverting the usual appellate process and requested that the entire Fifth Circuit "court reconsider, rehear, and decide this case *En Banc*." An en banc hearing, which includes all judges serving the circuit, would provide an opportunity for a discussion that would aid in maintaining uniform decisions, especially given that Gewin perceived the case to be exceptionally important in setting legal precedent.[37]

Chief Judge Tuttle polled the nine judges on the Fifth Circuit—Chief Judge Tuttle, Judges Rives, Brown, Wisdom, Jones, Gewin, Bell, and Cameron, and Senior Judge Hutcheson. The judges voted five to four against convening an en banc session in *Armstrong*, essentially closing the case.[38] When Judge Cameron learned in July 1963 that his brethren denied Gewin's proposal, he could no longer contain his professional impressions of what he perceived was happening on the court. Cameron erupted against what he saw as a trend of court-packing (slating a majority of liberal judges to serve on panels in Civil Rights cases to result in a favorable outcome for Black citizens).

Two weeks after Chief Judge Tuttle announced the majority decision against an en banc hearing of *Armstrong*, Cameron entered a severe dissent to the decision. A judge issuing a dissent to a three-judge panel decision on which he did not participate as a member was highly unusual. Cameron, perceived to be the most conservative judge on the circuit at that time, fully concurred with Gewin's dissent and lashed out at his fellow circuit judges. Cameron's comments were similar in kind to those he made in *Denton v. City of Carrollton*, wherein he attacked Rives's *Browder* bus desegregation decision. However, this time Cameron directed his comments at Tuttle, the most liberal judge on the circuit at that time. In *Armstrong*, Cameron accused Tuttle of engaging in questionable procedures "in cases involving racial problems."[39]

In his *Armstrong* dissent, Judge Cameron wrote that the Fifth Circuit decision denying the Birmingham Board of Education a rehearing by the full court, as recommended by Judge Gewin, gave rise to "questions of procedure which have for some weeks plagued and are still plaguing the Court." Judges on the Fifth Circuit were split on the issue of racial desegregation. Further, the judges were working with multiple cases in different public contexts that often overlapped on the judicial calendar. In a petition for rehearing in *Davis*, Judges Wisdom and Brown wrote "the School Boards of Mobile and Birmingham face substantially the same social, legal, and administrative difficulties. . . . There should not be one law for Birmingham [*Armstrong*] and another for Mobile [*Davis*]." They wanted the judges to present a unified front to the citizens in Alabama and across the Southern states; Gewin was less concerned about appearances. Cameron wrote to the other judges that he thought court-packing had been a practice since as early as 1961, approximately one year into Tuttle's tenure as chief judge of the circuit. As reported in the *Birmingham News*, Cameron believed Tuttle intentionally arranged the judges' Civil Rights panel assignments to "influence their outcome."[40]

Judge Cameron also asserted in his *Armstrong* dissent that Chief Judge Tuttle regularly excluded him from participating on three-judge panels related to Civil Rights issues in his home state of Mississippi. At that time, the Fifth Circuit had one judge from each state within the circuit. The circuit judge from the state in which lawyers filed an appeal was generally assigned to serve on the panel. Cameron wrote, "The idea that the Chief Judge may thus gerrymander the United States Judges of a State in order to accomplish a desired result is, I think, entirely foreign to any just concept of the proper functioning of the judicial process." Cameron was unaware that the chief judge had not undertaken responsibility for identifying members of three-judge panels since partway through Chief Judge Hutcheson's term. That practice continued during the terms of Hutcheson, Rives, and Tuttle. Cameron's dissent also included an appendix, providing evidence to support his charge of panel-stacking in which he identified twenty-five race-related cases (representing twenty matters) decided in the Fifth Circuit between June 1961 and June 1963. He later amended the appendix, including four additional cases. He noted that at least two of the four judges, which would comprise a majority on a three-judge panel, sat on each of the appeals.[41]

In addition, Judge Cameron's *Armstrong* dissent also discussed a July 20, 1963, newspaper article that appeared throughout the South. Although not identified by Cameron, a *Birmingham Post-Herald* published an article on that date titled, "Fifth Circuit Has Major Part in Civil Rights Conflicts," which praised the Fifth Circuit for blazing new trails in Civil Rights cases. Reporter Jack Steele credited a "hard core" majority of four members who "have stood together consistently in decisions on civil rights cases," identifying Chief Judge Tuttle of Atlanta, and Judges Rives of Montgomery, Wisdom of New Orleans, and Brown of Houston. Cameron wrote that the majority were following procedures that were, in his opinion, "not sanctioned by the law" and presented a "vexatious problem." He included a footnote in his dissent assigning a moniker to the four judges: "These four Judges will hereafter sometimes be referred to as 'The Four.'" His reference associated Tuttle, Rives, Wisdom, and Brown with the Four Horsemen of the Apocalypse, who would oversee the disastrous occurrences leading to the end time. Spivack interviewed Tuttle, who summarized Cameron's behavior saying, "he gave the impression of wishing he could start firing on Fort Sumter every Monday morning." Earlier, in *Sharp v. Lucky* (1958), Cameron described the South as a "conquered province" persecuted by the US Congress's "so-called Civil Rights Statutes" that his brethren had a "disposition to stretch . . . to cover doubtful cases." His view was that federal statutes must be narrowly applied to avoid becoming unconstitutional.[42] Cameron's exasperation at (what he thought was) Tuttle's selection of judges to serve on three-judge Civil Rights panels was escalated by another contention he had with court procedures.

Judge Cameron thought Chief Judge Tuttle was bypassing appropriate steps in identifying which cases were appropriate for emergency hearings. For example, Tuttle documented in *Woods v. Wright* (1964) that during the May 1963 Birmingham Children's Crusade, "approximately 1080" Black students left primary and secondary schools for several days to demonstrate in support of Civil Rights. Tuttle acted unilaterally in an emergency session to single-handedly stop a district court judge's decision to suspend the Black students who left school to protest in support of school desegregation. Then, in June 1963, Tuttle identified six cases as urgent and requiring emergency hearings; however, five of the six cases were already scheduled for hearings before the end of the month. Cameron viewed these as additional instances of Tuttle's attack on state rights.[43]

Judge Cameron warned white citizens in his dissent to *Armstrong*, "The Judges of the Court are sharply divided on these questions and not only the lawyers of the Circuit, but the public generally, are displaying open concern with respect to inconsistent positions which they conceive are being taken by the Court."[44] The inconsistent positions to which Cameron referred were the different views taken by individual judges regarding racial desegregation, wherein a result could potentially be determined by which three judges were serving on the panel. Cameron implied that he did not trust or respect the four judges' interpretation of the US Constitution, especially their applications of the law in light of the Tenth Amendment, which supports states' rights. Cameron's dissent made public what several judges on the circuit court already knew: judges on the Fifth Circuit were divided in decisions related to the racial desegregation of the public sphere.

When Judge Rives learned of Judge Cameron's charges against Chief Judge Tuttle in *Armstrong*, he sent a letter on March 8, 1964, to all judges on the court. Rives claimed that Cameron's "charges were not only unfounded but also 'inexcusable, impertinent, and reprehensible.'" Two weeks later, having obtained additional information, he withdrew his criticism of Cameron's comments and wrote a letter of apology to members of the court.[45] Cameron did not reply to either of Rives's letters, his silence reinforcing their differences in judicial philosophy.

In an unusual act, someone leaked the *Armstrong* school desegregation decision to the press prior to its official publication. On July 31, 1963, newspapers across the country carried stories about Judge Cameron's dissent in the case. Headlines proclaimed that Chief Judge Tuttle "stacks deck in race cases" and identified a "favored trio" of "crusaders" who decided racial cases using "unorthodox procedures." The *New York Times* reported that Cameron "attempted to discredit the Fifth Circuit" by claiming the court was "stacking civil-rights cases with the Four."[46] Cameron's dissent came to the attention of his friend, Mississippi senator James O. Eastland, a staunch segregationist and the chairman of the US Senate Judiciary Committee.

On Friday, August 2, 1963, the *Houston Chronicle* published a bold headline on the front page: "Senator to See if Court Stacked in Integration Cases." Chairman Eastland dispatched an investigator to the Fifth Circuit headquarters in New Orleans to find information that would warrant an impeachment of The Four, which is the only way a lifetime-appointed judge may be removed from the federal court. The investigation sought to uncover potential political misconduct and any possible "incriminating information about the Four's personal lives." Eastland, quoted in the *Atlanta Constitution*, claimed that "the rules . . . have been abused by the chief judge of the Fifth Circuit in order to circumvent due process and arrive at manipulated decisions."[47] As a result, potential impeachment proceedings were on the horizon that could destabilize the Fifth Circuit.

While Judge Cameron's allegations of court-packing in *Armstrong* were troublesome, they did not raise the ire of some Fifth Circuit judges as much as an incident reported in the Sunday, August 4, 1963, edition of the *Houston*

Chronicle. On page 1, an article by reporter Saul Friedman appeared, titled "Appeals Court Facing Revolt." Judge Brown, who lived in Houston, mailed a copy of the article to each of his brethren on the Court of Appeals. In the article, Judge Rives denied Cameron's court-packing allegations. Rives was quoted as saying that Chief Judge Tuttle was obliged to assign cases to judges "who will follow the law honestly and fully and without prejudice." The article also quoted an anonymous source "close to the court" as saying, "The chief judge wants honest judges to decide according to the law." Rives and the unknown source, which Emanuel indicated was generally thought to be Brown, seemed to focus on Cameron's character rather than his judicial philosophy. Two judges publicly casting aspersions against another judge was highly unusual. James P. Coleman, a clerk for Judge Cameron who later became a judge on the Fifth Circuit, stated in an interview with Spivack, "Judges don't go around talking about other judges on the same court, even if they may have some feelings on the subject." The division between judges on the Fifth Circuit had become public, and Judges Bell, Jones, and Gewin resented that their integrity had been publicly questioned without having an opportunity to address their colleagues' accusations in private before the information became public in the newspaper.[48]

On Wednesday, August 7, 1963, after Judge Jones received the letter and newspaper article from Judge Brown, Jones received a telephone call from Judge Bell. Jones and Bell both found the quotations in the newspaper to be offensive. Their more conservative judicial philosophies aside, the two men were concerned about how the general public would perceive the judges' accusations regarding strategic panel assignments. They knew that Edward W. Wadsworth, as clerk of court, would have access to information that would shed light on Judge Cameron's allegations.[49]

Wadsworth worked with Judge Brown in the panel assignment process and was aware of the collective content in the files related to scheduling three-judge panels. Law professor Joel William Friedman, informed by Judge Jones's diary and letters from Wadsworth to judges on the court, summarized the interactions. Wadsworth was unsure how to respond to Jones's questions. He did not want to be insubordinate to a senior member of the court, and he also did not want to speak without authorization. He delayed answering Jones's question by informing him that Chief Judge Tuttle was out of town vacationing in the Rocky Mountains and could not be reached. However, Wadsworth told Jones that if Acting Chief Judge Rives agreed, he would release a report of the case file information. Jones recorded in his diary that he was shocked at being snubbed by a court clerk and immediately called Rives, who had previously served as chief judge and was assisting Tuttle in his absence.[50]

Friedman wrote that Acting Chief Judge Rives agreed with Judge Jones's right to see the files. Rives then telephoned Wadsworth to direct him to comply with Jones's request. In the meantime, Wadsworth wrote to Jones that he had contacted Chief Judge Tuttle, who also told him that he must "fully and truthfully" respond to Jones's questions. Accordingly, Wadsworth called the deputy clerk to request assistance in preparing a detailed summary of panel assignments in all race cases. Jones recorded in his diary that several hours later, Wadsworth telephoned Jones to tell him he was working on an analysis of Civil Rights case panels. During the call, Jones asked Wadsworth again: Did Judge Brown suggest or direct him to assign or keep "any segregation or other civil rights cases . . . from any particular panels or judge?" Wadsworth answered, "Yes."[51]

Judges Jones and Bell, Friedman wrote, were outraged. Two days after Bell's telephone conversation with Jones, Bell mailed an angry six-page letter to the other Fifth Circuit judges. At the end of the letter, Bell called for a judicial conference in Houston.[52] The location would be convenient for Judge Hutcheson, now on senior status and in declining health, while also allowing an immediate response to the local newspaper that issued the story.

Friedman recounted that on Saturday, August 10, 1963, Wadsworth shared a summary table of judicial assignments with Acting Chief Judge Rives. The result, Jones recorded in his diary, revealed a condition worse than Rives had expected. As a result, Rives called Jones and asked if he would grant him "a personal favor" and wait to receive the report until after Rives had an opportunity to share the information with Chief Judge Tuttle. In reply, Jones declared, "If I do not get the information requested, I will consider whether to ask a member of Senator Eastland's staff to meet me in New Orleans," the headquarters for the Fifth Circuit Court. Rives promised to share the report with Jones as soon as Rives spoke with Tuttle. Jones agreed to wait.[53]

J. Robert Brown Jr. and Allison Herren Lee wrote in the *Texas Law Review* that what initially precipitated Judge Cameron's dissent in *Armstrong* was his frustration at being excluded from three-judge district panel hearings in Mississippi on race-related cases. His dissent then gave rise to the *Houston Chronicle* article. However, allegations of panel packing at the appellate court level soon overshadowed the issue of exclusion. Jones wrote in his diary that during Acting Chief Judge Rives's telephone conversation with him, Rives asked Jones to contact Cameron about his availability to attend the judicial meeting in Houston. Jones called Cameron on Monday, August 12, who reacted with evident surprise at the collective response to his dissent. During their conversation, Cameron said he regretted that Senator Eastland had "blasted off" by sending an investigator to look into panel assignments in the Fifth Circuit. Cameron's health was failing, and he told Jones that he "would not, in all likelihood, expose himself to the hazards of attending" the judicial conference regardless of whether the session was held later in August or postponed until the court's quarterly meeting in October.[54] Irrespective of whether Cameron would attend the meeting, the issue needed to be addressed.

Wadsworth finalized his report summarizing judicial assignments to race-related cases on August 17, 1963. He likely reflected on how the three-judge panels had been composed. When Judge Brown was confirmed to the Fifth Circuit, he offered to undertake slating three-judge panels to alleviate some of Chief Judge Hutcheson's duties. Brown, who excelled at administrative work, would forward the names of judges to serve on each panel to Wadsworth, who would schedule hearings throughout the circuit. When Rives became chief judge, he accepted Brown's offer to continue to identify judges to sit on three-judge panels. Judge Rives complimented Brown in a December 13, 1960, letter, writing, "It is really an excellent system for the assignment of judges and the approval of the calendar to be done by different judges." When Judge Tuttle became chief judge after Rives resigned from the post, Tuttle also asked Brown to continue to manage panel assignments. As time passed, Brown transferred more responsibility related to slating three-judge panels to Wadsworth.[55] Other judges on the Fifth Circuit were not yet privy to that information.

Acting Chief Judge Rives instructed Wadsworth to mail a copy of the report to each Fifth Circuit judge. A meeting was scheduled for August 22 and 23, 1963, in Houston. Even without Judge Cameron in attendance, the judges knew that the two-day meeting would be tense. Judge Wisdom took notes on the meeting, revealing that Chief Judge Tuttle requested that Rives convene the meeting of the Judicial Council for the Fifth Circuit and open the session with a prayer. Tuttle then addressed Cameron's charges regarding the composition of the three-judge panels. When Tuttle confirmed during the meeting that Judge Brown was overseeing the case assignments, several judges' suspicions arose about the creation of three-judge panels.[56] Yet, several factors needed to be considered in slating panels.

Personnel requests were extensive among the judges. Friedman stated that Judge Jones "asked Tuttle not to pair him with Cameron on any cases because of the delays caused by Cameron's demand for a lengthy siesta between morning arguments and afternoon conferences." Emanuel conveyed that Jones, representing Florida on the bench, also disliked traveling to Montgomery because of poor transportation options. Further, Judge Hutcheson's health limited him from participating on panels outside of Houston. In addition, Judge Cameron, the most conservative judge on Civil Rights, preferred not to sit with Tuttle, the most liberal judge on Civil Rights, on any panels.[57] These judicial requests added challenges to identifying a panel through a random assignment of judges.

Information was shared about Wadsworth's clerical assistance to Judge Brown in slating three-judge panels. Bass related that "Brown was shocked to find that Wadsworth had retained and filed . . . [his] cryptic memos relating to assignments," which revealed that Judges Bell and Gewin should not yet be assigned to three-judge panels on race-related cases. Bell and Gewin, nominated by President John F. Kennedy on an interim appointment and not yet confirmed by the US Senate, were excluded from race-related cases by Brown until their appointments passed through the Senate in early 1962. Yet even after they were confirmed by the Senate, Brown did not inform Wadsworth that Tuttle had lifted the restriction. That disclosure, Bass wrote, led Bell to state that "he had considered himself a full member of the court only to learn he was merely a judge under guardianship." As a result of the judges' requests, only Judges Brown, Rives, Tuttle, and Wisdom (The Four) were unrestricted in their appointment to panels.[58] Another consideration was Cameron's judicial philosophy on state rights.

Chief Judge Tuttle's refusal to assign Judge Cameron to hear racial desegregation cases in Mississippi created the impression of Court interference and disregard for the fundamental principles of judicial neutrality and impartiality. However, Tuttle believed that Cameron had admitted his inability to be impartial on Fourteenth Amendment cases in his twenty-six-page dissent in *Boman v. Birmingham Transit Co.* (1961). In that dissent, Cameron reviewed a series of cases in which he thought federal judges should not have intervened. Cameron expressed that the Fourteenth Amendment, ratified in 1868, was a result of political negotiations between "the extreme egalitarianism of the Radicals" and the "Moderates" in the US Congress. He thought the amendment was being deliberately interpreted by some judges in the Fifth Circuit "in a manner which the majority of our ancestors did not wish." Both Tuttle and Judge Brown perceived that Cameron's comments in that dissent revealed a bias in favor of state rights that would influence his assignment to judicial panels in Civil Rights cases. After Cameron admitted in *Boman* that he saw himself as a representative of the (white) people of Mississippi and did not believe *Brown I* should be enforced in that state, his judicial assignments began to change.[59] These limitations on Fifth Circuit panel assignments, possibly along with other requests that were not made public, influenced the assignment of judges who would hear appeals in various types of lawsuits in different states.

The Judicial Council meeting was strained and at one point, Bass revealed, Judge Jones threw a file to the floor in frustration and made accusations that some judges had neglected their judicial duties. Emanuel wrote that Judge Bell wanted Judge Brown to stop all involvement with docketing and thought it was appropriate that, as chief judge, Tuttle should resume assigning the three-judge panels. The room went quiet when Judge Wisdom supported Brown's continuation as assignment judge. Judge Rives knew firsthand that the workload of the chief judge could be overwhelming. According to Judge Wisdom's notes from the meeting, Rives implied that the outspoken judges should be part of the solution and take over the responsibility of composing the panels. On the conference's second day, the three judges forming the minority opinion—Jones, Gewin, and Bell—held a private discussion over lunch. When they returned to the meeting, Brown and Lee reported that the three judges supported Brown in continuing to slate panel assignments.[60]

As the two-day meeting neared an end, Judge Wisdom's meeting notes reveal a recommendation from Judge Rives that the judges issue a short news release because of the attention the issue had received in the media. Rives was concerned about legal consequences and the possibility that someone might challenge the legitimacy of prior court decisions. The judges agreed to issue a statement designed to protect the court's integrity and attempt to publicly close the issue. Wisdom wrote that Judges Jones, Gewin, and Bell drafted the initial language, and then the entire group refined the wording. The news release finally received the judges' approval and was later published, stating, "The problems alleged to exist in this Court have been considered by the Court. The Court believes that in no given case has there been a conscious assignment to accomplish a desired result. Action has been taken to avoid any appearance of inconsistency in the assignment of judges or the arrangement of the docket."[61] The remaining issue was to contact Judge Cameron to inform him about the result of the conference.

Judge Rives maintained a professional working relationship with Judge Cameron and called him at home to update him about the meeting. Following their conversation, Cameron talked with Senator Eastland. Bass interviewed Eastland, who stated that Cameron "was satisfied, and I was, too," with the outcome of the judicial conference. Spivack interviewed one of Cameron's clerks, who explained that Cameron revered the Fifth Circuit Court of Appeals. Cameron saw the court as "the highest, most respected Southern judicial institution" and as "an important part of the South, speaking for its judicial and legal traditions." The clerk elaborated, "Cameron saw that the Court could only be damaged as an institution by proceeding further, and he had no wish to do that." Eastland subsequently closed the investigation by the Administrative Office of the United States Courts.[62]

The news release brought the Houston Conference to a close. Never before had a public statement been made concerning the internal court matters of the Fifth Circuit.[63] Although the information Judge Cameron cited in his *Armstrong* dissent was available to the public, access to that information was fairly limited. The news release would reinforce that the judiciary attended to the issue and potentially increase the public's trust in the judiciary, which had begun to unravel. Future panels did not change much in their composition, but afterward, the Fifth Circuit judges knew they were being watched.

Nearly a decade after *Brown*, resistance to segregation had not subsided and litigation continued to ensue. In January 1963, *Lee v. Macon County Board of Education* was filed. The case began as a simple school desegregation case, heard in district court by Judge Johnson. In July the United States was added as a plaintiff-intervenor to the case. On August 22, 1963, Johnson ordered that members of the Board of Education make "an immediate start" to desegregate public schools in Macon County. He provided additional instructions, identifying deadlines for compliance.[64] However, the Macon County school system continued to face obstruction to desegregation by Alabama's State Board of Education, Governor George C. Wallace, and the state superintendent of education, Austin R. Meadows.

During the 1963–1964 academic year, the federal court was petitioned three times to intervene and stop state officials from interfering with "the peaceful and orderly desegregation of schools in Macon County." Citizens of the state witnessed Governor Wallace issuing executive orders; students being turned away from schools, assigned to other schools, and then turned away from those schools; reallocation of funding for education; the creation of foundations to fund private schools; and other maneuvers designed to uphold racial segregation in education.[65] The persistent interference led Judge Johnson to request that Chief Judge Tuttle assign a three-judge panel to the case.

In their July 16, 1964, per curiam *Lee* decision, Judges Rives, Grooms, and Johnson gave segregationist Alabama school authorities what Bagley called "a stern federal court ultimatum." The judges required authorities to desegregate classrooms with what the US Supreme Court justices announced in *Brown II* as "all deliberate speed." The *Lee* decision stated, "For the present time, this Court will proceed upon the assumption that" these state agencies "will comply in good faith with the injunction of this Court . . . and, through the exercise of considerable judicial restraint, no state-wide desegregation will be ordered at this time." Johnson had served on many cases with Rives and held him in high regard. In the area of educational decisions, Johnson followed Rives's lead. Rives and Grooms, both of whose views had shifted over time, were more restrained than Johnson in their opinions. Bagley suggested that if Johnson had been the only judge hearing *Lee* when a statewide desegregation order was requested, he "might have entered such relief." Rives and Grooms allowed segregationist white citizens time to prepare for the widespread social change that school desegregation would bring. The judges all recognized that a statewide order to desegregate public schools would enflame segregationists.

They also thought local school boards could act in good faith to desegregate public schools once the court "freed [·them] from state pressure and intimidation."[66] The unprecedented nature of a statewide court order was a critical element in withholding such a decision.

Four years after *Lee* was first filed, the case was still before the court. Lee's lawyers had filed a supplemental complaint challenging Act no. 252 and a second complaint "asking for a state-wide desegregation order and an injunction against the use of state funds to support a dual school system." The Southern Education Reporting Service documented the 1967 *Lee* hearing before Judges Rives, Johnson, and Grooms. They recorded that one of Lee's lawyers, Henry Aronson, an LDF lawyer, directly petitioned the court "to cut off state funds to cities and counties which continue to maintain a dual system." In his argument, Aronson said, "freedom of choice desegregation is not working." Judge Rives responded, "If the goal is to mix, I will concede that freedom of choice will not work, but if the goal is to abolish discrimination, then it is a different question—it might work." The way lawyers framed the legal question and their argument would shape the type of remedy the court could order. Rives's interest was to abolish discrimination by allowing individuals to choose whether they wished to attend a desegregated or segregated educational facility. In the hearing that day, Rives stated that the court would "give serious consideration" to the plaintiff's petition to order then-Governor Lurleen Wallace and other state officials to end racial discrimination in primary and secondary schools across the state of Alabama.[67]

Judges Rives, Grooms, and Johnson filed a per curiam decision in *Lee* on March 22, 1967. The court announced that since the previous decision in 1964, "it is now evident that the reasons for this Court's reluctance to grant the relief to which these plaintiffs were clearly entitled over two years ago are no longer valid." The judges could "conceive of no other effective way to give the [plaintiffs] the relief to which they are entitled" than to order "a uniform state-wide plan for school desegregation." The order covered the ninety-eight school systems not functioning already under a federal court order to adopt a racially desegregated educational plan "within 20 days from the entry of this decree." The educational plan would also apply to "the state's trade schools, vocational schools and state colleges" and all other educational institutions. Lawyers for the Macon County Board of Education appealed the judges' order to the US Supreme Court, which affirmed the ruling of Rives, Johnson, and Grooms. Although later litigation would ensue, the three-judge per curiam decision in *Lee* legally required administrators statewide to end all segregated classes for all students.[68] Litigation would continue, but essentially, racially segregated public schools had been legally abolished in Alabama.

Around the same time that *Lee* was moving through the legal process, the

US Office of Education issued its first regulations in April 1965 "providing guidance and standards regarding school desegregation." Revised guidelines issued on March 7, 1966, were intended to expedite the desegregation of public schools. The guidelines shortened the deadlines for actions such as requiring school boards to desegregate faculty members throughout the school system. In addition, administrators suggested that federal bureaucratic sanctions might be implemented (e.g., loss of federal funds) to overcome the segregationist consciousness of state and local school boards. The document further increased demands on school boards, which were already inundated by complaints from angry and frustrated white parents.[69]

In August 1966, during the eighth Special Session of the Alabama Legislature, Governor George Wallace proposed Act no. 252, also called the "Anti-Guidelines Act." The law "would forbid Alabama school districts from entering into desegregation agreements with the federal Office of Education." Educational boards in Alabama would no longer be required to complete the required federal forms that reported levels of racial desegregation in the public schools. The *Florence Herald* reported that Wallace spoke to the legislature after the bill was passed, declaring "We shall not retreat" in confrontations with the federal Department of Health, Education, and Welfare. Yet, support for Act no. 252 was not unanimous. State Senator Neil Metcalf served as chairman of the Senate Education Committee and was "an outspoken critic of the bill."[70]

The Southern Education Reporting Service recounted active resistance toward the new school policies from members of state school boards. This led Circuit Judge Rives and District Judges Johnson and Virgil Pittman of Mobile to conduct a one-day, eight-hour hearing on February 3, 1967. The hearing related, in part, to US Department of Health, Education, and Welfare (HEW) efforts to enforce compliance with the US Office of Education Guidelines for desegregation in public schools. Alabama educators petitioned the court to invalidate Alabama's 1966 anti-guidelines law and again formally requested that judges order Alabama school systems to racially desegregate their composition.[71]

During the hearing, the Southern Education Reporting Services observed that Judge Rives, who had authored many of the recent Fifth Circuit school desegregation rulings on behalf of the court and whose decisions they regarded as "bellwether rulings," put lawyers for the Justice Department and the LDF through their paces. Rives's opinion about the law differed from the lawyers seeking to enforce HEW guidelines. Rives thought the 1966 HEW guidelines "might transcend the legislative authority grant[ed] by Congress in the 1964 Civil Rights Act." He continued, noting that the "rules of general application made by the . . . [Office of Education] without approval of the

President might be outside the authority granted by Congress."[72] Rives was concerned about enforcing guidelines, the legality of which had not yet been determined.

According to the Southern Education Reporting Services, Rives asked about "the distinctions between 'freedom' and 'force' in desegregation" and commented, "It worries me . . . whether there is any *requirement* of integration beyond true freedom of choice." While some students may want to attend a desegregated school, Rives thought that some Black children would prefer to go to schools where only Black children attend, and some white children would prefer to attend schools where only white children attend. The report indicated that Rives referenced post-*Brown* litigation, where "the ultimate goal in court decisions has been the elimination of discrimination not the mixing of races [integration]."[73]

Rives thought that some of the revised guidelines would undoubtedly result, the Southern Education Reporting Services wrote, in "forced integration." He asked a lawyer for the US Department of Justice's Civil Rights Division, "If you classify students by race for the purpose of forced integration, aren't you coming close to depriving people of their rights under the equal-protection provision of the Constitution?'" His frequent questions led Court observers to believe that Rives was concerned about "integration" as distinct from "freedom-of-choice 'desegregation.'" Rives conceded that "some 'integration' is necessary 'to eliminate segregation.'" However, "When you go beyond that, aren't you denying the rights of others to equal protection?" He sought to clarify for himself the range of plausible interpretations of these words to comprehend if parties were defining terms in a similar manner, and also to define parameters of the law. During that time, Judge Brown told Read, "We were desperately trying to dispose of a lot of cases with genuine movement, an accelerated movement toward integration—I mean integration, not desegregation."[74] In contrast, Rives remained clear that his interpretation of *Brown* did not include integration.

Federal judges first distinguished between desegregation and integration in the July 1955 *Briggs v. Elliott* decision. US Supreme Court justices did not use the term "desegregation" in *Brown I*; they twice used the term "nonsegregated." Likewise, in *Brown II*, the justices did not use the term "desegregation" but referenced the need for a "racially nondiscriminatory school system," which was "not based on color distinctions." When Judge Rives first applied *Brown I* in the *Browder* transportation case, the only reference to desegregation in the decision came from a witness statement; Rives used the term "nonsegregated." He told Spivack that in early desegregation decisions he consciously followed the approach of Fourth Circuit Chief Judge Parker. Parker interpreted desegregation to mean "the prohibition of discriminatory segregation."[75] As time passed, Rives continued to prefer the word desegregation, while other judges used the term integration.

Judge Rives recognized that the general public did not distinguish between desegregation and integration, and that they viewed the two terms as synonymous. While the behaviors that indicate "desegregation" and "integration" are physically similar, the distinction between the two terms was legally important to Rives. In writing to Judges Jones and Brown about another issue in late 1957, Rives, a humble man, disclosed that "past experience forces me to admit that I have been confident before and have later found out that I erred." He understood that feelings about race ran deep in the South. The younger Rives likely advocated to his father that while desegregation is not integration, contact with a person of another race may lead to acceptance. Rives recognized that desegregation and integration both involved interracial contact. Read and McGough explained that as a judge, Rives perceived that one function of the law was to "make it as easy as possible for 'fair-minded' men to act responsibly." He had an "unfailing sense of the consequences of a particular decision, its 'enforceability quotient' in the teeth of southern resistance." Rives's character, concern for ethical behavior, and interest in common sense and fairness were undergirded by a principle of equality. He told Spivack that as time passed, he eventually came closer to the positions of the other members of The Four—Chief Judge Tuttle, and Judges Brown and Wisdom.[76]

After publication of the *Lee v. Macon* decision on March 22, 1967, Alabama school officials were mandated by the court to take proactive measures to desegregate the public schools within the state. Rives had been a member of the initial three-judge panel hearing *United States v. Jefferson County Board of Education* (hereafter *Jefferson*). On October 9, 1967, a Fifth Circuit en banc panel heard an appeal in *Jefferson*. After fifteen years as a judge on the Fifth Circuit, Rives assumed senior status on February 15, 1966, and did not sit on the en banc appeal in that case. In that appeal, judges on the Fifth Circuit began to command administrators of individual schools "to comply with uniform, rigorous HEW inspired guidelines intended to add teeth to weak 'freedom of choice plans' preferred by local boards of education." Without Rives's contribution, Spivack wrote that Fifth Circuit judges reversed their approach to school desegregation and moved "from passive desegregation to active integration." The *Jefferson* decision, which took Wisdom nearly a year to prepare, pushed for integration "lock, stock, and barrel."[77] While on senior status, Rives began to gradually support the per curiam decision of his colleagues in *Jefferson*.

In 1969, nearly fifteen years after *Brown II*, the US Supreme Court reentered the struggle for educational desegregation. The Supreme Court's order in *Alexander v. Holmes County Board of Education*, handed down in October 1969, ended the *Brown II* standard of "all deliberate speed." The justices deemed that approach to be "no longer constitutionally permissible. . . . the obligation of every school district is to terminate dual school systems at once and to operate now and hereafter only unitary schools."[78] Segregated school systems across the country had legally become a thing of the past.

From May 31, 1955, when the US Supreme Court handed down *Brown II*, until their October 29, 1969, decision in *Alexander*, Judge Rives and his colleagues marked a path in school desegregation decisions. Rives served on more educational panels during that time than any other judge, writing decisions that held school administrators and state officials accountable to the US Constitution. When the US Supreme Court finally reengaged to address the implementation of school desegregation, the justices essentially followed in the wake of Rives's and other federal judges' decisions regarding racial desegregation in public schools.

4

Demanding that the Executive Branch of Government Intervene

The Desegregation of Public Higher Education

Lawyers for the NAACP's Legal Defense and Educational Fund first used the Fourteenth Amendment to argue for the racial desegregation of the University of Maryland School of Law in *Murray v. Pearson* (1936). Then in 1950, the LDF won two additional higher education lawsuits, *Sweatt v. Painter* and *McLaurin v. Oklahoma State Regents for Higher Education*. Lawyers for those cases persuaded justices on the US Supreme Court to overturn the *Plessy v. Ferguson* (1896) "separate but equal" doctrine in graduate and professional schools. Despite the US Supreme Court's *Brown v. Board of Education* (1954, 1955) decisions desegregating public education, the LDF was forced to file additional lawsuits to desegregate higher educational institutions.[1]

Judge Richard T. Rives's first higher education racial desegregation appeal was a class action suit captioned *Board of Supervisors of Louisiana State University and Agricultural and Mechanical College v. Tureaud* (1953). In that case, Eastern District of Louisiana Judge J. Skelly Wright ordered the admission of Black students to the university's school of law, school of medicine, and graduate school. Upon appeal to the Fifth Circuit, a three-judge panel that included Rives was assigned to review Wright's decision. The majority of judges agreed with the university's board of supervisors to maintain a white student body. Rives dissented. He saw the case as "purely a factual question" about the equality of resources, "the decision of which was for the district judge." He stated that Wright commendably "shouldered the responsibility imposed upon him by law" in the US Supreme Court's *Murray*, *Sweatt*, and *McLaurin* decisions. In the appeal, Rives clarified that while a district judge must request a three-judge panel in cases involving the US Constitution, the US Code "does not require a district court of three judges" be assigned by the chief judge of a circuit simply because one was requested. *Tureaud* dragged on, and ultimately a 1956 en banc Fifth Circuit hearing that included Rives ordered the reinstatement of Wright's September 11, 1953, decision ordering the university to begin to admit Black students.[2] However, the court-ordered racial desegregation of one university did not sway segregationists from obstructing Black students at other universities.

After Judge Rives's involvement in *Tureaud*, he was informally drawn into the *Lucy v. University of Alabama* lawsuit. Rives was also involved in the lengthy appeals process of James Meredith, a Black military veteran who applied for admission to the University of Mississippi in 1961. The *Meredith* case would ultimately lead to Rives's reprimand of President John F. Kennedy for failing to comply with judicial instructions, and to US Attorney General Robert F. Kennedy filing civil contempt charges against Mississippi governor Ross Barnett. The purpose of charging someone with civil contempt, according to the Legal Information Institute, is to "persuade [a person] to comply with the court order." In addition to their full caseload, the lawsuits to racially desegregate public higher educational facilities placed what Rives told Orien S. Thiel was an "unusually heavy burden of work" on each of the Fifth Circuit judges. Rives's judicial patience was tested by the various strategies that lawyers, judges, and politicians used to roadblock justice. At times, Rives told Spivack, he supposed they were purposely misunderstanding the law.[3]

In September 1952, two years after the US Supreme Court rulings in *Sweatt* and *McLaurin*, Autherine J. Lucy and Pollie Anne Myers applied to attend the University of Alabama. Their scholastic applications were approved. However, when the dean of admissions met the two women and realized they were Black students, their admissions were rejected. As a result, in July 1953 the LDF filed *Lucy v. Adams*, a complaint against the dean of admissions at the University of Alabama.[4] The LDF had begun to move quickly to desegregate higher education in line with their internal 1930 Margold Report, a legal strategy document to attack "separate but equal" education.

Judge Rives would become involved behind the scenes in the *Lucy* case. Lawyers filed the case in Judge Grooms's Northern District of Alabama Court. Frank Sikora, journalist for the *Birmingham News*, characterized Grooms as "forthright and even-handed" in applying the law. In the *Lucy* decision, Grooms invoked the equal protection clause of the Fourteenth Amendment to grant a permanent injunction against the university, requiring them to admit Lucy and Myers. Two days later, he amended the decision to apply to all other Black students who were scholastically qualified to seek admission to the University of Alabama.[5]

Judge Grooms wrote in *Lucy* that he did not find a need to consider "the validity of any constitutional or statutory provision of Alabama under the Fourteenth Amendment." *Southern School News* reported that Grooms, who had served as a district judge for only two years, consulted privately with Judge Rives about the case. In their discussion, both men agreed that Grooms should grant the university a delay in implementing the court order. Accordingly, on September 6, 1955, Grooms granted the university's motion to suspend the admission of Lucy and Meyers for four months to allow time for an appeal of his decision. The *New York Times* reported that the university's lawyer immediately filed for a rehearing and identified twenty-three legal bases on which to appeal the district court injunction that required them to admit Lucy and Meyers. Lawyers for the university then appealed *Lucy* to the Fifth Circuit, and Chief Judge Hutcheson, and Judges Wayne G. Borah and John R. Brown upheld Grooms's decision allowing the delay. Lawyers for Lucy then appealed the case to the US Supreme Court. On October 10, 1955, US Supreme Court justices vacated the four-month injunction and required the university to begin immediately to admit qualified Black students.[6]

Judge Grooms was a relatively new judge on the Federal Circuit, and being overruled by a higher court was a public announcement that he, as the website Ballotpedia: Encyclopedia of American Politics explained, "did not properly apply or interpret a law or constitutional provision." Grooms, interviewed by a reporter for *Southern School News*, discussed Rives's input and was quoted as saying the US Supreme Court "promptly slapped both of us down." The justices' message was clear about the application of *Brown II*, decided May 31, 1955: a district court judge, Grooms said, "is not a free agent in the matter of segregation or integration."[7] Rives had been a gradualist in racial desegregation but when he and Grooms were overruled, the Supreme Court justices' message was clear: act more progressively toward racial desegregation. However, fundamental change in the South would take time.

Six years after the US Supreme Court's *Brown II* decision to desegregate public schools with deliberate speed, *Meredith v. Fair* was appealed to the Fifth Circuit. Higher education, which offers the opportunity to earn a baccalaureate or an advanced degree in a college or university, is generally seen by the public as preparing students to be citizens. Historian of education Johann N. Neem wrote that an advanced degree is one signal that a person is an American.[8] James Meredith had served in the US military but after his service, as a Black citizen Meredith was refused the right to attend Mississippi's flagship university. That refusal prompted him to seek legal action. *Meredith* proved to be one of the most complex educational desegregation cases during the modern Civil Rights era. Rives contributed to the voluminous legal file.

After Meredith left the Air Force in 1960, he wrote to the LDF in Washington, DC. Legal historian Tomiko Brown-Nagin explained that Meredith's application to attend the University of Mississippi was driven by his desire to "fight a 'war' against white supremacy." The University of Mississippi was the state's greatest symbol of white power and academic privilege. In the spring of 1961, Meredith applied for admission as an in-state transfer student from Jackson State College. As expected, his application was denied. On May 31, 1961, Meredith's legal team, which included LDF lawyer Constance Baker Motley, filed suit in the Southern District of Mississippi Court. The lawsuit charged Charles Dickson Fair, the president of the board of trustees of the state institutions of higher learning and of the University of Mississippi, with violating *Brown I* (1954), alleging that "the University of Mississippi is limited by policy and custom to admit students on a segregated basis only."[9] The case was first heard in Judge Sidney Mize's courtroom.

Judge Mize, born in Mississippi in 1888, accepted a position as a federal judge for southern Mississippi in 1937. As a conservative jurist, he was adamant about racial segregation and other protections of Jim Crow. Mize expressed his views plainly in *Evers v. Jackson Municipal Separate School District* in 1964, wherein he wrote that the "differences between Caucasians and Negroes are genetically determined and cannot be changed materially by [their] environment." Historian Howard Smead characterized Mize's "obstructionism from the bench" as setting "the standard" against which other judges' Civil Rights decisions were measured.[10] Mize issued his ruling against Meredith on December 12, 1961. Motley appealed the decision to the Fifth Circuit one week later.

Although the US Supreme Court's *Brown* rulings occurred in the mid-1950s, legal scholars Denny Chin and Kathy Hirata Chin note that many people including "politicians, the media, educators, attorneys, and even judges," would not accept that segregated public education was unconstitutional. Elmore Douglass Greaves, whom the Jackson, Mississippi, *Clarion-Ledger* identified as "a very outspoken" conservative from Mississippi, had a degree from Jackson School of Law. He articulated the perspective of many white Southerners who did not want to desegregate public spaces: "We know that once physical proximity with the negro is accepted, social integration will begin. That when social integration is accepted, racial intermarriage will follow. And that when racial intermarriage evolves on a large scale, the white race is damaged, and this is evil. We do not propose to let this degrading and atavistic process go any further among us." White supremacists openly condemned the *Brown* decisions. The newspaper called May 17, 1954, the date *Brown I* was decided, a "black day of tragedy."[11] Judge Rives had served on the bench for over a decade when *Meredith* was appealed to the Fifth Circuit.

In early January 1962, Judge Rives was assigned to a three-judge panel with Chief Judge Elbert P. Tuttle and Judge John Minor Wisdom. He had revealed his thinking about education in an earlier 1961 case, *Dixon v. Alabama State Board of Education*, writing, "It requires no argument to demonstrate that education is vital and, indeed, basic to civilized society. Without sufficient education the plaintiffs would not be able to earn an adequate livelihood, to enjoy life to the fullest, or to fulfill as completely as possible the duties and responsibilities of good citizens."[12] The three judges met in New Orleans, Louisiana, on January 9, 1962, to hear Meredith's petition.

During the previous year, the *Meredith* record had become convoluted by numerous legal actions filed by both sides. After the hearing, Judge Wisdom wrote on behalf of the panel of judges and three days later their decision was announced. The protracted litigation in *Meredith* led Wisdom to write that the case existed in "the eerie atmosphere of never-never land." He continued, "It is impossible to determine whether there were valid, non-discriminatory grounds for the University's refusing Meredith's admission." Mississippi historian James Silver interpreted Wisdom as "tartly" reprimanding Judge Mize for questionable continuances and long delays. The decision directed that a retrial be conducted in Mize's district court "in order to clarify the muddy record" and to clearly identify the legal issues at hand. The per curiam order charged Mize to "proceed promptly with a full trial on the merits and that judgment be rendered promptly" in the case.[13] The Fifth Circuit panel declined Motley's appeal to allow Meredith to attend classes while his case was underway, since there was still time for the district court to act before the February term began.

As required, Motley then filed for a retrial in the Southern District of Mississippi Court, alleging that Meredith was denied admission solely because of his race. A full trial was again held and on February 3, 1962, Judge Mize ruled against Meredith, maintaining that his admission had been denied for reasons other than race. Mize wrote, "The proof shows, and I find as a fact that the University is not a racially segregated institution . . . and find as a fact, that he was not denied admission because of his race."[14] Motley once again filed an appeal to the Fifth Circuit in which she sought to overturn the district court judge's decision. The record was now 1350 pages long.

On June 25, 1962, Judges Wisdom, Brown, and unwavering segregationist Judge Dozier A. DeVane, a federal judge for the Northern District of Florida Court, heard the appeal. Judges Wisdom and Brown formed a majority on a panel to reverse Mize, finding that Meredith's application to the University of Mississippi was rejected based on his race. After that opinion was issued, lawyers for the university did something unusual, but perhaps not unexpected given that Mississippi was well-known for what Brown-Nagin called "its vicious brand of racism and violent opposition to change."[15] Lawyers for the university's board of trustees went to see Fifth Circuit Judge Cameron in Mississippi.

The university lawyers petitioned Cameron, who had not participated in any of the *Meredith* hearings (despite being the circuit judge from the state of Mississippi), to issue a stay of the Fifth Circuit's directive to the district court.

They argued that Meredith should not be allowed on campus until his court case concluded. Cameron agreed with the university's lawyers, and on July 18, he issued a stay, which effectively obstructed Meredith's attendance on campus even though he had been accepted as a student. This time, the Fifth Circuit panel of Judges Wisdom, Brown, and DeVane issued a per curiam order on July 27 that vacated and set aside Cameron's stay order. The ruling directed the district court to issue an injunction that allowed Meredith to attend the University of Mississippi. The next day, July 28, Cameron issued another stay order, and the panel of judges set aside that order the same day. Then three days later, on July 31, Cameron issued another stay. On August 4, the three-judge panel set aside that stay, calling all three of Cameron's stays "unauthorized, erroneous, and improvident." Two days later, on August 6, Cameron issued a fourth stay. Cameron's behavior was unparalleled in the history of the Fifth Circuit.[16]

Judge Cameron believed the Fourteenth Amendment had never been validly adopted by the United States. Law professor Joseph A. Custer wrote that Cameron "never accepted *Brown* and believed that the Tenth Amendment reserved powers to the states to reject the Supreme Court's decisions." Cameron reasoned that Southern senators and representatives of the former Confederate States were not members of the US Congress that proposed and adopted the Fourteenth Amendment at the end of the Civil War. Hence, the amendment was invalid in Alabama and other Reconstruction states, and should not be honored by the Fifth Circuit. Cameron adhered to the Tenth Amendment of the US Constitution as the authoritative source for deciding racial segregation cases. Chin and Chin explained that Cameron "considered states' rights 'the bedrock of our constitutional system.'" Cameron and Judge Rives professionally disagreed with one another about state rights. American historian Charles W. Eagles wrote that Rives was one of the judges Cameron thought was "destroying the social order."[17]

After Judge Cameron's fourth stay denying Meredith's admittance to the university, Motley went to US Supreme Court Justice Hugo Black, the justice assigned as the circuit justice for the Fifth Circuit. A circuit justice attends to specific legal applications that may be handled by a single justice rather than requiring the entire Supreme Court to address an issue. Rives had contemplated the possibility of a culture war even before he voted in favor of the equal application of laws to desegregate public transportation in *Browder v. Gayle* (1956). Now he was witnessing the confrontation he suspected might transpire. Both Rives and Black understood the power of prejudice and likely found a reason to communicate about what the *Clarion-Ledger* called the "unprecedented judicial tug-of-war," in which a Mississippi district court judge, a Fifth Circuit judge from the state of Mississippi, and a Fifth Circuit three-judge panel were at an impasse for nearly three months.[18]

Justice Black intervened on September 10, 1962, to void the orders of Judge Cameron. Black wrote that he corroborated his opinion with his brethren on the court, who confirmed that the Fifth Circuit ruling was appropriate. He reinforced that it was highly improbable that the US Supreme Court would review the judgment of the Fifth Circuit's panel of judges. According to law professor Mitchell F. Crusto, Black's opinion "effectively served as a second court order" requiring university officials to enroll Meredith. On Thursday, September 13, as directed by Black with the backing of the other justices on the Supreme Court, Judge Mize filed an order at 5:30 p.m. that prohibited university officials from hindering or interfering with Meredith's admission to the university.[19] The court had temporarily settled the *Meredith* case, but Mississippi governor Barnett continued the fight to keep Meredith from enrolling at the University of Mississippi.

Two hours after Judge Mize filed his order to allow Meredith on campus, on September 13 at 7:30 p.m., Governor Barnett addressed the citizens of Mississippi live on television and radio. Barnett said he would take steps to refuse the federal court order and would work to keep the University of Mississippi, often referred to as "Ole Miss," racially segregated. That moniker hearkened back to slavery as a term that referred to the master's mother or grandmother—the "ole miss"—on the plantation. Any use of the phrase was a public declaration of white supremacy. In his address, Barnett declared, "no school in our state will be integrated while I am your Governor . . . we will not surrender to the evil and illegal forces of tyranny!" Further, he proclaimed, "There can be no real debate on issues for there is no issue beyond the supremacy of the white man." The next day was Friday, the beginning of the weekend on campus, and some white students hanged Meredith in effigy for the first time.[20] The effigies invoked the tradition of lynching and reaffirmed a culture of white supremacy.

Over the next few days, Governor Barnett called law enforcement from across the state of Mississippi to the town of Oxford and signed an executive order threatening to jail any federal agent who interfered with Mississippi state officials. By Wednesday, September 19, there were three hundred law enforcement officers in Oxford, in addition to Mississippi highway patrolmen, county sheriffs, and local policemen. FBI agents were also dispatched to Oxford. Both state and federal personnel were there to prepare for what Claude Sitton of the *New York Times* called "the now-unavoidable clash with federal authorities."[21]

Seeking to preserve the university as a white citadel of learning, Governor Barnett avoided complying with federal court orders to the point of nearly declaring war against the federal government. While US Supreme Court Justice Black had the authority to overrule lower court judges when they challenged the law, only the US attorney general had the authority to stop Barnett from engaging in behaviors that exhibited civil contempt of court. US Attorney General Kennedy had been placing telephone calls to Barnett for several weeks about Meredith's situation. In one of the conversations, author Wright Thompson reported that Barnett told the attorney general, "We have been part of the United States . . . but I don't know whether we are or not." Following a period of silence, Kennedy asked Barnett, "Are you getting out of the union?" Barnett's veiled threat to secede likely caused some alarm in the White House. Greaves sarcastically wrote that Attorney General Kennedy, who was unaware of the deep recalcitrance of the governor and citizens of the state, "appealed for peace and calm." Members of the Mississippi Senate despised the Kennedys.[22]

US Attorney General Kennedy filed a motion in the Fifth Circuit seeking a temporary restraining order against Governor Barnett and other government officials in Mississippi for civil contempt of court. The attorney general alleged that Barnett and other officials in Mississippi had enacted a "policy of massive resistance to the court's orders" in their professional capacity by enlisting various law enforcement agencies across Mississippi to serve in Oxford. Judge Rives and other members of the en banc court entered an order on September 24. Later that day an ancillary action was filed by the United States, alleging that Barnett's actions were causing "immediate and irreparable injury to the United States, consisting of impairment of the integrity of its judicial processes, obstruction of the administration of justice and deprivation of Meredith's declared rights under the Constitution and laws of the United States." The next morning, September 25, the court issued a temporary restraining order in *United States v. Barnett* (hereafter *Barnett*) that prohibited all parties from obstructing the Fifth Circuit order of July 28 and the district court order of September 13, 1962. Undeterred, later that afternoon Barnett blocked Meredith's application for enrollment and denied his registration. The next day, Wednesday, September 26, Meredith again tried to enroll at the university and register for classes. He was turned away by Mississippi lieutenant governor Paul Johnson. By Thursday, in addition to law enforcement in the town of Oxford, a reporter from the *Shreveport Journal* observed "more than 100 police cars stood parked around the gates" of the campus.[23] Judge Rives stayed informed of events on the campus.

On Friday, September 28, 1962, Judge Rives and all the other judges except Judge Cameron were present for the *Barnett* en banc hearing to determine if there was any reason that Governor Barnett should not be held in civil contempt of court for his efforts to obstruct the admission of Meredith to the University of Mississippi. A summons had been issued requiring Barnett to appear that day, but he did not acknowledge receipt of the document.

During the hearing, as the justices tried to determine whether Barnett was aware of the summons, witnesses for the Department of Justice testified that they had mailed and tried to deliver the papers personally, but Barnett had refused them. The court ruled that Barnett's failure to appear negated his right to a defense by lawyers.[24]

Chief Judge Elbert Tuttle did allow John C. Satterfield, former president of the American Bar Association, to appear as amicus curiae for Barnett. According to the Legal Information Institute, amicus curiae generally refers to "a person or group who is not a party to an action, but has a strong interest in the matter" and wishes to file a brief or participate in the argument to influence the outcome of a case. When judges questioned Satterfield about his association with Barnett, Satterfield objected and asked to be sworn in as a witness to Barnett's actions regarding the summons. Judge Rives, for one, overruled Satterfield's objection. Rives was aware of the tactics of delay and denial that Barnett could use to keep *Meredith* in the courts and Meredith out of the University of Mississippi. Rives directed Satterfield to respond as an officer of the court. Satterfield again objected, declining to answer unless he had the status of a participating lawyer. Inquiring about Satterfield's association with Barnett, Rives succinctly replied, "Yes, you may object, but I still ask for an answer." Finally, Satterfield acknowledged that Barnett knew about the court's order to appear even though he had not accepted the summons.[25]

Once again the judges found Governor Barnett in civil contempt of court. The judicial order stated that Barnett must obey the court's directive to stop interfering with Meredith and his case by 11:00 a.m. on Tuesday, October 2, 1962, or he would be arrested and placed in the custody of federal authorities. There were no indications that Barnett would comply with the court order, so Rives and four other judges concluded that Barnett should be assessed a fine of $10,000 per day for as long as he continued to exhibit contempt behavior. The decision was per curiam, although Judges Warren Jones, Walter Gewin, and Griffin Bell, who generally voted conservatively on Civil Rights issues, dissented from the part of the order that imposed a fine on Barnett.[26] The temporary restraining order and daily fine to be imposed reveals the judges' frustration at Barnett's lack of deference to the court.

Chief Judge Tuttle contacted US Assistant Attorney General Burke Marshall to force Barnett to comply. Tuttle explained to law professor Frank T. Read that he talked with Marshall to determine what "can be done by the Court to see that its orders are carried out, and also . . . what can be done by the Executive Department to see that the Court's orders are carried out." Marshall reassured him, "The executive branch . . . will use whatever force, physical force, is required." However, President Kennedy and his brother, the US attorney general, wanted to desegregate the university without using military force. President Kennedy contacted Barnett in an effort to negotiate an end the escalating crisis, but the telephone call did not sway Barnett.[27]

Without a resolution to the crisis, Governor Barnett attended the University of Mississippi Rebels' home football game against the University of Kentucky Wildcats on Saturday, September 29. Silver observed that "the hysteria whipped up in Jackson was unbelievable." At the game, members of the White Citizens Council distributed Confederate flags to people in the stadium. During halftime, Barnett could have "turned the populace aside from its madness," but instead, as journalism professor Kathleen W. Wickham observed, the "stadium lights were dimmed for a candlelight ceremony exalting the 'Southern way of life.'" From center field, the governor delivered his "I Love Mississippi" speech, stating that he would never allow a Black student into the University of Mississippi.[28] Barnett reenergized the crowd in support of state rights in a speech of fewer than twenty words. That night, the people at the game made their states' rights position clear; they did not want Meredith to attend the University of Mississippi. President Kennedy preferred to remain detached from the situation.

President Kennedy was reluctant to get involved in Civil Rights issues and delegated Meredith's racial desegregation dispute to the Justice Department. During the Kennedy era, journalist Jack Bass commented, "Congress was in no mood to pass new civil rights legislation, and the policy of the . . . administration began as a strategy 'to litigate, not legislate.'"[29] At long last, the Mississippi governor and the US attorney general reached an agreement. Meredith would relocate to the University of Mississippi on Sunday evening, September 30, 1962, and he would register for classes the next morning.

Judge Rives had discussions throughout the *Meredith* case with US Attorney General Kennedy. One of Rives's clerks, Lawrence R. Levin, recalled events that Rives had shared with him. In preparation for Meredith's move to campus, Rives talked with Kennedy on the telephone. Rives told him that a strong federal law enforcement presence would be needed to maintain peace on the campus. Kennedy replied that James O. Eastland, a US senator from Mississippi and chair of the US Senate Committee on the Judiciary, had assured him that Governor Barnett would provide adequate Mississippi Highway Patrol protection to support the US marshals during Meredith's registration at the university.[30]

Judge Rives was familiar with Mississippi senator Eastland from Rives's days in politics before being appointed to the Fifth Circuit. Levin said Rives was steeped in Southern politics; he "knew all the politicians, he knew the politics, and he knew how the South worked." Rives anticipated Eastland's potential for further complicating the situation. Brown-Nagin described Eastland as a "wealthy plantation owner" known as much "by the 'trademark' cigar that dangled from his lips" as for "his daily consumption of scotch." He fiercely opposed the *Brown* decisions, which he thought had "destroyed the Constitution." Reporter Mike Wallace, in an interview with Eastland, characterized him as the "Voice of the White South" for his segregationist leadership.[31] Rives knew that Eastland and Governor Barnett would both construct obstacles to stop desegregation on the Mississippi campus.

According to Levin, Judge Rives told US Attorney General Kennedy in one of their conversations that he was familiar with Governor Barnett. Rives told Kennedy that he should not trust Barnett's pledge to Eastland that he would provide enough state police to keep the peace on campus. Levin recalled that Rives emphasized to Kennedy that "he knew the people of Mississippi well and if there was a very strong federal presence there would be no trouble, but if there was not, then the Klan could cause a riot." Vigilante groups had already publicly offered their services to the governor to keep Meredith and federal escorts off campus. For example, the Greenville, Mississippi, *Delta Democrat-Times* reported that William T. Rainach, a leader in the Louisiana Citizens' Council, contacted Barnett to offer their group's assistance. When presented with offers of support, Barnett explained, "I would not invite outside groups because it would make discipline impossible. But I would not tell them not to come." Having delegated the responsibility for university desegregation to the attorney general, the president distanced himself from this situation and seemed to be unaware of the intensity of the mounting conflict. Levin recalled that the attorney general reiterated to Rives that the president trusted Eastland and "was sure the Governor would provide the necessary security" on the University of Mississippi campus when Meredith arrived.[32] Rives had attempted to preempt the potentially impending riot.

On Sunday afternoon, September 30, 1962, an estimated four hundred US marshals and helicopters carrying approximately sixty soldiers arrived in Oxford. As planned, later that day Meredith was moved to campus, nearly unnoticed. While Meredith was settling into his dormitory room in Baxter Hall, word of his presence began to spread throughout campus. Silver commented that students returning to campus could have heard Citizens' Council members appealing to them on car radios to "form a human wall around the mansion" to protect the governor from arrest. Greaves, a deep-dyed segregationist, reflected the attitudes of some of the students. He wrote, "Call it what it is—military occupation, the beginning of our second 'Reconstruction'—and strip our star from the field of the Union, and leave there a torn, mutilated space—[a] fit emblem of our degradation and demise!"[33] Students began to gather outside of the Lyceum. The building, constructed before the Civil War and located at the heart of the university, housed the registrar's office. The presence of the Mississippi Highway Patrol had not quelled students' anger, and the gathering was turning into a riot.

At that time, the town of Oxford was populated by approximately five thousand people. The number of participants involved in the riot continues to be a source of debate. The *Clarion-Ledger* reported that about twenty-five hundred students gathered outside the administration building, "jeering and joking" while US marshals held guard. Bob Carter of the *Delta Democrat-Times* estimated the number at two thousand to four thousand people. As the size of the crowd increased, Judge Rives told Levin that he again contacted US Attorney General Kennedy with a cautionary message to send more federal troops. Despite Rives's warning, Kennedy explained that he could not find adequate federal resources in the Mississippi area. Governor Barnett's segregationist rhetoric surged throughout the public sphere, despite his civil contempt conviction two days earlier for disobeying a court order.[34]

As Sunday evening wore on, the crowd became increasingly unmanageable, as Judge Rives predicted, due to the limited presence of federal law enforcement personnel. The crowd turned into a riot that journalist Dick Gentry called "the last battle of the Civil War." Any person on campus whom students recognized as being an outsider, including journalists and photographers, was threatened and roughed up. Aram Goudsouzian quoted Meredith as hearing shouts of "*We want Meredith! . . . Get a rope! . . . Burn the Kennedys and the niggers!*" People "screamed insults, brandished shotguns, tossed bottles and bricks, and hoisted a Confederate flag atop the pole in the Lyceum Circle." US marshals came under gunfire as members of the crowd emboldened one another. Governor Barnett told President Kennedy that one man had been shot and died. Kennedy was inaccurately informed that the man was a Mississippi Highway Patrol officer. The man who was murdered was actually Paul Guihard, a journalist for Agence France- Presse. He was shot in the back from a distance of about one foot.[35]

Judge Rives would wait no longer for federal action after he learned that a newsman had been shot and killed and that the US marshals guarding Meredith in his dormitory were concerned for his safety. Rives depicted the conversation to Levin. During the confusion after the death of the journalist, Rives again called the US attorney general at the Justice Department, telling him to go to the White House and after he arrived to call Rives back and then put the president on the phone. When President Kennedy returned Rives's call, Rives admonished both the president and the attorney general for failing to provide the level of federal law enforcement directed by the court in preparation for Meredith's admission to the university. Rives then said to the president that it was clear to him that either the governor of Mississippi was in contempt of court for not keeping his word to provide state police, or the president of the United States, whom the attorney general advises on all legal matters, was in contempt of the Fifth Circuit's order to stop Barnett's interference with Meredith's admission to the university.[36]

The *Clarion-Ledger* reported that President Kennedy had previously scheduled a "15-minute television-radio broadcast to the nation at 5:15 p.m. Mississippi time Sunday night" to address the university desegregation crisis. Until that point in his administration, Kennedy was not known for supporting Black citizens' Civil Rights. Rives recalled to Levin that he told the president that if he did not see him on television in the next twenty minutes announcing that he had ordered ten thousand federal troops to restore order, the president would be in contempt of court. President Kennedy told Rives that he was running for reelection and did not want the public to think he acted disrespectfully toward a court of law.[37]

In his television-radio address, President Kennedy quickly mentioned the Fifth Circuit's ruling in *Meredith v. Fair* and said that the US government would support the decision of the court to desegregate the public university. In responding to the violence underway in Mississippi, the president said, "Americans are free, in short, to disagree with the law—but not to disobey it. For in a government of laws and not of men, no man, however prominent or powerful, and no mob, however unruly or boisterous, is entitled to defy a court of law."[38] During the speech Kennedy announced that he had federalized the Mississippi National Guard to enforce the court's order to desegregate the University of Mississippi. Judge Rives placed legitimate judicial pressure on the president, but the federal response did not come soon enough.

The rioting lasted well into Sunday night, resulting in damage to property and injury to people. A United Press International reporter on the scene observed that by Monday morning "at least 15 automobiles lay smashed . . . campus was strewn with broken glass, soft drink bottles, sticks and small boulders that were used by the rioters. Some windows in the Lyceum building . . . were smashed." Two men had been killed. The number of people injured or arrested remains in dispute. The *Delta Democrat-Times* reported at least seventy-five people were wounded and a dozen arrested. Journalist Susan M. Weill wrote that 160 US marshals sustained injuries. The *Clarion-Ledger* reported vandalism that resulted in the arrest of approximately 215 people, of which fewer than one-third were students at the university. Ultimately, only twenty-five people were charged, and all others were released. There were no convictions following the riot.[39] The events were probably seen by Governor Barnett as an unavoidable representation of the will of the citizens of Mississippi; the events were probably seen by Rives as totally unnecessary.

The agreement between the US attorney general and Mississippi Governor Barnett was to have Meredith registered and begin classes on Monday morning, October 1. At 8:15 a.m., registrar Robert B. Ellis enrolled Meredith as a student in the Department of Political Science of the College of Liberal Arts. At 9:00 a.m., with a US marshal on each side of him, Meredith walked to an American history class amid epithets shouted by white students.[40] Barnett was relentless in his effort to keep higher education racially segregated in Mississippi and was angry that federal troops had been dispatched to the town of Oxford.

The next day, Tuesday, October 2, Governor Barnett was scheduled to appear before an en banc hearing of the Fifth Circuit in New Orleans to address civil contempt charges against him by the US attorney general for refusing to admit Meredith to the University of Mississippi. On the one hand, Barnett did not want to concede that the court had jurisdiction over him, which would make him appear as if he had acquiesced to the government's desegregation position, so he did not appear. On the other hand, he wanted to be represented, so he sent lawyers to argue on his behalf. Judge Rives served as the presiding judge and as the hearing began, he notified Barnett's counsel that some of the other judges on the Fifth Circuit were hearing arguments in other cases. Rives had, however, polled all judges by telephone, except for Cameron who was too ill to attend the hearing, and they agreed to delay action in Barnett's contempt charge until the Fifth Circuit could convene en banc.[41] Barnett's lawyers reported to him that the court had thus delayed the hearing on his contempt charge for ten days.

After the delay, Judge Rives and the other judges assembled in New Orleans on Friday, October 12 to address the civil contempt charge against Governor Barnett. Barnett's lawyer, Charles Clark, appeared, but once again, his client did not. During the hearing, lawyers for the Justice Department acknowledged that the governor had allowed Meredith to enter campus and register as a student. However, according to the *New York Times*, the governor "failed to order the police to abide by the court's order to maintain law and order around the university and to ensure that Meredith was treated like all other students." Bass recounted that in defending Barnett, Clark declared that "Barnett would comply with the court's order unless he felt that compliance would be inconsistent with his duties and obligations as governor of Mississippi." Judge John R. Brown remarked to Clark, "That is impossible, isn't it, . . . [that Barnett] can determine when it is that a court's order is to be obeyed?" Judge Wisdom's linguistic theme of *Alice in Wonderland*, introduced in the January 1962 *Meredith v. Fair* decision, was picked up by Rives. During the hearing, Bass reported that Rives exclaimed, "We have indeed entered the field of Alice in Wonderland where language doesn't mean what it says when you tell me . . . that the governor will comply . . . to the best of . . . [his] ability."[42] Rives's statement exhibited his growing irritation at Barnett's lack of respect for the court.

Newspaper journalists latched on to Judge Rives's *Alice in Wonderland* metaphor and included it in the Saturday, October 13, morning newspapers. Over the weekend, people found time to write letters to Rives about his comment. The letters he received resemble what must have been Alice's experience. One segregationist writer interpreted Rives to mean that the language of desegregation made no sense and "at least one Federal Judge has at long last seen the light." Another person wrote, "You spoke a truth that is apparent to the man in the street. For the past several years, federal judges are guilty of saying that the Constitution means one thing when there is absolutely no basis for such a decision." The writer continued, "I shall be happy to buy you the best Stetson hat in your city if you will show me just one federal law that the people of Mississippi violated about integration."[43] While that letter was courteous in its mockery, some messages were filled with vitriol. Rives continued to receive crank letters throughout the *Barnett* case expressing hatred toward him. Meanwhile, a decision on the governor's contempt of court hearing could not wait.

On Monday, October 15, Chief Judge Tuttle distributed a draft en banc decision in *Barnett* to his colleagues, in which the Fifth Circuit adopted the Justice Department's recommendations. He wrote that Governor Barnett had not yet purged himself of the civil contempt charge, had not complied fully with the Court's previous rulings, and would be arrested on October 24.[44] The decision delayed Barnett's arrest, which would allow some time for him to potentially appeal the decision to the US Supreme Court. However, Tuttle's draft was now met with strong objections from several Fifth Circuit judges, who recommended changes in the document.

Between the September 25 contempt order and the October 2, 1962, hearing, Barnett had complied with the most serious aspect of the court's orders—Meredith was, in fact, enrolled and attending classes. Judges Rives and Brown thought such compliance made his arrest unnecessary. They thought that "further sanctions would yield no practical value." Judge Walter P. Gewin, a conservative judge, thought that Meredith's registration at the university minimized Barnett's "unrepentant attitude" and "the court should not attempt to humiliate the state's chief executive." Wisdom did not agree with any of the other judges' proposals. Law professor Joel William Friedman wrote that Judge Wisdom perceived the "imprecise language contained in each of these drafts was likely to generate insuperable interpretive problems."[45] The extraordinary events of the past few weeks had transpired quickly, and another en banc meeting would need to be held to determine whether to arrest and fine Barnett for his actions.

In the meantime, Governor Barnett did not let up in his resistance to desegregating the university. As the *Cullman Times Democrat* reported, when the

University of Mississippi dean of students directed students to comply with the court's order "to halt the harassment" of Meredith, Barnett appointed a legal committee "to protect students' rights on campus." Barnett argued that following "the invasion and occupation of the university campus by Federal troops," reports emerged that "white students' constitutional rights to freedom of speech and freedom of assembly are also being threatened." The *Anniston Star* quoted Barnett, who carefully insisted that his claims were based on "what I believe to be the law" and were not to be interpreted as actions in contempt of the court.[46]

A few days later, on Friday, October 19, Chief Judge Tuttle and Judges Rives, Jones, Brown, Wisdom, Gewin, and Griffin Bell met in New Orleans. The meeting was not productive. By now, six judges had made their decisions on whether Governor Barnett should be held in civil contempt of court. No longer open to persuasion, they simply restated their previous positions. Among the seven judges, the vote was three to three; Rives remained undecided. He first sided with Tuttle, Brown, and Wisdom, who thought Barnett should be jailed for his extended acts of civil contempt. Then between the original appeal and the judicial hearing, Rives shifted his thinking to side with Gewin, Jones, and Bell, who insisted that since Barnett allowed Meredith to enroll at the university, continuing the contempt of court charge would serve no good end. At that point, Bass wrote, Rives agreed that "imprisonment was unnecessary in light of Barnett's eventual acquiescence" to Meredith's enrollment at the University of Mississippi. Rives continued to interrogate legal sources to seek his own understanding of the law. He appreciated suggestions from others, but now that everyone had decisively declared their position he did not have anyone who would open-mindedly reason with him about the situation. Rives's indecisiveness troubled his colleagues. Wisdom and Brown, two of Rives's allies, were disappointed by his reversals.[47] Until Rives reached a conclusion, the judges were at a stalemate in writing the decision.

Military politics changed the United States on Monday, October 22, 1962, three days after the entire group of Fifth Circuit judges met in New Orleans to determine the consequences of Mississippi Governor Barnett's actions. The Soviet Union had created a defensive military buildup in Cuba, increasing their expansion to the level of offensive military capabilities, which presented a potential threat to the United States. As a result, the US military dispatched a fleet to blockade the incoming Soviet arms shipments to Cuba. That evening, President Kennedy delivered a televised address in which he confirmed the presence of "a series of offensive missile sites" in Cuba that allowed the Soviets to have "nuclear strike capability against the Western Hemisphere."[48] This event shaped the international political background in which the Fifth

Circuit court operated. As the country faced a possible nuclear threat, Judge Rives stayed abreast of the developments and focused on the judicial work ahead of him.

On October 24, five days after the court met in New Orleans, Judge Rives wrote a letter to his six colleagues self-consciously confessing that he "continued to 'flip and flop' between the two camps" on *Barnett*. After reviewing a draft of Judge Jones's opinion supported by Judges Bell and Gewin, Rives considered what an arrest with fines would mean to Barnett's supporters. Rives wrote that he had finally concluded that sanctions were no longer needed to secure compliance by Governor Barnett since Meredith was now attending the University of Mississippi. The next day, October 25, Chief Judge Tuttle sent a letter to members of the court, suggesting that they delay any official decision or action in the *Barnett* case due to the unstable nature of international events. In his letter Tuttle wrote that he thought the court should provide "a great degree of solidarity behind the efforts of the President" and that an order to imprison a governor would threaten that show of democratic solidarity. Further, Tuttle expressed that Judge Wisdom was willing to redraft the opinion for the civil contempt hearing to construct an argument that would hopefully generate a greater than one-vote majority between the seven judges.[49]

On November 5, 1962, Judge Rives offered an alternative solution to Governor Barnett's contempt of court charge. Rives was a member of the en banc panel that found Barnett in contempt six weeks earlier. Rives reminded Chief Judge Tuttle in a letter that the court could order the incarceration of a person found guilty of civil contempt of court. Rives suggested that although the imprisonment of a governor for a charge of civil contempt might be unrealistic, there was enough evidence of defiance by Barnett to warrant a charge of criminal contempt of court. In civil contempt, the court seeks to induce future compliance with the court's orders, and guilt is established by a preponderance of the evidence. The purpose of charging someone with criminal contempt, South Carolina Supreme Court Justice E. C. Burnett explained, is "to preserve the court's authority" and to punish the person "for disobedience of its orders"; guilt is established when evidence points beyond a reasonable doubt. A civil charge may escalate to criminal status depending on the level of willfulness associated with the person's behavior. The court may charge a person with civil or criminal contempt of court for the same act. Rives wrote that one course of action could be to terminate the civil proceedings and instead issue a citation to Barnett for criminal contempt.[50]

In Judge Rives's letter to Chief Judge Tuttle, he pointed out "the practical consequences of further contempt proceedings" against Governor Barnett, noting that additional proceedings would be "a serious step" that raised two important questions. First, the Fifth Circuit would have to determine if Barnett would be entitled to a jury trial for criminal contempt. Second, if a jury trial was appropriate, "would the original three-member panel conduct the trial, or would that responsibility belong to the [en banc] circuit court?"[51] Although there were challenges with Rives's proposal, his initiative appears to be driven in part by his desire to find a resolution that would be just and also to offer the possibility of breaking the entrenched positions of the judges.

Judge Rives worked to maintain a positive relationship with each of his brethren, recalled Levin, "whether they agreed with each other philosophically or not." Maintaining professional civil relationships allowed the members of the Fifth Circuit to sustain their collegiality and potentially reach greater consensus on complex issues. Rives wrote to his colleagues, Levin continued, to offer suggestions when the judges were "in a snarl" and tried to help clarify complex legal matters. The most critical aspect for Rives was that the judges "must get . . . [the lawsuits] decided right." On opinions he wrote on behalf of the court, he regularly included the request that other judges contact him with "any suggestions or criticisms." Rives was generally able to help negotiate philosophical differences between the judges. He worked to reason through cases in a way that would hold defendants accountable and also be acceptable to various judicial orientations.[52] The *Barnett* case was one of many times when Rives sought to hold a party to the litigation accountable without creating further discontent among the judges.

Judge Rives's suggestion of closing the civil contempt charge and opening a criminal contempt charge against Governor Barnett was favored by five of his six colleagues. Only Judge Gewin, the most conservative judge on Civil Rights issues in Judge Cameron's absence, refused to be persuaded as to the merits of filing a criminal contempt charge against Barnett. A majority decision was written closing off the civil contempt charge, and on December 21, 1962, the Justice Department applied for an order charging Barnett with criminal contempt of court in line with the Fifth Circuit's judgment. The order required Barnett to appear in the US Court of Appeals for the Fifth Circuit on February 8, 1963, to show why he should not be held in criminal contempt for the charge of obstructing Meredith's admission to the University of Mississippi. But before Barnett's hearing on a criminal contempt charge, the Fifth Circuit sought clarification from the US Supreme Court as to whether Barnett had a constitutional or statutory right to a jury trial.

Amid the monthslong *Barnett* contempt case, *Alabama Journal* reporter Ray Jenkins talked with Judge Rives about the charge against Governor Barnett. Rives repeated his conversation with Jenkins to Bass. Rives and Jenkins discussed what kind of sentence the governor might get if he were convicted. Rives thought, "perhaps three years or so in a federal prison." Rives recalled that Jenkins was surprised at the length of the suggested sentence. Rives, a man who left Tulane University after his first year and appreciated what a university education meant and the opportunities a degree could offer, replied, "You sentence a man to three years for stealing a car, and here's a man who almost destroyed a university."[53] Rives's speculation on a possible sentence was conjecture; the US Supreme Court had yet to respond to the Fifth Circuit's request for information.

Many Alabamians had supported Mississippi Governor Barnett since the beginning of the *Meredith v. Fair* case in 1961. On November 19, 1962, columnist W. J. Mahoney Jr. wrote in the *Alabama Journal*, "The 'Fifth US Circuit Court of Appeals' at New Orleans 'has directed the Justice Department to bring criminal contempt charges' against the Governor and Lieutenant Governor of Mississippi." Mahoney referred to the judges as "assorted scalawags" and continued, "If Dick Rives's conduct at the [original] hearing . . . of the Barnett case is as it was described to me by an alleged eye-witness (who said that he openly solicited advice from one side and turned his back while Mississippi's lawyers spoke), then he is guilty of conduct that would put to shame any self-respecting police-court judge." Mahoney obliquely threatened Rives, writing that he "need feel no personal nervousness about residing in Montgomery," and attempted to insult him by writing that "his side . . . [was] not the White Southerner's side." Mahoney also attacked the judiciary as "guilty of every proved criminal act against the persons of the opposition."[54] This was not the first time Rives experienced attacks on his character arising from his involvement in racial desegregation cases.

The next day, November 20, Rives wrote to the president of the Alabama State Bar, James Carter. Rives defended himself against Mahoney's accusations, writing, "The reference to my conduct is utterly false. Being discourteous to lawyers certainly is not one of my many faults." Rives referred Carter to Governor Barnett's lead counsel, Charles Clark, a lawyer of "the highest ethical standards." Carter replied to Rives, stating, "I have known, and observed, you too long, as a lawyer, judge, and gentleman, ever to be impressed that you would under any circumstances be discourteous or inattentive, on or off the bench." Rives also forwarded a copy of the information to former Chief Judge Hutcheson, who replied, "You have been right in the middle of all this stuff." He praised Rives's composure, observing that Rives had been "in the place of, and acquitted . . . [himself] like, old St. Paul when he said, 'I have fought a good fight, I have kept the faith,' and I certainly feel sure that you will not let attacks of this kind disturb you."[55] Rives undoubtedly felt professionally supported after reading Hutcheson's letter, yet the public pressure for him to stop ruling in favor of desegregation, which would apply the law equally to all citizens, was unyielding.

Nearly one and a half years later, on April 6, 1964, the US Supreme Court delivered an answer to the questions posed by the Fifth Circuit regarding potential criminal contempt procedures against Governor Barnett. In a five to four vote, the justices held that "the alleged contemners are not entitled to a jury as a matter of [constitutional or statutory] right."[56] Therefore, the Fifth Circuit judges needed to determine whether to prosecute the governor of Mississippi for his original civil contempt of court charge or for a criminal contempt of court charge for interfering with Meredith's admission to the university.

The Fifth Circuit judges did not meet until 1965 to address Governor Barnett's contempt of court charge. Over two years had passed since the September 25, 1962, civil contempt judgment and the November 15, 1962, criminal contempt discussion. In the interim, Judge Cameron had died, Judge Hutcheson had retired, and their positions were still vacant.[57] Barnett was no longer governor, although he remained politically active in Mississippi. Changes in court personnel had occurred, but the judges were once again split on the vote.

After the meeting, Judges Jones, Gewin, and Bell recommended terminating the contempt proceedings. Judges Tuttle, Brown, and Wisdom vigorously opposed closing the file. Judge Rives once again remained the swing vote. Friedman explained that following a careful review of a letter from Judge Jones, Rives agreed that there was an unlikely chance that another person would commit a similar act of contempt. Therefore, as Jones wrote, "prosecuting Barnett no longer would serve any useful purpose" and may induce even greater public resentment of the courts by segregationists. In addition, Barnett had substantially complied with the court order by allowing Meredith to enter the university and enroll as a student there until he graduated with his bachelor of arts degree in August 1963.[58]

Even if Barnett were to have a jury trial, Judge Rives explained to Bass, he thought that no jury would unanimously convict Barnett of criminal contempt (regardless of the evidence) under the jury selection procedures in Mississippi. Further, the maximum sentence for a criminal contempt charge was six months in jail or a $500 fine. Such a minimal sentence "would be nothing more than a slap on the wrist," potentially making Barnett a martyr and destroying the moderate political element in Mississippi. Rives continued, "Barnett was as racist as a man could get, but . . . [further contempt hearings] would accomplish nothing. It was better to let him go." On May 5, 1965, the Fifth Circuit judges voted four to three to allow the civil contempt judgments to stand but did not impose sanctions. Accordingly, the judges dismissed the criminal contempt proceeding against Barnett. Rives drafted an unsigned majority opinion, which declared that because of Barnett's "substantial compliance with this Court's orders," as well as the improbability of further contempt, there was no reason to continue criminal contempt proceedings. Although Barnett would not be punished, Rives told Levin that nothing might upset Barnett more as a politician than "being consigned to the ashbin of history."[59]

The government's judicial, legislative, and executive branches were all drawn into the University of Mississippi racial desegregation conflict. The case started in the courts, led to a campus riot involving US military troops, involved private meetings with President Kennedy and US Attorney General Kennedy, moved President Kennedy to shift his public position on Civil Rights, and concluded with contempt proceedings against Barnett.

Rives was involved in racial desegregation lawsuits in the context of higher education before *Brown I*. An early case, *Tureaud*, illustrates how the courts defined procedural requirements for desegregation cases. Rives's dissent pointed to the LDF's earlier cases of *Sweatt* and *McLaurin*, the importance of district judges in making decisions, and his support of the US Constitution's supremacy clause over state rights. His behind-the-scenes consultations with Judge Grooms about *Lucy* prompted him to move from a gradualist position on requiring compliance in higher education racial education to a more active stance. In addition, his contribution to the *Meredith* and *Barnett* decisions reveals his political awareness and judicial influence in swaying the executive branch of government to actively engage in constructing a democracy for all citizens. While Rives's discernment in *Barnett* took longer than his colleagues would have liked with the workload facing them, his willingness to use a dialectical method to form his decision allowed him to conclude what would be the best course of action for the development of democracy—emerging as a reason that his opinions continue to remain well-respected.

The constitutional principle of equality addressed in *Brown* and other legal cases required that district and circuit judges extend racial desegregation throughout higher education. The US Supreme Court intended the *Brown* orders to be the law of the land. Judges in federal district and circuit courts continued to disagree about desegregation, and the US Supreme Court regularly declined to review race cases decided by the Fifth Circuit. That decision by the justices, by extension, also judicially shielded Black citizens who wanted to exercise their right to vote in elections from elected state representatives who discriminated against them.

Figure 1. Rives family, ca. 1896: (*left to right*) Alice Bloodworth Taylor Rives, Richard Taylor Rives (baby on lap), William Gordon Rives, Janie Louise Rives, Ellen Rives, Tom Christopher Rives, William Henry Rives Jr. Photograph courtesy of Ginny Granade.

Figure 2. Richard T. Rives, high school portrait, ca. 1911. Photograph courtesy of Ginny Granade.

Figure 3. First Sergeant Richard T. Rives and fellow soldiers at the mobilization camp in Montgomery, Alabama, before World War I, 1916: (*front row, left to right*) Richard Taylor Rives, N. W. L. Thompson, Monroe Meek. (*back row, left to right*): Bray (?), Turner Barrett (?), Colin Carter. Photograph (Q91497) courtesy of the Alabama Department of Archives and History.

Figure 4. Richard T. Rives, ca. 1925. Photograph courtesy of Ginny Granade

Figure 5. Richard T. Rives Jr. with his father, Richard T. Rives, ca. 1945. Photograph courtesy of Ginny Granade.

Figure 6. Richard T. Rives shaking hands with Judge Leon C. McCord the day Rives was sworn in as a judge of the US Court of Appeals for the Fifth Circuit. Rives's wife, Jessie, is standing between the men. Photograph (Q91498) courtesy of the Alabama Department of Archives and History, Montgomery, Alabama.

Figure 7. *Browder v. Gayle* (1956) panel: (*left to right*) Judges Richard T. Rives, Frank M. Johnson, and Seybourn H. Lynne. *Birmingham News*, May 12, 1956. Unknown photographer.

Figure 8. *Shuttlesworth v. Birmingham Board of Education* (1958) panel: (*left to right*) Judges Seybourn Lynne, Richard Rives, and H. H. Grooms, Historic Images (website), April 5, 1958. Unknown photographer.

Figure 9. Judges on the US Court of Appeals for the Fifth Circuit: (*front row, left to right*) Judge Richard T. Rives, Joseph C. Hutcheson Jr., and Elbert P. Tuttle; (*back row, left to right*) Warren L. Jones, Benjamin F. Cameron, John R. Brown, and John M. Wisdom, May 9, 1959. Photograph (Q94078) courtesy of the Alabama Department of Archives and History.

5

Adjudicating Representation in State Legislatures

Making Strides in Reapportionment

In the 1960s South, racism undergirded political discourse. The white elite were unwilling to share political power with Black citizens. As a result, the Alabama state legislature had not been redistricted since the 1901 Alabama constitution was passed. Redistricting relies on decennial US Census data to include approximately the same number of people within the boundaries of each voting district. This ensures that each citizen has an equal opportunity to influence the outcome of an election. Reapportionment relies on the population in each district to determine the number of representatives allotted to that district for different political offices. These two processes are often collectively referred to as "reapportionment." Lack of reapportionment placed all Alabama citizens, white and Black, in a position of being inequitably represented in the state legislature. White legislators—who frequently proclaimed state rights in response to the perceived tyranny of the federal government—often employed their own tyrannical strategies within the state to retain their power.[1] Their strategic inaction was one means used to prevent any representation of Black citizens in the state legislature, even if they were able to gain the right to vote.

The Alabama constitution requires a bicameral state legislature. In the 1960s, the House of Representatives had 106 representatives: each of Alabama's sixty-seven counties had one representative, and the remaining thirty-nine seats were to be distributed among counties with the largest populations. The state senate, one-third the size of the house, included thirty-five senators who each represented a district. State demographics had changed dramatically between 1900 and 1960. Journalist Dewey W. English Jr. wrote that in 1900 less than 12 percent of the state's population lived in urban areas, which had increased to nearly 52 percent in 1960. For the first time, in 1960 the number of Alabamians living in urban areas surpassed the entire rural population. As economic opportunities arose in urban areas, the number of Alabamians employed in agriculture lessened as they found employment in urban manufacturing and trades. The Student Nonviolent Coordinating Committee (SNCC) reported that between 1950–1960, although the state's population of Black citizens in Alabama stayed nearly the same, those living in urban areas of Alabama increased by over 20 percent, while those living in rural areas was down by almost 20 percent. At the same time, white citizens living in urban areas of Alabama increased by nearly 40 percent, while those living in rural areas of Alabama were down over 10 percent. This gave rural citizens greater representation in the legislature and allowed their representatives to gain a larger portion of state taxpayer funds for infrastructure, such as roads, bridges, and schools.[2]

Judge Richard T. Rives's knowledge of state politics provided indispensable background information as he considered cases that involved issues of citizens' representation in the legislature. In 1962, Rives was assigned to hear *Sims v. Frink* (hereafter *Frink*), a case filed against the Alabama secretary of state related to inequities in Alabama voting procedures. *Frink* remained in the courts for over a decade in various iterations. Over time, that case would become attached to *Reynolds v. Sims* (1964), *Sims v. Baggett* (1965), and *Sims v. Amos* (1972). Each of these cases related to the reapportionment of the Alabama legislature and was heard by the same judicial panel of Circuit Judge Rives and District Judges Frank M. Johnson and Daniel H. Thomas. While these cases were not overtly racial, they would reveal racial connotations that echoed the inequalities first remedied by the US Supreme Court in *Brown I* and *II*.[3]

As a lawyer in Montgomery, Rives was actively involved in politics, often campaigning statewide on behalf of his friends Hugo Black, Bibb Graves, and Lister Hill, as they prepared for elections in Alabama. As a judge, Rives was not far removed from the political scene although, as the Hatch Act of 1939 requires, he could no longer be politically active. He was aware of the voting patterns of citizens in various districts, as well as inequities in the system that emerged as the population shifted. In 1960, *Gomillion v. Lightfoot* (1960) was heard by the US Supreme Court, which ruled that the Alabama legislature's replacement of Tuskegee's square voting district boundaries with a twenty-eight-sided figure—essentially excluding all Black citizens from the city limits of Tuskegee—was unconstitutional. During Rives's time on the bench, the Civil Rights Movement had brought about a change in the social climate of the state. Some white citizens in Alabama, opposed to the *Brown I* and *II* decisions and angry at the repercussions the case brought to the state, sought to energize resistance to desegregation.[4]

One way Southerners raised opposition to racial equality was to promote a grassroots interest in the centennial anniversary of Alabama's involvement in the Civil War. The state entered the war in March 1861 and historian Robert J. Cook wrote that centennial events "peaked in the spring and early summer of 1961." The events were designed to raise "the [white] public's awareness that the southern way of life was more threatened at this time than it had been since the 1860s and 1870s." The election of George Wallace as governor revealed "that a majority of whites in the state were still determined to maintain segregation at apparently any cost." Alabama's promotion of Confederate "idealism and bravery," Cook explained, served to increase the unity of white citizens and to impede any attack against Confederate values.[5]

The social context favoring racial segregation had little changed despite the US Supreme Court justices' decisions, Judge Rives's *Browder v. Gayle* (1956) decision to end the Montgomery bus protest, and the passage of the Civil Rights Act of 1960. Cook wrote, "Most Alabama blacks . . . [were] still routinely humiliated and disfranchised by Jim Crow regulations and practices."[6] As a result, Black university students began to engage in Civil Rights activities across the South. Student sit-ins at the Woolworth Department Store in Greensboro, North Carolina, began in February 1960. That April, Ella Baker invited student Civil Rights activists to Shaw University in Raleigh, North Carolina, where together they founded SNCC. Other protests were occurring across the country, but even as students pushed for racial equality, political affairs in Alabama were still controlled by white legislators.

In July 1961, M. O. Sims, a white taxpaying voter residing in Birmingham, Alabama, filed a lawsuit in Judge Johnson's federal district court to correct inequities of representation in the state legislature. Sims claimed he was underrepresented due to the inaccurate boundaries that delineated voting districts. The defendants in the lawsuit were Bettye Frink, who served as secretary of state for Alabama, and other Alabama state officials who were charged with responsibilities in connection with elections.[7] Johnson contacted Fifth Circuit Chief Judge Elbert P. Tuttle to request the appointment of a three-judge panel to hear the case.

In September 1961, Chief Judge Tuttle named Judges Rives, Johnson, and Thomas to hear *Frink*. Law professor Tony A. Freyer commented that the question of law to be decided by the panel would center on "whether the state's failure to reapportion its electoral districts in keeping with population shifts . . . violated the Fourteenth Amendment's Equal Protection Clause." With centennial events winding down, Rives may have reflected on history: when Alabama rejoined the Union following the Civil War, much more was required than soldiers simply putting down arms against one another. Reformation of the United States required pulling the states together under a single rule of law that brought justice to all citizens. The population in Jefferson County, where Sims resided, had substantially increased since 1901, yet the number of legislative representatives remained the same. The *Frink* case resembled *Baker v. Carr*, a lawsuit recently adjudicated in the US District Court for the Middle District of Tennessee.[8]

In the 1959 *Baker* case, the plaintiffs' lawyers argued that the lack of redistricting in Tennessee led to legislative distribution that was "grossly disproportionate to the distribution of population" in the state: 37 percent of Tennessee citizens of voting age controlled over 60 percent of the members of the state senate. Reapportionment issues had come before various courts on numerous occasions, but the judges identified the subject as a legislative matter. As such, the case was inappropriate for hearing by the judicial branch of government: "With the plaintiffs' argument that the legislature of Tennessee is guilty of a clear violation of the state constitution and of the rights of the plaintiffs the Court entirely agrees. . . . But even so the remedy in this situation clearly does not lie with the courts. It has long been recognized and is accepted doctrine that there are indeed some rights guaranteed by the Constitution for the violation of which the courts cannot give redress." When Judge Rives was assigned to *Frink* in 1961, the *Baker* decision was still on appeal to the US Supreme Court. The Fifth Circuit delayed Alabama's reapportionment case until the justices ruled in *Baker*.

The "reapportionment revolution" of the 1960s, according to *Redistricting in the South*, was so-named due to "a series of Supreme Court decisions that established the principle of 'one-man-one-vote' in the districting of congressional and state legislative seats." This activism occurred in response to the nationwide malapportionment of state legislatures. In 1946 the US Supreme Court justices allowed malapportionment in *Colegrove v. Green*, which permitted state legislatures to ignore redistricting and reapportionment obligations without any consequences.[9]

Colegrove was filed on Fourteenth Amendment grounds against state officials in Illinois over the distorted congressional districts that remained following the 1940 Census. That court order, written over fifteen years earlier, already signaled disagreement between justices on the relationship between the judicial and political branches of government. In a fractured vote, a decision written by Justice Felix Frankfurter stated that the US Supreme Court would not enter what he described as a "political thicket" by considering claims that state legislatures were malapportioned. Frankfurter wrote for himself and Justices Stanley Reed and Harold Burton: "We are of the opinion that the appellants ask of this Court what is beyond its competence to grant." The divided Court saw "the remedy for unfairness" in *Colegrove* as lying in "state legislatures that will apportion properly," or in "the ample powers of Congress."

Rives's friend, Justice Hugo Black from Alabama, dissented in *Colegrove*, perhaps thinking of legislators with whom he was familiar in his home state. Black attributed malapportionment to "willful legislative discrimination," which would not end with the Supreme Court's order that state legislatures should act. But now the justices agreed to hear an appeal of *Baker*, questioning whether they should overrule *Colegrove*.[10]

The US Supreme Court justices who would hear *Baker* differed from those who had heard the *Colegrove* appeal in 1946. The plaintiff's lawyers asked the justices to determine whether the issue of defining state electoral district boundaries was justiciable. Justiciability addresses whether the courts can rule on an issue or whether an issue falls within the domain of another branch of government. On March 26, 1962, the Supreme Court justices decided in a six to two vote that state redistricting was, in fact, a controversy that fell within the oversight of the courts. Justice William Brennan Jr. wrote for the majority.

In *Baker* (1962), Justice Brennan stated that the Fourteenth Amendment's equal protection clause was valid ground for reapportionment lawsuits seeking to ensure that each citizen's vote carries equal weight. Brennan relied on US Supreme Court decisions dating back to 1901, stating, "An unbroken line of our precedents sustains the federal courts' jurisdiction of the subject matter of federal constitutional claims of this nature." He wrote that the plaintiffs were seeking "protection of a political right"—a "guaranty of a republican form of government"—which is not the same as "a political question." A citizen's political right to ensure the continuation of a republican form of government is "within the federal judicial power" of the courts when members of the legislative branch of a state government are unable or unwilling to do so. *Baker* led to *Gray v. Sanders* (1963), in which Supreme Court Justice William O. Douglas wrote that "the conception of political equality" in our constitutional documents "can mean only one thing—one person, one vote."[11] These decisions required the federal courts to enforce fair legislative redistricting plans.

Ray Jenkins of the *Montgomery Advertiser* perceived *Baker* to be the most significant legal step in racial desegregation since the *Brown I* (1954) decision. In *Baker*, the US Supreme Court opened the lower federal courts to lawsuits and possible appeals from voters seeking to redraw election maps. Many white Southerners' reaction to the case was similar to their response to the *Brown I* decision: in their view, the Court created a needless conflict between two amendments to the US Constitution. National attention to the equal protection clause of the Fourteenth Amendment resulted, some Alabamians argued, in a devaluation of the Tenth Amendment's focus on states' rights. Citizens who privileged the Tenth Amendment, which was included in the original Bill of Rights, sought to curb federal authority over how the state of Alabama conducted reapportionment.[12]

The US Supreme Court's *Baker* decision allowed Sims's lawsuit concerning the reapportionment of representatives and senators in the Alabama legislature to move forward in federal court. Unfortunately, as Jenkins wrote, in the 165 pages in which the *Baker* decision was contained, "there is not the slightest suggestion as to what the lower [federal district and circuit] courts are supposed to do once they determine that a State Legislature is illegally apportioned." The situation was comparable to that following *Brown II*, when justices delegated what the *Alabama Journal* called the "implementation and enforcement" of their school desegregation order to the lower federal courts.[13] As in the *Browder* (1956) bus desegregation case, the judges were in legally uncharted territory.

Some Southerners believed that Circuit Judge Rives and other federal judges were out of control. To them, the judges were meddling in political matters by confusing the responsibilities of the legislative branch of government with the duties of the judicial branch of government. The editors of the *Montgomery Advertiser* opined that court actions were increasingly perceived by states' righters in Alabama as "dictatorial" in demanding that citizens of the state surrender their constitutional rights. In a letter to the editor published in the *Montgomery Advertiser*, John Peavy Wright summarized the view held by some citizens in Alabama: no court possesses the right to reapportion any state legislature, "Richard Rives to the contrary notwithstanding."[14] The invisible yet palpable wall of hatred toward the judiciary continued to intensify. Rives recognized that if state legislators did not act to reapportion the state legislature, the courts would be required to do so—and that could potentially lead to an even greater public resentment of the judiciary.

Judge Rives had been on the receiving end of ostracism in the press and in daily life since he signed the *Browder* court order six years earlier. Many Alabamians identified Rives as the reason their way of life was changing. Rives told one of his former clerks that some people who worked in the same building in which his office was housed did not even make eye contact with him when they passed in the hallways each day. Historian John M. Spivack wrote that Rives's "forgiving nature" allowed him to overlook the shunning to which people subjected him.[15] If people's behavior bothered Rives, he did not often acknowledge it to others.

Clifford and Virginia Durr were friends of the Rives family in Montgomery. In her autobiography, Virginia recalled that "living in Montgomery [during that time] was like living in the midst of a storm. You never knew what was going to happen." A native of Alabama, she described people who lived in the city: these were "just ordinary Montgomery people" who had become filled with "hatred . . . bigotry and meanness." As a result, several white racial desegregationists were forced to leave Montgomery, and others willingly left because of their views. Judges Rives and Johnson stayed to follow their judicial consciences. As legal historian Liva Baker wrote, a "new coalition" was emerging in the Fifth Circuit, "an alliance of men committed to no longer reading the Fourteenth Amendment the way Southern law schools had traditionally taught it since Plessy, but in the revolutionary way the US Supreme Court had read it in May of 1954."[16] With growing support from some other judges, Rives did not back down from his principles.

Sims's lawsuit against Alabama secretary of state Frink would be the first test of principles outlined by US Supreme Court justices in *Baker* and *Gray*. As *Frink* gained publicity, the case attracted the attention of other citizens who found themselves in a similar position to Sims. Their votes were also underrepresented in the Alabama legislature. As a result, the case file began to expand. Plaintiffs Sims and the Jefferson County Democratic Campaign Committee, an intervenor who entered the lawsuit, filed an injunction requesting the postponement of the May 1962 Alabama primary elections until either the legislature or the court determined reapportionment procedures. A hearing was scheduled for April 14, 1962, to determine if the May 1962 elections would be deferred.[17] Despite the public's interest in the case, the panel of Judges Rives, Johnson, and Thomas was not willing to be hurried by election deadlines.

Judge Johnson told one of Judge Rives's clerks, Lawrence R. Levin, that the *Frink* decisions were authored primarily by Rives. Johnson remarked that no other judge could have written that opinion. Rives was highly knowledgeable about Alabama politics and knew how to address the needs of the court to allow both sides to be fairly represented. To emphasize the importance of citizens' involvement in a democracy while at the same time following the parameters of the law, the court ordered that the Alabama legislature must have a "reasonable but prompt opportunity" to comply with the Alabama constitution by redistricting and reapportioning itself. The decree required representatives in the state legislature to do their duty: "It is necessary that any action taken by the legislature comply with constitutional standards, and it is important that such standards be met not halfheartedly but fully" since the legislators could not alter their proposed plan until after the 1970 Census. The court also advised the governor to call a special session of the state legislature urging representatives to accomplish their responsibilities related to reapportionment.[18]

The April 14, 1962, *Frink* opinion attempted to retain a separation between the state legislature and the federal court. In the per curiam decision, the judges recommended that legislators follow a strategy proposed by US Supreme Court Justice Thomas C. Clark in *Baker*: "One plan might be to start with the existing assembly districts, consolidate some of them, and award the seats thus released to those counties suffering the most egregious discrimination." As if to forewarn the legislators not to modify the Alabama constitution to conform to the current malapportionment practices, the judges cited Section 284 in their decision: "Representation in the legislature shall be based upon population, and such basis of representation shall not be changed by constitutional amendments."[19] The order required the Alabama Democratic primary elections to be held in May as scheduled.

The court slated a rehearing of *Frink* for July 16, 1962. The three-month interim would allow the legislature a reasonable amount of time to propose reapportionment plans that could be implemented before the November election. If the legislature was unable to do so, the court would have still time to generate a plan before the general election in November. The July deadline would also keep the lawsuit under the court's jurisdiction and stall any immediate appeal to the US Supreme Court since that court typically recesses from late June/early July until early October each year. Judges Rives, Johnson, and Thomas encouraged legislators to approve a constitutional plan for redistricting, writing that after so doing, "the duty resting on us will be at an end and the case can be dismissed."[20] The judges likely hoped that the incentive of dismissing the case would persuade legislators to take the court's order seriously and, potentially, redirect some of the increasing public scrutiny of the courts toward the state legislature.

Alabama governor John M. Patterson called a special session of the state legislature to address reapportionment. Tom Gordon of the *Birmingham News* called Patterson "one of Alabama's most outspoken segregationists," who did not want the public to see the legislative branch of government as subservient to the judicial branch. Patterson delayed a month before convening the legislators. He finally announced that legislators would begin their work in special session on June 12, 1962. The *Birmingham Post Herald* observed that Patterson opened the Alabama Legislature with a statement, declaring, "as long as I am Governor of Alabama, no Federal Court will be permitted to set the policies of this state." He denounced the court's decision as "dictatorial" and "unwarranted." Patterson stated that the federal government had "no intention to cease and desist" and he urged legislators to "beat the federals to the draw" by passing a plan to meet the court's deadline. Bob Ingram of the *Montgomery Advertiser-Journal*, reported that Patterson continued, "In the interest of conserving time and money, I urge you to consider meeting in legislative session five consecutive days each week until we work out a solution."[21] In response to that appeal, members of the state legislature agreed to meet in special session for the five weeks that remained until the July 16 deadline set by the court. As likely expected by the judges, legislators, and general public, the meetings were filled with animosity.

The legislators argued among themselves in daily sessions. Ingram wrote, "Just when it appeared that either the House or Senate had finally agreed on a reapportionment route to follow there would be an abrupt change of sentiment." Representatives proposed numerous bills that then fell short of the votes required to pass as legislation. Historian J. Douglas Smith quoted Charles Morgan, Sims's lawyer in *Frink*, who confirmed the meetings were "a fight for self-preservation on behalf of the men who sit in those legislative halls." The legislators changed coalitions and reversed positions, depending in part on the personal impact that the reapportionment proposal would have on each man. If a proposal better protected a legislator's seat, he might change his coalition and vote in favor of it. Ingram characterized the sessions as follows: "Black Belters [were] fighting Black Belters, and by the same token, North Alabama legislators were at each other's throats."[22] The legislature was at a standstill.

Arthur Osgoode of the *Montgomery Advertiser* reported that on Friday, June 29, 1962, with patience worn thin and tempers at their peak, Senate Speaker Virgis M. Ashworth called for "a voice vote on one of the bills" and amid a cacophony, he "ruled that the resolution [to adjourn for the July 4 holiday] had been carried." Their long weekend would be, Ingram wrote, "a paid vacation without a roll call vote," and citizens would not know how each district representative voted. With this confusing ending, both chambers adjourned in observance of the holiday, resuming work on Thursday, July 5 at 12:00 noon.[23] Upon return, only a few working days remained until reapportionment plans were due to the federal court.

The Monday, July 16 hearing was rapidly approaching, but legislators had not yet agreed on a reapportionment plan to submit to the court. Following a month of heated debate, the House and the Senate each adopted a different plan for the Alabama legislature, designed to take effect for the 1966 elections. The Senate plan was referred to as the Sixty-Seven-Senator Amendment to the state constitution. If voters did not pass the amendment—or if the court found the amendment was not in compliance with the Fourteenth Amendment—then a backup plan, the Crawford-Webb Act, proposed by the house of representatives, would become effective. Prior to the court hearing, the Crawford-Webb Act was signed into law by Governor Patterson. The act would alter only a few of the districts and would be effective, law professor Doug Linder explained, "until the legislature is reapportioned according to law." The act gave no specific guidelines or timeline for reapportionment.[24]

While the legislature struggled with reapportionment plans, Judge Rives sought out the opinion of Fifth Circuit Chief Judge Tuttle. Tuttle and Rives were nearly always in agreement—but not in the *Frink* case. One of Rives's law clerks explained that following *Baker*, "Judge Rives was of the opinion that . . . [reapportionment] applied to both the House of Representatives and to the Senate of the state legislature. And Judge Tuttle didn't agree." Tuttle's position was that the US Senate was malapportioned, and federal judges could not ask state senates to do something that the US Senate was unwilling to do. The clerk shared that Rives insisted to Tuttle that the inclusion of Black citizens in the political system "is about a democratic revolution, this is not about being consistent."[25] If a state has a malapportioned senate, there would be no value in having a state house of representatives apportioned by population. Such a configuration would continue the problem of the rural areas of the South controlling the state legislatures and preventing the passage of progressive legislation.

On July 16, Judges Rives, Johnson, and Thomas met at 10:00 a.m. to rehear the *Frink* case. In addition to the legislative plans for redistricting and reapportionment, various parties had filed a series of motions with the court. The lawsuit originally included fourteen Birmingham business leaders. Intervenors included the Jefferson County Democratic Campaign Committee, four city officials from Mobile, and the United Steelworkers of America union. The courtroom overflowed with people who were both curious and concerned about how electoral districts might be reapportioned.[26] All parties, including the general public, were waiting for the case to be heard.

The fervor that the legislature had been in for the past few weeks was matched by a heat wave outside. Temperatures in the mid to high nineties and high humidity had gripped Alabama since July 7 with no end in sight. Before beginning the oral arguments, the *Anniston Star* reported that Judge Rives, who directed the court proceedings, cautioned the lawyers, "We want light and not heat." Alluding to the long holiday that legislators took in the middle of the special legislative session against the advice of Governor Patterson and the court, Rives instructed, "There is no use to make a Fourth of July speech."[27] Rives's admonishment revealed his frustration with legislators for their lack of serious attention to generating an acceptable redistricting and reapportionment plan.

Judge Rives divided the arguments related to the reapportionment of voting districts into two categories. First, the court would need to address whether the two parts of the legislative plan met the standards of the US Constitution. Second, if neither proposal met the conditions of the Fourteenth Amendment, the judges would need to determine what action to take. In writing for the *Montgomery Advertiser*, Osgoode explained that Rives "was chiefly interested in a reapportionment plan which conformed to constitutional requirements, whether or not it became effective immediately."[28] Citizens need to be represented equally in a state's legislative body.

Osgoode recounted the court proceedings in the July 17 issue of the *Montgomery Advertiser*. State legislators had appointed Senator Douglas Webb of Escambia County to explain and defend the assembly's proposals to the court. Webb began, "Our problem was not one simply of math or geography as some people insist upon but that there exists in our state today a very real and very serious personality conflict between some of the contiguous counties of Alabama." To obtain the necessary votes to pass legislation, he continued, "an attempt had to be made, if possible, to avoid as many of these personality conflicts as possible." For example, he observed that representatives of Bibb County were "'extremely reluctant' to be connected with Shelby County in a senatorial district." In addition, "no counties wanted Lowndes . . . [or] Macon County in their district." According to statistics compiled by SNCC for 1960, Lowndes and Macon Counties, both rural counties, were two of the three counties in Alabama in which Black citizens numbered over 80 percent of the population.[29] Legislators' hesitance to affiliate with these counties was due, in part, to a lower tax base, relationships between officials in those counties and other counties, and a general history of racism.

Listening to State Senator Webb's argument, Osgoode wrote that Judge Rives asked how legislators had managed to pass the sixty-seven senator plan. Webb replied, "I think the legislators felt the odds were that the . . . [voters] would turn it down anyway," as they had twice before. Webb's unspoken message, Smith wrote, was that malapportionment served "as a cornerstone of white supremacy in the South." In Morgan's rebuttal on behalf of the plaintiffs, he referred to Webb's comments as "evidence that the present legislature was incapable of passing a constitutional plan of apportionment."[30] The legislature was at an impasse.

An *Alabama Journal* article stated that during the hearing "the Court apologized" for having to intervene in legislative affairs. Judge Rives had acknowledged the difficulty of state legislators working to apportion a new legislature due to "the complexity of the task and the political and selfish struggle inevitable in the distribution of power where there is rivalry and competition between agriculture and industry." Rives expressed that the court had "no desire," nor was it the court's responsibility, "to criticize the present or previous Legislatures for any failure to heed the clear mandate of both the Constitution of the United States and the Constitution of Alabama." Clarke Stallworth wrote in the *Birmingham Post-Herald* that Rives told the defendants "nothing the court did would reflect [poorly] on action taken by the Legislature . . . he knew it did the best it could."[31] Rives's lack of criticism disclosed a separation between his professional responsibility as a judge and his personal associations with individual legislators and citizens of his home state.

The hearing took the entire day. At the end of the session, Osgoode reported Judge Rives as saying, "the court will not be able to render an immediate decision." Rives expressed that the judges would need time to study the evidence, but he also recognized the need for an early decision. He explained that the court would dedicate "practically its entire time" to the case "because we realize the paramount importance of it" and promised all parties a prompt court ruling.[32]

From Judge Rives's involvement in politics as a lawyer, he would have understood that some politicians were deeply invested in maintaining generational traditions that supported a narrative of racial inequality. He likely empathized with some people's internal and external conflict about what may have been seen as a too-rapidly changing culture. Even though he was perhaps sympathetic of the perspective of rural legislators, Rives could not support that view as a federal judge. His position required him to determine how to give the US Constitution meaning in that historical moment. In so doing, the court had to determine how social and moral questions such as legislative redistricting (which in Alabama directly involved race relations) would be practically implemented.

The *Frink* decision was announced on July 21, 1962, in a twenty-eight-page per curiam order. The opinion acknowledged that the judges "took note of the delicacy of upsetting Federal and State relations." After *Baker*, the court could no longer accept delay and inaction. Jenkins covered the story for the *Alabama Journal*, quoting Judge Rives: "This Court has reached the conclusion that neither the '67-Senator Amendment,' nor the 'Crawford-Webb Act' meets the necessary constitutional requirements." The decision was straightforward: "We find that each of the legislative acts, when considered as a whole, is so obviously discriminatory, arbitrary and irrational that it becomes unnecessary to pursue a detailed development of each of the relevant factors of the test." In addition to violating tenets of the US Constitution, both proposals delayed any change in representation until after the 1966 election, which was also unacceptable to the court.[33]

The court ultimately revised the state legislature by adopting portions of both the Sixty-Seven-Senator Amendment and the Crawford-Webb Act, even though both plans were individually considered to be, according to a draft of the decree, "void, invalid and ineffective." The Alabama House of Representatives would remain at 106 members and be temporarily reapportioned according to relevant sections in the Sixty-Seven-Senator plan. The Alabama Senate would stay at thirty-five members and be temporarily reapportioned according to relevant portions of the Crawford-Webb Act, which allowed larger urban counties to attain some advantage over their current representation. In their decision, the judges hoped these "moderate steps" would be enough "to break the strangle hold" in the Alabama Legislature. Legislators could then provide what the court called a "true reapportionment" of the legislature after the November 1962 general election. If the legislators still did not propose an acceptable plan, the judges wrote in *Frink* that they would be required to take "very drastic reapportionment" steps to relieve the plaintiffs and others similarly situated from being denied equal protection of the laws.[34]

Alabama was the first state to require the modification of electoral district boundaries and reapportionment of representatives following the US Supreme Court ruling in *Baker*, which provided that legislative reapportionment was a justiciable issue. Tom Johnson, reporting for the *Memphis Commercial-Appeal*, revealed that one of the three judges confided to him following *Frink* that in states not required by their state constitution to reapportion after each national Census, the ruling would have been different. The same judge "expressed fears from time to time that the United States Supreme Court would not uphold the Alabama decision since he feared that the decision went too far" in addressing responsibilities of the state legislature.[35] The continued internal deliberations of that anonymous judge, who may have been Rives, reflected that he was still privately working through how to implement equitable redistricting and reapportionment if he and his colleagues were ultimately required to do so.

Soon after the *Frink* decision ordered a temporary redistricting arrangement for the Alabama legislature to be used in the 1962 elections, Alabama county probate judges Bernard A. Reynolds and Frank Pearce (rather than the state) contested the decision. *Frink* was thus escalated to the US Supreme Court as *Reynolds v. Sims*. The probate judges asserted through their lawyers that the federal court plan continued to violate the US Constitution.[36] The Supreme Court heard the appeal on November 13, 1963.

As the US Supreme Court justices were finishing a discussion related to *Reynolds* on November 22, Smith revealed that Chief Justice Earl Warren was informed and shared with his colleagues that President John F. Kennedy had been shot and killed in Dallas, Texas. Vice President Lyndon B. Johnson, a Texan and member of the US Congress since 1949, would become the next president of the United States. Before Johnson became vice president, political scientist Irving Bernstein wrote that the general public viewed him as "a gas and oil, anti-civil rights senator" who opposed every Civil Rights proposal in Congress from 1937–1957. Political historian Keith M. Finley recalled that in public Johnson was avowedly anti–Civil Rights when representing his constituents. However, in private, Johnson "illustrated a commitment to racial tolerance and to many aspects of" President Franklin Delano Roosevelt's New Deal philosophy. After becoming president, Johnson had the platform to expand Civil Rights initiatives nationwide. He began to use the phrase "Great

Society" to refer to a set of proposed reforms that involved enhanced medical care (such as Medicare and Medicaid), improved education, housing, transportation, equal rights, and voting rights for all citizens.[37] At the time, a majority of US Supreme Court justices held a perspective similar to the incoming president.

The US Supreme Court decision in *Reynolds* became public on June 15, 1964. The justices affirmed the lower court's decision in *Frink*, written by Judge Rives. That early decision, the *Alabama Journal* newspaper reported, "took the longest step of any of the Federal courts considering reapportionment cases when it decreed new legislative seat assignments."[38]

Two weeks after the US Supreme Court's decision in *Reynolds*, Judge Thomas received a motion from the Birmingham business leaders who initially filed *Frink*. The motion requested that the three-judge panel expedite implementation of the *Frink* decision to allow time to prepare for fall elections. Shortly after the plaintiffs' filing, lawyers for the state requested that additional time be granted for the legislature to act. On June 30, Thomas wrote to Judges Rives and Johnson, "I am sure that the plaintiffs have a right to file this supplemental pleading. I have not thoroughly studied the Supreme Court's affirmance; however, I realize it will require further action on our part. I would appreciate ideas from both of you as to when we should again take up this matter."[39] Rives responded to Thomas's letter before the end of the week.

Judge Rives's July 3 reply to Judges Johnson and Thomas indicated that he perceived the plaintiffs' motion and the defendants' answer to be "premature" in the process. He conjectured that "the <u>mandate</u> from the Supreme Court's decision of June 15" had probably not even been received by the appellants before their appeal was written and submitted. He wrote, "The parties are stirring about a good deal, I believe, purely as political propaganda." Rives read the plaintiffs' motion as a legal tactic used by politicians to stall redistricting and reapportionment of the state legislature. He reiterated that the Alabama legislature should be given the opportunity to generate "a constitutionally valid, permanent apportionment scheme." Rives suggested that after the US Supreme Court *Reynolds* decree was published and received, the district court might enter an order to permit supplemental pleadings to be filed while reinforcing the judges' intention for the legislature to determine the protocol for reapportionment. In addition, he methodically suggested steps the judges might take: "In brief, we should take the earliest opportunity to spell out in plain and simple language what is required to be enacted as a permanent apportionment plan. We should make that so plain and definite that the Legislature will have no excuse in submitting to us any plan except one under which both the House and the Senate are reapportioned according to population as nearly as practicable, even though that may, and doubtless will, require ignoring a number of the restrictions contained in the State Constitution."[40] Rives was willing to give the legislators additional time to adhere to the US Constitution, despite both parties anxiously pushing to close the lawsuit given the upcoming elections. The legislators needed time to change a process that was older than many of the representatives themselves.

Judge Rives accepted that after two years of inaction, the chances were small that the state legislature would arrive at a suitable proposal for redistricting and reapportionment. In his July 3, 1964, letter to Judges Johnson and Thomas, Rives recommended that Johnson, in whose court the case was filed, "should take the initiative in preparing any proposed order" for the judges to consider. Rives's work style was courteous and negotiable, open to persuasion. Rives wrote, "Of course, these are merely tentative views and if either of you have different ideas, or if the parties convince us otherwise, we can proceed in some different manner."[41] The other two judges agreed with Rives's suggestions and, as the state legislature remained gridlocked, Johnson went to work on a proposal.

The justices affirmed the *Frink* ruling of July 21, 1962, in their "one person, one vote" ruling in *Gray v. Sanders* (1963), and in their 1964 *Wesberry v. Sanders* order requiring members of the US House of Representatives to be chosen from districts approximately equal in population. Chief Justice Warren delivered the *Reynolds* opinion, which would necessitate a thoroughgoing full redistricting and reapportionment for both houses of the Alabama legislature to meet the US constitutional requirements. The justices voted eight to one that regardless of the state constitution, "the seats in both Houses of a bicameral state legislature must . . . be apportioned on a population basis." Each citizen has a right to "substantially equal legislative representation . . . in a State regardless of where they reside."[42] The US Supreme Court once again upheld a decision by Judge Rives, much to the annoyance of some white Southerners.

Judge Rives was targeted for his professional desegregation decisions with one definitive act of indecency, which was atrocious when compared to the everyday slights and snubs he experienced. Rives recalled to law professor Frank T. Read that the grave of his son, Richard T. Rives Jr., who died in 1949 due to an automobile accident, was "desecrated. We found it painted red and garbage thrown on his grave and that kind of thing. Although the sexton was compelled to report the incident to the police, there was not much publicity." During the Cold War between the United States and the USSR, the color red often symbolized the political and economic ideology of communism, in contrast to the capitalist ideology of the United States. People who supported state rights often referred to the Civil Rights Movement and the 1964 Civil Rights Act, which "prohibits discrimination on the basis of race, color, religion, sex or national origin," as a Communist conspiracy. Some white citizens saw Rives as colluding with Communists to implement racial equality, which would eliminate socioeconomic classes and undermine American democracy—handing a slap in the face to hardworking white citizens. A later reference to the desecration of the younger Rives's grave appeared in a *Time* magazine article titled "Courts: The Fascinating and Frenetic Fifth." In response, Rives wrote a letter to the magazine's editor. He did not ascribe the act of violence to be representative of the citizens of Alabama but attributed it to a specific malicious person, "Alabamian or not," who was "mentally ill." John Daniel Reaves, one of Rives's clerks, shared that the judge recognized that while citizens of Alabama held a variety of different opinions, he thought they were fair-minded people.[43] Rives cared about the community in which he had spent his life.

Judge Rives was financially generous, regardless of how some people treated him. This kindness may have stemmed from his religious faith, his expanding definition of human equality, or a desire to help others, white or Black. For example, one of Rives's former clerks shared that each year in June, when the peach crop in Chilton County, Alabama, would ripen, the peach farmers loaded up their trucks with peaches. Farmers would drive to Montgomery, park their trucks on the side of the road, and sell the peaches. Rives would leave home early in the morning, find a farmer, and buy every peach on his truck. He would pay the farmer, and after securing a promise not to tell anyone who purchased the peaches, Rives would give the person some extra money to deliver peaches to people in all of the nursing homes in Montgomery. The clerk also disclosed that Rives anonymously had Christmas gifts delivered to the children of the manual laborers who worked in the federal courthouse. He was steeped in the ways of the South yet had been internally transformed by the racial awareness his son helped him cultivate. The personal attacks may have bothered Rives but Neil T. Bradley, one of his clerks, said Rives told him that the people who ostracized him should feel the loss, not him.[44] Rives's family had established themselves in Alabama three generations before his birth. As he matured, Rives discarded the Southern views held by his mother and adopted the newer Southern opinions held by his father, from whom he learned to treat each person fairly as an individual.

During the years Judge Rives judicially implemented racial desegregation, he retained an identification with Southerners. Law professors Frank T. Read and Lucy S. McGough perceived that Rives had "a keen appreciation of the realities confronting the southern 'fair-minded' man caught between his conscience and the necessity of making a livelihood dependent upon the goodwill of the general community."[45] Rives shared with Read an example of a young lawyer who once approached him. The lawyer conveyed his desire to openly support the federal courts while public outrage against the judiciary was at its peak. Rives said, "I told him, 'Well if I were in your position, I would not. Now you are just committing suicide so far as your law practice is concerned, and we don't have to have that. We are protected by life tenure. We are going on and doing our job anyhow. I appreciate your position, but I frankly don't think you should do it. You don't owe that much sacrifice to come out and almost destroy your practice,' which he would have done, I think."[46] Rives's position protected him in ways that other people's livelihoods did not.

Professionally, Judge Rives provided a symbolic physical target for people who disagreed with the legal system and had lost trust in the courts, especially as desegregation rulings changed the public sphere. He was a foil for how race functioned in society during this time and came to signify a changing culture, which some Southerners found unacceptable. In return, he recognized that in an evolving democracy, at times the judiciary would be a necessary vanguard to guide people in their thinking and acting.

As judicial decisions on reapportionment moved ahead, legislators continued to struggle. On April 5, 1965, the *Anniston Star* reported that the Middle District of Alabama Court would follow the 15 percent rule identified in *Toombs v. Fortson*, a case decided in the Northern District of Georgia federal court four days earlier. The decision required that "in apportioning voting districts, . . . [district boundaries] must, in the final analysis, all wind up within 15 per cent of each other in population totals." While the rule was perceived as straightforward, the politics for achieving that statistic were not. The newspaper reported that the task challenged even the best politicians in doing what legislators "were legally and morally bound to do." Senators would propose bills, filibuster, and following a failed vote, adjourn.[47]

On July 27, 1965, with nine days remaining in the annual session of the Alabama legislature, the House and Senate still needed to be reapportioned. The court had previously stipulated that both chambers of the legislature were required to file proposals by August 23. Bettye Frink's term as Alabama secretary of state had expired and Agnes Baggett was next elected to that position. The 1962 *Frink* decision had served as a temporary solution, and a lawsuit captioned *Sims v. Baggett* (hereafter *Baggett*) was recently entered into the judicial system. Judge Rives set a pretrial hearing for August 25 at 10:00 a.m. in Judge Johnson's chambers. Then another demographic consideration was added into the mix: on August 6, the Voting Rights Act of 1965 was passed by the US Congress. The act required that the issue of race be incorporated into redistricting and reapportionment plans.[48]

At the Wednesday, August 25, 1965, short pretrial hearing on *Baggett*, the *Selma Times-Journal* reported that presiding Judge Rives "pointed out . . . that the court will insist on reapportionment of both houses" and not simply with "reshuffling of the Senate alone" as proposed by the Alabama legislature. After the hearing, Governor Wallace convened a special session of the legislature to begin Thursday, September 9. The session would open with Wallace delivering a televised speech in front of legislators at the Alabama state capitol building at 7:00 p.m. The *Anniston Star* stated that given this legislative effort, as well as requirements issued in the recently passed 1965 Voting Rights Act, Rives allowed attorneys additional time to submit their proposed reapportionment plans. He required concise briefs that would assure equal representation in the state legislature to be submitted no later than Monday, September 13.[49]

With the 1965 Alabama legislative session coming to a close, members of the state legislature quickly considered nine reapportionment proposals in the Senate and eleven in the House, each intentionally designed to dilute the influence that Black citizens could have on political discourse. Ingram wrote that Governor Wallace's staff members examined each of the redistricting plans and concluded that "all would create one or more districts in which Negroes would outnumber whites." The *Selma Times-Journal* reported that a proposal widely recognized as the White Supremacy Bill was gaining support in the Senate. Lieutenant Governor James Allen explained the bill as meaning that each county with a majority of Black citizens would be placed "in districts where the electorate is predominantly white." Ingram of the *Montgomery Advertiser* opined, "It is no secret that one of the features some senators found most attractive about this plan is that [the large districts almost guarantee] . . . that no Negroes would be elected to the senate any time in the near future. There is a white majority in all of the congressional districts, and since candidates for the senate would have to run in the entire district, Negro aspirants would be at a disadvantage. If smaller districts should be created, such as now exist, it is very probable that one or more Negroes might be elected to the senate."[50] Alabama legislators struggled with various configurations that would meet the 15 percent rule and stop Black citizens from being able to influence political outcomes.

As suggested by Judge Rives in July 1964, Judge Johnson had begun to prepare the first draft of a constitutional reapportionment plan. In constructing the proposal, he considered population as well as geographic and economic matters. On September 8, 1965, he submitted a draft to his two colleagues on the panel for their input: "This represents the best I have been able to come up with as far as the Senate is concerned. I have an open mind, and if you have any suggested changes, or an altogether different plan, I will, if it comes nearer equalizing the representation of the various areas, be happy to change or withdraw the plan as now proposed." Rives reviewed Johnson's plan and jotted a note to himself, "Do not like Frank's Senate Plan." Rives's working draft of an alternate apportionment plan reveals his thinking: "nine counties have half the population of the state. The only way I think that you will be able to get a fair reapportionment is by division of counties into total population; but I do not think this is practical." The challenge was daunting and necessarily time-consuming. Jonathan R. Harkavy, a clerk for Rives, explained that Rives was "very intense" when he worked and allowed nothing other than a family matter to disrupt him. On the one hand, whatever solution the court could find would receive what the *Alabama Journal* called an "indignant outcry" from legislators.[51] On the other hand, the legislators who would likely protest the loudest were members who did not fulfill their responsibility as stated in the Alabama constitution.

As the September 13, 1965, deadline for parties to submit briefs in *Baggett* neared, Alabama legislators passed bills to reapportion both houses and submitted their proposals to the court. In addition, several parties bypassed the legislative body and submitted potential reapportionment plans directly to the court. Johnson compiled information that he determined to be appropriate for consideration and forwarded the documents to Judges Rives and Thomas.[52]

Judges Rives, Johnson, and Thomas met to hear testimony in *Baggett* regarding legislators' progress on their court order for reapportionment on September 17 at 10:00 a.m. During the hearing, Rives listened to the representatives' proposed plans. He questioned the legislators' logic in their redistricting proposal for the State House of Representatives. For example, he inquired about the representatives' reasoning for putting Macon County in a district with Elmore and Tallapoosa Counties. Macon County was the only county in the state with Black citizens elected to city and county political offices. Both Elmore and Tallapoosa Counties had predominantly white populations. Columnist Rex Thomas wrote that lawyer McLean Pitts, an "unabashed segregationist" from Selma who held political influence, "questioned the wisdom of going into the racial issue." Since the case was initially filed before the 1965 Voting Rights Act was passed, Pitts asked the court to set aside the issue of race "until there is evidence of gerrymandering because of race."[53] The State House of Representatives still did not have a plan that met US constitutional requirements. The hearing lasted for over two hours and ended without any indication of how the judges might rule.

On September 28, Judge Thomas wrote to Judges Johnson and Rives about *Baggett*. Thomas explained that he and Rives had spoken and agreed upon a revision to Johnson's reapportionment plan. Prompting movement in the case, on September 30, Rives replied to Thomas that the state legislature had failed to reapportion both houses in accordance with the US Constitution, and the "time has now arrived" for the court to act.[54] With offices in the same building, Rives likely collaborated with Johnson to develop an equitable plan for the House of Representatives that included race as a demographic consideration.

On Monday, October 2, 1965, the court ruled in *Baggett*. The eighteen-page per curiam decree was accompanied by a twenty-six-page opinion explaining the judges' findings. Levin recalled that Rives once again took the lead on writing the per curiam decision. The court ultimately accepted the legislators' plan for reapportioning the State Senate but found that the proposal for reapportioning the State House of Representatives exhibited "discrimination" and was in violation of "equal protection of the law accorded" in the Fourteenth Amendment.[55]

Commenting on the legislature's proposal, the judges stated in *Baggett*, "It is apparent that the framers of the Constitution had at least two purposes in mind: First, to prevent gerrymandering, and second, to insure compact geographic districts with legislators attuned to local problems." The court's decision was highly critical of redistricting proposals that would prevent the election of Black representatives to offices in counties populated predominantly by Black citizens. The decision concluded that the house redistricting plan "adopted by the all-white Alabama Legislature was not conceived in a vacuum. If this Court ignores the long history of racial discrimination in Alabama, it will prove that justice is both blind and deaf." Referring to district boundaries that placed Macon County with Tallapoosa and Elmore Counties, the court held that such action was intended "for the sole purpose" of locking Black citizens out of representation in the House. The decision continued, "Historically, counties have been the voting unit, but suddenly we find without any apparent reason a number of counties that are entitled to their own representatives on a population basis aggregated, turning Negro majorities into minorities. It would be unfortunate if Alabama's Negroes were to find, just as they were about to achieve the right to vote, that that right had been abridged by racial gerrymandering." Citing the US Supreme Court's 1939 decision in *Lane v. Wilson*, a case in which justices found that discriminatory treatment resulted from electoral legislation in Oklahoma, the *Baggett* decision declared, "What the Constitution forbids is 'discrimination,' 'sophisticated as well as simple-minded.'" Following *Baggett*, the State Senate would be reapportioned by the legislators' plan, and for a second time the judges' plan would reapportion the State House. The new configuration would take effect for the 1966 election and remain in place until the state legislature had time to redistrict after the 1970 US Census.[56]

Following the census, but before the Alabama legislature could meet in their regular session to address reapportionment, Judges Rives, Thomas, and Johnson heard several new reapportionment cases filed against the state of Alabama. The first case, *Nixon v. Brewer*, was filed in January 1970 to contest the 1965 reapportionment decision in *Baggett* and demand that the Alabama legislature reapportion the governing body as required by state law. Judges

Rives, Johnson, and Thomas determined that *Nixon* was not filed "within a reasonable time" following *Baggett* and that any further court action would be inappropriate. However, the complaint was not dismissed because "the evidence offered in support of the plaintiffs' claims . . . makes out a strong case for the consideration of the Legislature of Alabama."[57]

A second case, *Sims v. Amos*, was filed against Mabel Sanders Amos, the new Alabama secretary of state, for her connection to the election of Alabama legislators. The district court consolidated *Sims v. Amos* with *Nixon* and a similar case by J. Elbert Peters—all petitioning the court to reapportion the state legislature. In the 1972 *Amos* decision, the court adopted the plaintiffs' plan, a computer-drawn proposal "based on enumeration districts of the US Census Bureau rather than on county or precinct lines."[58] State officials immediately attacked the court's decision.

Governor Wallace supported Alabama attorney general Bill Baxley in filing an appeal of the district court's order to the US Supreme Court in a 1974 lawsuit captioned *Wallace v. Sims.* The US Supreme Court upheld, without comment, the district court's per curiam ruling in *Sims v. Amos.*[59] The federal courts had implemented plans to redistrict and reapportion the Alabama legislature for the third, but not the final, time.

The *Brown II* decision, which required public officials to exercise deliberate speed in revamping education, opened the door for Southerners to drag their feet in desegregating the public sphere, including the reapportionment of state legislatures. While *Frink* was initially filed by white Birmingham business leaders who contested the representation of rural and urban interests in the state legislature, the case exposed a deeper conflict about race in Alabama. Legislators in the former Confederate state actively resisted overhauling the state government's system of representation in the legislature, exercising filibusters and recesses during the tenure of three different secretaries of state. Serving on panels that heard cases related to reapportionment, Judge Rives privileged the rights of citizens over the manufactured rush of election deadlines. He respected the separation of powers at the state and federal levels yet recognized the importance of the US Constitution as the preeminent document that guides federal court decisions. After the US Supreme Court's ruling in *Baker*, which required the judicial branch of government to reapportion state legislatures if a state legislature failed to act, the general public came to view the court as a deeply partisan and political institution.

Judge Rives modeled a constructive response to the criticism he received from members of his community. When people directed hate toward him for doing his judicial duty, he understood that such behavior was not entirely propagated by personal hatred toward him but was, at least partially, a response to cultural change. To those who viewed Rives's life from a distance, the death of his son and the ostracism he felt from people with whom he had participated in Montgomery's civic life had brought about in him a demeanor of quietude and self-containment. Historian John A. Salmond wrote that Clifford Durr thought Rives "upheld the law fearlessly and faced the ostracism and hatred of his former colleagues at the Alabama bar for so doing." Rives's point of view was regularly supported by the US Supreme Court, who agreed with his sound judgment. Federal courts continue to rely on rulings in reapportionment cases decided by Judges Rives, Thomas, and Johnson to require equity in the apportionment of legislators representing voting districts. Rives could not have foreseen that rulings he wrote on the representation of citizens in state legislatures would be expanded by the US Supreme Court into a nationwide decree following *Wallace*.[60]

6

Addressing State-Sanctioned White Supremacy in Elections

Refuting Discrimination against Black Voters

The suppression of Black voters in Alabama dates back to the formation of the state in December 1819. The portion of the Alabama Constitution of 1819 relevant to voting rights begins, "Every white male person . . . shall be deemed a qualified elector." After the Civil War, Congress ratified the Fifteenth Amendment to the US Constitution, which assured all citizens that their right "to vote shall not be denied or abridged by the United States or by any State on account of race, color, or previous condition of servitude." Large numbers of Black citizens secured the right to exercise their vote in that Reconstruction amendment and elected representatives to stand for them in the state legislature. Some white citizens were furious that elections would be open to Black citizens who could, theoretically, change state laws that upheld white supremacy.[1]

During Reconstruction (1865–1874) white citizens in Alabama clamped down on the potential voting power of Black citizens, often by engaging in election fraud to secure their desired outcome. White officials participated in practices that the Birmingham *Age-Herald* wrote included "the strongest and most flagrant measures of bribery" to gain the cooperation of white citizens who worked at polling places. The practice was commonly accepted, as indicated in a letter to the editor of the *Montgomery Advertiser*. General C. M. Shelley reinforced approval of the system by announcing that "ministers of the gospel" endorsed stuffing the ballot box to maintain white supremacy.[2] Many white citizens turned a blind eye to the fraud and quietly accepted the behavior as part of the political process. They may have feared repercussions for speaking out or perhaps accepted dishonesty as a suitable means to maintain white supremacy.

The conservative wing of the Alabama Democratic Party firmly controlled state politics in 1900. Politicians identified a solution to eliminating fraudulent elections and maintaining white supremacy. If they could reduce or eliminate voting by Black citizens, historian Edwin C. Bridges wrote, "white Alabamians could then resume honest elections among themselves." To disfranchise Black citizens, in 1900 the Alabama State Democratic Executive Committee passed the formal Democratic pledge, which stated, "Resolved, That it is hereby understood and declared that no white man in Alabama shall be disenfranchised for want of property, education, or any other cause, except the commission of a crime." Democrats followed a strict strategy of support for states' rights, while also reminding audiences that the political party would disfranchise only Black citizens.[3]

According to political scientist William H. Stewart, a principal purpose for revising the state constitution in 1901 was "to make sure that governing Alabama would be the business of white men only, especially white men from the southern areas of the state where human slavery had been most prominent before the Civil War." Alabama voters approved the new state constitution, which required a voter applicant to pay a cumulative poll tax, to demonstrate literacy or to own $500 in property, to document a two-year residency requirement, and to provide evidence of gainful employment for the prior year, in order to register to vote. Another provision in the state constitution disfranchised citizens convicted of a list of crimes, including misdemeanors. The inclusion of this provision addressed behaviors perceived to be committed more often by Black citizens than white citizens. The revisions were designed, as Sarah A. Warren wrote in the Encyclopedia of Alabama, to "enshrine white supremacy" in Alabama.[4]

William H. Rives Jr. (1854–1922), Judge Rives's father, was a longstanding member of the Montgomery County Democratic Party. For numerous years he served as the representative of Ward 4 of the City of Montgomery. When Rives was six years old, his father served as secretary of the Montgomery Democratic Executive Committee. One of the committee's responsibilities was to establish voting procedures in the county. Members of the statewide organization worked diligently to implement the new Alabama constitution, passed in November 1901, to prevent Black citizens from registering to vote, without which they could not cast a ballot. The new constitution swiftly disfranchised over 45 percent of the population of the state.[5] William's involvement made him complicit in voter suppression. In response, lawsuits were filed against the use of discriminatory practices used to deny Black voter registration.

Jackson Giles, president of the Colored Men's Suffrage Association, filed *Giles v. Harris* (1903, hereafter *Harris*) and *Giles v. Teasley* (1904, hereafter *Teasley*) against the Montgomery County Board of Registrars in response to the requirements added to the 1901 Alabama Constitution. The lawsuits claimed that the laws governing who could register to vote were arbitrary and racially discriminatory. The US Supreme Court dismissed both cases, given that the changes applied to all citizens in the state. This action affirmed the legality of Alabama's voting requirements and politicians effectively maintained white supremacy at the voting polls.[6]

Registrars used many additional strategies to prohibit Black citizens from registering to vote. Jack Bass explained that the rationale registrars used to decline applicants included failing a literacy test, not perfectly filling out complex registration forms, not paying the required poll tax before registration, or other tactics. He offered an example of blatant discrimination against registrants: A Black female college graduate was rejected because the registrar heard her respond to the question "Will you support and defend the Constitution" as though she would "support and defend the constitution"—with a lowercase c. Though this was an oral pledge, the registrar rejected her application because the applicant failed to signpost the capital "C" that specifically referenced the US Constitution rather than pledging her support to an unspecified constitution with a lowercase "c." The *Congressional Record* identified a Louisiana applicant who was "rejected for not computing his age in years, months, and days," and a woman who was blind "was rejected for the way the registrar filled out her form."[7] These examples illustrate the types of occurrences that led to Rives's cognitive dissonance and informed his intellectual evolution.

Rives had lived in Alabama his entire life, except during the time he was at Tulane University or serving in the military. During the late 1930s and early 1940s, before he became a judge Rives experienced several personal and professional events that contributed over time to alter his view on equality in the public sphere. His interpretation of these experiences, melded with previous personal knowledge and other information in the social complex, gradually and decisively began to align with individual equality, regardless of race. Rives had already experienced significant loss in his personal life, and his friends were moving on with their careers. His friend Hugo Black had left Alabama in 1937 to take a seat on the US Supreme Court. In 1938, his friend Lister Hill relocated to become a member of the US Senate. The political landscape in Alabama was altered when a long-standing political rival, William A. Gunter Jr., died in 1940. Then in 1942 Bibb Graves, a close political associate, died while Rives was leading Graves's campaign for governor. Most significantly, Rives's mother, who was known to support the Confederacy and remained unReconstructed, died in October 1943. With both of his parents dead, Rives may have, as sociologist Debra Umberson wrote, "transition[ed] to a new adult identity." These losses likely contributed to personal reflection and an awareness of what he had or had not yet accomplished in his own life.[8]

In January 1945 Rives turned fifty years old. His son had led Rives to reinterpret what he read and saw in everyday life and as a lawyer. For example, Rives may have altered his interpretation of President Franklin D. Roosevelt's State of the Union speech to the US Congress in January 1944. World War II was raging in Europe and Black soldiers were returning from service overseas. Roosevelt politically provided, as he stated, "a second Bill of Rights [also called a Bill of Economic Rights] under which a new basis of security and prosperity can be established for all regardless of station, race, or creed." Professionally, Rives had been a partner at Hill, Hill, Whiting, and Rives for twenty years. He had developed a reputation as "a person of decorum, cordial and courteous."[9] As part of his legal work, Rives was involved in a case defending voter registrars for their racially discriminatory practices.

In 1944, LDF lawyer Thurgood Marshall filed *Mitchell v. Wright* against the Macon County voter registrars. Black voter applicants had accused the registrars of requiring them "to submit to tests not required of white electors applying for registration" and of "refusing to register qualified [Black] electors while at the same time registering white electors with less qualifications." The Hill law firm represented George C. Wright and Virgil M. Guthrie, and a motion was filed with the court to dismiss the case. The district court complied. Marshall then appealed the case to the Fifth Circuit. In 1946, Rives and other cocounsel defended Wright and the Macon County Board of Registrars in *Mitchell v. Wright*. The judges denied Mitchell's petition on the ground that he failed "to exhaust his administrative remedy in the state courts of Alabama" and remanded the case back to the district court, which ultimately ruled for the registrars.[10] Rives helped win the case for the Macon County board and Black citizens did not receive relief in court. At that time, Rives thought that all who were eligible and qualified to vote—according to criteria established by white politicians and judges—should be able to register to vote. However, he was becoming increasingly aware that the law was unjust.

As Rives was reconsidering his orientation toward individual equality and the issue of race in the law, *Smith v. Allwright* was filed in Texas in 1942. Lonnie E. Smith alleged that Texas's Democratic primary system, which did not allow Black citizens to vote in primary elections, violated the Fourteenth and Fifteenth Amendments. On appeal to the Fifth Circuit, a three-judge panel affirmed the lower court decision. The case was then appealed to the US Supreme Court, in 1944 the justices ruled in favor of Smith and ordered that state primary elections were desegregated.[11] That decision prompted Alabama legislators to propose a change to Section 181 of the state constitution, to appear on the November 1946 ballot as Amendment Four.

Amendment Four was popularly known as the Boswell amendment. The amendment was written by the state Democratic Executive Committee and introduced during a meeting of the 1945 Alabama legislature by Representative Elmo C. ("Bud") Boswell, who prominent Tuskegee community leader Vera Chandler Foster characterized as "a man with a gospel to save white supremacy." Political scientist Tinsley E. Yarbrough described the amendment, which would allow registrars to deny a voter applicant for any of three reasons: (1) if an applicant could not "understand and interpret" a portion of the state constitution, (2) if an applicant was perceived as not being of "good character," or (3) if an applicant could not comprehend "the duties and obligations of good citizenship." Law professor Anne S. Emanuel wrote that the mechanics of the amendment were "ruthless," giving white registrars complete discretion to require tests of people they selected, along with the power to reject at will the results of any test. This unlimited power was directed squarely against Black applicants. The *Alabama Journal* identified Boswell amendment supporters, including a Grand Cyclops of the Ku Klux Klan (unnamed, but identified by Emanuel as a "prominent Birmingham lawyer") and Alabama Governor Frank Dixon, who were transparent about the true intentions of the amendment: to "insure [*sic*] white supremacy."[12] Democratic politicians had long maneuvered in the Alabama legislature to construct a culture that would affirm that social ideal.

As a lawyer, Rives opposed the Boswell amendment on legal grounds and soon began a personal statewide campaign to persuade white voters to reject the proposed amendment to the state constitution. Law professor Tony A. Freyer described Rives as a quintessential "establishment Democrat" who held memberships in all the appropriate clubs to affirm his social status. He knew people throughout the state, to whom he asserted that the state amendment would conflict with the US Constitution and would not be upheld by the courts. Rives delivered a public address at the Montgomery Museum of Fine Arts on April 18, 1946, that was later published in *The Alabama Lawyer*. He explained that in his experience defending the Boards of Registrars of Montgomery and Macon Counties "against the efforts to force the registration of Negro voters, . . . [he] necessarily studied the principles involved much more thoroughly than has the average citizen." Rives, a man attentive to personal and professional ethics, continued, "I would be derelict in my duty if I remained silent." He reasoned that the Boswell amendment was so blatantly unconstitutional that passage of the amendment would invite further action by the US Supreme Court.[13] Rives publicly went against the conservative Democratic tide to support President Roosevelt's New Deal.

When Rives spoke on radio programs and to civic clubs, the *Birmingham News* reported that he cautioned voters that the proposed amendment "could be used against all men, not just Black men." Rives had seen poor white men disfranchised by measures in the 1901 Alabama Constitution intended to disfranchise Black men. He warned white voters against sacrificing their own liberties if they could not meet the Boswell amendment requirements. Boswell's strategy, Rives said, would disallow "qualified" Black citizens to register to vote, but could also disallow white "unqualified" citizens to register to vote.[14]

By the fall of 1946, Rives was traveling across the state at his own expense, at times debating with Birmingham attorney Horace Wilkinson at meetings of civic organizations on the question, "Should the Boswell Amendment be Adopted?" On one occasion, the debate was broadcast on the North Alabama Radio Network. A debate in Florence, Alabama, required an outside loudspeaker system for the overflow crowd. Wilkinson argued that the amendment would further the Democratic Party's motto of "White Supremacy." Rives, identified in *Davis v. Schnell* (1949) as a "distinguished Alabama Lawyer," used direct language: "Let us be frank and honest with ourselves. You and I know that the people of our State are expected to adopt the Amendment in order to give the registrars arbitrary power to exclude Negroes from voting." He called the proposal "dangerous and undemocratic." He repeatedly spoke against the Amendment but did not challenge the idea of white supremacy.[15]

Rives publicly established his interest in social, political, and legal equality when campaigning against the Boswell amendment. He relied on the potential threat against white citizens to support the voter registration of Black citizens. On this issue, Rives may have agreed with Jim Folsom, a liberal Democrat who would later become an Alabama governor. Historian George E. Sims wrote that Folsom believed "Negroes were citizens and entitled to all the rights of citizenship. This meant that blacks were entitled to a ballot, to equal justice before the law, and to the educational and economic opportunities that whites enjoyed." However, Folsom "did not seek a fundamental shift of political power or a revolution in social mores."[16] Rives was an astute lawyer, who in private likely saw the necessity and inevitability of both.

In public addresses against the Boswell amendment, Rives drew from the Bible to reach Alabamians who relied on religion to justify Black oppression. He adapted the biblical parable of the wise and foolish builders from Jesus's Sermon on the Mount (Matt. 7:24–27) to sway his listeners to vote against the Boswell proposal. The *Montgomery Advertiser* quoted Rives: "When we use arbitrary law as the basis for white supremacy, we are building on quicksand. But when we assert the white man's leadership in terms of intelligence, character, and sense of justice, we are building upon a solid foundation of rock. . . . The chains we forge to shackle qualified Negroes can be used to keep white voters of Alabama from walking to the polls." Emanuel recalled that Rives predicted racial segregation would become a "moral cancer" on white citizens, a practice that slowly carves away a person's principled stance until one eventually becomes amoral.[17]

In one of his speeches, Rives explained that he favored a "gradual registration of qualified Negroes," using "a more stringent literary test, impartially administered to prevent mass black voting" to maintain white supremacy but prevent moral cancer. Foster wrote that he used the "understand and explain" clause of the Boswell amendment as an example. Rives claimed that "'understanding and explaining the constitution under a republican form of government'—those pious words . . . are just a lot of legalistic mumbo-jumbo . . . impossible of accurate application. . . . How can any citizen be sure that his idea of the proper understanding and explanation of any article of the constitution is the same as the opinion of a majority of the Board of Registrars?" Rives argued that the Boswell amendment was unnecessary. The voting record at that time did "not show any immediate threat to white supremacy" under the state constitution.[18]

Wilkinson, Rives's opponent, was a sitting judge—and, like Rives, a former Klansman—who spoke in favor of adopting the Boswell amendment. Historian Scotty E. Kirkland wrote that Wilkinson disparaged any idea of racial equality as "a communistic theory." Wilkinson argued, "The negro wants to vote primarily because political equality leads to social equality, and social equality leads to intermarriage." Therefore, Wilkinson pronounced, "I earnestly favor a law that will make it impossible for a Negro to qualify [to register to vote], if that is possible." Such a law, he said, was necessary "to keep this inferior, unreliable, irresponsible, easily corrupted race from destroying the highest civilization known to man."[19] Wilkinson's comments on race prompted audience members to ask Rives, whose focus had been on the law, about his personal rather than legal views.

Rives responded to those who questioned him about his stand on race: "For the purpose of this discussion it is not necessary that I take a stand, but I feel that I would be lacking in moral courage if I did not say frankly that I am not one of those who would deny the ballot to those Negroes who are qualified under the law." Rives offered an alternative to the Boswell amendment of "a high school education or its equivalent." This proposal modified Rives's earlier proposition in the 1930s to a state legislative committee, which Bass wrote would "allow anyone to register who had at least a sixth-grade education."[20] Education was important to Rives, but he recognized that daily life can also help prepare citizens to engage in democratic processes.

In November 1946 the Boswell amendment to the Alabama constitution was passed by 54 percent of Alabama voters and became state law. The amendment changed voter registration procedures, Sims explained, by giving local registrars "complete discretion in assessing the qualifications of voter applicants." A Mobile voting group called the Voters and Veterans' League and the Alabama branch of the NAACP immediately prepared separate lawsuits to test the legality of the new amendment.[21]

The Southern District of Alabama court tried the first of the two cases filed, *Davis v. Schnell*. The Voters and Veterans' League's complaint was against voter registrars in Mobile County. Rives suspected that a three-judge panel would declare the Boswell amendment unconstitutional, and he was proven correct: he correctly predicted that the judicial panel would find the "understand and explain" requirement of the amendment to be deliberately ambiguous and intentionally directed at circumventing *Smith*. Milton Schnell, a Mobile Board of Registrars member, appealed the ruling to the US Supreme Court as *Schnell v. Davis* and the justices upheld the district court's decision. The justices ruled that the Boswell amendment violated the right of Black citizens to register to vote as guaranteed in the Fifteenth Amendment to the Constitution. Rives explained to law professor Frank T. Read that he recognized the Boswell amendment for what it was: "nothing on earth but to keep Negroes from registering" to vote.[22]

Rives's support of individual equality as an objective and impartial principle of democracy was markedly strengthened when Alabama citizens passed the Boswell amendment and the US Supreme Court invalidated the legislation. Even Wilkinson, who disagreed with Rives during their public debates, characterized him as an honest man with a "brilliant legal mind." Rives explained to Read that the Boswell amendment "was just too much for me. I thought that was just totally unfair."[23] Rives's thinking about equality was evolving and during his public presentations he openly split with the conservative faction of the Democratic Party. As a lawyer and politician, Rives realized that different meanings may be packed into words and his awareness of the reciprocal relationship between politics and economics—acquired from his father and his own experiences in politics—aided his understanding of the motivations of racial segregationists. He knew that Black citizens with access to their political right to vote could change the structure of democracy.

Judge Rives's thinking continued to change during his time on the bench as voter registrars ramped up their resistance to registering Black citizens to vote. Civil Rights activists placed pressure on the federal government to protect the voting rights of Black citizens. On May 17, 1957, six years after Judge Rives took the bench, Martin Luther King Jr. marked the third anniversary of *Brown I* (1954) by delivering a speech in Washington, DC, at the Lincoln Memorial. King's speech, titled "Give Us the Ballot," articulated the relationship between voting rights and a vision of more freedoms for Black citizens. King asserted that "many states [had] risen up in open defiance. The legislative halls of the South [rang] loud with such words as 'interposition' and 'nullification,'" preventing the promise of *Brown* from being fulfilled.[24] In that speech, legal historian Tomiko Brown-Nagin wrote, King "envisioned how the Black vote would transform American democracy."[25] King rallied the crowd by arguing that voting rights are essential to social justice, environmental protection, and peace—and that voting rights were a Civil Right that must not be delayed.

On September 9, 1957, the US Congress passed the Civil Rights Act of 1957, the first Civil Rights legislation since Reconstruction. The act specified the creation of a Civil Rights Division within the Department of Justice (DOJ), which "empowered federal prosecutors to obtain court injunctions against interference with the right to vote." Officials in the DOJ charged members of the Civil Rights Division with enforcing Civil Rights through litigation. The act also established a bipartisan US Commission on Civil Rights, which was authorized to investigate discrimination and make recommendations to the US Congress.[26] The two groups worked in tandem to investigate and prosecute racial discrimination in voting processes. Passage of the act raised the perception among some white Alabamians that the number of potential Black voters in Alabama posed a threat to their way of life.

In Alabama, some white citizens recognized that if Black voters had the ability to vote, they could influence elections and possibly elect Black officeholders, especially in counties with more Black than white residents. Black voters could also potentially pass laws unfavorable to white citizens. Therefore, white authorities were anxious to identify new legal barriers that would block Black citizens from registering to vote in local and state elections. One form of terrorizing Black citizens who registered to vote was the inclusion of "the names of persons eligible to vote in state and county elections" in local newspapers such as Montgomery's *Alabama Journal*, whereby individuals could be potentially targeted for retribution. Applicants also had to list their employers on their voter registration form, which invited retaliatory firings. In addition, registrars implemented the policy that an application was one-and-done: a previous denial of registration was grounds to deny a new application.[27] White supremacists in Alabama counties exhibited their apprehension in acts of hatred and violence toward those who caused their unease. However, Black citizens, with the support of the LDF and the DOJ, continued to file lawsuits to gain the equality that was theirs as written into the US Constitution.

Within a few months, the Civil Rights Act of 1957 was passed. Dick Hines of the *Montgomery Advertiser* later wrote that the US Commission on Civil Rights received "'a substantial number' of complaints" from prospective Black voters in Alabama counties. This provoked the commission to evaluate Alabama voter registration practices and election processes. When officials for the DOJ required that registrars in Macon, Lowndes, Wilcox, Bullock, Barbour, and Dallas Counties submit their records for review, the registrars declined to do so. In 1958, US Attorney General William P. Rogers filed Civil

Action no. 1487N, *In Re: George C. Wallace*, to be heard in Judge Johnson's Middle District of Alabama courtroom in Montgomery.[28]

On December 11, 1958, the *Montgomery Advertiser* reported that lawyers working for the US attorney general's office petitioned Johnson in *In Re: Wallace* to direct "reluctant registration officials from the six Black Belt counties to produce voter records and to testify before the Civil Rights Commission." A hearing was scheduled, and on Monday, January 5, 1959, Johnson ordered the registrars to comply with the DOJ's request. The records of Barbour and Bullock had been transferred from the county registrars to George C. Wallace, then judge of the Third Judicial Circuit of Alabama. Judge Wallace refused to comply with the federal court order, and on Friday, January 9, Johnson ordered the transfer of records.[29] Alabama county registrars continued to deny Black registrants in anticipation of the 1960 presidential election, even as the federal government continued to enhance Civil Rights protections.

The Civil Rights Act of 1960, passed in May of that year, extended the life span of the Civil Rights Commission, which was established in the Civil Rights Act of 1957. The 1960 act continued the practice of allowing federal inspectors to examine voter registration records and to issue a penalty for obstructing the equal right to vote. Judge Johnson heard cases alleging racial discrimination in registering voters in Macon County, Bullock County, and Montgomery County. Ruling as a single judge in each of the three cases, Johnson developed what became known as the "freezing doctrine."[30]

United States v. Alabama was the first test in Alabama of the efficacy of the Civil Rights Act of 1960. The DOJ brought the case against the state of Alabama for alleged voter registration violations in Macon County. Records showed that less than 10 percent of the nearly twelve thousand Black citizens eligible to vote in the county were registered to do so. Judge Johnson addressed the discrimination, ruling that white Alabama registrars "deliberately engaged in acts and practices designed to discriminate against qualified Negroes in their efforts to register to vote." Yet, Johnson declined the DOJ's petition to appoint voting referees for Macon County. Instead, Johnson gave the state of Alabama, acting through the Macon County Board of Registrars, an opportunity to adopt other registration practices. The decision ordered the defendants to "act fairly" and follow "the directions spelled out in this Court's decree." Johnson's 1961 ruling followed the 1958 approach of Judge Rives in *Shuttlesworth v. Birmingham Board of Education*. The two judges focused on the law, each man ruling in a different context that the law under consideration was just and that an honest person could fairly implement the requirements. Johnson's decision warned registrars not to circumvent the law by appropriating discriminatory registration practices to promote white supremacy. In response to Johnson's decision, lawyers for the state of Alabama asserted that the US government was impeding the rights of their state as granted in the Tenth Amendment to the US Constitution, and they appealed the case to the Fifth Circuit.[31]

The appeal, *Alabama v. United States*, was heard by a three-judge panel that included Judges Rives, Benjamin F. Cameron, and John R. Brown. The panel reviewed "over nine hundred pages of testimony from 53 witnesses plus two huge boxes of documentary exhibits." On behalf of himself and Rives as the majority, Brown wrote, "we are of the clear view that this order was within the power of the Court to grant, and that the exercise of that power was eminently proper." Brown noted that in the lower court ruling, the aspect most disturbing to Judge Johnson was that the voter registration situation was worsening: "There was not even a slight ray of hope that conditions would improve, and that specifically, despite evident shortcomings in the past, the Registrars would not undertake to operate voter registration without conscious race discrimination." Cameron, swiping back against Rives and Brown in a lengthy nine-part dissent, accused the majority of "attributing to the words of a statute a meaning not contained in them, by embracing the thesis that the end justifies the means."[32] Although Rives's and Cameron's correspondence was professional, their judicial philosophies would continue to prompt disagreements between the two men. On appeal, the US Supreme Court justices upheld Johnson's district court decision. Voter registrars must allow Black applicants an equal opportunity to register to vote. During the two years that the case moved through the courts, the Macon County Board of Registrars remained recalcitrant even as the DOJ filed additional lawsuits.

The second complaint to inform the freezing doctrine, also captioned *United States v. Alabama*, was filed by the DOJ against the Board of Registrars in Bullock County. Lawyers for the DOJ petitioned the court for Black citizens' right to register to vote in Bullock County without being discriminated against based on race. White registrars routinely aided white applicants in completing the forms; they did not assist Black applicants. On September 13, 1961, Judge Johnson ruled that the registrars "perpetuated the existing disparity in voter registration . . . by adopting and applying arbitrarily strict and technical standards in grading applications, and by arbitrarily rejecting qualified Negro applicants while registering white applicants no better qualified."[33] Registrars were once again ordered to fairly implement the law.

United States v. Penton, brought against registrars in Montgomery County, was the third case that helped to shape Judge Johnson's freezing doctrine. Johnson once again ordered registrars to apply uniform standards in registering citizens to vote. The right to vote, he wrote, "is not a privilege to be granted or denied at the whim or caprice of state officers or state governments." In an interview with Bass, Johnson reiterated his principle of equality in voter registration practices: "The only way to straighten it out was to apply the same standards [to Black applicants] that had been applied to white applicants." He ordered registrars to act consistently, regardless of the applicant's race, using the least restrictive standard previously applied to any registrant. The decisions in these three cases constituted a temporary solution to racial discrimination in voter registration.[34] As Johnson was developing his freezing doctrine, other cases were concurrently being heard in federal court.

In March 1961 lawyers for the DOJ alleged in *United States v. Atkins*, heard in Judge Daniel Thomas's Southern District of Alabama court, that a pattern of racial discrimination was occurring in voter registration practices in Dallas County. According to the 1940 Code of Alabama, registrars could decline applicants due to a failure "to establish by evidence to the reasonable satisfaction of the board of registrars that he or she is qualified." The code stated that to qualify to register to vote, a person must be a United States citizen; a minimum of twenty-one years old; a resident of the state, county, and precinct or ward in which one is registering; able to read and write English; of good character; and support the "duties and obligations of citizenship" under both the state and federal constitutions.[35]

Overseeing the district court trial of *Atkins*, Judge Thomas was caught between what Wolfgang Saxon of the *New York Times* called "an impatient Justice Department and recalcitrant local authorities." Many Civil Rights advocates deemed Thomas "hostile to their cause." As expected, Thomas did not provide the requested relief to the plaintiffs, but he did rule that applicants who were rejected by registrars could reapply to vote after sixty days, which was previously impossible. Time passed, and newly inaugurated Alabama governor Wallace and other officials of his administration appointed three new members to the Dallas County Board of Registrars. Before the new board members officially took office, outgoing Dallas County Board members changed several procedures in the voter registration process.[36] The changes did not satisfy the DOJ lawyers, who sought restitution for Black applicants who were denied the right to vote by previous registrars.

Lawyers for the DOJ asserted that the practices instituted by the new Dallas County Board of Registrars were "merely a more sophisticated form of discrimination than that practiced in the past." The DOJ relied on Johnson's freezing doctrine to appeal Judge Thomas's ruling to the Fifth Circuit: "1) that an order be used compelling the immediate enrollment of named Negroes who had applied in the past and who possessed, at the time of application, the qualifications of the least qualified white person who applied during the same year and was registered," and "2) that the Registrars be ordered to register Negroes in the future who possess the qualifications required of whites during the period 1952–60."[37] The freezing doctrine would be held to scrutiny upon appeal.

When *Atkins* was appealed to the Fifth Circuit, a three-judge panel was assigned to the case. Judge Rives would hear the appeal with his segregationist colleague Judge Cameron, and Judge Paul R. Hays of the Second Circuit, sitting in lower Manhattan, New York. Hays participated as a visiting judge on the panel, which law professor Marin K. Levy indicated is also called "by designation." While district judges may sit on three-judge panels in circuit courts of appeals as visiting judges, designating a judge from another circuit is less common.[38] However, following the Houston Conference held two months earlier, in which Judge Cameron accused Chief Judge Elbert P. Tuttle of court-packing on Civil Rights appeals to the Fifth Circuit, the court likely cautioned against any appearance of impropriety.

Judge Hays, a 1961 Kennedy appointee, specialized in labor arbitration and dispute resolution in labor law. Hays's judicial style resembled that of Judge Rives. Hays was devoted to his task and sought to dispatch business efficiently. Hays's colleague on the bench, Henry Friendly, wrote that Hays was driven by "a mind of his own . . . [one] that is always ready to listen, and to yield when convinced that the other side has the better of the argument or even that the issue does not warrant an expression of disagreement." Friendly summarized Hays's judicial philosophy: "The dominant note in his opinions is that the agencies of government should be held to a high degree of responsibility in the performance of their duties, but once they have discharged this, the courts should not interfere."[39] Rives and Hays disagreed with the freezing doctrine that Judge Johnson had developed for Macon, Bullock, and Montgomery Counties.

Judge Rives addressed voter registration practices in his October 1963 *Atkins* decision on behalf of the court. He referenced the use of literacy tests as a prerequisite to voter registration. He was aware that voter registrars assisted some white citizens in preparing their applications and were thereby acting illegally when registering some voters. Rives did not support freezing that illegal activity in place. His goal was to achieve individual equality by stopping voter registration processes that favored white citizens and discriminated against Black citizens.

In *Atkins*, Judge Rives would overrule his protégé, Judge Johnson. Rives explained his disagreement with Johnson's freezing doctrine, which held in place the current registrar process in Macon, Bullock, and Montgomery Counties. Although Governor Wallace's recent appointees discontinued some discriminatory practices, the new Dallas County registrars did not allow previously declined applicants to reapply. Rives wrote that limiting the reapplication process was a practice that was "designed to retain the status quo." He was responding, in part, to the illegal behaviors in which "the Registrars, themselves, furnished the answers to and filled out the questionnaire" for some white applicants but for no Black applicants. The idea of evaluating Black registrants against the least restrictive practices for white applicants was incommensurate; there was no uniform baseline in counties across the state of Alabama from which to assess qualified applicants. Writing on behalf of himself and Hays, Rives stated, "The effect of the relief now asked would be to 'freeze' the unlawful practices of the prior Boards into a permanent policy." As Johnson recalled in an interview with Bass, Rives thought that "two wrongs"—allowing unqualified white citizens to register and not allowing any Black citizens to register—"don't make a right." In contrast, Johnson's thinking was, "Two wrongs don't make a right, but" the temporary solution of freezing, if legally applied, "corrected a greater wrong—to eliminate the effects of past discrimination" against Black citizens.[40] Rives did not distinguish one wrong as greater than another; for him, the registrars' inconsistent behavior was unconstitutional and, therefore, illegal.

Judge Rives cautioned in *Atkins* against applying "the freezing idea too freely." He suspected that the outcome of the temporary freezing practice might not allow the Alabama Legislature or the citizens of Alabama to later alter registration processes, which ultimately meant voter suppression would continue. Supporting Judge Johnson's freezing doctrine would imply that the Board could "continue to violate state law," all the while claiming adherence to Judge Thomas's court order. Rives foresaw that registrars would likely suspend registering Black applicants who would otherwise be qualified, and retain a voting bloc of wealthy, educated white citizens. Rives wrote that if the freezing principle could be legally justified, such an approach should be used "only if there were no other alternative by which justice can be reached." Howard M. Feuerstein, one of Judge Rives's clerks, said Rives preferred that registrars follow the law fairly for all applicants. He thought everyone must be treated equally under the US Constitution, and registrars must be held accountable for following the law.[41] Rives's 1963 majority opinion in *Atkins* was written two years after he first encountered Johnson's freezing doctrine. During that time, many white Southerners conflated Rives's adherence to the US Constitution with racial sympathy toward Black citizens, which produced a hostile response toward Rives from his professional colleagues as well as some members of his community.

Indeed, while some white people in Montgomery may have been sympathetic to racial equality, Feuerstein recalled that many people "were literally afraid to get involved" in Civil Rights. They feared that if they supported Black citizens' Civil Rights, members of organizations such as the KKK and the White Citizens Council (a white-collar Klan) might target them or their businesses. They feared their friends and neighbors would not acknowledge them and worried their children might be in danger. Although some

Alabamians were beginning to be receptive to the idea of racial equality, Judge Rives acknowledged in an interview with Read that court decisions in matters of Civil Rights were leading to "a complete social revolution in the Deep South." Rives continued, "It takes a little time for . . . even fair-minded people, to get their thinking turned about, because nobody had ever dreamed of such a complete change here."[42] He held out hope for white citizens in his community, across Alabama, and throughout the South. Still, even places where Rives had previously found respite were increasingly becoming closed off to him, including his local church.

Religion was a significant force shaping different opinions of the Civil Rights Movement. Journalist Ralph McGill wrote that the Southern region of the US was labeled "the Bible Belt" to reflect that the area "has always been a strongly churchgoing region." Before the Civil War, many white citizens "honestly persuaded themselves that Christianity endorsed and made slavery obligatory." They continued to justify racial segregation with Christian principles that supported their point of view.[43]

Judge Rives was a member with strong ties to Montgomery's Trinity Presbyterian Church. In April 1949, his son's funeral had been conducted there. Henry Edward ("Jeb") Russell, pastor of Trinity Presbyterian Church and brother to Georgia's Senator Richard Russell, had served on Montgomery's mediation committee during the bus boycott. Civil Rights scholar Mary Stanton wrote that in one sermon, Russell "denounced Rives from the pulpit." Despite being chastised, Rives continued to attend the church. After serving Trinity for fourteen years, Pastor Russell relocated to Second Presbyterian Church in Memphis, Tennessee. The *Alabama Journal* wrote that in 1958 Reverend Robert Strong succeeded Russell. Strong was also a proponent of segregation and would preach negatively about the federal court. During the spring of 1965, Black citizens picketed churches across the city to desegregate worship services. Although two Methodist and one Presbyterian church in Montgomery were desegregated, Trinity Presbyterian Church still seated Black worshippers in the balcony. This troubled Judge Rives, who had joined the church when he and Mrs. Rives were married. Rives's clerk, John Daniel Reaves, recalled that Mrs. Rives told her husband, "I don't know why you go," since she "belonged to the church before he did." When Trinity refused to desegregate the congregation, Virginia Durr wrote, "Judge Rives . . . got up and walked out of his church." She explained that while Rives "acted according to his conscience," he was distraught: "He simply loved 'The Church.'"[44] Soon after, Rives made an important decision about his religious membership.

On April 17, 1965, the evening before Easter Sunday, Judge Rives attended a meeting in Reverend Strong's home. Strong was remembered in his memorial as "faithful in the courts of the Church" and privileged church law over secular law. His interpretation of religious law favored segregation—and, therefore, public law should require segregation. Rives recalled that the reverend instructed church deacons and others at the meeting "to confront people who obviously come [to church] for sociological demonstrations and tell them that they are not welcome."[45] Rives perceived this directive as a targeted attack against him. Strong had suggested that Rives was not welcome because he supported the US Constitution above the reverend's interpretation of religious teachings.

Judge Rives contemplated Strong's directive over the Easter holy days. On Tuesday, April 20, he wrote the reverend a letter that stated, in part, "Dear Dr. Strong: Thank you again for our visit at the manse last Saturday, and especially for the copy of your Palm Sunday sermon. After reading, and re-reading and praying over it, I find myself still thinking not of race but of all sinners, a class to which each of us belongs. Feeling very deeply that no sinner who professes to come to church to worship should be told that he is not welcome, I cannot, for the present, attend worship at Trinity without feeling myself a hypocrite." Rives's letter clearly articulated his religious beliefs and ethical principles. His concern was not with race, but with all of humanity. When pushed to choose between his church and his character, Rives refused to go against what his convictions required of him as a man and what the US Constitution required of him as a judge. He then joined Westminster Presbyterian Church in Montgomery, which was desegregated and adhered to a religious doctrine similar to that of his previous congregation.[46]

Although Judge Rives could not control what others thought of him, he could choose to uphold his own principles, which invariably emerged during his conversations with others. Judge Ginny Granade shared that if Rives did not go home to eat lunch around midday, his usual practice was to join other judges to eat at the Francis Cafeteria on South Lawrence Street or in the back section of the Elite (pronounced e-light) Café on Montgomery Street.[47] The restaurant was popular in downtown Montgomery, close to the Alabama State House and to the federal building. The café was frequented by lawyers, federal and state judges, legislators, and other people who worked downtown and found it a convenient location to meet. Norman L. Blumenfeld, a clerk for Rives, recalled that during lunchtime, "back then, it was just a café. Meatloaf and potatoes, gravy, corn, and iced tea." The setting was plain: there was no carpet on the floor and the food was good. E. Lloyd Sutter, another of Rives's clerks, explained that the café had an area in the back separated from other diners where government workers sat. That area was generally considered to be "neutral territory."[48] No one caused trouble there, but that would not prevent diners at one table from potentially overhearing what other patrons were discussing. Some of those conversations invariably were related to racial desegregation cases.

Judge Rives's circle of friends included Judge John Godbold, with whom he had briefly practiced law and who was appointed to the Fifth Circuit in 1966. Sutter mentioned that Rives was sometimes joined by Judges Johnson and Godbold for lunch at the Elite Café. His close friendships with the other judges did not deter Rives from being aligned on different sides of issues in three-judge panels on which they served together. Governor George Wallace, whose 1963 inaugural address is best known for his phrase "segregation now . . . segregation tomorrow . . . segregation forever," would also have lunch there with the president pro tempore of the Alabama Senate. Rives told Sutter that one day while Wallace was "walking past the table of three judges, Wallace said to them, 'We're going to pass a bill today in the legislature that says thus and so.' And one of the judges looked up from his soup or beans and said, 'Well, we'll have it declared unconstitutional before the sun sets.' Then they would go back to eating their lunch. They would shake hands and go back to work." The men had all known each other a long time—Wallace and Johnson had been friends in law school at the University of Alabama.[49] But beyond their professional courtesy lay a fundamental disagreement about the US Constitution.

Judge Rives was known to handle court matters with uniform calmness and composure, according to Neil T. Bradley, one of Rives's clerks. A person would be mistaken, however, to equate Rives's self-control with an acceptance of arguments that he deemed were not within the scope of the law. Rives's demeanor aided him in reasoning through conflicting principles in lawsuits, allowing him to determine propriety with respect to the US Constitution, legislative statutes, and legal precedent. These he aligned with an emphasis on ethical behavior and a commitment to common sense, fairness, and equality. He retained a newspaper article by Anthony Lewis published in the *Louisville Courier-Journal*, wherein Lewis discussed the relationship between the judiciary and a nation's conscience. He wrote that the framers of the Constitution and the Bill of Rights "deliberately chose to use phrases such as 'due process' and 'equal protection'—phrases that express no more than moral ideals, that must be given content by each generation."[50] These ideas must have resonated with him. Although Judge Rives was perceived by the general public to be liberal because he regularly sided with other Fifth Circuit judges to form The Four in race cases, the judicial philosophy he used to arrive at his positions under the common law was more conservative than his liberal colleagues.

Judge Rives followed legal precedent and legislative statutes impartially, as required by his oath of office, and advocated for an equal application of the US Constitution regardless of race. Lawrence R. Levin, one of Rives's clerks, recalled that Rives was also guided by the impact that court decisions would have on human beings within a historical and cultural context. Levin relayed that Rives would ask himself, "'What did the framers intend to accomplish?' and 'How can we accomplish that in this day and age, given how things resonate within the southern mind?'"[51] Rives perceptively read social trends through that lens. The early 1960s were a time of remarkable change, driven by activists' determination to obtain equal Civil Rights for all citizens.

The Civil Rights Act of 1964 was passed by the US Congress on July 2. Passage of the act was preceded, Joe Hall of the *Alabama Journal* wrote, by several months of "Senate debate and cloakroom bargaining" and included some vaguely written voting rights protections. For example, "the Act required that registrars administer literacy tests equally and accept applications that contained minor errors." This created a presumption—consistent with Rives's position thirty years earlier—that anyone who had completed sixth grade had met the education requirement for voting eligibility. Nevertheless, each time the federal legislature or judiciary required white registrars to allow Black citizens to apply to vote, white registrars across the state would devise another means to block their registration. White segregationists, who opposed the *Brown* decisions and were angry at Black citizens' attacks on Jim Crow, developed a strong coalition of resistance.[52] Black citizens, beyond frustrated, acted to strengthen community ties between citizens in disfranchised areas.

Southern Christian Leadership Conference (SCLC) Civil Rights activists arrived in Selma in early 1965. Reverend Cordy Tindell (C. T.) Vivian was one of the activists in the SCLC who worked for change at the grassroots level. On Thursday, February 18, 1965, Vivian was scheduled to speak at an evening rally in Zion United Methodist Church in Marion—about twenty-five miles northwest of Selma. The church where the rally was held was adjacent to the Perry County Courthouse Square. James Orange, a field organizer for SCLC who worked for the voter registration effort, had been arrested for contributing to the delinquency of minors, disturbing the peace, and other infractions resulting from encouraging young people to participate in voter registration drives in the county.[53]

After Vivian's speech, amid rumors that jailers planned to lynch Orange, several hundred people marched to the Marion jail where Orange was being held. The nonviolent protesters intended to walk the two blocks from the church to the jail and sing outside to protest Orange's arrest. Their presence would let jailers know that citizens were watching and make Orange aware they were there to support him. The protesters had not walked very far when Dallas County Sheriff Jim Clark and other officers accused the marchers of an attempted jailbreak to free Orange, and a squad of twenty-one state trooper cars appeared. Black citizens dispersed from outside the Marion jail. A young Black man named Jimmie Lee Jackson followed other demonstrators into a Black restaurant, Mack's Café. Jackson, who had unsuccessfully attempted to register to vote in Perry County for four years, was followed inside the restaurant by Alabama state troopers. He was shot twice in the abdomen by James Bonard Fowler and later died.[54] The Black community was outraged.

Civil Rights leaders had previously suggested a march to Montgomery to petition Governor Wallace for the right to register to vote. After Jackson's murder, SCLC's Director of Direct Action James Bevel advocated for a march from Selma to the Alabama state capitol building, a distance of about fifty-four miles on the roadway of that time. The march would symbolize, in part, the number of Black citizens whose right to vote was withheld by white supremacists. Southern historian J. Mills Thornton III wrote that a march "seemed to many blacks an inspiring gesture and to many whites a menacing one." The protest march began in Selma, which SNCC reported was a town of 28,385 at the time. The town, located in Dallas County, was home to 13,969 Black citizens (49.2 percent of Selma's total population).[55]

The Dallas County political system terrorized any Black person who dared to try to register to vote. Civil Rights activists Barbara Arnwine and Marcia Johnson-Bianco reported that as a result, less than 2 percent of eligible Black citizens in Selma, the Dallas County seat, were registered to vote in 1965. On March 6, 1965, Governor Wallace called a press conference, telling reporters, including Steven Otfinoski, that the march "could not be tolerated" because it "would interrupt the orderly flow of traffic and commerce" on US Highway 80. After the press conference ended, Wallace pulled aside state trooper Colonel Al Lingo, head of the Alabama Highway Patrol. According to Otfinoski, Wallace told Lingo to "use whatever measures are necessary to prevent the march." Jim Clark, the sheriff of Dallas County, organized his officers and posse to aid Lingo's men. The message Wallace conveyed to Selma's mayor, Joe Smitherman, was different. Thornton wrote that Wallace told the mayor that although "the state troopers intended to prevent the march, they would do so calmly and prudently."[56] White politicians crafted their messages carefully, which allowed them to shift the blame for any illegal activity that may occur to Black citizens.

The first march was organized by Bevel, activist Diane Nash, and others, and was led by John Lewis of SNCC and Hosea Williams of SCLC. The march began at Brown Chapel AME Church in Selma on Sunday, March 7, 1965, around 4:00 p.m. The day would become known as "Bloody Sunday." Thornton recalled that the live television footage of the "brutal suppression" by state and county law enforcement personnel evoked disgust in citizens across the United States. King, who had not participated in the first march, issued a call asking "sympathetic Americans" to meet him in Selma to renew the march. Religious leaders and citizens from across the country began arriving in Selma.[57]

The next day, Monday, March 8, people in more than eighty cities across the United States, enraged by the previous day's events, participated in demonstrations demanding a federal response to the unprovoked violence. In addition, Williams filed a lawsuit against the governor of Alabama styled *Williams v. Wallace*. Williams sought "relief from the denial of the equal protection of the laws under the Fourteenth Amendment" and "redress of the deprivation of rights, privileges, and immunities guaranteed by the First, Fourteenth, and Fifteenth Amendments" in the planned march from Selma to Montgomery. The marchers intended to present Governor Wallace with a list of complaints about violations of Black citizens' Civil Rights, including a demand for the right to register to vote. Judge Johnson issued a temporary restraining order that forbade the organizations from holding a second march until the *Williams* case was heard.[58] However, the activists would not wait.

Bevel, Nash, King, and others began organizing a second march for Tuesday, March 9. Intermediaries for President Lyndon B. Johnson, Assistant Attorney General John Doar, and former Florida governor LeRoy Collins went to Selma to try to persuade King to call it off. Yet some SCLC and SNCC members insisted that the demonstration occur as planned. King did not want either to refuse the activists or disobey the court order. Historian Taylor Branch relayed that at around two o'clock early Tuesday morning, King agreed with President Johnson's representatives "to confine any march that day to the city limits of Selma—thus avoiding another confrontation across the Pettus Bridge." Later that day, King led the group from the church and across the Edmund Pettus Bridge to the point of the March 7 attack. There they kneeled and prayed. As they rose, law enforcement personnel and marchers faced one another. According to historian James T. Patterson, when troopers stepped to the side to allow marchers to continue to Montgomery, King shouted, "We will go back to the church now!" Civil Rights historians Christopher M. Richardson and Ralph E. Luker wrote that while some marchers were outraged by this action, now known as "Turnaround Tuesday," King did not want to defy the court order.[59]

Judge Johnson heard Williams's petition to allow the march from Selma to Montgomery on Thursday, March 11, 1965. Johnson authorized the fifty-four-mile march in *Williams v. Wallace* on March 17 and ordered the state of Alabama to protect protesters. In addition, he set parameters for the demonstration. On Sunday, March 21, demonstrators, along with troops and marshals, set off from Selma to Montgomery.[60] The protest march ended five days later in front of the Alabama state capitol building.

On March 25, the first wave of men and women began passing within view of Judge Rives's window on the fourth floor of the US Post Office and Courthouse building in Montgomery. Rives telephoned Judge Johnson, whose office was on the second floor on the opposite side of the building. Bass wrote that Rives told Johnson, "You have ordered one of the largest parades in the nation's history. . . . Now I want you to come up to my floor and view it. Because you ordered it, you ought to at least be able to see it." Johnson joined Rives to watch as thousands of people gathered in front of the Alabama capitol building. Rives promoted equality for all people under the US Constitution and recognized that state laws had been manipulated to keep certain citizens from experiencing those rights. Blumenfeld explained that Rives approved citizens marching and petitioning as a form of legal protest against any legislation violating the Constitution. He only recommended dissolving public protest when demonstrators acted in illegal ways.[61]

Judge Rives had stated his position about freedom of speech and assembly a year earlier in *Cameron v. Johnson*. In 1964, in an effort to draw attention to discrimination in voter registration of Black citizens, Reverend John Earl Cameron had been regularly picketing the Forrest County Court House in Hattiesburg, Mississippi. *Cameron* addressed the passage of the 1964 Mississippi Legislature's "House Bill 546: An Act to Prohibit the Unlawful Picketing of State Buildings, Courthouses, Public Streets, and Sidewalks." The bill was approved on April 8, 1964, by Mississippi governor Paul B. Johnson Jr. On April 9, the state statute went into effect, and Cameron was warned about the law and threatened with arrest. The next day, when he again picketed the courthouse, he was arrested for violating the statute. The *Montgomery Advertiser* reported that Cameron filed the lawsuit against Governor Johnson to "wipe out" House Bill 546.[62]

That case was heard in the Southern District of Mississippi court by a three-judge panel of Circuit Judge Rives and District Judges Sidney Carr Mize and William Harold Cox. Mize and Cox, ardent segregationists, formed the majority decision in *Cameron* in support of the state. Southern historian Raymond Arsenault wrote that by then, Judge Rives, the third member of the panel, was "widely regarded as a traitor to the white South." As in other cases on which Mize served with Rives, Mize likely made "no effort to conceal . . . [his] disdain" for Rives's "heretical views." In dismissing Cameron's complaint, Mize concluded there was "no need or necessity for this Court to pass upon the constitutionality of House Bill 546 . . . and this Court, therefore, declines to do so." In his dissent, Rives referred to a case heard in the same courtroom in 1961, *Bailey v. Patterson*. In that case, the plaintiffs argued that sections of the Code of Mississippi were unconstitutional. Rives's dissent referred to the supremacy clause in the US Constitution, which establishes the authority of federal law over state law. He wrote, "The rights asserted here [in federal court] are based on the Constitution which itself creates the cause of action for equitable relief."[63] If a judge in a federal court were to order that a state statute is superior to the US Constitution, the judge would be violating the federal judges' oath of office. The plaintiff's lawyer, agreeing with Rives's dissent, appealed the Mississippi anti-picketing statute decision to the US Supreme Court, which reversed the judgment of the district court majority in *Cameron* and remanded the case back to the Southern District of Mississippi court for another trial.

On October 14, 1966, the three-judge panel hearing the case included Judges Rives, Cox, and Fifth Circuit Judge James P. Coleman, former governor of Mississippi. Leslie H. Southwick, a former judge on the Mississippi Court of Appeals, wrote that Coleman was a "dedicated and effective segregationist shaped by the racial views of his state." Coleman (designated to the panel after Mize's death) and Cox formed the majority and refused to adhere to the US Supreme Court's 1965 reversal of their 1964 decision. Instead, the Southern District of Mississippi judges again dismissed the complaint, this time with prejudice—which, as the Legal Information Institute defines, means "the plaintiff cannot refile the same claim again in that court."[64] Rives again dissented and supported the exercise of free speech.

In Judge Rives's 1964 *Cameron* dissent, he addressed the line between the state government and the US Constitution and indicated what would be needed to make Mississippi House Bill 546 constitutional. Rives reminded lawyers for the state of Mississippi that "a statute against picketing must be exact and precise, for example, by limiting the pickets to a certain designated reasonable number or by prescribing that they must walk at a certain named reasonable distance from each other. Broad, sweeping, and inexact terms of a statute regulating picketing necessarily encroach on freedom of speech and press." Rives declared, "Broad prophylactic rules in the area of free expression are suspect." In his 1966 dissent he reiterated his position, "The danger to freedom of speech and assembly of such a broad and vague delegation of power as here involved is too great to expose it to the long road of case-by-case litigation in the hope that some day the statute's reach will be narrowed to constitutionally permissible limits." Further, "The Court's injunction may always be narrowed if and when the appropriate appellate courts of Mississippi construe the statute in all its vague peripheries. The real answer is that if the legislature desires to legitimately protect access to its public buildings, it must do so by a statute appropriately drawn." Perhaps encouraged by Judge Rives's dissent, Cameron's lawyer again appealed the case to the US Supreme Court. In 1968, the justices affirmed Rives, overruling the district court order.[65] Cameron's case was in the courts for four years. While the majority of judges in the district court interpreted the anti-picketing law as valid and charged Cameron with violating the statute, Rives considered the more significant issue to be freedom of speech.

Judge Rives had twice expressed his common-law position on the relationship between state and federal governments and the chilling effect that overly broad statutes present on citizens' freedom of speech and assembly as identified in the First Amendment. In a common-law approach, a living Constitution metaphor allows legislators to modify the US Constitution to adapt to a changing society. According to legal scholar David A. Strauss, "There is a legitimate role for judgments about things like fairness and social policy" in developing the law. In the courtroom, common-law judges are obliged to make a judgment about what is a fair outcome or what would be good policy, "why one result makes more sense than another, why a different ruling would be harmful to some important social interest." A judge with a common-law philosophy interprets the law in the light of precedent and statutes as well as impressions of fairness—an idea that Rives's father instilled in him.[66] Rives endorsed the right of citizens to express dissent in lawful ways to attain their Civil Rights, such as the Selma-to-Montgomery march.

In this, however, he was not in the majority in his state. Members of the federal government soon realized that even under court order, voter registrars in Alabama were not going to suspend their racially discriminatory practices. Working in unison to dismantle inequalities in the voting system, the Montgomery County Democratic Conference (MCDC), the Montgomery Improvement Association, and the NAACP contacted the DOJ. In early October 1965, Rufus Lewis, chair of the MCDC, told a reporter for the *Montgomery Advertiser* that federal registrars had been contacted to request oversight of voter registration practices in Montgomery county "some time ago."[67] The 1965 Voting Rights Act passed by Congress earlier that year did not change the voter registration practices in Alabama.

The right to vote is a significant part of a citizen's ability to influence the development of democracy in local, state, and federal governments. Section 4 of the Voting Rights Act of 1965 provided guidelines to address white citizens' activities that were designed to prohibit voting by Black citizens, such as literacy tests and poll taxes. The act targeted specific state and local governments that "encompass the most pervasively discriminatory jurisdictions" related to voting as a right of citizenship. Federal examiners would be dispatched to oversee elections and counteract registrars who supported state rights and refused to register Black citizens to vote. A population requirement within the act aided lawyers in the DOJ's Civil Rights Division in determining the specific areas of the country to which federal examiners would be dispatched. At the point when more than 50 percent of Black citizens in a particular county were registered, examiners would physically vacate the site but retain certain oversight conditions.[68] Alabama was one of the places to which US Attorney General Nicholas Katzenbach sent federal examiners to monitor voter registration procedures and ensure that registrars did not discriminate against Black applicants.

Federal examiners dispatched to Montgomery began to register voters on October 1, 1965. Applicants who wanted to register to vote in Montgomery County could do so through two channels, either with the Montgomery County Board of Registrars or with federal examiners, who set up registration offices in the federal Post Office—the same building in which Rives had his office. Federal examiners registered many applicants who had been previously declined by registrars. By the end of October, federal examiners provided Montgomery registrars with a list of more than eleven hundred names to add to the voting rolls. Joe McFadden of the *Montgomery Advertiser* reported that Barbara Dent, chairman of the Board of Registrars for Montgomery County, had a staff of eight clerks double-checking the list of names provided by the federal examiners to determine which names "ought to be challenged under county rules." The *Alabama Journal* wrote that federal examiners across the state submitted lists including the "names of some 23,000" Black citizens to be added to the voting rolls. State probate judges, told by their respective state circuit judges not to add the names to the voting rolls, were caught between opposing orders from the federal and state governments.[69]

The probate judges filed a lawsuit captioned *Reynolds v. Katzenbach* to question the certification of citizens registered to vote by federal examiners. Fifth Circuit Chief Judge Tuttle, Circuit Judge Rives, and District Judge Thomas were assigned to hear arguments in *Reynolds* in the Southern District of Alabama courtroom. Judith Helms of the *Alabama Journal* reported that on November 16, 1965, Mobile lawyer Charles Arendall argued in court for plaintiff Bernard Reynolds that the probate judges "have been enjoined by [state] circuit judges in their counties from registering illiterates but at the same time face fines or prison terms under federal law if they fail to comply with the Voting Act." Frank Mizell, who represented Alabama governor Wallace, asserted to Helms that federal examiners "were listing not only illiterates but persons ineligible under residence requirements and some who were registered twice." Sue Seale, serving as chair of the Hale County Board of Registrars was reported as saying that "her investigation of more than 2,000 names submitted to her revealed about 50 who were registered twice, 62 who had committed disqualifying crimes, and several persons who lived in other counties." Conflicts between state and federal law were compounded by incomplete or incorrect information on some registration forms. The federal government, represented by Assistant Attorney General John Doar, filed a counterclaim on behalf of defendant Nicholas Katzenbach, the US attorney general, asking the court to order probate judges to include the names of all people certified by federal voting examiners on the official voting lists.[70] The three-judge panel filed a per curiam decision in the case.

On November 23, 1965, the judges ruled in *Reynolds* that state circuit court injunctions, which prohibited probate judges from accepting the names of eligible voters, are "entirely null, void, and of no effect." The judges ordered that the court "must assume the Voting Rights Act of 1965 to be constitutional and valid." The voters' roll must include all additional names submitted by federal examiners. The *Montgomery Advertiser* reported that judges did not have the authority to "issue declaratory judgments on the Voting Rights Act." Voter registration continued apace, and by December 29, the Montgomery County Board of Registrars and federal voting examiners had registered 63,181 people to vote. Approximately one-third of the newly registered voters were Black citizens.[71]

The registrars' unwillingness to fairly identify all qualified citizens to vote was aided by the use of literacy tests. Accordingly, Civil Rights litigators contested the legitimacy of a law under which the Alabama Boards of Registrars required voter applicants to pass a literacy test as a prerequisite to registering to vote. Following *Atkins* (1963), lawyers for the DOJ filed *United States v. Baggett* and *Dent v. Duncan*. Judge Rives had been assigned to all three judicial panels.

The *Atkins* case, discussed earlier, a complaint that ultimately disallowed Judge Johnson's freezing doctrine, continued in the courts from April 1961 through October 1963. In addition to ordering legal voting procedures for all applicants, in writing the majority decision Judge Rives observed that registrars had been using a questionnaire provided by the Alabama Supreme Court "as a test" without "any standards whatsoever" for evaluation. At the time the judges heard the case, the Dallas County Board of Registrars' policy did not allow a person to reapply to vote once an application had been rejected. In *Atkins*, after including a set of instructions to bring voter registration practices in line with the US Constitution and the 1964 Civil Rights Act, Rives ordered the registrars "to keep records of the exact reasons for the rejection of any applicant and to reveal these reasons to any applicant who inquires as to specific reasons for his rejection."[72] He likely hoped to achieve at least some modicum of fairness from registrars despite the rampant injustices of voter discrimination. However, even after this federal decision, state boards of registrars continued their practice of administering literacy tests in an inconsistent manner.

In January 1965, over a year after the *Atkins* decision, the federal government filed *United States v. Baggett*. Agnes Baggett, secretary of state of Alabama, remained under an order by the Supreme Court of Alabama to administer one of several newer literacy tests to each applicant registering to vote. In *Baggett*, the DOJ sought to prohibit the newer tests, alleging "the tests are too tough," which resulted in "freezing out" Black citizens after most whites of voting age were already registered under an older, easier test. The *Alabama Journal* wrote that even Alabama attorney general Richmond Flowers Sr. admitted that the test "is rigged." He opined, if "every voter in Alabama passed this test, we would have the most intelligent electorate in the nation." Yet in doing his job, Flowers said the state would defend the registrars who administered the test "with every faculty we have."[73] The fight by white politicians to retain their political power via states' rights was unyielding.

Voter registrars took no action to change their procedures while *Baggett* remained under review. As already discussed, ten months later on October 1, 1965, federal examiners were dispatched to Montgomery to oversee the voter registration process. The next day, an interview with Barbara Dent, chairman of the Montgomery County Board of Registrars, appeared in the *Montgomery Advertiser*. She verbally chastised the DOJ for assigning examiners to oversee registrars. Dent asserted, "There is no justification for the appointment of examiners in Montgomery County. . . . This board has operated under a federal court injunction since November 20, 1962, and every person, regardless of race, who is eligible under the law and who has applied for registration has been registered. The appointment of examiners in this county would be to register persons who are not eligible under the law to vote because they cannot read or write." She pointed to the Alabama Constitution, which "specifically state[s] that the ability to read and write is a necessary requirement to register in Alabama."[74] Using tests ordered by the Alabama Supreme Court, a registrar would determine whether an applicant was literate. Dent contended that having a federal examiner look over her shoulder would not change whether she deemed an applicant able to read and write.

Federal examiners, Dent said, submitted the names of citizens she knew could not read or write as registered voters. To seek clarification on voter registration procedures, Dent filed a petition to the US Civil Service Commission calling for an interpretation of the Voting Rights Act of 1965. The *Montgomery Advertiser* covered the story. Dent inquired "whether the act abolishes literacy as a voting qualification or whether it only suspends the use of tests, requiring an applicant to demonstrate [an] ability to read and write." Lyman C. Duncan Jr., a hearing officer for the US Civil Service, denied Dent's assertion that literacy was a necessary condition for voting based on the 1965 Voting Rights Act. Dent appealed Duncan's decision to the Fifth Circuit as *Dent v. Duncan*. Montgomery County district attorney David Crosland represented the Montgomery Board of Registrars, arguing that county registrars had not required applicants to prove their ability to read or write. Instead, the registrars asked, "'Can you read and write?' If the applicant answers 'yes' he can register, but if he answers 'no' he cannot register." On March 29, 1966, Judges

Rives, Coleman, and Orie Leon Phillips of the Tenth Circuit heard the case. While Coleman was a segregationist, Phillips's habit was to state material facts, identify the controlling principles of the law, and then apply those principles to the facts. The judges relied on the US Supreme Court's decision in *State of South Carolina v. Katzenbach* to affirm their *Duncan* decision: literacy tests cannot be used as a qualification for registering to vote.[75] Over ten years after *Brown*, the per curiam decision of the three-judge panel in *Dent* was one sentence long. Rives wrote a rare special concurrence to that court decision.

In his *Dent* concurrence, Judge Rives recalled the words of US Attorney General Katzenbach in a hearing before the US Congress prior to the passage of the 1965 Voting Rights Act. Katzenbach explained that a majority of states do not use a literacy test. Places using literacy tests, he explained, implemented them to discriminate against Black applicants: "The literacy test is demonstrably unrelated to intellectual capacity. It is directly related only to one factor: color." Rives echoed Katzenbach's sentiments in his reprimand of the Montgomery Board of Registrars. The judge wrote, "It is not this bill—it is not the Federal Government—which undertakes to eliminate literacy as a requirement for voting in such States or counties. It is the States or counties themselves which have done so and done so repeatedly, by registering illiterate or barely literate white persons." He argued that the registrars' unfair administration of tests led to the suspension of literacy tests as a prerequisite for voter registration. Rives concluded, "I look forward to the day when the state and its political subdivisions will again take up their mantle of responsibility, treating all of their citizens equally, and thereby relieve the federal government of the necessity of intervening in their affairs. Until that day arrives, the responsibility for this intervention must rest with those who through their ineptitude and public disservice have forced it."[76] He placed the burden for needing to remove literacy tests squarely on the shoulders of white citizens engaged in public service. But this was not the only obstacle Black citizens faced in exercising their right to the franchise.

At the same time that literacy tests were being challenged, Alabama voter registrars were also collecting poll taxes as a means to significantly inhibit Black citizens' right to vote. The poll tax (also known as a "head tax") dates back to Colonial America, when the fee was originally instituted in Massachusetts in 1646. Instead of levying taxes against property or income, a fixed amount was levied against each adult citizen, without regard to the resources one may have. The funds were generally used as a source of revenue to offset governmental expenditures that were in the interest of taxpaying citizens. Many other states later adopted this practice. In Alabama, the poll tax was first codified in Article 9 of the 1868 Alabama constitution, following readmission to the Union after the Civil War, but the state constitution did not make the tax a prerequisite for voting. In the 1901 revision of the Alabama constitution, Article 8 declared payment of the poll tax to be cumulative as well as a prerequisite for voting. Each voter was required to pay a tax for 1901 and for each succeeding year. The Twenty-Fourth Amendment to the US Constitution, ratified in January 1964, abolished payment of a poll tax as a prerequisite for voting in federal elections. However, states could still implement a poll tax to be paid prior to registering to vote in local and state government elections.[77]

In 1964, Alabama was one of five states that retained the poll tax as a prerequisite to voting. The Voting Rights Act of August 6, 1965, directed the US attorney general to "challenge the use of poll taxes in state and local elections." Supporters of state rights immediately disputed the Voting Rights Act, and Alabama county registrars insisted on waiting to change any registration procedures until the US Supreme Court ruled on the legality of the legislation.[78] That insistence further discriminated against some voters by delaying the approval of applications.

Several cases were filed to address the unconstitutionality of the poll tax. Nearly thirty years earlier, in 1937, US Supreme Court justices reasoned in *Breedlove v. Suttles* that since states grant voting rights and the poll tax applied to all voters as a fee for government services, the tax did not violate the Fourteenth or Fifteenth Amendments to the US Constitution and was therefore valid. In 1966, *Harper v. Virginia Board of Elections* was pending in the Supreme Court.[79] At the same time a similar case, *United States v. Alabama*, was under review in the Fifth Circuit.

Circuit Judges Rives and Walter P. Gewin and District Judge Johnson heard preliminary arguments on December 20, 1965, in a pretrial hearing for *United States v. Alabama*. The judges were charged with determining whether Congress's Voting Rights Act of 1965 outlawing a poll tax in federal elections should also apply to state elections. After the hearing, a reporter for the *Alabama Journal* stated, "A majority of this court is unwilling to hold the provisions of the constitution and statutes of Alabama imposing a poll tax as unconstitutional at this point in the proceedings." The judges wanted to hear additional evidence about the issues presented, Helms wrote, including "arguments which dealt primarily with the application of the tax." They were interested in whether the law was, as the *Montgomery Advertiser* added, "improperly administered" or whether the law was, in effect, to keep Black citizens from voting. A hearing on the merits of the case was scheduled for February 14, 1966.[80]

After the February hearing, Judge Rives began to draft the majority decision in *United States v. Alabama* on behalf of himself and Judge Johnson. To provide context for the argument, Rives provided a brief history of voting and racial discrimination in Alabama. He quoted the Alabama constitution, which required "a poll tax in the amount of $1.50" to be "imposed annually" on residents "between the ages of 21 and 45." Payment of the tax was voluntary, but a person could only vote if the tax was paid. Poll tax receipts were dedicated to education and, in 1966, provided the state with annual revenue of approximately $300,000 for those purposes. Although not addressed in Rives's decision, SNCC had previously distributed a report that documented the median income for the white and nonwhite population. The median annual income of Black citizens living in rural areas of Alabama in 1960, such as Dallas and Perry County, was $669. The median annual income of white citizens living in rural Alabama was $1,737. Further, the median annual income of white citizens living in urban areas was nearly three times that of Black citizens living in urban areas. Rives's draft decision stated, "The poll tax was born of an effort to discriminate on the basis of race or color and it has had just that narrow effect."[81] The judges agreed that legislators installed the tax to take advantage of economic disparities between white and Black citizens.

Judge Rives also identified restrictive aspects of the poll tax in the draft of his majority decision, such as the payment timetable, given that the tax could "be paid only between October 1 and February 1." Requiring payment within these specified dates presented a separate issue from one's economic status, both of which, Rives noted, are unrelated to qualifications for voting. The language of the Alabama Constitution declared that a "prospective voter must have paid the poll taxes due for the previous two years in order to vote in an election in the ensuing year." In Rives's draft decision, he wrote, "On May 21, 1901, a State Constitutional Convention assembled largely, if not principally, for the purpose of changing the 1875 Constitution so as to eliminate Negro voters." Helms reported that in 1901 the state legislature identified public education as the reason for imposing the tax. Rives responded in *United States v. Alabama*, "The alleged interests [in education] amount to no more than ingenious afterthought."[82] The majority opinion made clear the intersections between race, economics, and voting.

Judge Rives continued his draft, writing, "If this court ignores the long history of racial discrimination in Alabama, it will prove that justice" is indifferent, not impartial—and that those with legal power are ignoring Black citizens' demands for equality. These words exhibit Rives's anger with legislators in local, county, and state offices who, against the US Constitution, intentionally manipulated words and meanings in the Alabama constitution to discriminate against marginalized groups of citizens. He also discussed the relationship between state rights and the Fourteenth and Fifteenth Amendments to the US Constitution. Rives ordered that people in service of the state of Alabama "must exercise their powers so as not to discriminate between their inhabitants," as they had been, because "race can never be a reasonable ground for discrimination." He admonished registrars who used tactics that would interfere with "the right to vote 'on account of race, color, or previous condition of servitude.'" He concluded that "the poll tax abridges the right to vote on account of race."[83]

Judge Rives balanced his conservative and liberal impulses on race cases. In *United States v. Alabama* he wrote, "It is important to recognize that the Supreme Court has *only recently* determined that the Fourteenth Amendment limits the power of the states to fix voting requirements for state elections." He continued, "the states have the power to impose only reasonable limitations on the exercise of the franchise, and that any limit or condition on the exercise of that right which does not bear a reasonable relationship to the intelligent exercise of the ballot is not a 'qualification.'" Therefore, he reasoned, a poll tax violates the due process clause of the Fourteenth Amendment.[84] Rives balanced the Tenth and Fourteenth Amendments to the US Constitution and required the removal of a poll tax stipulation across Alabama as required by the Twenty-Fourth Amendment (ratified January 23, 1964) and the Voting Rights Act of 1965. In his draft, Rives described Alabama's poll tax as "one of the last great pillars of racial discrimination."[85] His argument was clear and straightforward, designed so that all persons who read the decision would understand the court's order.

After Judge Rives completed his draft of the *United States v. Alabama* decision, he shared his work with Judges Johnson and Gewin as a professional courtesy and as a way to invite other points of view and receive recommendations that might inform his interpretation of the case. All three men were natives of Alabama. As Gewin read through the draft, he came across Rives's history of the Alabama poll tax. Levin, who was in the room when Rives and Gewin met, recalled that Gewin thought Rives's comments would "make Alabama look bad" nationwide. Gewin also took exception to the inclusion of Rives's summary of the Alabama Constitutional Convention, which revealed that legislators adopted the 1901 state constitution to protect segregation and keep Black citizens from voting. After listening to Gewin's argument to delete that portion of the majority decision, Rives refused to do so. He felt it was necessary to include the information to properly explain why the judges ruled as they did. Gewin then responded that if the constitutional convention material was not removed to avoid embarrassing Alabama, he would have to dissent to the majority opinion, and he would include in his dissent "terrible things about Abraham Lincoln and how he was a segregationist." Regarding this interaction, Levin recalled that Gewin turned to him and said, "That should bother you, Larry. You're from Illinois." Rives then laughed and said to Gewin, "No, no, Larry and I think alike. We think, Judge, that Abraham

Lincoln's ideas on segregation were bad and that it is for history to judge him. . . . We're not judging Abraham Lincoln. We're judging the Alabama poll tax. And history has to know the principles" on which the majority decision was made.[86] Gewin then began to write his dissent.

The published decision in *United States v. Alabama* includes Judge Rives's history of the 1901 Alabama constitution as well as Judge Gewin's reference to President Lincoln. Gewin dissented from the majority opinion, partly because the US Supreme Court was still considering *Harper*, a case involving the use of a poll tax in Virginia. Gewin wrote, "The principle of judicial restraint dictates that we await the action of the Supreme Court." Gewin thought Judges Rives and Johnson were engaging in judicial overreach. He stressed, "We should follow the decisions of the Supreme Court and not seek to anticipate what future rulings may be, especially in cases involving the validity of a state constitutional provision." Gewin quoted a sentence written by Rives in *Howard v. United States*, a 1956 case related to determining "the proper test of criminal responsibility" when a defendant asserts insanity. In that case, Rives wrote on behalf of the court, "This Circuit follows the law as stated by the Supreme Court and leaves any need for modification thereof to that Court." Judge Lynne referenced the same passage ten years earlier in the *Browder* (1956) bus desegregation case.[87]

Three weeks after the *United States v. Alabama* decision, the US Supreme Court ruled in *Harper*. The justices followed Rives's lead and overruled *Breedlove v. Suttles* (1937). The justices declared in *Harper* that using a poll tax in the state of Virginia, and therefore across the nation, violates the equal protection clause of the US Constitution, regardless of the use to which funds were put.[88]

The legal strategy used by Civil Rights activists for enfranchising Black citizens as voters relied on principles set forth in *Brown*; Amendments Fourteen, Fifteen, and Twenty-Four of the US Constitution; and the Voting Rights Act of 1965—making their argument legally indisputable. As a lawyer, Rives protested the Boswell amendment, and as a circuit judge, he overruled Judge Johnson's freezing doctrine, worked to remove literacy tests, and eliminated the poll tax as a prerequisite to registering to vote. He was met with a fierce backlash for his stance on equality but he was not deterred from his judicial duty to dismantle racial discrimination against voter applicants. Rives was instrumental in ending the era of politicians relying on the state judiciary and the laws of Alabama to sanction white supremacy in public elections.

The Fifteenth Amendment to the US Constitution was not empty sentiment. The Constitution explicitly granted Black men—and with the Nineteenth Amendment granted all women—the right to vote to shape the structure of democracy. Over eighty years lay between the passage of the Fifteenth

Amendment in 1870 and the US Supreme Court's 1954 mandate for public equality in *Brown I.* With that decision, the justices ordered discrimination in the public sphere to be un-American. Joel W. Motley III, the son of Civil Rights lawyer Constance Baker Motley, said the 1965 Voting Rights Act, was "a capstone of legal and legislative achievement." Before the end of 1965, county registrars and federal examiners had added the names of 250,000 new Black voters across the South to the voting rolls.[89] Desegregating the juror selection process, which relied on voter rolls to identify a pool of potential jurors, also required the attention of the court.

7

Ordering Conditions that Allow for an Impartial Jury

Desegregating Juror Selection Processes

In the South of the 1950s and 1960s, as we have seen, judges could intentionally misinterpret the law to draw conclusions in line with their personal biases. An impartial jury can protect against the partiality of a judge. The right to a jury trial is one means of preventing government oppression of an individual. The democratic institution of a trial by jury was so revered at the founding of the United States that delegates installed this right in the Sixth and Seventh Amendments to the US Constitution. The Sixth Amendment ensures, in part, that in all criminal prosecutions a citizen has the right to a "speedy and public trial, by an impartial jury of the State and district wherein the crime shall have been committed." The Seventh Amendment, in part, addresses a person's right to a jury trial in civil cases and the types of civil cases and claims that require a jury trial.[1] A citizen's right to a jury trial in criminal and certain civil cases is an important institution of the judicial system. Fairness is necessary for justice to occur and was a critical factor in Judge Richard T. Rives's common-law approach to jurisprudence.

Before becoming a judge, Rives leaned politically toward New Deal liberal Democrats against the conservative Democrats who were their rivals in state politics. He knew that voting records were a primary source of names on lists from which potential jurors were drawn to hear cases. In 1901, members of the Alabama Constitutional Convention intentionally altered the Alabama constitution to exclude Black citizens from voting. In addition, voter registrars also implemented additional obstacles, requiring payment of a poll tax, passing a literacy test, and ownership of property, among other qualifications. These requirements severely limited Black citizens' prospect of registering to vote, and reduced their opportunity to serve on a jury to near nil. The jury selection process had become an unquestionable pretext for intentional discrimination. Since white lawyers rarely raised the issue of Black citizens serving on juries, judicial attention to all-white juries seemed to recede in the context of other, seemingly more pressing, issues.[2]

As a lawyer in the 1930s, Rives was undoubtedly influenced by the Scottsboro trials, which brought national attention to all-white juries in Alabama. In March 1931, nine Black youths ranging in age from twelve to nineteen were charged with assault and attempt to murder, to which were added the charge of raping two white women on a freight train near Paint Rock, Alabama.[3] The boys and men were transported to Scottsboro and separated into four groups for trial. The cases were tried and appealed across several years, involving Alabama courts and the US Supreme Court. Despite the April 1933 testimony of an alleged victim, Ruby Bates, that she and her companion had not been assaulted, the defendants continued to be found guilty by all-white juries and repeatedly sentenced to death. In April 1935, the Supreme Court ruled in *Norris v. Alabama* that "for this long-continued, unvarying, and wholesale exclusion of negroes from jury service, we find no justification consistent with the constitutional mandate." The justices ruled that systematic exclusion of Black citizens from jury pools violated the Sixth Amendment right to a fair trial and the Fourteenth Amendment right to equal protection under the law.[4]

Disallowing Black citizens' right to serve on a jury persisted even though US congressional representatives passed the Fourteenth Amendment in 1868, which prohibited states from enacting laws that discriminate against formerly enslaved people. To reinforce the Fourteenth Amendment, seven years later, federal legislators passed the Civil Rights Act of 1875. The US Supreme Court made illegal the tactic of excluding a person from jury service by reason of race. In response to state actions that violated Black citizens' right to serve on a jury, in 1880 the judicial branch of the federal government strengthened the legislature's Civil Rights Act of 1875 in three pivotal decisions.

The US Supreme Court decided three cases related to the composition of a jury on the same day. On March 1, 1880 the justices ruled in *Strauder v. West Virginia*, *Virginia v. Rives*, and *ex parte Virginia*. Opinions in each of these cases barred individual states from denying Black citizens' right to serve on juries. However, state legislators realized that if their state's juror selection policy did not specifically refer to race and if Black citizens were systematically excluded through covert practices, the state's actions did not impair the integrity of the US Constitution. In Alabama, state legislators reasoned that the Tenth Amendment protecting state rights would allow them to act autonomously from the federal government to determine Alabama jury procedures. All-white juries were pervasive in Southern states as late as the 1960s. US Supreme Court justices were generally unwilling to hear appeals that addressed differences between state and federal laws on racial matters. The justices primarily accepted appeals, as the US Commission on Civil Rights stated, that "dealt with administrative practices rather than State laws"—cases that related mainly to the administration and regulation of government agencies.[5] This allowed the Supreme Court to avoid the issue of a citizen's inclusion in a jury pool and the composition of juries.

The historical context of state-sponsored and -condoned violence, in the form of white lynch mobs and extrajudicial killings, is reflected in the presence of all-white juries. Impartiality is especially important in cases involving Civil Rights activity or crimes that might arouse hostility in a community. While the Alabama constitution was clear—"the right of trial by jury shall remain inviolate"—the everyday practices of lawyers and judges in trial courts revealed rogue intent in jury selection processes.[6]

In a 1959 decision on behalf of the court, Judge Rives called attention to jury discrimination in *United States ex rel. Goldsby v. Harpole* (hereafter *ex rel. Goldsby*), a case centered on a Black man accused of murder in the state of Mississippi. Rives used this case to address the absence of Black jurors because he thought each person deserves to access their rights as identified in the US Constitution. Excluding citizens from potentially participating on juries violates the right of the accused person and the rights of citizens who are not allowed to participate. At that time, Rives had been writing decisions on behalf of the court for nearly a decade. He had become aware that the courts were going to be the dominant vehicle that established racial desegregation as set out in *Brown v. Board of Education of Topeka I* and *II*. After Rives addressed the need for an impartial jury in *ex rel. Goldsby*, he reiterated the need for inclusive juries in *United States ex rel. Seals v. Wiman* (1962), and in *Rabinowitz v. United States* (1966) and its companion case *Jackson v. United States*. In *Rabinowitz*, Rives wrote on behalf of the majority on an en banc Fifth Circuit panel, confirming his position on the importance of impartial juries, which would significantly inform the US Congress's Jury Selection and Service Act of 1968.[7]

Judge Rives became involved in the Robert Lee Goldsby case, *ex rel. Goldsby*, several years after the preliminary hearing in 1954. Goldsby, a Black man, had been sentenced to death by an all-white jury for killing Mozell McCorkle Nelms in the parking lot of her husband's service station and coffee shop.[8] There was no question that Goldsby killed Mozell Nelms; the question was whether he committed murder or whether he acted in self-defense. Making that decision would take two trials, over twenty court appeals, and numerous rescheduled execution dates over seven years.

The dispute was covered by the Greenville, Mississippi, *Delta Democrat Times*. On the morning of September 4, 1954. Goldsby, age twenty-eight, was riding in the front passenger seat of a car traveling south from St. Louis, Missouri, on Highway 51 toward Canton, Mississippi. In the car were four other Black adults and a child. The driver of the vehicle, Robert Gilliam, pulled into Bryant Nelms's gas station and café outside of Vaiden, Mississippi, so sharply that it created a cloud of dust and sprayed the building and an employee's car with gravel. Nelms, a white man, went outside to investigate. He asked Gilliam "what he meant by coming in like that" and found that the people in the car had been drinking alcohol. Nelms ordered them to leave his property.[9] They refused to do so and an argument ensued.

The Jackson, Mississippi, *Clarion-Ledger* provided additional details. Nelms left and returned gripping a rubber tire hammer in his hand and concealing a pistol in his pocket. When he reached the car, he found not Gilliam but Goldsby in the driver's seat. Nelms again demanded they leave his property, and Goldsby reached over and pulled a gun out of the glove compartment. Nelms struck Goldsby on the side of his head with the hammer. Goldsby then fired his pistol out of the car window, hitting Nelms twice; he was wounded and fell to the ground. Mozell heard the gunshots and ran from inside the café toward the car. Goldsby fired a fourth bullet that killed Mozell. Then Goldsby sped out of the parking lot onto the highway.[10]

Goldsby's car was stopped by law enforcement officials a few miles south of Lexington, Mississippi, between 9:30 and 10:00 a.m. Everyone in the vehicle was arrested and taken to Hinds County jail. Later that day, Goldsby was taken to the State Highway Patrol Headquarters, where he signed a statement admitting he shot and wounded Bryant Nelms and killed Mozell Nelms, although Goldsby claimed the crime occurred in self-defense given that he had been hit with a hammer. Goldsby later testified in court that he did not see Mozell while shooting: "I was nervous and scared, . . . I shot as fast as I could pull the trigger." He stated that he just "started shooting" and then drove away. The community's reaction to the injury of Bryant Nelms and the death of Mozell Nelms at a local business was personal. A person from outside of the community had attacked one of their own.[11] This bias would make obtaining an impartial jury difficult for Goldsby's defense team.

The adjudication of Goldsby was convoluted. The incident occurred in the jurisdiction of the Mississippi Judicial Circuit for the District of Carroll County. Goldsby was initially represented by a Jackson, Mississippi, law firm. His lawyer immediately filed a motion for a change of venue, seeking to move the trial to a location where the Nelmses were not as well-known and in which Goldsby might receive a fair jury trial. Fifth Circuit Judge Leslie Southwick wrote that Judge Henry Lee Rodgers, who "stood for states' rights concepts of the Tenth Amendment," denied the motion. Goldsby would be required to stand trial in Carroll County, where Mozell was killed.

The case was first heard by a grand jury, whose role is to determine whether probable cause exists to believe an offense has been committed.[12] The jurors were to conclude whether Goldsby would be charged with the felony offense of murder.

When members of Goldsby's family living in Indiana learned of his arrest in Mississippi, they contacted the NAACP, which had been instrumental in Civil Rights cases since before *Brown*. The NAACP referred them to George Leighton, a Black lawyer from Chicago, Illinois. A month later, Claude Hatcher, clerk of the Second Judicial Circuit in Mississippi, confirmed that a grand jury had been "properly drawn, as required by law" for the trial. Leighton was present with Goldsby on November 8, 1954, when members of the grand jury found probable cause to believe that Goldsby had murdered Mozell Nelms. Their indictment would lead officers to charge Goldsby with murder; he would stand trial in state court.[13]

Leighton prepared a motion challenging the grand jury indictment and the trial location based on discrimination he witnessed when people were selected to serve on the jury. Before Leighton could file his motions, other members of Goldsby's family retained John Prewitt, a white lawyer from Vicksburg, Mississippi as cocounsel. Prewitt revealed to Goldsby's relatives that he refused to work with a Black lawyer.[14] As a result, Leighton was asked to withdraw from the case. His motions were never filed, but the issue of juror discrimination remained. A lack of communication between family members and their uncertain knowledge of appropriate legal procedures continued to complicate Goldsby's legal representation.

After Leighton withdrew from the case, the court presumed Goldsby had no representation and appointed Luther Ringgold of Winona, Mississippi, to defend him. Ringgold then learned of the family's insistence that Prewitt also appear on Goldsby's behalf, and Ringgold obtained the judge's consent for dual representation. The trial was set for Wednesday, November 17, 1954, and Goldsby entered a not guilty plea to the charge of murder. The lawyers completed their closing arguments on Friday afternoon. The trial jury left the courtroom to deliberate and returned to the courtroom less than fifteen minutes later. Goldsby was found guilty of murder and sentenced to die on December 24, 1954. The day after Judge Rodgers rendered a guilty verdict, Goldsby's lawyers filed a motion for a new trial, citing a complaint similar to that which Leighton had previously prepared. The judge denied their motion.[15]

Goldsby's lawyers next filed a petition with the Mississippi Supreme Court. They alleged that Goldsby was erroneously convicted because of the systematic exclusion of Black citizens from both the grand jury and the trial jury. The state did not dispute Goldsby's claim. On March 28, 1955, Judge

Percy Mercer Lee of the Supreme Court of Mississippi held in *Goldsby* that since Goldsby's lawyers did not raise the issue of excluding Black citizens from the jury before Goldsby's original trial or in the lawyers' appeal on the merits of the case prior to the trial, Goldsby "had effectively waived" his right to raise the issue of jury composition. Lee denied the petition filed by Goldsby's lawyers and set May 13, 1955, as the date for Goldsby's execution. On May 11, an appeal was granted, providing for another stay of execution. Goldsby next appealed the case to the US Supreme Court, and on December 12, 1955, the justices declined to hear the appeal. Instead, they referred Goldsby's matter back to the Supreme Court of Mississippi to set another date for his execution.[16]

The Mississippi Supreme Court scheduled Goldsby's execution for February 24, 1956. That date elapsed, as did several additional petitions, hearings, and dates for execution before the court set an execution date of Thursday, May 29, 1958. Two days before Goldsby was sentenced to die, Goldsby's lawyers again appealed to the US Supreme Court. Chief Justice Earl Warren granted Goldsby a stay of execution "until [the] petitioner has had an opportunity to exhaust his federal rights."[17] Once again, Goldsby was given a reprieve.

The appeal was now in the Fifth Circuit. Judges Rives, John R. Brown, and John M. Wisdom would hear *ex rel. Goldsby* and decide two issues in the case. The first issue the court was required to determine was "whether Negroes were systematically excluded from the grand jury and from the petit [or trial] jury." The second issue concerned "whether those objections were waived as to both the grand jury and the petit jury" since Goldsby's lawyers did not raise them before the trial.[18] This case hinged on a lack of representation of Black citizens on juror pool lists drawn from voter rolls on which Black citizens were very rarely included.

In *ex rel. Goldsby*, Rives wrote on behalf of the three-judge panel, addressing the issue of the systematic exclusion of Black citizens on juries. He referred to evidence that Black residents comprised 57 percent of residents in Carroll County. In the earlier trial, the state officials had called several witnesses, including the circuit clerk, the chancery clerk, the sheriff, the ex-sheriff who had served for twenty years, the district attorney, and the circuit judge. Not one of those witnesses could recall an instance of a Black man serving on a jury. The county court ruled that this situation was apparently due to Black citizens' inability to meet one or more of the qualifications to be a registered voter in Mississippi and thus be included in the jury pool. Rives wrote that the only two Black citizens "ever proved registered as electors" and thus eligible for jury service in the county "were two [men] who had died before 1954." The three-judge federal panel rejected the defense lawyers' assertion that Black citizens "voluntarily abstained" from registering to vote, thus making themselves ineligible for jury duty. As a lifelong resident of Alabama who had worked in the courts as a lawyer and a judge for over forty years, Rives was aware of this situation. He wrote that although his "familiarity with such a condition thus prevents shock," the continued existence of racial discrimination heightened his intolerance of Black citizens being "excluded from serving as jurors solely because of their race or color."[19]

In the court's *ex rel. Goldsby* order, Judge Rives cited Alexis de Tocqueville's *Democracy in America*, wherein Tocqueville saw the main evil of democracy in the United States as "the inadequate securities one finds there against tyranny."[20] The tyranny Tocqueville referred to is the abuse of power that the founders exploited when determining and making laws and then breaking those laws when doing so suited their own interests. Earlier in his career as assistant city lawyer for Montgomery, Rives supported county boards of registrars against Black suffrage. As a judge, he viewed such action as unconscionable. For Tocqueville, privilege and power are entwined in the political fabric of the United States. Both Rives and Tocqueville were interested in enriching democracy and in the challenges inherent in creating equality for all people.

In *ex rel. Goldsby*, Rives required the state of Mississippi to prove that it did not discriminate against Black citizens in selecting jury pools. Writing on behalf of the court, Rives chastised Southern lawyers: "As Judges of a Circuit comprising six states of the deep South, we think that it is our duty to take judicial notice that lawyers residing in many southern jurisdictions rarely, almost to the point of never, raise the issue of systematic exclusion of Negroes from juries." Judicial notice indicates a point that the court accepts as true without evidence to support the claim.[21] Rives cited two reasons that lawyers did not raise the issue of jury discrimination in Southern courts.

Southern lawyers were silent about jury discrimination, Judge Rives acknowledged, partly because "the prejudicial effects on their client . . . outweigh any practical protection in the particular case." He cited *Shepherd v. State of Florida*, wherein US Supreme Court Justice Robert H. Jackson, writing on behalf of the court in 1951, recognized the prejudice at play in jury selection. Even if a Black citizen were selected to serve, Jackson wrote, "I do not see, as a practical matter, how any Negro on the jury would have dared to cause a disagreement."[22] Jackson understood that simply including Black people on a jury would not ameliorate any injustice rendered by a white majority. Further, white jurors may render their own extralegal "justice" toward a Black juror outside the courtroom.

A second reason that lawyers did not raise the issue of a desegregated jury for a Black client was the likelihood that such action would create an impact that would extend beyond the courtroom. Judge Rives wrote that lawyers who "fight against the systematic exclusion" of Black jurors may risk personal sacrifice that may extend to "loss of practice and social ostracism."[23] A lawyer who raised the issue may find oneself without friends or business. In these two scenarios, Justice Jackson and Judge Rives succinctly summarized the arguments against lawyers petitioning the court for desegregated Southern juries.

The *ex rel. Goldsby* case preceded the Legal and Educational Defense Fund's focus on voting rights. Judge Rives ordered that relying on the condition of voter registration as a precursor to jury service violates the US Constitution and must no longer be followed as law. The Fifth Circuit gave the state of Mississippi eight months to retry Goldsby's case, ordering that "any such re-trial must of course be before a jury from which Negroes have not been systematically excluded." Rives was cognizant of the importance of adhering to the Sixth Amendment to the US Constitution, which provides a speedy trial for all defendants. Goldsby had already "been confined to jail or in the penitentiary for more than four years." Rives observed that Goldsby had yet to receive due process. The Fifth Circuit's decision in January 1959 ruled that Goldsby "had not been tried before a legally constituted petit jury, nor has his right to such a trial been effectively waived." Rives reminded the lower court of the importance of a defendant's right to a prompt trial: "If the appellant has not been re-tried within such period, this Court will consider and decide whether or not he should be discharged."[24] What Rives may have meant as a promise to the defendant was perceived as a threat by the people of Mississippi.

The public grew increasingly frustrated with the federal courts as Goldsby's appeals spurred additional appeals and more court decisions. The ongoing case raised animosity against the judicial system from white citizens in Alabama and Mississippi, especially those who lived near Vaiden, the site of the killing and trial. They feared the *ex rel. Goldsby* decision meant that any Black person tried in the future before an all-white jury could potentially have a guilty verdict reversed without regard for actual guilt.[25]

The general public's perception was that lawyers used the multiple appeals allowed by law to evade justice. One person commented in the *Conservative*, a newspaper published in Carrollton, Mississippi, "We expect there will be some other scheme forthcoming to keep . . . [Goldsby] out of the gas chamber. We believe in giving a man every opportunity when his life is at stake but such cases as this . . . are inclined to make us lose respect for the laws we have." Supporters of the Nelms family became wary of the legal system due to the seemingly drawn-out justice for Mozell Nelms. An editorial in a later issue of the same newspaper identified a question regarding Goldsby's case that many white citizens were asking: "What does it take to exhaust his rights?" One point of contention was Goldsby's purpose in filing his appeals. Was he intentionally dragging out the process to stay alive, or was the legal team using his case as a public argument for jury desegregation? The public's annoyance, in part, pertained to the conflation of race with the question of guilt. A journalist wrote, "It seems of small if any consequence whether he was guilty of the slaying of which he is charged." The *Conservative* articles revealed public sentiment that in Goldsby's guilt for killing Mozell Nelms—whether murder or self-defense—"the race question . . . [was] paramount" over justice.[26]

The Fifth Circuit's 1959 decision in *ex rel. Goldsby* stated that the defendant must be retried before a jury on which Black citizens had not been systematically excluded. Judge Rives told William H. McDonald, a reporter for *Southern School News*, that he experienced increasing criticism after each of the racial desegregation decisions he had written. Rives said that of all the decisions he wrote between 1956–1962 on behalf of the majority of judges on panels emanating from the US Supreme Court's *Brown* decisions, he was "most criticized for the Goldsby decision."[27] The pushback Rives received for requiring fair juries eclipsed even the comments directed to him on decisions related to the desegregation of public transportation, public educational facilities, and voter registration.

Judge Rives's decisions did not endear him to some white Alabamians who claimed state rights as a defense for all-white juries. He endured some white citizens' vitriol, exhibiting remarkable courage. The only precaution Rives felt necessary to take against such animosity was to have his home mail delivered to a box at the post office. He refused to have an unlisted telephone number. Rives told law professor Frank T. Read that despite the threatening calls that would "keep . . . [them] up all night," Rives thought public servants should be available to their constituents, even when hatred, revulsion, and inappropriate timing were the focus of that contact.[28]

Historian John M. Spivack wrote that some people believed Judge Rives "paid a rather heavy price" because of his legal opinions. Still, Rives, who was an unassuming man, did not think he suffered any more than any other judge on the court. Considering the tumultuous time, Rives told Spivack he believed judges had "to expect some unpleasantness when they made rulings that were unpopular in the community."[29] Neither the general public nor his brethren on the court uniformly supported Rives's interpretation of the US Constitution, but even those who did not support Rives respected him and his work.

Judge Rives laid aside personal and political beliefs to create a camaraderie with his colleagues based on impartiality and faithfulness to the US Constitution. Yet on the bench, Rives and some of his colleagues were deeply divided in their interpretations. They were conflicted, in part, about which aspect of the Constitution to emphasize in specific deliberations. Article VI of the Constitution, the supremacy clause, states that when federal and state laws conflict, federal law will supersede state law or a state constitution. Yet the Tenth Amendment asserts that any powers not delegated to the federal government are the purview of an individual state.[30] That amendment raises the question of identifying specific powers that are delegated to a state government. For Rives, the supremacy clause, which resides within the body of the Constitution, should prevail over the Tenth Amendment. The disagreement led to a hostile response toward Rives from citizens who felt oppressed by federal oversight. He interpreted the backlash projected at his character as anger some citizens felt toward the federal Constitution. Rives's behaviors reveal that he would rather be a target of public animosity than vote on three-judge panels in ways he thought were inconsistent with the Constitution and its amendments. Citizens' responses to Rives's decisions came from across the circuit and beyond.

Mississippians, in general, adhered to a view of state rights and objected to oversight by the federal government. Historian Robert E. Luckett Jr. notes that Mississippi attorney general Joseph T. Patterson attempted to mount a legal defense of Southern states against judicial decisions that were perceived to dismantle state sovereignty. *Ex rel. Goldsby* was one case that Patterson feared would threaten the state's right to govern itself. Judge Rives's 1959 court order required that Goldsby receive a new trial. This led Patterson to prepare an appeal to the US Supreme Court requesting a review of the three-judge decision, given the interposition of the state of Mississippi against the federal government.[31]

Segregationist Southerners resurrected the doctrine of interposition as a by-product of the US Supreme Court's *Brown* decisions. The term "interposition" was coined by Thomas Jefferson in his Kentucky Resolutions of 1799. Civil Rights historian Robert Brisbane wrote that Jefferson distrusted a government with "powerful centralized authority." Interposition, Brisbane explained, is the idea that states have the right and "are in duty bound, to interpose for arresting the progress of the evil." According to this theory, a state may place itself between the federal government and the citizen whenever representatives of a state determine "a federal statute or court decision to be unconstitutional or harmful within its specific jurisdiction." In this way, states could pass an ordinance of nullification, which would cancel out the law, and state officials would "simply refuse to obey them." Brisbane observed, "In the South . . . this doctrine was generally considered to be next in importance to the Ten Commandments. It was an article of political faith for every true Southerner and one who did not accept it was suspect." After state legislatures passed Jefferson's Resolutions, in 1809 the US Supreme Court "repudiated interposition as a valid constitutional doctrine" in *United States v. Peters*.[32]

Yet, between 1956 and 1957, seven Southern states passed interposition declarations to ensure inequality in the public sphere. State interposition was directed toward retaining racial segregation and, as explained in 1960 by Circuit Judge Rives and District Judges Herbert William Christenberry and J. Skelly Wright in *Bush v. Orleans Parish School Board*, would "not recognize the Supreme Court's decision in *Brown v. Board of Education* . . . [or court orders] issued pursuant to the mandate of that case." A strategy of interposition essentially "denies the constitutional obligation of the states to respect those decisions of the Supreme Court with which they do not agree." The judges wrote, "The conclusion is clear that interposition is not a *constitutional* doctrine. If taken seriously, it is illegal defiance of constitutional authority. . . . However solemn or spirited, interposition resolutions have no legal efficacy." Interposition resolutions lack legal standing and cannot override the US Constitution.

As Goldsby's case wore on, his lawyers continued to press for a desegregated jury to hear his fast and fair retrial.[33] Mississippi Attorney General Patterson sought to delay Goldsby's retrial by attempting to overturn the Fifth Circuit's *ex rel. Goldsby* decision. Court records for *Harpole v. ex rel. Goldsby* recount Patterson as saying the decision gave Black citizens a "license to commit any crime and escape prosecution" if they served as a racial majority on juries. He argued that Black citizens did not serve on juries in Carroll County because none met the necessary qualifications, not because the selection process was discriminatory and unconstitutional. When appealed to the US Supreme Court, the justices refused to review the ruling of the Fifth Circuit and allowed the court's decision to stand.[34]

Goldsby's execution date had been postponed five times in four years. In seeking clemency, Goldsby simultaneously nudged forward the cause of Civil Rights. Indeed, *Time* magazine reported that some people thought Goldsby had "one abiding concern: Saving his skin." Numerous motions were filed in courts of law, including writs of habeas corpus, motions on the grounds of newly discovered evidence, and requests based on the systematic exclusion of Black citizens from jury service. Each action resulted in the Mississippi Supreme Court resetting Goldsby's execution date. The case moved recursively through the state supreme court, US district court, US Court of Appeals for the Fifth Circuit, and US Supreme Court.[35] Finally, Goldsby's case was remanded back to Judge Rodgers's Mississippi Circuit Court for the District of Carroll County for a fair trial with a desegregated jury.

The *Conservative* covered Goldsby's second trial for the death of Mozell Nelms, committed nearly five years earlier. The trial began with additional motions that included one for a change of venue. Judge Rodgers granted the request, and the case was transferred to the Mississippi Judicial Circuit for the

District of Hinds County for trial. As the second trial began in early December 1959, a court clerk was quoted as saying he was "almost sure" the 150-man pool of potential jurors included "some" Black citizens. In fact, the pool did include the names of five Black men. From the pool, twenty-four prospective jurors were drawn, including two Black men. After the state made peremptory challenges, twelve white male jurors remained. Following the trial and additional appeals, the court sentenced Goldsby to die in a gas chamber on May 31, 1961, for the seventh time in nearly seven years.[36]

The prominence of Goldsby's case and the media's reporting of trial details informed the public of discriminatory issues associated with jury selection. For many white citizens, a Black man found guilty of killing a white woman in Mississippi was automatically guilty of murder; self-defense was inconceivable. Racial history in the South shows us that Black on white crime was treated more egregiously than white on Black crime. Nuances of Goldsby's case raised racial concerns for posterity. Although Goldsby did not directly lobby for the larger cause of Civil Rights, his case was instrumental in advancing Black citizens' right to a jury of their peers.

The *ex rel. Goldsby* case lasted seven years and raised two significant issues for jury selection: the systematic exclusion of Black citizens from juries, and the waiver of one's right to fair representation on a jury. While these two issues were common at the time, they were nonetheless sticking points for Judge Rives. He thought the purposeful exclusion from jury pools and mistreatment of Black citizens by white juries threatened to dismantle the US Constitution. Rives made professional decisions based on the rights guaranteed in that document, believing that the Constitution superseded an individual's beliefs and cultural distinctions.

In correspondence with Judge Brown several years earlier, Judge Rives wrote, "Juries are great shock absorbers and as long as we cannot have any more perfect system of criminal law than presently seems possible, juries are the best practical means of administering substantial justice to the individual without abandoning protection to the public."[37] Rives called attention to the imperfect system that he recognized as inherently withholding protections from Black citizens. At the same time, he asserted that desegregated jury trials are the only means of providing additional Constitutional protection for marginalized citizens in criminal trials. Rives was adamant that a citizen has a Constitutional right to justice through an equitable jury selection process.

Judge Rives sat on other judicial panels in which he reinforced that jury discrimination was unconstitutional as *ex rel. Goldsby* moved through the courts. One of those cases was *Seals v. State of Alabama*, in which an all-white jury sentenced Willie Seals, a Black man, to death in 1960 for the capital rape of a white woman. During the legal process, Seals learned that his lawyer did not file the appropriate motions necessary for an adequate defense. In addition to other actions that Seals's lawyer could have filed, he failed to request that the decision be rendered void because of jury discrimination, nor did he ask for a change of venue. Seals obtained a new lawyer, and in 1961 he appealed the ruling to the Alabama Supreme Court as *ex parte Seals*.[38]

In the *ex parte Seals* decision, Alabama chief justice J. Edwin Livingston ordered that while Seals's lawyers could have appealed for a new jury or change of venue earlier based on jury discrimination, "it now comes too late." Livingston decided that not only did Seals's lawyers' request for a change of venue come too late in the trial proceedings, it also did not convince the Court that the "proposed attack on the judgment" of the white jury was "meritorious" and, therefore, did not warrant a new trial.[39] For Livingston, the right to register to vote and the right to potentially serve on juries were separate issues.

After Alabama Supreme Court Chief Justice Livingston refused to rehear *ex parte Seals*, Seals was sent to prison. During his incarceration, Seals and his lawyer continued to advocate for a new trial heard by a desegregated jury. As part of this defense, Seals argued that the warden of the prison, Martin J. Wiman, was complicit in detaining him without a fair trial. After following other legal processes, in 1962 lawyers appealed *United States ex rel. Seals v. Wiman* (hereafter *ex rel. Seals*) to a three-judge panel of the Fifth Circuit that included Judge Rives. The judges were to decide three claims related to the case, including the plaintiff's declaration of "racial discrimination in jury selection."[40] Rives's involvement in this case is noteworthy because, against the view of Livingstone, Rives perceived voter registration rolls and jury composition as intertwined, given that voter registration lists contained the names of people eligible to serve on a jury.

In working on a draft of the *ex rel. Seals* decision, Judge Rives wrote to his colleagues on the panel, Judges Brown and Wisdom, admitting that he had held the case "entirely too long." He had worked on the decision "so much that I have grown stale." He also acknowledged, "Even now I do not want to turn out the opinion until after our Alabama primary on May 1, 1962. If turned out sooner, it would probably become a political football to the detriment of the Court and it would also be unfair, I believe, to McDonald Gallion," a candidate for Alabama governor. Rives suggested, "As the case is a preferred case, we probably should not hold it beyond May 1."[41] The judiciary does not exist in a vacuum, and public opinion was still running against the courts. As such, judges needed to consider the timing of the release of decisions.

The majority opinion in *ex rel. Seals*, written by Judge Rives, was published on May 30, 1962. In the decision, Rives reviewed the process for selecting juries in Mobile County, Alabama, where the trial was held. He noted that 31 percent of Black citizens were qualified for jury service, but fewer than 2 percent were in the venire (the group of people from which a jury is drawn). No Black citizens served on the eighteen-man grand jury that first indicted Seals. Of greater significance, only two Black men were included on the list of 110 citizens from which the jury was selected. Following jury selection, only white men were included on the trial jury that ultimately convicted and sentenced Seals. Rives looked for a reasonable explanation for the underrepresentation of Black citizens in the jury pool, but lawyers for the state of Alabama did not provide one. Rives explained that the method of jury selection in place "inevitably resulted in systematic exclusion of all but a token number of Negroes from the jury rolls."[42] For Rives, this was an intentional strategy used by white citizens to retain power in the legal system.

Ex rel. Seals affirmed the principle that Black defendants have the right to be heard by people who are selected from a jury pool that includes Black citizens. The judges' decision established guidelines for determining whether a minority group had, in fact, been excluded from the jury pool. The *New York Times* quoted law professor Harvey C. Couch, who complimented Judge Rives: "This was the first time anyone had gotten down and wrestled with the question of how you prove jury discrimination with regard to minorities."[43] Rives's careful thinking resulted in the advancement of equality in jury desegregation.

Judge Rives's determination to get *ex rel. Seals*, as well as other cases, "right" did not go unnoticed by his colleagues. Judge Brown wrote to both Judges Rives and Wisdom about the lawsuit, expressing his "profound appreciation for the painstaking, patient, thorough manner in which Judge Rives does this serious business."[44] On behalf of the court, Rives carefully articulated the question of law, parsed legally relevant issues in the case, and referenced legal precedent and state codes to write the court's decision. The day after publication of the decision, Rives wrote to Clifford Durr. In his May 31, 1962, letter, Rives revealed his intention to call attention to two of his recent opinions, which he saw as an "unseemly" move but hoped would "have some far-reaching practical effect" in future trials involving Black defendants. Rives suggested that his opinions on behalf of the court in *ex rel. Goldsby* and *ex rel. Seals* had the ability "to work against the systematic exclusions of Negroes from juries." He likely thought that providing information about these decisions to Durr as soon as possible would aid lawyers who were beginning to raise the issue of jury exclusion so they could work to change the legal system.[45]

Several years would pass before Rives would write a decision on behalf of the majority on an en banc panel in *Rabinowitz v. United States* (hereafter *Rabinowitz*) and its companion case *Jackson v. United States*, which would inform the Jury Selection and Service Act of 1968. The situation leading to Judge Rives's *Rabinowitz* decision began in Albany, a city in southwestern Georgia with a population of about fifty-five thousand. Lawyer Victor Rabinowitz wrote in his memoir that white citizens living in that geographical area had an extreme reputation for "racist brutality" toward Black citizens that was only rivaled in "two or three other locations in the deep South." Reporter Vanessa Murphree, writing about SNCC, documented that field coordinators Charles Sherrod, Cordell Reagon, and Charles Jones arrived in Albany in the fall of 1961 in response to the discrimination and repression of Black citizens, to aid them in attaining their Civil Rights. In so doing, they initiated what would become the Albany Movement. SNCC was different from other Civil Rights organizations of the 1960s. The group used direct action and, as Civil Rights activist Julian Bond explained, was a "hands-on organization, helping local leadership in rural and small-town communities across the South participate in a variety of protests, as well as in political and economic organizing campaigns." Members of SNCC worked to address efforts to register local voters and raise awareness of Civil Rights activities.[46]

One of the SNCC members was civil liberties lawyer Victor Rabinowitz's daughter Joni Rabinowitz, a student from Antioch College in Yellow Springs, Ohio. In his memoir, Victor recalled that part of Joni's college degree required off-campus fieldwork, and she arrived in Albany at the beginning of April 1963 to work for SNCC's voter registration drive.[47] She would later find herself involved in a complex federal perjury trial that would result in Judge Rives writing the court's decision that overturned how juries were composed for federal trials. Joni's case emerged from a situation in which SNCC activists picketed a grocery store owned and operated by Carl Smith.

Smith had been selected to serve on a federal grand jury in Albany to consider *Ware v. Johnson*. In that case, Charles Ware was arrested without a warrant by Sheriff L. Warren Johnson on July 4, 1961. Ware, a Black man, was taken to the jail, but before going into the building Johnson pistol-whipped and shot Ware three times in the neck. Ware survived and sued Johnson for $125,000 in damages in the US district court in Albany, charging that the sheriff violated Ware's Civil Rights. The federal grand jury on which Smith served did not indict Johnson.[48]

Smith's South Albany grocery store was located in a segregated neighborhood known as Harlem. For several months, SNCC had led Black citizens to boycott the store because Smith would not promote Black employees beyond the level of menial jobs. The organization was also boycotting other white store owners with similar policies. Victor Rabinowitz explained that Smith's vote on the unanimous jury refusal to return a true bill against Sheriff Johnson, meaning that the grand jury members did not find enough evidence to indict Johnson of a crime, "added an additional grievance and provoked more militant action" from Civil Rights workers. Lawyer Townsend Davis wrote that about one hundred SNCC members picketed Smith's store for an hour on Saturday afternoon, April 20, 1963. The following Monday, the *Detroit Tribune* reported that "Smith began to move out of the store contending that he had been driven out of business by the boycott."[49] Smith was well-connected in Georgia's Democratic Party and contacted his friends in the organization, likely asking them to support his claim.

A report by the National Committee for the Albany Defendants about the Albany cases explained that Smith was active in Georgia's Democratic Party, which advanced John F. Kennedy in his political aspirations. James H. Gray, a leading segregationist and former chairman of the Georgia State Democratic Committee, helped John F. Kennedy raise campaign funds when he was a US senator. Before the 1960 presidential election, Smith and Albany Mayor Asa D. Kelly Jr. "promised to carry Southwest Georgia" for Kennedy in his presidential race, and they fulfilled their promise. Smith's attorney, B. C. Gardner, was a member of the legal firm of Smith, Gardner, Kelly, and Wiggins. The National Committee for the Albany Defendants report stated that Taxi Smith, the managing partner, "was closely allied" with Democratic US Senators Richard Russell—brother to Henry Edward ("Jeb") Russell, former reverend of Trinity Presbyterian Church in Montgomery—and Herman Talmadge of Georgia. A week after Smith closed his store, the Albany Bar Association contacted the DOJ, headed by US Attorney General Robert Kennedy. The bar association charged that nine SNCC members (the Albany Nine) who picketed Smith's store violated the federal law as an act of juror intimidation and insisted that the Justice Department conduct an immediate and complete investigation.[50] Smith and other Democratic Party members in Georgia had reason to believe the US attorney general would provide relief against SNCC protesters.

US Attorney General Kennedy was reluctant to have the DOJ intervene in Albany. A year earlier, Judge Rives had contacted Kennedy about James Meredith's enrollment at the University of Mississippi, another instance in which the DOJ was hesitant to become involved. Given the abundant and persistent racism in Albany, William G. Anderson, president of the Albany chapter of SNCC, later reflected on the "magnitude of the physical and emotional abuse to which Southwest Georgia blacks were subjected" that warranted SNCC's actions. The *Indianapolis Recorder* reported that despite SNCC's repeated appeals to the DOJ to prosecute law enforcement officers in Albany and the surrounding area who had engaged in "violence and brutality against civil-rights workers," the DOJ refused. SNCC reported incidents that included sworn victim statements to the FBI, which is responsible to the US attorney general. While "the FBI always said it was investigating," members of SNCC perceived that no help was forthcoming.[51]

The Albany Civil Rights Institute stated that US Attorney General Kennedy's position had been that as long as Laurie Pritchett, Albany's chief of police, "avoided violence in opposing and suppressing the initiatives of the Albany Movement," the DOJ would take a "hands off" approach. Historian Michael Chalfen wrote that after the Albany Movement had been in the news for over a year, Kennedy urged Albany mayor Kelly to "resolve Albany's racial conflicts" given that the protests and violence "tainted America's democratic image abroad." On July 19, 1963, Kennedy "declared that voter registration was the preferred way to fight racial discrimination, not civil disobedience." On July 29, Anderson appeared on *Meet the Press*, a national one-hour news interview program, with Civil Rights leader Ralph Abernathy, a close friend of Martin Luther King Jr. During the interview, Anderson criticized the federal government for inaction while clear violations of constitutional rights were occurring.[52] Given this string of events, Smith and his colleagues in the Democratic Party had reason to think the DOJ would support their claims of juror intimidation by SNCC.

Presumably in response to the political pressure by Smith and others, US Attorney General Kennedy approved the indictment of the Albany Nine for juror intimidation. However, the DOJ continued to distance itself from other cases involving Civil Rights violations in southwest Georgia. Meanwhile, the 1963 March on Washington was nearing. In that public demonstration, an alliance of Civil Rights, labor, and religious organizations sought to bring nationwide attention to the issues of jobs and freedom for Black citizens. Martin Luther King Jr. was scheduled to keynote the event. American studies scholar Peter J. Ling wrote that a few days before the March on Washington, Kennedy announced that the Justice Department "would seek criminal indictments against nine civil rights activists in Albany, Georgia, on charges including intimidation of a federal juror." The announcement's timing reinforced that the DOJ would process criminal charges but preferred that local leaders address what they saw as local problems. Their approach had been that the federal government would not intrude in Civil Rights matters that state officials could handle.[53] The politics of the Albany investigation threw a wrench into this course of action.

The Justice Department charged that SNCC's picket line outside of Smith's store was an obstruction of justice, conducted to intimidate Smith because of his vote on the grand jury in *Ware*. Given the charge of juror intimidation, the case came up through DOJ's Criminal Division, headed by US Assistant Attorney General Herbert ("Jack") Miller, as an obstruction of justice charge rather than through US Assistant Attorney General Burke

Marshall's Civil Rights Division as a Civil Rights violation. The difference in charges between the two units would alter the federal government's response to SNCC's behavior. Soon after the DOJ became involved in Smith's case, SNCC reported at least thirty-five FBI agents in Albany. The agents were supposed to establish whether there was sufficient evidence of juror intimidation to bring a lawsuit against Anderson and other protesters. The agents interviewed hundreds of witnesses, compiled thirty thousand pages of evidence, subpoenaed over fifty members of the Black community as witnesses, and convened a grand jury to determine whether to indict members of SNCC's picket line outside Smith's grocery store, in retaliation for his refusal to indict Sheriff Johnson for shooting Ware.[54] Many Black citizens subpoenaed by lawyers were members of SNCC.

Law professor Leonard S. Rubinowitz, along with Michelle Shaw and Michal Crowder, wrote that Chevene Bowers (C. B.) King, a Civil Rights attorney in Albany, was chief counsel for the SNCC chapter and represented the arrested demonstrators. Early in his practice King developed a reputation, historian Taylor Branch wrote, for being "the only black lawyer south of Atlanta who would take on civil and criminal cases." King scheduled a meeting in his law office with the subpoenaed people to discuss "their rights and duties as grand jury witnesses." King was suddenly called away for a "mass trial of young people arrested at a library sit-in," and Elizabeth Holtzman, a summer law clerk from New York seeking experience in Civil Rights litigation, met with the witnesses who were subpoenaed for the grand jury hearing. The meeting was designed to help witnesses familiarize themselves with the legal process. Joni Rabinowitz was one of the people called to testify in front of the grand jury. She had arrived in Albany in April 1963 to complete work for academic credit, and her work for SNCC was completed in July 1963, when she returned home to New Rochelle, New York. Joni was in New York when Holtzman met to prepare subpoenaed witnesses and did not attend that meeting. She returned to Albany shortly before the grand jury hearing.[55]

The grand jury convened on July 29, 1963, in the federal courthouse in Macon, Georgia. As stated in the civil subpoena, evidence was presented by an attorney for the federal government "concerning charges of violation of federal law, which made it a crime to coerce or threaten anyone because of his or her vote on a federal jury." Victor Rabinowitz recalled Smith's testimony, in which he stated "a white girl had been at the picket line" outside his store and that she "seemed to be directing it." During a recess of the grand jury, Smith saw Joni "standing in the court corridor awaiting her turn to testify, and he identified her as the white girl on the line." When lawyers called Joni before the grand jury, she denied having been on the picket line and said she was not at Smith's store on the day of the protest. When SNCC worker Joyce Barrett, a white woman, testified at the trial, she stated that she, and not Joni, had been picketing at the store. After ten days of hearings, the grand jury found reasons for lawyers to charge the nine Civil Rights workers with intimidation of a federal juror. SNCC members Anderson, Luther Woodall, and Robert Colbert were indicted for obstruction of justice. In addition, Slater King, Elza L. Jackson, Rev. Samuel B. Wells, Thomas C. Chatmon, Robert Thomas, and Joni Rabinowitz were charged with perjury before the grand jury for not remembering whether they had attended a meeting in King's office or not remembering whether they were present at the picketing.[56]

Joni Rabinowitz was indicted on three counts of perjury for denying that she was present at the protest in front of Smith's store and could not tell the court the name of the woman at the protest since she was not present. However, Barrett had already testified that she was the white woman outside the grocery store that day. King, lawyer for the Civil Rights activists, contested that the charges were politically motivated. Dennis Roberts, a SNCC member who worked with King, identified a possible subtext of the charge against Joni: she and her father were believed to be Communists due to his involvement in Fair Play for Cuba and in efforts for "peace, free speech and socialism." Victor had represented Fidel Castro at trials held in the United States concerning the federal embargo on Cuba. During the 1960s Red Scare, J. Edgar Hoover, director of the FBI, equated "any kind of protest with communist subversion," targeting Martin Luther King Jr. and Civil Rights groups.[57]

Throughout mid-July 1963, the US Senate held hearings on what would become the 1964 Civil Rights Act. Historian David J. Garrow wrote that segregationists, including Mississippi Governor Ross Barnett, "repeatedly made wild accusations that the Civil Rights movement was a Communist conspiracy." In response to this rising belief, on July 25, US Attorney General Kennedy "released a carefully worded statement to the effect that civil rights leaders were not 'Communists or Communist-controlled.'" At that time, the allegation of Communism was enough to convict a person of a crime in southwestern Georgia. Since Joni's alleged perjury was committed before a grand jury in Macon, the case would be tried there on October 28. The maximum penalties, if convicted, were five years in prison and a $2,000 fine.[58]

Victor Rabinowitz wrote that he was confident the jury would return a guilty verdict in the district court trial. He and his partner in the case, Leonard Boudin, recognized a "direct challenge to a jury verdict on a simple factual issue is not likely ever to be successful on appeal, and so we turned our attention to an attack on the jury system, which seemed to be our best (and perhaps our only) bet." Before Joni's district trial for perjury, her lawyers challenged the method by which the court selected grand jurors and trial jurors: "If the grand jury was illegally selected, then they couldn't return a legal indictment."[59] District Judge William A. Bootle denied the petition, and Joni's lawyers appealed her case to the Fifth Circuit.

Achsah Posey, a reporter for the *Atlanta Constitution*, covered the Fifth Circuit three-judge hearing on Victor Rabinowitz's motion asserting that the grand jury panel needed to include Black citizens to return a valid indictment. According to Posey, at one point Chief Judge Tuttle commented, "This lady [Joni Rabinowitz] is white. . . . Explain if you will how she will be injured by not having enough Negroes on the grand jury?" Boudin responded, "As a white girl she will be regarded more as a traitor to her class" and therefore "be subject to more prejudice 'than any Negro would be' in such a case." He continued, "The fact that she's a young woman and mingles socially with Negroes . . . would prejudice a [white] jury against her." Tuttle replied, "all these elements would be irrelevant (and therefore inadmissible) in a trial of her case."[60] He thought lawyers should not consider the social pressures that could potentially be placed on a juror when selecting a jury in southwest Georgia.

The court granted lawyers a two-week extension, and *Rabinowitz* was tried in federal district court at 9:30 a.m. on November 12, 1963, in Macon, Georgia. Of those summoned for jury duty, lawyers questioned forty-two citizens; no Black citizens were included. Again, an all-white jury was selected. When questioned, Joni Rabinowitz responded that she was not involved in the picketing and had been truthful in her statements to the grand jury. The *Macon Telegraph* documented that twelve additional witnesses also testified that Joni "was not at the scene during the picketing of a grocery last April." The *Macon News* echoed that observation. Once again, Barrett—who was from Philadelphia, Pennsylvania—said Joni was not at the site of the picketing and that "she herself was the only white girl on the scene." The trial took four days, and Victor Rabinowitz described the proceedings as largely routine. Eleven white men and one white woman deliberated for nearly three hours.[61]

Joni Rabinowitz was convicted on all three counts of perjury. Lawyer Manley F. Brown interviewed Judge Bootle, who translated the jurors' feelings: Joni "came down as a part of the movement to register black voters, and so forth, and she came to Albany, and she chose to live with the blacks in Albany. And that probably outraged all [residents of Albany]." Charles Salter of the *Macon News* reported that Bootle sentenced Joni "to the custody of the attorney general for treatment and supervision until discharged by the Youth Corrections Division of the Board of Parole." As expected, her lawyers filed a notice of appeal to the Fifth Circuit because of discrimination against Black citizens in the selection of jurors for the Middle District of Georgia federal courts.[62]

By the end of 1965, discrimination against Black citizens in jury selection had reached the general public's attention. The public was outraged over the acquittal of Collie LeRoy Wilkins by an Alabama state circuit court in the murder of white Civil Rights activist Viola Liuzzo following the Selma-to-Montgomery voting rights march. Earl C. Dudley Jr. wrote that President Lyndon B. Johnson responded to the public rage over Wilkins's not guilty verdict with "a call for new legislation designed to eliminate discrimination in the selection of both federal and state juries." Robert B. Semple Jr. of the *New York Times* reported Johnson's assertion that trial by jury is "the cornerstone of our system of justice. If its composition is a sham, its judgment is a sham . . . And when that happens, justice is a fraud." The president was also responding to a 188-page report issued by the US Commission on Civil Rights in 1965 addressing law enforcement in the South. That report recommended, in part, that "the Attorney General be given increased power to initiate suits in state court proceedings to obtain equal treatment and racial balance on juries."[63] Federal legislators were prepared to address this Civil Rights issue, even though earlier legislation had already done so.

The states had already lost control over the qualifications of federal jurors with the passage of the Civil Rights Act of 1957, which amended Title 28 of the US Code, Section 1861: Federal Juror Qualifications. That act, together with *Glasser v. United States* in 1942, which established the rule that a jury must represent a cross-section of the community from which it was selected, had previously set forth criteria for juror selection. The question remained, however, if Section 1861 set a minimum standard or if states were allowed to augment the jury rule with additional criteria for juror selection.[64]

The Fifth Circuit had been hearing jury desegregation appeals frequently enough that according to one of Judge Rives's clerks, Lawrence R. Levin, Rives wanted to limit such instances. Rives saw a pattern of juror discrimination and recommended that the court select several cases from states across the Fifth Circuit, prepare each of them for an en banc hearing in New Orleans, and "remake the judicial system in the entire Fifth Circuit for how juries are selected." The outcome of the hearing would have extensive implications for previously tried cases and for cases yet to be heard by district trial courts. The five cases the court selected included appeals from state courts in Louisiana (*LaBat v. Bennett* and *Scott v. Walker*), Alabama (*Billingsley v. Clayton*), Texas (*Brooks v. Beto*), and Georgia (*Davis v. Davis*). The sixth case, *Rabinowitz*, added the federal courts into the mix.[65] Legal teams filed briefs, and the lawsuits moved forward.

The Civil Rights Division of the DOJ represented the federal government in the five state cases, and the Criminal Division of the DOJ represented the federal government in the *Rabinowitz* case. Lawyers from the Civil Rights Division filed to desegregate state juries, while lawyers from the Criminal Division supported the finding of a segregated jury. In the appeals, the DOJ found itself both defending and prosecuting verdicts from all-white juries that did not represent a cross-section of people in the judicial district. Rives told his clerk, Levin, to ask John Doar, the Assistant Attorney General of the Civil Rights Division, "if he was aware that the Criminal Division was filing briefs in the federal case that conflicted with . . . [Doar's] briefs in the state case." Doar was unaware that the Criminal Division was using the same argument to support the opposing side of the issue. When Doar returned to Washington, DC, he set out to resolve how the federal government found itself on both sides of such an important matter. At Doar's request, the solicitor general, Thurgood Marshall, took over the case. Marshall transferred the *Rabinowitz* case out of the Criminal Division and argued the complaint on behalf of the United States in December 1965.[66] The cases were heard by an en banc panel of judges in the Fifth Circuit.

At the time, according to federal statute, juries in federal courts were to be selected under the laws of the state where the judges were hearing a case. States across the country, including Georgia, used what was known as a "key-man" system to procure prospective jurors' names. Judge Bootle explained the key-man method of jury selection in Georgia to Manley F. Brown, who said the system "boiled down to this: They put in that jury box only folks they knew or those recommended to them by folks they knew." As Victor Rabinowitz wrote, "Judges Wisdom, Tuttle, and Rives were outraged at the facts presented as to the composition of the jury and the method of its choice."[67] The key-man system for selecting jurors was discriminatory and, therefore, unconstitutional.

The key-man list of prospective jurors used in the Macon Division of the Middle District of Georgia, from which state and federal juries were drawn, included less than 6 percent Black citizens. In comparison, the population of Black citizens over the age of twenty-one totaled nearly 35 percent of the population. The question for the court to decide in *Rabinowitz* focused on the qualifications that the clerk of court, his deputy, and the jury commissioner "required of prospective jurors and on the method by which the jury list was compiled."[68] The list of prospective jurors had been most recently updated in 1959 using the key-man system. An en banc court for the five state cases and the one federal case was bound to bring forth a variety of opinions; *Rabinowitz* evoked five separate judgments.

After the en banc hearing and circulation of the draft opinions, but before judges made decisions in the six cases, Judges Rives took senior status. Since Rives participated on the three-judge panel in *Anderson v. The City of Albany* in 1963 (an appeal filed by SNCC's lawyer, Anderson, against the court ruling that allowed racial discrimination, which encompassed Elza L. Jackson's perjury case), he was eligible to rehear an appeal of *Jackson v. United States*, a case identical in nature to *Rabinowitz*. The *Jackson* decision, written by Rives on behalf of himself, Tuttle, Wisdom, and Thornberg as the panel majority, was announced on July 20, 1966. The court ultimately adopted Rives's opinion in *Jackson* as the holding of the court in *Rabinowitz* and published the two cases in one decision.

In his *Rabinowitz* decision on behalf of the court, Judge Rives carefully documented extant law. He provided an extensive analysis of the history of jury selection processes used in the Fifth Circuit for the past twenty years. He also assessed the statutory history of the US Congress to establish uniform standards for federal jury selection. In his argument, Rives cited the 1942 US Supreme Court *Glasser* decision mentioned earlier, wherein Justice Frank W. Murphy wrote, "our democracy itself, requires that the jury be a 'body truly representative of the community,' and not the organ of any special group or class." Later in 1945, additional efforts were made by the court to improve how the jury system functioned. That work ultimately failed "because the divergent laws of the several States still imposed 48 separate standards for federal jury service."[69] Individual states controlled qualifications for federal jury service until 1957.

As stated earlier, Congress's Civil Rights Act of 1957 amended the US Code on federal juror qualifications. One purpose behind that effort was to overcome differences between federal and state laws by adopting "uniform national standards for service on juries." When *Rabinowitz* raised the issue of racial exclusion from federal jury service, the Middle District of Georgia Court interpreted the act as "merely . . . a minimum qualification . . . and that the jury commissioners were not compelled to use only that; that they could then go on their own experience and their own judgment." The jury commissioners then "added their own ideas as to good character, intelligence and ability to 'understand the cases that are tried in court.'" Officials who compiled the 1959 list of prospective jurors for the Middle District of Georgia Court testified that "many more Negroes than whites failed to meet the increased standards of character and intelligence." Alabama county registrars had used the same justification to prevent Black citizens from registering to vote. Judge Rives pointedly stated that the 1957 Civil Rights Act was not primarily a judicial statute. "On the contrary," Rives wrote in *Rabinowitz*, "Congress was enacting a Civil Rights Act and intended to confer an additional civil right, i.e., the right to be a federal juror."[70]

The Fifth Circuit majority did not agree whether the 1957 Civil Rights Act's prescribed standards were a minimum qualification for inclusion in a jury pool in the 1966 *Rabinowitz* decision. If state officials who were primarily responsible for compiling jury lists could freely add "broad and vague subjective tests" to those established in Section 1861, "the same disunity would result that Congress sought to proscribe." The federal qualifications were seen as "objective and precise, requiring in their application no discretion on the part of the court clerk and the jury commissioner," and "intended to be lower" than those used in many states. The modified standards would increase the number of Black citizens in the jury pool so federal juries could better reflect "a fair cross-section of the community." Victor Rabinowitz summarized Rives's argument on behalf of the majority: The 1957 Civil Rights Act provided "the maximum qualifications" for inclusion in the venire. By adding other qualifications, the state was "acting contrary to the intention of the statute, with the result that in the South, large numbers of poorly educated citizens, both black and white, were improperly excluded from jury duty."[71] State jury commissioners could not raise the standards for prospective federal jurors.

Much to the annoyance of some of Judge Rives's brethren on the bench, Rives's 1966 decision on behalf of the majority in the en banc hearing did not identify a particular method for identifying prospective jurors. The majority agreed only that the sources must provide "a representative cross-section of the community" and that the list does not systematically exclude "a cognizable group or class of qualified citizens." Rives would have been aware of a 1953 appeal heard by the US Supreme Court decision captioned *Brown v. Allen*, which stated, "Our duty to protect the federal constitutional rights of all does not mean we must or should impose on states our conception of the proper source of jury lists, so long as the source reasonably reflects a cross-section of the population suitable in character and intelligence for that civic duty."[72] Rives and other judges in the *Rabinowitz* majority thought providing a method for identifying members of a jury pool went too far in federal oversight of the states.

Rives quoted the 1951 US Supreme Court order in *Universal Camera Corp. v. National Labor Relations Board* in *Rabinowitz* to further support the argument against a prescriptive technique for compiling potential juror lists. The *Universal Camera Corp.* decision read, in part, "It is fair to say that in all this Congress expressed a mood. And it expressed its mood not merely by oratory but by legislation. As legislation that mood must be respected, even though it can only serve as a standard for judgment and not as a body of rigid rules assuring sameness of applications. Enforcement of such broad standards implies subtlety of mind and solidity of judgment," which are characteristic of federal judges.[73] The inclusion of this section further irritated minority members of the panel.

Judges Bell, Gewin, and Coleman, the three most conservative judges on the bench, filed dissents to the majority opinion in *Rabinowitz*. Judge Bell seemed to take direct aim at Rives's *Universal Camera Corp.* reference when he wrote, "It is difficult to understand just what the majority opinion holds [regarding 'mood'], much less what it says." Judge Gewin concurred with Bell's opinion. Coleman, the most conservative of the three, concurred in part and dissented in part with the majority decision. He agreed to reverse the convictions "solely because the Government recommends it." Minority opinions expressed displeasure that the government admitted the key-man system was flawed. Bell and Gewin did not fault the system of prospective juror selection, although they agreed that the method had not worked well in this instance. The three judges each argued that, as in voting, intelligence and literacy should be considered as prospective federal juror qualifications. Despite these contestations by judges in the minority, the majority agreed that the court should order a new trial. The decisions reversed the district court's convictions and dismissed the indictments of Joni Rabinowitz and Jackson. The federal government then dropped charges against other members of the Albany Nine.[74]

Two years later, the US Congress again undertook to consider the issue of juror qualifications. Levin shared that federal legislators adopted passages from Rives's *Rabinowitz* (1966) opinion when writing the Jury Selection and Service Act of 1968. Until the passage of that act, federal courts had not established a uniform method of jury selection. Lawyer Fred A. Summer wrote that the act was primarily a "response to the inability of the prevailing jury selection process to achieve the goal of a representative jury." The statute requires that all states use voter registration lists and lists of actual voters as the primary source of names for jury selection in federal courts. Lists that did not include or underrepresented Black citizens were prohibited. In such cases, the voter registration list should be augmented with other sources of names (e.g., utility customers, motor vehicle registrations, payers of income tax, etc.).[75] Rives's decision on behalf of the majority in *Rabinowitz* further cemented the right of Black citizens to serve on juries.

In the 1950s South, despite the passage of the Reconstruction Amendments eighty-five years earlier, Black residents were not seen by the law as full citizens. When Black citizens were brought to trial for alleged crimes in Southern states, they routinely appeared in front of an all-white jury. For Judge Rives, the issue of jury exclusion violated the Sixth, Seventh, and Fourteenth Amendments to the US Constitution. That finding was bolstered by US Supreme Court decisions and federal legislation. Rives believed jury pools and juries (grand juries, civil juries, criminal juries) should not intentionally exclude Black citizens.

In *Rabinowitz*, the principle of equality undergirding the US Supreme Court justices' decisions in *Brown* was extended to include Black citizens' presence on juries. While Goldsby's legal proceedings were aimed at prolonging his life, they also pressed forward the issue of a desegregated jury. The case of Seals, first charged with capital rape in 1958, further affirmed the right of a Black defendant to be heard by a jury that potentially includes Black citizens. Judge Rives's decision on behalf of the court in the 1966 *Rabinowitz* case, as Summer wrote, "was recognized by the Senate Committee on the Judiciary as the basic factor in convincing the legislators that it was necessary to replace the key man selection system." Although Rives and members of the majority stipulated that the selection committee "did not consciously engage in discriminatory practices," the evidence of jury discrimination was "enough to sound the call for reform." Rives's decision on behalf of the majority in *Rabinowitz*, in particular, laid the groundwork for the 1968 Jury Selection and Service Act, an extension of the principle of equality that guided the Supreme Court justices in the *Brown* decisions.[76]

8

Judge Richard T. Rives

A Civil Rights Legacy

Judge Richard T. Rives served the federal courts in a challenging judicial position at a tumultuous time in American history. His Civil Rights legacy was shaped primarily during his fifteen years of full-time service on the US Court of Appeals for the Fifth Circuit from 1951–1966. Rives's intellectual evolution led him to write groundbreaking Civil Rights decisions on behalf of three-judge panels that often emerged from a split, two-to-one, majority vote. His judicial philosophy reflected Rives's ethical interest in common sense, fairness, and legal application of the principle of equality. Rives used everyday language when writing his decisions and dissents, striving to assure that all citizens could understand his court orders. Foremost in his opinions was an adherence to the US Constitution and the clause that begins the preamble to that document: "We the People," who continually shape the United States. His courageous leadership worked toward ending the legal rationing of justice to Black citizens in the public sphere. This monograph emphasized decisions that Rives wrote on behalf of the court to racially desegregate public transportation; elementary and secondary schools; and higher education—as well as equitable reapportionment of electoral districts; voting rights procedures including voter registration, poll taxes, and literacy tests; and the composition of jury pools.

A significant first Civil Rights lawsuit in Judge Rives's career was *Board of Supervisors of Louisiana State University and Agricultural and Mechanical College v. Tureaud*, first decided by Judge J. Skelly Wright of the US District Court for the Eastern District of Louisiana in 1953. In that case, Wright ruled that the university must admit qualified students to the school regardless of race. The case was appealed to the Fifth Circuit. Chief Judge Joseph Chappell Hutcheson Jr. and Judge Robert Lee Russell, a brother of Georgia's Senator Richard Russell, overruled the lower court, supporting the status quo. In their decision, the judges also ordered that a three-judge panel (instead of a single federal judge) was required to decide cases in which a conflict emerges between federal and state law. In contrast, Rives agreed with the lower court's admission decision and in his dissent he reasoned that a single district judge could try such cases. On appeal to the US Supreme Court, the justices overruled the circuit court majority, agreeing with Rives's dissent. Upon hearing the case a second time in the Fifth Circuit, Rives authored a decision on behalf of the court that upheld the district court judge; ruling, in part, that a single district judge may address federal issues involving state law.[1] That case initiated Rives's public record of Civil Rights decisions.

Judge Rives's 1956 decision with his protégé, Judge Frank M. Johnson Jr., for the majority in *Browder v. Gayle*, which desegregated public transportation in Montgomery, would become the first decision to implement the US Supreme Court's *Brown v. Board of Education of Topeka I* and *II* decisions. The *Browder* decision would result in overthrowing *Plessy v. Ferguson*, a racial segregation decision in effect since 1896.[2] Rives interpreted the justices' application of the legal principle of equality in *Brown* to apply to all citizens acting in the public sphere.

Between 1955 and 1966, Judge Rives participated in more educational desegregation panels than any other Fifth Circuit judge. These included early cases such as *Borders v. Rippy* (1957), *Shuttlesworth v. Birmingham Board of Education* (1958), and *Gibson v. Board of Public Instruction of Dade County, Florida* (1959), wherein he held out hope that school administrators would act in good faith to apply the law. After Rives recognized that such compliance would not occur, in 1963 he ruled in *Armstrong v. Birmingham Board of Education*. Eight years after *Brown II*, the *Armstrong* case was a tipping point for segregationist Judge Benjamin F. Cameron. Cameron dissented to the court decision even though he was not a member of the three-judge panel. He alleged that court-packing led to consistent desegregation rulings in elementary and secondary education lawsuits. Cameron's public intervention prompted the Houston Conference, at which judges on the Fifth Circuit addressed Cameron's charges. Few administrative changes were made following the conference, and Rives continued to serve on educational desegregation panels. His involvement in educational desegregation lawsuits came to an end in 1967 in *Lee v. Macon County Board of Education*, which desegregated all public schools in Alabama.[3]

In 1955, two years after Judge Rives ruled in *Tureaud*, Judge Harlan H. Grooms of the Northern District of Alabama consulted with Rives and affirmed gradualism in *Lucy v. University of Alabama*. However, the US Supreme Court overturned Grooms's decision and required immediate action toward desegregation in higher education. This undoubtedly led Rives to begin to question his perspective on racial desegregation. He was also involved in *Meredith v. Fair*, James Meredith's lawsuit to desegregate the University of Mississippi. A riot on the campus of the University of Mississippi in September 1962 led to confrontations between Rives, Attorney General Robert F. Kennedy, and President John F. Kennedy. In addition, legal confrontations occurred between Rives and Governor Ross Barnett of Mississippi in *United States v. Barnett* that addressed the governor's obstruction of Meredith's right to attend the university.[4] Ultimately, Rives and his colleagues dismissed all charges against Barnett.

Reapportionment revolution lawsuits, activated in part by *Gomillion v. Lightfoot* (1960), which ruled against gerrymandered voting districts, also landed on Judge Rives's desk. Malapportionment placed all Alabama citizens, white and Black, in a position of being inequitably represented in the state legislature. M. O. Sims of Birmingham was a plaintiff in several lawsuits (*Sims v. Frink*, 1962; *Reynolds v. Sims*, 1964; *Sims v. Baggett*, 1965; *Sims v. Amos*, 1972) that kept reapportionment in the public eye for over a decade.[5] Rives heard numerous cases with District Judges Johnson and Daniel H. Thomas in which he took the lead on writing court opinions. Those decisions, affirmed by the US Supreme Court, expanded the role of the courts in legislative reapportionment issues.

Judge Rives also tackled voting rights issues, which recalls his involvement as a lawyer in a campaign against the 1946 Boswell amendment, adopted by white Alabama citizens in response to *Smith v. Allwright*, a 1944 Texas case that eliminated white primary elections. When voting registrars in Macon, Bullock, and Montgomery Counties in Alabama refused to submit voter registration records to the US Department of Justice, cases were filed against registrars in each county. In these three decisions, Middle District of Alabama court Judge Frank M. Johnson Jr. fashioned what became known as the "freezing doctrine." The doctrine required that the least restrictive voting registration methods used for white applicants should also be used for Black applicants. Rives disagreed with Johnson, conscious that registrars were already engaging in illegal actions by aiding white citizens in completing their applications. Writing on behalf of a three-judge panel, Rives overruled Johnson's freezing doctrine in *United States v. Atkins* (1963). This interpretation of the law intensified some white citizens' hatred toward Rives, including the minister of his church. In spite of people's animosity toward him, Rives dutifully continued his federal service. In 1966, he wrote panel decisions in *Dent v. Duncan*, which negated the use of literacy tests, as well as *United States v. Alabama*, forbidding the use of poll taxes as a prerequisite for voter registration.[6]

In addition, Judge Rives was passionate about the importance of a fair jury trial. In his 1959 decision *United States ex rel. Goldsby v. Harpole*, Rives drew a line that required judges and lawyers to act in ways consistent with the law.

He also stated that excluding people from jury pools violated the right of the accused person's Civil Rights as well as the Civil Rights of citizens who were not allowed to potentially participate on juries. Rives's 1962 decision on behalf of the court in *United States ex rel. Seals v. Wiman* and his 1966 decision in *Rabinowitz v. United States* reinforced the law requiring desegregated jury pools. Yet Rives's decisions were not always in the majority. In his 1969 dissent to *Boeing Co. v. Shipman*, a personal injury case that addressed the requirements of evidence for submitting a case to a jury, Rives offered his standpoint, "There are many who do not agree with my almost reverential attitude toward jury trial, but this is no occasion for a debate on that subject, because our forefathers wrote into our Constitution the right of trial by jury in both criminal and civil cases." Rives worked to remove legal pillars of racial segregation in the United States, prompted in part by the US Supreme Court's *Brown* decisions.[7]

From a contemporary vantage point, other judges could have interpreted cases in a similar manner, leading to similar decisions. However, except for a few other judges across the South and several other judges with whom Judge Rives worked closely, they did not. As the longest-serving active judge on the Fifth Circuit during that time, Rives exercised enormous influence in the area of Civil Rights. His conversations with Judge Johnson, several colleagues on the Fifth Circuit court, and with other people who held perspectives similar to and different from him enabled Rives to expand the US Supreme Court's *Brown* (1954, 1955) decisions throughout the public sphere. Rives's passion for democracy and the perpetual construction of the United States, his lifetime position, his character and demeanor, and his judicial philosophy enabled him to do what other judges would not.

Judge Rives's judicial oath professionally bound him to support the US Constitution, "the supreme law of the land." Rives spoke to Cumberland Law School in 1976, explaining that according to Article VI of the Constitution, "the judges in every state shall be bound" by the supremacy clause. As a federal judge, Rives did not directly discuss his judicial philosophy, but he did provide glimpses into his thinking. One may infer his approach to the law by reading his decisions, drawing upon scant references he made in writing, reviewing the articles he wrote, and considering the speeches he made. Rives's legal reasoning was shaped by the letter and spirit of the law and of the US Constitution. This approach guided his recognition of the Constitution as a living, evolving document. In 1966 Rives shared his views in *White v. Crook*, a case that addressed racial discrimination in the composition of jury pools: "The Constitution of the United States must be read as embodying general principles meant to govern society and the institutions of government as they evolve through time. It is therefore this Court's function to apply the

Constitution as a living document to the legal cases and controversies of contemporary society." Rives reiterated this sentiment when he spoke to Cumberland Law School. He explained that judicial decisions resulting from the addition of the Reconstruction Amendments to the US Constitution provide evidence that "we now have a living Constitution."[8]

Working from the premise of a living constitution, Rives also addressed an aspect of his judicial philosophy in his *Boeing Company v. Shipman* (1969) dissent. In that case, an employee in one state charged his employer headquartered in another state for personal injuries allegedly incurred due to unsafe working conditions. While discussing the importance of desegregated jury pools and juries, Judge Rives described himself as a common-law lawyer who, as a judge "armed with the Constitution," felt compelled to try to persuade the majority of judges to his way of thinking.[9] Rives's common-law approach situated the legal system within the historical moment in which he made judicial decisions. He sought to ethically and equally apply legal precedent that was infused by the Charters of Freedom—the Declaration of Independence, the US Constitution, and the Bill of Rights—along with federal legislation and a common sense understanding of justice as fairness.

As discussed in earlier chapters, Judge Rives's record indicates that he felt a tenuous pull between legal precepts and the interworking of everyday social systems. He pursued the reconciliation of these differences by drawing upon a rationality that was conceived in his personal experience and in the community of lawyers and judges. Rives's decisions were based on his understanding of common sense as a means to derive what is fair (right or wrong, just or unjust). He was a strategic thinker who considered the direction of the law and what he perceived would best shape democracy. Jonathan R. Harkavy, one of Rives's clerks, praised Rives's thinking and patience. He stated that Rives "was very clever about how to advance a legal doctrine by sometimes not taking a complete step but taking only a smaller step" in pushing the law forward. Rives was not afraid to make a trail in his decisions but also knew that in some instances an incremental approach may be necessary to advance the law in a democratic direction.[10]

Judge Rives made common sense a substantial consideration in his legal decisions. Shortly after Rives wrote the decision in the *Browder* bus desegregation case, Levi S. Udall, a longtime chief justice of the Arizona Supreme Court, wrote, "A judge will never go far wrong if he applies the test: 'Does my proposed action square with good common sense?'" Born just a few years before Rives, Udall claimed, "All in all, common sense is the best tool in our judicial kit. We might be able to get by as judges if we don't know much law, but we just can't make it without common sense." The common sense to which Udall referred includes considering social norms, a judge's personal and professional experiences, and professional sources of the law when making a decision. Rives relied on common rationality (observation, inductive generalizations, and inference) to determine the best explanation and yield sound judgment related to social norms. He conscientiously conducted his own research, tracking down background law on cases in which he served as a judge.[11] His common sense was shaped, in part, by fairness, a noteworthy contributor to Rives's approach to judicial reasoning.

Early in his life Judge Rives learned the lesson of fairness toward each individual. As political scientists Deborah J. Barrow and Thomas G. Walker wrote, "Perhaps what kept him from joining the segregationist forces in his state was a profound commitment to basic human fairness."[12] Fairness guided his ethical desire to act impartially, free from favoritism or discrimination toward any group. Rives attended not only to procedural fairness by using honest and impartial practices but also to distributive fairness, ensuring that equal outcomes were adjudicated for the same type of case. He sought to fairly and equally apply the law. When parties to litigation refused to implement the court's orders, Rives required that the law be followed and that litigants do what was right.

At the turn of the 1900s when Judge Rives was young, families strove to be respected by other members of their communities. Coming as he did from an aristocratic Montgomery family, that respect was granted to him by others who observed family members doing what was right, which included following his religious faith, being honest, and working hard. He adhered to these characteristics when engaging in his judicial responsibilities. His autonomy as a federal judge gave Rives a professional independence toward justice when deciding his panel votes and writing opinions and dissents on behalf of the court. When historian John M. Spivack asked Rives about his approach to justice, Rives said, "I don't know if it's just been in me. I knew what's right and wrong, I suppose. And I've lived with that . . . right is right."[13] A judge continually faces the challenge of applying a general law to an individual case, which always deviates in some sense from the law. A right or just application of the law is not simply a technical skill; a living constitution also requires adhering to the spirit of the law. Such applications were not always popular with the general public.

Judge Rives worked to attain justice, regardless of the public outcry against his decisions. Judge Johnson recalled to journalist Linda Parham that on three-judge panels, Rives "never hesitated to render an unpopular decision if the ends of justice require it." He added, "On principle, Richard T Rives does not know how to yield." Some members of the general public balked at his translations of abstract legal principles into everyday life. Yet, Rives had learned what Judge E. J. Devitt called "the art of judging," which incorporates introspection and critical thinking in conjunction with federal judicial procedures and rules, and Rives was not swayed away from what he considered to be just.[14]

Judge Rives was careful in his decision-making and thoughtful in his deliberations. His attention to detail and desire to understand issues thoroughly may have slowed his work pace, led some of his legal decisions to be more conservative than others, and resulted at times in being overturned on appeal by the US Supreme Court. He was also known to change his mind as he deliberated about cases prior to arriving at his final conclusions. This was due, in part, to his dialectic thinking and contemplation about how the law may change society and how to best shape democracy for all citizens. For example, Rives wrote to his colleagues Judges John R. Brown and John Wisdom, "further study and deliberation and a thorough review of the record" in the 1960 appeal of *Hall v. United States*, a case in which the judges were to determine whether evidence presented was sufficient to sustain the judgment of conviction, brought him to change his mind between hearing the oral arguments and the time he wrote the order of the court. Rives would research and reflect on issues, thinking through the ideas carefully, seek additional information, and glean insights that were not immediately apparent to him and perhaps other judges.[15]

Judge Rives's background and life experience allowed him to understand multiple perspectives on the issue of racial justice. That is not to say he was without blind spots. Rives was an anomaly; he was a grandson of a white man who owned enslaved people, was born and reared in the South, and was a liberal Democrat prior to becoming a judge who supported racial equality. Although Rives often sat on three-judge panels with more liberal colleagues, at times he filed a minority dissent in court decisions.

The US Constitution does not articulate *how* to understand the meaning of words in written documents. Legal processes, procedures, and content, along with the relationship between the law and justice, are, within limits, interpretive in nature. The meanings contained within words are not static. Judge Rives recognized how that flexibility of words could open aspects of linguistic meaning to push equality within the Southern lexicon. He translated the abstract questions of law into concrete examples to be implemented within the structures of society.

Judge Rives was attentive to words, sometimes to the detriment of a larger issue. For example, *Miller v. Amusement Enterprises* (1968) addressed whether a privately owned amusement park must allow access to Black citizens. The legal definition of "entertainment" led Rives to dissent from his brethren on the Fifth Circuit. In his dissent, Rives wrote, "The judicial function is to determine not what the law should be, but what Congress, after hearings, conflict, compromise and change, finally enacted into law."[16] The extant definition of entertainment resulted in his voting against the racial desegregation of an amusement park. While this exhibits that Rives was not a Civil Rights activist on the bench, his dissent also points out that there are numerous forces influencing a common-law approach to justice.

There were also times that Judge Rives sided with more conservative members of the court. For example, *United States v. Cox* was originally brought in the Southern District of Mississippi Court. US Attorney Robert E. Hauberg refused Judge W. Harold Cox's court order to prepare indictments against several individuals for perjury as requested by a grand jury. Hauberg told the court that he "respectfully declined" to initiate indictments based on instructions given to him by Nicholas Katzenbach, the acting US attorney general. On appeal to an en banc panel of the Fifth Circuit, the judges dismissed the lawsuit against Hauberg. The 1965 decision reveals partial concurrences and dissents among the judges. In the minority, Rives sided with conservative Judges Walter P. Gewin and Griffin B. Bell, concurring in part and dissenting in part to the majority decision. The dissent would have affirmed Cox's judgment of civil contempt against Hauberg, and required the district attorney to sign a grand jury indictment, even though the US attorney general holds the power to move for a dismissal of an indictment. John Daniel Reaves, one of Rives's clerks, recalled, "Conservative judges on civil rights applauded him for being attuned to what the law provided."[17] Rives judicial philosophy was not neatly liberal or conservative in nature.

When Judge Rives's decisions were appealed to the US Supreme Court, the justices nearly uniformly aligned themselves with Rives's opinions. However, his decisions were not approved without exception. For example, Rives's 1966 opinion on behalf of the court in *White v. Crook* granted women the right to serve on juries in Alabama. Yet in Rives's 1972 *Frontiero v. Laird* decision, his traditional view of a man as the primary wage earner in a family resulted in the US Supreme Court justices overturning his decision on behalf of the majority. No judge likes to have their decision overruled by a higher court. Rives would later explain to one of his clerks that his *Frontiero* decision was the opinion he regretted most in his career.[18] At the time, Rives viewed race as an egalitarian concept, but his view of gender equality was still nascent. His understanding of justice continued to evolve throughout his time on the bench.

Despite these limitations, Judge Rives's general record of decisions in Civil Rights evidences that, as his clerk Jonathan R. Harkavy shared, he was "a clever common-law judge"—a maverick for racial equality in the United States. Harkavy highlighted the work ethic Rives exuded, coupled with his writing skill, which allowed Rives "to pull others along" by articulating the law in such a way that others "wouldn't disagree" with his reasoning. Lawrence R. Levin, another of Rives's clerks, agreed with Harkavy. Levin commented that Rives worked with members of the public and the judiciary in ways that allowed him to construct arguments and ideas—such as those developed when he actively campaigned against the Boswell amendment—"that normally would be met with hostility" as legitimate approaches to racial desegregation. Governmental structures often serve as gatekeepers of truth and knowledge, and Rives additionally recognized the importance of transparency and the significance of behind-the-scenes negotiation. That is to say, Rives knew when to ease against the lines of Southern tradition and heritage and when to force a different approach in his decisions. Harkavy explained that though Rives "was not afraid to make a path-breaking decision, he also knew when a more incremental approach might be necessary to push the law in a favored direction."[19] Expanding legal Civil Rights is one way to alter social customs, but legal injunctions alone cannot accomplish wholistic societal change.

Throughout his career, Judge Rives tried to persuade people to be guided, as he was, by the first three words in the preamble to the US Constitution, "We the People." The Constitution does not identify degrees of citizenship that differentiate groups of people. One group does not have, as historian John J. Patrick wrote, "first-class citizenship with superior rights and privileges relative to different classes of citizens with different rights." There is only one legal system, and the Constitution does not discriminate between citizens. In his speech to the Cumberland Law School, Judge Rives asserted that the "impossible dream" of a democratic United States can only flourish when citizens consider collective governance to be paramount. The preamble records that democracy is sustained by those who desire justice, peace between the states, defense of the country against threats both foreign and domestic, promotion of the well-being of the nation, and the responsible uses of one's freedom under the law for self and others—in the present and in the future.[20]

Judge Rives's elucidation of insights conveyed in the US Constitution exhibits that he was a student of words, examining their meanings and uses in different contexts. As he said in his speech to Cumberland Law School, "To be frank and honest, originally" the words "We the people" "did <u>not</u> mean what they say. For it is impossible to harmonize those three words . . . with several provisions of the body [of the document] itself." Here Rives explained that the text of the Constitution is at odds with the preamble; Black citizens were excluded from the collective of what was, at the time the Constitution was written, "We the People." The subtext of Rives's argument is that since "We" tacitly referred to white citizens only, Black citizens were not protected by the Constitution because "in the event of conflict [within the document] the body of any instrument prevails over its preamble." He noted that the courts are responsible for harmonizing "provisions for the protection of slavery in the very body of the Constitution not only with its nobly worded preamble but also with the Declaration of Independence." He saw his duty as a member of the judiciary as "to attempt reconciliation of the irreconcilable."[21] Rives's responsibilities required him to resolve complexities within the Constitution, Declaration of Independence, Bill of Rights, and other federal documents, and between state and federal laws as they governed all citizens.

Before becoming a judge, Rives was active in community organizations and recognized by professional groups, including the Alabama Bar Association and the Montgomery Bar Association. Although he was considered a pariah by many people during his judgeship, people later saw the significance of his work. Rives received an honorary doctor of law degree from the University of Notre Dame in 1966, the same year he became a senior judge on the Fifth Circuit. He also received an honorary doctor of law degree from Cumberland School of Law at Samford University in Birmingham in 1975. One of his clerks shared that Rives continued to receive letters from organizations wishing to acknowledge his contributions to the field of law with honorary degrees. In response to the invitations Rives told him, "I'm tired of being eulogized" and that he "didn't want any more accolades." The judge had performed his duty and recognition, for which he was very grateful, was not necessary.[22] Rives's sense of duty sustained his work habit.

As Judge Rives passed milestones in his career, he received telegrams and letters of appreciation from political leaders and presidents. Rives served under seven presidents, most actively under Presidents Harry S Truman, Dwight D. Eisenhower, John F. Kennedy, and Lyndon B. Johnson. As Rives moved to senior status, US Attorney General Kennedy, who Rives had to persuade to send law enforcement personnel to the University of Mississippi several years earlier, wrote to him, "You have been one of the unsung heroes of our country and we are grateful for your quiet courage and strong leadership." President Johnson wrote to Rives, "All of those who have watched your service . . . know how much wisdom, courage and high patriotism you have brought to the bench. While the issues have been difficult ones, you have just reason to be proud of the judicial qualities you have offered your nation." Johnson affirmed that Rives's "outstanding service is a credit to his country, to his fellow citizens of Alabama, and above all, to his own high ideals."[23] Rives wanted the law to be right, and he worked to make it so. His interest in common sense and fairness as justice were interwoven with an ethical concern for equality.

Numerous judges served with Judge Rives on three-judge panels in federal court. Judge Wright, who served the Eastern District of Louisiana from 1949 to 1962, sat on Civil Rights panels with Rives. Wright wrote to Rives that he had been "an inspiration" to all citizens "who believe in the essential dignity of the human being as well as the rule of law." Rives was conscientious in his work and exhibited what a *Birmingham News* reporter wrote was a "most earnest application of the best that was within him." Judge Wisdom also complimented Rives on his "great judicial talents, steadfast character and immeasurable humanity . . . in a time of trial when these qualities were so sorely needed on the bench." In 1965, Judge Brown wrote to Rives, "The ultimate test of the Appellate Judge—[is] the quality of his judicial opinions." By that litmus, Brown as well as Hugo L. Black Jr., whose father was a member of the US Supreme Court during that time, affirmed that Rives's leadership on the Fifth Circuit elevated him to a status as one of the most influential appeals court judges in the history of the United States.[24]

Rives's juridical record, for which he received numerous laurels, supports the need for historical recognition of his legacy. While he underwent extreme criticism during the Civil Rights years, he was later thanked for his assistance, integrity, and service to the country. He was recognized by professional organizations, universities, and people who felt his influence. Rives's personal demeanor, legal expertise, and judicial leadership prepared him to take on Civil Rights issues with poise. His interpretation of the US Constitution, judicial decisions, and collegiate rapport with other judges allowed him and his colleagues to press equality into democracy in areas that lacked justice.

In the end, Judge Rives's decisions reveal a man who interpreted the law in ways that prohibited the continuance of institutionalized race bias. He contributed to democracy as a judge by agitating what had become a one-party political system in Southern states and by supporting the US Constitution. Rives allowed his opinions to change as he matured, gained additional information, and learned through experience. He was never a confirmed segregationist, although he was influenced by his Alabama heritage. Rives worked to bring consensus on three-judge and en banc panels; however, when that was not possible, he forged a course that was necessary to attain a fuller democracy. Rives's body of numerous landmark Civil Rights decisions bears credit to his legal thinking and to his fearless yet humble demeanor. His Civil Rights legacy endures as "We the People" continue to shape the constitutional form of government that is the United States.

Notes

Introduction

1. Hugo L. Black Jr., "The Final Judgement: Richard Taylor Rives, 1895–1982," *Alabama Lawyer* 44, no. 1 (1983): 59; *Brown v. Bd. of Educ.* (*Brown I*), 347 U.S. 483 (1954); *Brown v. Bd. of Educ.* (*Brown II*), 349 U.S. 294 (1955).

2. Committee on the Judiciary, "Testimony of Althea T. L. Simmons, Director, Washington Bureau, National Association for the Advancement of Colored People," Hearing before the Subcommittee on Courts, Civil Liberties, and the Administration of Justice of the Committee on the Judiciary House of Representatives, 96th Cong. 2nd sess., August 22, 1980, 11.

3. US Constitution, amend. XIV.

4. *Brown I*, 347 U.S. 483; *Brown II*, 347 U.S. 483.

5. Boeing Co. v. Shipman, 411 F.2d 365 (5th Cir. 1969) at 378, 379; David A. Strauss, "The Living Constitution," University of Chicago Law School (website), September 27, 2010; idem, *The Living Constitution* (Oxford: Oxford University Press, 2010), 38, 35, 43; "Living Constitution," Choose Your Judges, accessed July 18, 2024; US Constitution, preamble; *Brown I*.

6. E.g., "Courts: The Fascinating and Frenetic Fifth," *Time*, December 4, 1964, 46; "Richard T. Rives, Judge on Court That Helped Integrate the South," *New York Times*, October 30, 1982.

7. Browder v. Gayle, 142 F. Supp. 707 (M.D. Ala. 1956); Plessy v. Ferguson, 163 US 537 (1896); *Brown I*; Euel Screws Jr., quoted in "Richard T. Rives, Judge on Court That Helped Integrate the South."

8. Frank T. Read and Lucy S. McGough, *Let Them Be Judged: The Judicial Integration of the Deep South* (Metuchen, NJ: Scarecrow Press, 1978), 619–22; Borders v. Rippy, 247 F.2d 268 (5th Cir. 1957); Shuttlesworth v. Birmingham Bd. of Educ., 162 F. Supp. 372 (N.D. Ala. 1958); Gibson v. Bd. of Public Instruction of Dade Cty, Fla, 272 F.2d 763 (5th Cir. 1959); Armstrong v. Birmingham (330 F.2d 333 (5th Cir. 1963); Lee v. Macon, 267 F. Supp. 458 (M.D. Ala. 1967).

9. Bd. of Supervisors v. Tureaud, 207 F.2d 807 (5th Cir. 1953); Lucy v. Univ. of Ala., 134 F. Supp. 235 (N.D. Ala. 1955); Meredith v. Fair, 298 F.2d 696 (5th Cir.

1962); Meredith v. Fair, 313 F.2d 532 (5th Cir. 1962); United States v. Barnett, 330 F.2d 369 (5th Cir. 1963); United States v. Barnett, 346 F.2d 99 (5th Cir. 1965).

10. "Introduction," in *Redistricting in the South*, Rose Institute of State and Local Government, Claremont McKenna College (website), accessed December 4, 2024; Gomillion v. Lightfoot, 364 US 339 (1960); Sims v. Frink, 205 F. Supp. 245 (M.D. Ala. 1962); Sims v. Frink, 208 F. Supp. 431 (M.D. Ala. 1962); Reynolds v. Sims, 377 US 533 (1964); Sims v. Baggett, 247 F. Supp. 96 (M.D. Ala. 1965); Sims v. Amos, 336 F. Supp. 924 (M.D. Ala. 1972).

11. Smith v. Allwright, 321 US 649 (1944); United States v. Ala., 192 F. Supp. 677 (M.D. Ala. 1961); United States v. Ala., Civil Action no. 1677-N (M.D. Ala., 1961); United States v. Penton, 212 F. Supp. 193 (M.D. Ala. 1962); United States v. Atkins, 323 F.2d 733 (5th Cir. 1963); Dent v. Duncan, 360 F.2d 333 (5th Cir. 1966); United States v. Ala., 252 F. Supp. 95 (M.D. Ala. 1966).

12. Norris v. Alabama, 294 US 587 (1935); United States ex rel. Goldsby v. Harpole, 263 F.2d 71 (5th Cir. 1959); United States ex rel. Seals v. Wiman, 304 F.2d 53 (5th Cir. 1962); Rabinowitz v. United States, 366 F.2d 34 (5th Cir. 1966).

13. Richard T. Rives, "Law Day Remarks, Cumberland Law School," unpublished ms courtesy of Jonathan R. Harkavy, April 29, 1976, 1.

Chapter 1

1. Waller, *Adm'r de bonis non v. Ray, Farley*, in *Reports of Cases Argued and Determined in the Supreme Court of Alabama*, vol. 48, *January Term, and at June Term, 1872* (Montgomery: Barrett and Brown, 1874), 469.

2. Richard T. Rives, interview by John M. Spivack, July 27, 1977, audiotape courtesy of John M. Spivack; James Rives Childs, *Reliques of the Rives (Ryves): Being Historical and Genealogical Notes of the Ancient Family of Ryves of County Dorset and of the Rives of Virginia, an Essay: Sociological and Historical, of a Family's Contribution to the Making of a Nation* (Lynchburg, VA: J. P. Bell, 1929), 480–81.

3. J. Wayne Flynt, "Religion in Alabama," *Encyclopedia of Alabama*, May 25, 2022; Childs, *Reliques*, 481; Jeffrey C. Benton, *Respectable and Disreputable: Leisure Time in Antebellum Montgomery* (Montgomery: NewSouth Books, 2013), 13; Richard T. Rives, quoted in John Michael Spivack, "Race, Civil Rights, and the United States Court of Appeals for the Fifth Judicial Circuit" (PhD diss., University of Florida, 1978), 258n*; Rives, interview by Spivack; Richard T. Rives, quoted in Tinsley E. Yarbrough, *Judge Frank Johnson and Human Rights in Alabama* (Tuscaloosa: University of Alabama Press, 1981), 53. Cf. Donnie Williams with Wayne Greenhaw, *The Thunder of Angels: The Montgomery Bus Boycott and the People Who Broke the Back of Jim Crow* (Chicago: Lawrence Hill Books, 2006), 208: while Williams and Greenhaw state that James McLemore was Rives's "great-great-grandfather," he was actually Rives's great-grandfather-in-law.

4. Rives, quoted in Yarbrough, *Judge Frank Johnson*, 53.

5. Bill Blanchard, email to Bobby Segal, October 29, 2018; Rives, interview by Spivack; Ray Jenkins, "Decade on Bench Has Brought Rives Wide Recognition," *Alabama Journal*, May 8, 1961.

6. Rives, interview by Spivack.

7. Deborah J. Barrow and Thomas G. Walker, *A Court Divided: The Fifth Circuit Court of Appeals and the Politics of Judicial Reform* (New Haven, CT: Yale University Press, 1988), 15; Rives, interview by Spivack; Minna Roth Hill, "A Significant History," Sidney Lanier High School (website), accessed March 12, 2021; Jonathan R. Harkavy, email message to Pat Arneson, January 6, 2023.

8. Rives, interview by Spivack; Joe Simmons, "Senior US Judge Rives Dies," *Montgomery Advertiser*, October 28, 1982.

9. Rives, interview by Spivack; Peggy Roberson, "Retired Judge Pleased at Progress," *Birmingham News*, April 9, 1975; Simmons, "Senior US Judge."

10. Jenkins, "Decade on Bench"; Rives, interview by Spivack: Rives said he worked in the pressing business for "a year," but that length of time does not allow him two years to complete his apprenticeship prior to taking the bar examination. He may have meant he worked in the pressing business for a summer, which would be long enough to determine if the business would be profitable and also better fit his chronology. See also William H. McDonald, "Judge Rives Gets Lots of 'Fan Mail,'" *Southern School News* 8, no. 9 (March 1962), Richard T. Rives Papers, Alabama Department of Archives and History, Montgomery, AL (hereafter RTR Papers); Anne S. Emanuel, *Elbert Parr Tuttle: Chief Jurist of the Civil Rights Revolution* (Athens: University of Georgia Press, 2014), 131.

11. David A. Strauss, "The Common Law Genius of the Warren Court," *William and Mary Law Review* 49, no. 3 (2007): 845; Rives, quoted in Spivack, "Race, Civil Rights," 249; Virginia Foster Durr, *Outside the Magic Circle: The Autobiography of Virginia Foster Durr*, ed. Hollinger F. Barnard (New York: Simon and Schuster, 1985), 291.

12. Rives, interview by Spivack; McDonald, "Judge Rives Gets"; Debra Cassens Weiss, "Students Try to Avoid Law School Costs with 'Reading Law' Path to Law License," *ABA Journal*, July 30, 2014.

13. Strauss, "Common Law Genius," 858–59.

14. Rives, interview by Spivack; "Capitol Profile," *Montgomery Advertiser*, June 14, 1959; Spivack, "Race, Civil Rights," 249.

15. Rives, interview by Spivack; Richard T. Rives, "Commonplace Book," RTR papers.

16. David A. Strauss, *The Living Constitution* (Oxford: Oxford University Press, 2010), 34; Rives, interview by Spivack.

17. Law clerk for Richard T. Rives, interview by Pat Arneson, February 22, 2017 (this clerk graciously allowed me to conduct an interview with them, but wished to remain anonymous in this book); Roberson, "Retired Judge Pleased"; McDonald, "Judge Rives Gets."

18. Rives, interview by Spivack; Dan Abrams and Fred D. Gray with David Fisher, *Alabama v. King: Martin Luther King Jr. and the Criminal Trial That Launched the Civil Rights Movement* (Toronto: Hanover Square Press, 2022), 54.

19. "Tribute to Judge John Harris (Senate-March 13, 1991)," *Cong. Rec.* 137, pt. 5: 5930; Richard T. Rives, "Trying a Case for the Plaintiff," *Alabama Lawyer* 2, no. 4 (1941): 413; Boeing Co. v. Shipman, 411 F.2d 365 (5th Cir. 1969) at 378.

20. US Dept. of Veterans Affairs, AL, "National Guard Index Cards, 1897–1924," Alabama Department of Archives and History, Montgomery, AL; "One Cent a Word," *Montgomery Daily Advertiser*, October 27, 1888; Rives, interview by Spivack. Cf. Steve Welz, "Judge Rives Is Honored," *Pro Confesso* [Cumberland School of Law at Samford University, Birmingham, AL] (April 1975): 1, 4: while Welz states that Rives served in the US Army Signal Corp at the rank of lieutenant before attending Tulane University, he actually served as first class sergeant after attending Tulane University.

21. Rives, interview by Spivack; "1915 Bulletin of the Alabama Polytechnic Institute State College for the Benefit of Agriculture and Mechanical Arts," Alabama Mosaic (website), accessed December 30, 2023; US Dept. of Veterans Affairs, AL, "National Guard Index Cards."

22. "Attorney's Office: Legal Department's Function," City of Montgomery, AL (website), accessed March 12, 2021; Rives, interview by Spivack; "Capitol Profile"; US Dept. of Veterans Affairs, AL, "National Guard Index Cards."

23. Rives, interview by Spivack; "County Marriage Records 1828–1978," *Bibb County, Marriages (White), Book O, 1917–1920*, Georgia Archives, Morrow, GA, Alabama Department of Archives and History, Montgomery, AL; Richard Rives to Mrs. Richard T. Rives, postcard, n.d., RTR Papers.

24. "Rives, Richard T.," *US City Directories, Montgomery City Directories* (Montgomery: R. L. Polk, 1920), Alabama Department of Archives and History, Montgomery, AL; "Infant Daughter Rives," Find a Grave (website), October 8, 2008. Over the years Hill, Hill, and Whiting underwent numerous name changes including Hill, Hill, and Whiting; Hill, Hill, Whiting, and Stern; Hill, Hill, Whiting, Thomas, and Rives; Hill, Hill, Whiting, and Rives; among others.

25. Childs, *Reliques*, 478; "Legislators Who Have Represented Montgomery County," *Montgomery Advertiser*, April 14, 1901; "Democratic and Conservative Party," *Montgomery Daily Advertiser*, April 3 and 5, 1883; "Election Notice!" *Montgomery Daily Advertiser*, July 26, 1878; "Election Notice," *Montgomery Daily Advertiser*, October 11, 1882; Glenn Feldman, *Politics, Society, and the Klan in Alabama, 1915–1949* (Tuscaloosa: University of Alabama Press, 1999), 117–24; J. Mills Thornton III, "Challenge and Response in the Montgomery Bus Boycott of 1955–1956," *Alabama Review* 67, no. 1 (2014): 40–41; J. Mills Thornton III, interview by Pat Arneson, August 14, 2015; Anne Permaloff, "Black Belt-Big Mule Coalition," Encyclopedia of Alabama (website), last modified March 30, 2023;

Marie B. Owen, "Twenty-Eighth District: Montgomery County," *Alabama Official and Statistical Register, 1919* (Montgomery: Brown Printing, 1920), 101.

26. Thornton, "Challenge and Response," 40–41; Thornton, interview by Pat Arneson, August 14, 2015.

27. "Former Publisher R. F. Hudson Dies," *Montgomery Advertiser*, December 16, 1965; "History of the Montgomery Advertiser," *Montgomery Advertiser* (website), accessed November 5, 2022; Coke Ellington, "The Montgomery Advertiser," Encyclopedia of Alabama (website), last modified April 11, 2022; "Newspaper's Tradition Weighed Heavily on Ambitious, Hard-Working R. F. Hudson," *Montgomery Advertiser*, December 16, 1965; J. Mills Thornton III, "Hugo Black and the Golden Age," *Alabama Law Review* 36, no. 3 (1984–1985): 904; Thornton, interview by Pat Arneson, August 14, 2015. See Jesse B. Hearn, "William Albert Bellingrath," Alabama Business Hall of Fame (website), accessed November 10, 2022. Bellingrath was a "deacon and elder in the Presbyterian Church."

28. Thornton, "Hugo Black," 903, 906; Linda Gordon, *The Second Coming of the KKK: The Ku Klux Klan of the 1920s and the American Political Tradition* (New York: Liveright, 2017); Edwin C. Bridges, *Alabama: The Making of an American State* (Tuscaloosa: University of Alabama Press, 2016), 124.

29. Thornton, "Hugo Black"; Gordon, *Second Coming*; Bridges, *Alabama.*

30. US Constitution, amend. XVIII: The amendment prohibited the manufacture, sale, and transport of intoxicating liquors but not their consumption; A. James Reichley, *The Life of the Parties: A History of American Political Parties* (New York: Rowman and Littlefield, 2000); Thornton, "Hugo Black," 906; Thornton, interview by Pat Arneson, August 14, 2015.

31. Rives, interview by Spivack; Barrow and Walker, *Court Divided*, 15; George E. Sims, *The Little Man's Big Friend: James E. Folsom in Alabama Politics, 1946–1958* (Tuscaloosa: University of Alabama Press, 1985), 14–15.

32. "Hugo L. Black," Oyez (website), accessed March 12, 2021; Thornton, "Hugo Black," 902; Tony A. Freyer, *Hugo L. Black and the Dilemma of American Liberalism* (New York: Pearson, 2008), 47. See Feldman, *Politics*, 66: "Charlie McCall, Hugh Locke, Ben Ray, George Frey, A. G. Patterson, Richard Rives, Walter Brower, and Cooper Green rushed to become members of the secret order."

33. Ray Jenkins, email to Pat Arneson, May 17, 2017; E. Lloyd Sutter, interview by Pat Arneson, May 15, 2017; Freyer, *Hugo L. Black*, 43, 44; Barrow and Walker, *Court Divided*, 16.

34. Thornton, "Hugo Black," 902–4; Jack Bass, *Unlikely Heroes: The Dramatic Story of the Southern Judges of the Fifth Circuit Who Translated the Supreme Court's Brown Decision into a Revolution for Equality* (New York: Simon and Schuster, 1981), 73; "Rives Re-Appointed Judge Advocate of State's Legion," *Alabama Journal*, August 3, 1942, RTR Papers; Rives, interview by Spivack.

35. Law clerk for Richard T. Rives, interview by Pat Arneson, February 22, 2017; A. G. Danish, "Common Sense: The Most Uncommon Virtue," LinkedIn

(website), October 9, 2023; "Callie Dougherty Rives," FamilySearch (website), accessed June 7, 2023; "Rives, Richard T.," *US City Directories: Montgomery City Directories* (Montgomery: R. L. Polk, 1925), 613, Alabama Department of Archives and History, Montgomery, AL; "Jesse Dougherty Rives," Find a Grave (website), September 29, 2010. Cf. "Richard T. Rives, Judge on Court": this source says that Rives "married Jessie H. Daugherty [*sic*] of Georgia around 1920. The couple would have three [*sic*] children, two of whom died in infancy." But Jessie's last name was actually spelled "Dougherty," and the couple had four children. Lonewalker, "Jessie Hall Dougherty Rives," Find a Grave (website), October 7, 2010, accessed December 30, 2023, states that the Riveses named their fourth child Callie Dougherty Rives. In fact, the Riveses named their fourth child Jesse Dougherty Rives. Their offspring include an unnamed first child (1920–1920); a son, Richard Taylor Rives Jr. (1922–1949); a daughter, Callie Dougherty Rives (1924–1987); and a son, Jesse Dougherty Rives (1926–1926). Callie Dougherty Rives was the mother of Callie Virginia Smith ("Ginny") Granade (b. 1950), who herself became a judge.

36. Richard T. Rives, quoted in Frank T. Read and Lucy S. McGough, *Let Them Be Judged: The Judicial Integration of the Deep South* (Metuchen, NJ: Scarecrow Press, 1978), 32. This litigation is referred to in several publications; however, I have been unable to locate the case citation. The lawsuit likely occurred sometime between 1913 and 1921 based on Sweeney v. Erving, 228 US 233 (1913), and the first edition of *ASME A17.1 Safety Code for Elevators and Escalators* (New York: American Society of Mechanical Engineers, 1921).

37. Parke v. Dennard, 218 Ala. 209 (1928); Richard T. Rives, interview by Ginny Granade, n.d., digital file courtesy of Ginny Granade.

38. Rives, interview by Granade.

39. Rives, interview by Granade; Neil T. Bradley, interview by Pat Arneson, February 6, 2017.

40. Carl Grafton and Anne Permaloff, *Big Mules and Branchheads: James E. Folsom and Political Power in Alabama* (Athens: University of Georgia Press, 1985), 80; Ferrel Guillory, "On the Temper of the Times: Jack Bass," *Southern Cultures* 18, no. 3 (2012): 34; Spivack, "Race, Civil Rights," 252; Thornton, "Hugo Black," 903. Rives would also actively participate in Lister Hill's 1938 political campaign for US senator.

41. Sims, *Little Man's Big Friend*, 17; "Graves Administration Paid Lawyers $751,873: Matt Murphy Drew Largest Sum in State: Horace Wilkinson Got $54,000 from Alabama Treasury, Report Shows," *Anniston Star*, May 28, 1939; "Auditor Lists $751,880 in Lawyer Fees," *Montgomery Advertiser*, May 27, 1939.

42. "US Court of Appeals for the Fifth Circuit—Legislative History," US Court of Appeals for the Fifth Circuit (website), accessed December 30, 2023; Richard T. Rives, "The Scope of Review of Facts by United States Courts of Appeals," *Alabama Law Review* 11, no. 1 (1958): 71; "About the US Courts of Appeals," US Courts (website), accessed January 5, 2023.

43. Lister Hill to Richard Taylor Rives, May 15, 1938, RTR Papers; Richard T. Rives, quoted in Bass, *Unlikely Heroes*, 70.

44. Virginia Van der Veer Hamilton, *Lister Hill: Statesman from the South* (Chapel Hill: University of North Carolina Press, 1987), 106–7, 89.

45. William D. Barnard, "The Old Order Changes: Graves, Sparks, Folsom, and the Gubernatorial Election of 1942," in *From Civil War to Civil Rights: Alabama, 1860–1960: An Anthology from "The Alabama Review"*, ed. Sarah Woolfolk Wiggins (Tuscaloosa: University of Alabama Press, 1987), 425n40; McDonald, "Judge Rives Gets"; Roberson, "Retired Judge Pleased"; Hamilton, *Lister Hill*, 89.

46. "1940 United States Federal Census," Alabama Department of Archives and History, Montgomery, AL; "History of the MCBA," Montgomery County Bar Association (website), accessed December 30, 2023; "Past Presidents," Alabama State Bar (website), accessed November 10, 2022; Pat Boyd Rumore, *From Power to Service: The Story of Lawyers in Alabama* (Montgomery: Alabama State Bar and the Alabama Bench and Bar Historical Society, 2010), 178, 179, 183, 180; Spivack, "Race, Civil Rights," 250.

47. Allison Marston, "Guiding the Profession: The 1887 Code of Ethics of the Alabama State Bar Association," *Alabama Law Review* 49, no. 2 (1997): 481; "The Code of Legal Ethics: Thomas Goode Jones," Alabama Judicial System (website), accessed March 12, 2021; Oakley Melton Jr., "President's Message," *Alabama Lawyer* 41, no. 1 (1980): 9; Rives, interview by Spivack.

48. Spivack, "Race, Civil Rights," 250; Harvey C. Couch, *A History of the Fifth Circuit, 1891–1981* (Washington, DC: Bicentennial Committee of the Judicial Conference of the United States, 1984), 84; confidential communication, quoted in Spivack, "Race, Civil Rights," 250; Armory Commission of Alabama, State Military Department: Functional Analysis and Records Disposition Authority, January 27, 2010, 1 (website); "Red Cross Unit to Hold Parley," *Alabama Journal*, January 16, 1939, RTR Papers; "Rives Re-Appointed Judge Advocate of State's Legion," *Alabama Journal*, August 3, 1942, RTR Papers; "Richard Rives Heads Enemy Alien Board," *Alabama Journal*, December 24, 1941, RTR Papers.

49. Freyer, *Hugo Black*, 27; "David Bibb Graves," Find a Grave (website), November 12, 2022; Sims, *Little Man's Big Friend*, 17; "David Bibb Graves," Geni (website), accessed November 8, 2020.

50. Sims, *Little Man's Big Friend*, 18; Rumore, *From Power*, 183; Barnard, "Old Order Changes," 425n40.

51. Sims, *Little Man's Big Friend*, 17; Freyer, *Hugo L. Black*, 39; William D. Barnard, *Dixiecrats and Democrats: Alabama Politics, 1942–1950* (Tuscaloosa: University of Alabama Press, 1974), 20; Bradley, interview by Pat Arneson, February 6, 2017.

52. Sims, *Little Man's Big Friend*, 18, 20; Bradley, interview by Arneson; Barnard, *Dixiecrats*, 20. Cf. Freyer, *Hugo L. Black*, 20, 21: "Sparks was to prove an independent governor [from 1943–1947] . . . and his administration disappointed some and surprised others by its progressive cast."

53. "Madison Family Collection," Trenholm State Community College (website), accessed February 21, 2021; Bryan Lyman, "The Believer: Arthur Madison Launched a Montgomery Voter Registration Drive in 1944—and Paid a Price," *Montgomery Advertiser*, February 21, 2021: The citizens included "13 men and women, many of them his family members"; Wesley Phillips Newton, *Montgomery in the Good War: Portrait of a Southern City, 1939–1946* (Tuscaloosa: University of Alabama Press, 2000), 137.

54. Thornton, interview by Pat Arneson, August 14, 2015.

55. Thornton, interview by Arneson; "Negro Vote Lawyer Put in Jail Here: Arthur H. Madison of New York Is Arrested for Violating Statute: Faces $2,500 Fine: Act Forbids an Attorney's Appearing for Person without Being Retained," *Montgomery Advertiser*, April 9, 1944, 1, 15; Newton, *Montgomery*, 137; Lyman, "Believer."

56. Rives, quoted in Read and McGough, *Let Them Be Judged*, 32.

57. Jack Bass, *Taming the Storm: The Life and Times of Judge Frank M. Johnson, Jr., and the South's Fight over Civil Rights* (Athens: University of Georgia Press, 2002), 113; Ginny Granade, email message to Pat Arneson, June 5, 2023; "R. T. Rives, Jr., Killed, 5 Hurt in Car Mishap: Vacationists Involved in Three-Way Crash at Jacksonville, Fla.," Richard T. Rives, Vertical Name Files, Birmingham Public Library, Birmingham, AL. Cf. Jack Bass, "Richard T. Rives," Encyclopedia of Alabama (website), last modified January 16, 2015, which incorrectly states that Richard T. Rives Jr. attended the University of Exeter in England; he in fact attended Phillips Exeter Academy in New Hampshire for his secondary education.

58. Rives, quoted in Yarbrough, *Judge Frank Johnson*, 53; Frye Gaillard, *Cradle of Freedom: Alabama and the Movement That Changed America* (Tuscaloosa: University of Alabama Press, 2004), 33; Bass, "Richard T. Rives."

59. "The Lawyers Club, 1948–1949," Miscellaneous Law School Publications, University of Michigan Law School (website), last modified August 17, 2017; Bass, "Richard T. Rives"; Gaillard, *Cradle of Freedom*, 33; Gunnar Myrdal, *An American Dilemma: The Negro Problem and Modern Democracy* (New York: Harper and Bros., 1944).

60. Emanuel, *Elbert Parr Tuttle*, 132; Myrdal, *American Dilemma*, 3–4; Gaillard, *Cradle of Freedom*, 33; Black, "Final Judgement," 59.

61. Richard T. Rives, "Bureaucracy," *Alabama Lawyer* 5, no. 4 (1944): 420; John Rawls, *A Theory of Justice* (Cambridge, MA: Belknap Press, 1971). Rawls's work was published after Rives assumed senior status in 1961. Rawls, an American philosopher, in developing his theory of "justice as fairness," wrote little about race or how to rectify injustice in his works. See *Fordham Law Review* 72, no. 5 (2004), a special issue that includes over thirty essays delivered at a symposium held at Fordham University School of Law in November 2003 titled "Rawls and the Law."

62. Spivack, "Race, Civil Rights," 251, 252; Geoffrey Birt, "Hill-Rives Firm Dissolved," RTR Papers; Richard T. Rives, quoted in Roger K. Newman, *Hugo Black: A Biography* (New York: Pantheon Books, 1994), 690n14.

63. Kari Frederickson, *The Dixiecrat Revolt and the End of the Solid South, 1932–1968* (Chapel Hill: University of North Carolina Press, 2001), 134.

64. Thornton, interview by Arneson; Rumore, *From Power*, 198.

65. "Rives Funeral Slated Sunday: Body Being Returned to Montgomery Today," *Alabama Journal*, April 2, 1949; law clerk for Richard T. Rives, interview by Pat Arneson, February 22, 2017. Cf. Emanuel, *Elbert Parr Tuttle*, 132: Richard T. Rives Jr. was with a friend traveling to his parents' beach home in Mary Esther, Florida: other reports indicate that the younger Rives was with a car of friends heading to Miami, Florida, for spring break. "R.T. Rives, Jr., Killed, 5 Hurt," RTR Papers identify him as being in his "junior year of law school," but he began studying law in fall 1947 and was likely at the end of his second year of law school. Bass, *Unlikely Heroes*, 70: identifies the time of year as summer: the spring season (March–May) would put his death as occurring in the spring.

66. Gaillard, *Cradle of Freedom*, 33; "Rives and Godbold Organize Law Firm," *Alabama Journal*, July 5, 1949, Richard T. Rives, Vertical Name Files, Birmingham Public Library, Birmingham, AL; Tony Freyer and Timothy Dixon, *Democracy and Judicial Independence: A History of the Federal Courts of Alabama, 1820–1994* (Brooklyn: Carlson, 1996), 142; Spivack, "Race, Civil Rights," 252n*.

67. Black, "Richard Taylor Rives," 59; Bass, "Richard T. Rives"; Bass, *Taming the Storm*, 114.

68. Strauss, "Common Law Genius," 852; Walter V. Schaeffer, "Precedent and Policy," *University of Chicago Law Review* 34, no. 1 (1966): 3–25; Benjamin Nathan Cardozo, *The Nature of the Judicial Process* (New Haven: Yale University Press, 1921), 133–34; Strauss, *Living Constitution*, 84.

69. Mark V. Tushnet, *The NAACP's Legal Strategy against Segregated Education, 1925–1950* (Chapel Hill: University of North Carolina Press, 1987); Sipuel v. Bd. of Regents of the Univ. of Okla., 332 US 631 (1948); Briggs v. Elliott, 98 F. Supp. 529 (E.D.S.C. 1951); Briggs v. Elliott, 342 US 350 (1952).

70. Rumore, *From Power*, 195.

71. Rumore, *From Power*, 195–96.

72. Rumore, *From Power*, 197; Richard T. Rives, "An Argument against the Adoption of the Boswell Amendment," *Alabama Lawyer* 7, no. 3 (1946): 291–97.

73. Rives, quoted in Read and McGough, *Let Them Be Judged*, 32.

74. "Fair Dealing Called Key to Prosperity by Rives at Rally: Hill Cites Progress toward Peace; Huge Parade Marks Labor Day Event," *Alabama Journal*, September 5, 1949; Harkavy, email message to Pat Arneson, January 6, 2023.

75. Bass, *Unlikely Heroes*, 70; Ray Jenkins, "McCord Insisted on Naming Rives When He Retired," *Alabama Journal*, May 9, 1961; Hamilton, *Lister Hill*, 182; Rives, quoted in Spivack, "Race, Civil Rights," 252–53.

76. Rives, quoted in Read and McGough, *Let Them Be Judged*, 32; McDonald, "Judge Rives Gets"; Geoffrey Birt, "Rives Would Be among US's First Magistrate," *Montgomery Advertiser*, March 11, 1951, Courts-Federal-Alabama Clippings File,

Birmingham Public Library, Birmingham, AL; "Richard T. Rives," *United States Register of Civil, Military, and Naval Service, 1863–1959* (May 1, 1952): 666, Alabama Department of Archives and History, Montgomery, AL.

77. Emanuel, *Elbert Parr Tuttle*, 132; Richard T. Rives to John Sparkman, November 5, 1950, RTR Papers. Only the draft letter was available in RTR Papers. Rives may not have finalized or mailed the letter; Bass, *Unlikely Heroes*, 70.

78. Bass, *Unlikely Heroes*, 71; Hamilton, *Lister Hill*, 182. Cf. Couch, *A History of the Fifth*, 84, and Emanuel, *Elbert Parr Tuttle*, 132: Rives reported back to Judge McCord, who said he experienced being "sold down the river." Although McCord was a lawyer before becoming a judge, a career politician such as Hill would seem more likely to have been betrayed by other politicians in Montgomery.

79. "'Dick' Rives and Leon McCord," *Montgomery Examiner*, March 1, 1951, Richard T. Rives, Vertical Names File, Birmingham Public Library, Birmingham, AL; Daniel H. Thomas to Richard T. Rives, April 27, 1951, RTR Papers.

80. Ala. Public Service Comm'n. v. Southern Ry. Co., 341 US 363 (1951); Rives, quoted in Spivack, "Race, Civil Rights," 252–53.

81. Rives, quoted in Spivack, "Race, Civil Rights," 253; Rives, quoted in Bass, *Unlikely Heroes*, 72; Barrow and Walker, *Court Divided*, 16–17; John Daniel Reaves, interview by Pat Arneson, April 11, 2023; Bradley, interview by Pat Arneson, February 6, 2017.

82. "Senate, Tuesday, May 1, 1951," *Cong. Rec.* 97, pt. 4 (Washington, DC: US Government Printing Office): 4613; Freyer and Dixon, *Democracy and Judicial Independence*, 143; Rives, quoted in Spivack, "Race, Civil Rights," 253.

83. "Judge Richard T Rives, Left, Is Sworn In," *Alabama Journal*, May 8, 1951, Richard T. Rives, Vertical Names File, Birmingham Public Library, Birmingham, AL; Ralph Kennamer, "Richard T. Rives Becomes a Federal Judge," *Alabama Lawyer* 12, no. 3 (1951): 298.

84. Brown v. Bd. of Educ., 347 US 483 (1954); Brown v. Bd. of Educ., 349 US 294 (1955); Browder v. Gayle, 142 F. Supp. 707 (M.D. Ala. 1956).

Chapter 2

1. Plessy v. Ferguson, 163 US 537 (1896) at 537; US Constitution, amend. XIV.

2. Leland B. Ware, "Setting the Stage for *Brown*: The Development and Implementation of the NAACP's School Desegregation Campaign, 1930–1950," *Mercer Law Review* 52, no. 2 (2001): 631–73; José Felipé Anderson, *Genius for Justice: Charles Hamilton Houston and the Reform of American Law* (Durham, NC: Carolina Academic Press, 2022); Dan Abrams and Fred D. Gray with David Fisher, *Alabama v. King: Martin Luther King Jr. and the Criminal Trial That Launched the Civil Rights Movement* (Toronto: Hanover Square Press, 2022), 39; Plessy, 163 US at 537; U.S. Constitution, amend. XIV; *Brown v. Bd. of Educ.* (*Brown I*), 347 US 483 (1954).

3. *Brown I*, 347 US 483; "Earl Warren," Oyez (website), accessed November 12, 2022; Boeing Co. v. Shipman, 411 F.2d 365 (5th Cir. 1969) at 378.

4. *Brown I*, 347 US 483; US Constitution, amend. X; Alabama Legislature, "Senate Joint Resolution: Act no. 894," *Alabama Laws (and Joint Resolutions) of the Legislature of Alabama* 2, pt. 3 (1953): 1204.

5. *Brown I*, 347 US 483; *Brown v. Bd. of Educ.* (*Brown II*), 348 US 294 (1955) at 301; Kahlil G. Chism, "Using Primary Records to Understand Brown et al. v. Board of Education of Topeka et al.," in *The Unfinished Agenda of Brown v. Board of Education*, ed. The Editors of *Black Issues in Higher Education* with James Anderson and Dara N. Byrne (Hoboken, NJ: John Wiley and Sons, 2004), 10; Richard T. Rives, quoted in John M. Spivack, "Richard Taylor Rives and Benjamin F. Cameron: The Varieties of Southern Judges," *Southern Studies: An Interdisciplinary Journal of the South* 1, no. 3 (1990): 232.

6. *Brown I*, 347 US 483; *Brown II*, 349 U.S. 294; David Cunningham, *Klansville, U.S.A.: The Rise and Fall of the Civil Rights-Era Ku Klux Klan* (New York: Oxford University Press, 2013), 13; J. Mills Thornton III, "Challenge and Response in the Montgomery Bus Boycott of 1955–1956," *Alabama Review* 67, no. 1 (2014): 90; Abrams and Gray with Fisher, *Alabama v. King*, 135, 197; James W. Silver, *Mississippi: The Closed Society* (New York: Harcourt, Brace, and World, 1964), 36; J. Mills Thornton III, "Selma's Smitherman Affair of 1955," *Alabama Review* 44, no. 2 (1991): 112.

7. Jack Bass, *Taming the Storm: The Life and Times of Judge Frank M. Johnson, Jr. and the South's Fight over Civil Rights* (New York: Doubleday, 1993), 86.

8. Robert F. Kennedy Jr., *Judge Frank M. Johnson, Jr.* (New York: G. P. Putnam's, 1978), 66.

9. Lawrence R. Levin, interview by Pat Arneson, May 1, 2017; Kennedy, *Judge Frank M. Johnson*, 67.

10. "Johnson, Frank Minis, Jr.," Federal Judicial Center (website), accessed March 12, 2021; Bryan A. Stevenson, "Emphasis and Integrity: Frank Johnson and the Administration of Criminal Justice," *Alabama Lawyer* 52, no. 6 (1991), 338.

11. David S. Caudill, "Judge John R. Brown: Enjoyment of Law as Enjoyment of Life," *Mississippi College Law Review* 14, no. 1 (1993): 20; Stephen J. Rowe, "Questions and Answers with Judge Frank Johnson," *Alabama Lawyer* 52, no. 6 (1991): 330; Ginny Granade, email message to Pat Arneson, June 5, 2023; Richard T. Rives, interview by Ginny Granade, n.d., digital file courtesy of Ginny Granade.

12. Richard T. Rives to John R. Brown, September 9, 1955, John R. Brown Papers, O'Quinn Law Library at the University of Houston Law Center, Houston, Texas (hereafter JRB Papers); Richard T. Rives to John R. Brown, October 22, 1955, JRB Papers.

13. Rives to Brown, October 22, 1955.

14. Ginny Granade, email message to Pat Arneson, June 5, 2023; Jonathan R. Harkavy, interview by Pat Arneson, February 15, 2017.

15. "Streetcars: Montgomery, Alabama," Hawkins Rails (website), last modified April 3, 2022; Butler Browder, interview by Pat Arneson, March 17, 2023; J. Mills Thornton III, "Challenge and Response," 65.

16. Jo Ann Gibson Robinson, *The Montgomery Bus Boycott and the Women Who Started It: The Memoir of Jo Ann Gibson Robinson* (Knoxville: University of Tennessee Press, 1987), ix, 25; David J. Garrow, "The Origins of the Montgomery Bus Boycott," *Southern Changes* 7 (October–December 1985): 22.

17. Thornton, "Selma's Smitherman," 129; Thornton, "Challenge and Response," 106; Samuel Momodu, "Baton Rouge Bus Boycott (1953), BlackPast (website), February 4, 2018.

18. Martin Luther King Jr., *The Papers of Martin Luther King Jr.: Birth of a New Age: December 1955–1956*, vol. 3 (Berkeley: University of California Press, 1997), 3; Robert Jerome Glennon, "The Role of Law in the Civil Rights Movement: The Montgomery Bus Boycott, 1955–1957," *Law and History Review* 9, no. 1 (1991): 59–112; Rosa Parks v. City of Montgomery, 92 So. 2d 683 (Ala. Ct. App. 1957); "Browder v. Gayle Filed," African American Registry (website), accessed December 29, 2923; Abrams and Gray with Fisher, *Alabama v. King*, 23.

19. Abrams and Gray with Fisher, *Alabama v. King*, 43.

20. "Bus Segregation Act Faces Test," *Alabama Journal*, May 10, 1956.

21. Browder v. Gayle, 142 F. Supp. 707 (M.D. Ala. 1956); Ex Parte Young, 209 US 123 (1908); Tony Freyer and Timothy Dixon, *Democracy and Judicial Independence: A History of the Federal Courts of Alabama, 1820–1994* (Brooklyn: Carlson, 1995), 202–3; Abrams and Gray with Fisher, *Alabama v. King*, 322; *Brown I*, 347 U.S. at 488.

22. George E. Sims, *The Little Man's Big Friend: James E. Folsom in Alabama Politics, 1946–1958* (University: University of Alabama Press, 1985), 183; Alabama Legislature, "House Joint Resolution: Act no. 42," *Alabama Legislative Acts, Special Session* 71, pt. 1 (1956). This resolution became an act on February 2, 1956, without approval by Governor Jim Folsom.

23. Legal Information Institute, "28 US Code § 2284—Three-Judge Court; When Required; Composition; Procedure," Cornell Law School (website); Michael E. Solimine, "The Three-Judge District Court in Voting Rights Litigation," *University of Michigan Journal of Law Reform* 30, no. 1 (1996): 113; "Former 5th Circuit Chief Judge is Dead at 87," *Times-Picayune/The States-Item* [New Orleans, LA], October 29, 1982, Fifth Circuit Library, Richard T. Rives Clippings, New Orleans, LA.

24. Frank M. Johnson to Joseph C. Hutcheson Jr., February 1, 1956, Frank M. Johnson Papers, Collections of the Manuscript Division, Library of Congress, Washington, DC (hereafter FMJ Papers); Joseph C. Hutcheson Jr. to Frank M. Johnson Jr., February 3, 1956, Richard T. Rives Papers, Alabama Department of Archives and History, Montgomery, AL.

25. Richard T. Rives to Frank M. Johnson Jr., February 21, 1956, RTR Papers;

Cleveland v. United States, 323 US 329 (1945) at 332; Frank M. Johnson Jr. to Joseph C. Hutcheson Jr., February 22, 1956, RTR Papers.

26. Joseph C. Hutcheson Jr. to Frank M. Johnson Jr., February 28, 1956, RTR Papers; Frank M. Johnson Jr. to Joseph C. Hutcheson, March 8, 1956, quoted in Joseph C. Hutcheson Jr. to Frank M. Johnson Jr., March 12, 1956, FMJ Papers.

27. Brion McClanahan, "National Democratic Party (NDP)," *LewRockwell*, April 7, 2009; Democratic National Committee, *Campaign Text-Book of the National Democratic Party, 1896*, 2nd rev. ed (Chicago: National Democratic Committee, 1896), 1–2; Freyer and Dixon, *Democracy*, 254, 229, 227; Frye Gaillard, *Cradle of Freedom: Alabama and the Movement That Changed America* (Tuscaloosa: University of Alabama Press, 2004), 33.

28. Gaillard, *Cradle of Freedom*, 32; "Frank M. Johnson Jr., Judge Whose Rulings Helped Desegregate the South, Dies at 80," *New York Times*, July 24, 1999.

29. Gaillard, *Cradle of Freedom*, 34; Tinsley E. Yarbrough, *Judge Frank Johnson and Human Rights in Alabama* (Tuscaloosa: University of Alabama Press, 1981), 26; J. Mills Thornton III, *Dividing Lines: Municipal Politics and the Struggle for Civil Rights in Montgomery, Birmingham, and Selma* (Tuscaloosa: University of Alabama Press, 2002), 204; Joseph Mark Bagley, "School Desegregation, Law and Order, and Litigating Social Justice in Alabama, 1954–1973" (PhD diss., Georgia State University, 2014), 134; Richard C. Cortner, *Civil Rights and Public Accommodations: The Heart of "Atlanta Motel" and "McClung" Cases* (Lawrence: University Press of Kansas, 2001), 72.

30. Freyer and Dixon, *Democracy*, 229.

31. David A. Strauss, "Common Law Constitutional Interpretation," *University of Chicago Law Review* 63, no. 3 (1996): 895.

32. Harkavy, interview by Arneson.

33. Sweatt v. Painter, 339 US 629 (1950); McLaurin v. Okla. State Regents, 339 US 637 (1950); Henderson v. United States, 339 US 816 (1950); *Brown I*, 347 U.S. 483 at 495; Bolling v. Sharpe, 347 US 497 (1954); Muir v. Louisville, 202 F.2d 275 (6th Cir. 1953) at 275; Muir v. Louisville, 347 US 971 (1954), quoted in Steiner v. Simmons, 35 Del. Ch. 83 (Del. 1955) at 90; Dawson v. Mayor and City Council of Baltimore, 350 U.S. 877 (1955); Rice v. Arnold, 340 US 848 (1950); Holmes v. City of Atlanta, 350 US 879 (1955).

34. Rives to Lynne and Johnson, May 5, 1956, RTR Papers; Legal Information Institute, "Doctrine," Cornell Law School (website), accessed January 17, 2023; *Brown I*, 347 U.S. 483; *Brown II*, 349 U.S. 294.

35. Richard T. Rives to Seybourn H. Lynne and Frank M. Johnson, May 5, 1956, RTR Papers; *Plessy*, 163 US at 552; Seybourn H. Lynne to Richard T. Rives, May 7, 1956, RTR Papers.

36. Seybourn H. Lynne, quoted in Yarbrough, *Judge Frank Johnson*, 26, 55; Rives to Lynne and Johnson, May 5, 1956; Lynne to Rives, May 7, 1956; Richard T. Rives to Seybourn H. Lynne and Frank M. Johnson Jr., May 9, 1956, RTR Papers.

37. Richard T. Rives to Frank M. Johnson Jr., May 18, 1956, RTR Papers;

Donnie Williams with Wayne Greenhaw, *The Thunder of Angels: The Montgomery Bus Boycott and the People Who Broke the Back of Jim Crow* (Chicago: Lawrence Hill Books, 2006), 209, 208; Harkavy, interview by Arneson; Abrams and Gray with Fisher, *Alabama v. King*, 48.

38. *Brown I*, 347 U.S. 483; *Plessy*, 163 US 537; Richard A. Posner, *The Problems of Jurisprudence* (Cambridge, MA: Harvard University Press, 1990), 307.

39. *Plessy*, 163 US 537; Ruth Johnson, "Anecdotes from Judge Johnson's Wife, Ruth," *Alabama Lawyer* 52, no. 6 (1991): 322.

40. Lawrence R. Levin, interview by Pat Arneson, March 27, 2017; Frank M. Johnson, quoted in Yarbrough, *Judge Frank Johnson*, 55. Cf. Bass, *Taming the Storm*, 110, indicates that Johnson was unfamiliar with Rives and unsure of how Rives would vote in *Browder*. However, Johnson knew Rives and was aware that Rives was going to vote in support of desegregating public buses.

41. "Southern Manifesto on Integration (March 12, 1956)," *Cong. Rec.* 84, pt. 4 (Washington, DC: Governmental Printing Office, 1956): 4415–416; "The Decision of the Supreme Court in the School Cases—Declaration of Constitutional Principles," *Cong. Rec.* 85 (March 8, 1956, to March 27, 1956): 4459; Tony Badger, "'Closet Moderates': Why White Liberals Failed, 1940–1970," in *The Role of Ideas in the Civil Rights South*, ed. Ted Ownby (Jackson: University Press of Mississippi, 2002), 100.

42. Jack Bass, *Unlikely Heroes: The Dramatic Story of the Southern Judges of the Fifth Circuit Who Translated the Supreme Court's Brown Decision into a Revolution for Equality* (New York: Simon and Schuster, 1981), 65; Virginia Van der Veer Hamilton, *Lister Hill: Statesman from the South* (Chapel Hill: University of North Carolina Press, 1987), 284.

43. Levin, interview by Pat Arneson, March 27, 2017; "State Laws Held Constitutional: Circuit Judge Orders Bus Line to Halt Integration Policy," *Alabama Journal*, May 10, 1956; *City of Montgomery v. Montgomery City Lines*, *Race Relations Law Reporter* 1, no. 3 (1956): 537; Flemming v. South Carolina Electric and Gas Co., 224 F.2d 752 (4th Cir. 1955); Legal Information Institute, "Injunction," Cornell Law School (website), accessed November 12, 2024; Robert Jerome Glennon, "The Role of Law in the Civil Rights Movement: The Montgomery Bus Boycott, 1955–1957," *Law and History Review* 9, no. 1 (1991): 70. Cf. *US Reports: Decisions Per Curiam*, "Decisions Per Curiam and Orders from April 18 through June 11, 1956," South Carolina Electric and Gas Co. v. Flemming, 351 U.S. 901 (1956): 901: The record states simply, "Per Curiam: The Appeal is dismissed. *Slaker v. O'Connor*, 278 U. S. 188"; Cameron McGowan Currie, "Before Rosa Parks: The Case of Sarah Mae Flemming," in *Matthew J. Perry: The Man, His Times, and His Legacy*, ed. W. Lewis Burke and Belinda F. Gergel (Columbia: University of South Carolina Press, 2004), 90–91: While newspaper articles across the nation "viewed the Supreme Court's dismissal as a decision on the merits," others thought the dismissal was made "on purely procedural grounds" because the dismissal cited a

decision that the US Supreme Court could not entertain appeals of suits for damages unless damages had actually been awarded.

44. Abrams and Gray with Fisher, *Alabama v. Gray*, 323; Gaillard, *Cradle of Freedom*, 34; Frank Sikora, *The Judge: The Life and Opinions of Alabama's Frank M. Johnson, Jr.* (Montgomery: NewSouth Books, 2007), 28.

45. Abrams and Gray with Fisher, *Alabama v. King*, 96–97; Gray, *Bus Ride to Justice*, 81; Fred Gray, "Alabama v. King: The Trial That Launched the Civil Rights Movement," YouTube video, 1:01:58, uploaded by Alabama Department of Archives and History, February 16, 2023.

46. Abrams and Gray with Fisher, *Alabama v. King*, 192, 205.

47. "Court Reporter's Transcript of Hearing Held May 11, 1956," *Browder v. Gayle*, Civil Action no. 1147-N (M.D. Ala., 1956), Civil Rights Digital Library, Items 3 and 31, 3, 5; "Testimony Completed Quickly in Segregation Act Attack: No Immediate Ruling Planned by US Court," *Alabama Journal*, May 11, 1956; Thornton, "Challenge and Response," 82.

48. Browder, interview by Pat Arneson, March 17, 2023.

49. Abrams and Gray with Fisher, *Alabama v. King*, 98, 29, 47, 94; Butler Browder, interview by Pat Arneson, April 5, 2019.

50. Mark Hilton, "Aurelia Eliscera Shines [*sic*] Browder: Civil Rights Pioneer," *Historical Marker Database*, last revised August 30, 2020; Browder, interview by Arneson, March 17, 2023 (last name was Shine, not Shines); Browder, interview by Arneson, April 5, 2019; Kathleen M. Blee, email message to Arneson, April 2, 2023; Abrams and Gray with Fisher, *Alabama v. King*, 98, 29, 47, 94, 326; Butler Browder, "Butler Browder Reflects on Browder v. Gayle," in Jonathan Gold, "'Browder v. Gayle': The Most Important Civil Rights Case You've Never Heard Of," Learning for Justice 53 (Summer 2016) at 2:23, accessed March 12, 2021; "Court Reporter's Transcript," 4.

51. "Court Reporter's Transcript," 5, 6, 8 (emphasis added).

52. Butler Browder, Jonathan L. Entin, and Robert O. White II, "Browder v. Gayle: An Example of Legal, Political and Economic Radicalism," in *Highway 80: A Drive through Alabama's Civil Rights Corridor*, 2nd ed., ed. Robert O. White II (Ronkonkoma, NY: Linus Learning, 2018), 42; Abrams and Gray with Fisher, *Alabama v. King*, 256.

53. US Constitution, amend. XIV; Abrams et al., *Alabama v. King*, 24.

54. Thornton, "Challenge and Response," 82; Steve Lesher, "U.S. Judges Deliberate Bus Segregation Fate: Race Hearing in Court Here Ends Session," *Montgomery Advertiser*, May 12, 1956; US Congress, "Browder v. Gayle," *Civil Rights—1959: Hearings before the Subcommittee on Constitutional Rights of the Committee on the Judiciary: United States Senate: Eighty-Sixth Congress*, pt. 2 (Washington, DC: United States Government Printing Office, 1959): 2558; "Court Reporter's Transcript," 48.

55. "Court Reporter's Transcript," 25; *Flemming*, 224 F.2d 752; Abrams and Gray with Fisher, *Alabama v. King*, 332; Hugh W. Sparrow, "Case Under Study—Two of Judges Indicate Bus Laws in Force," *Birmingham News*, May 12, 1956.

56. Sparrow, "Case under Study," May 12, 1956; *Brown I*, 347 US 483.

57. Lucy v. Adams, 350 US 1 (1955). Myers's first name was spelled "Pollie," but it was misspelled as "Polly" in the decision. According to Autherine Lucy, it was Myers's idea for the two of them to apply to graduate school at the University of Alabama ("An Indomitable Spirit: Autherine Lucy," *Our American Story* (blog), undated, Smithsonian National Museum of African American History and Culture). After Myers's marriage to Robert Pinkins, she was known as Pollie Anne Myers-Pinkins; she died in 2003.

58. *Brown I*, 347 U.S. 483; *Brown II*, 349 U.S. 294; Lucy v. Adams, 350 US 1 (1955); Abrams and Gray with Fisher, *Alabama v. King*, 330; Steve Lesher, "US Judges Deliberate Bus Segregation Case: Race Hearing in Court Here Ends Session," *Montgomery Advertiser*, May 12, 1956; Thomas Jefferson, *The Papers of Thomas Jefferson: 1760–1776*, ed. Julian P. Boyd (Princeton, NJ: Princeton University Press, 1950), 426: Jefferson wrote against King George, who in supporting the enslavement of people was "paying off former crimes committed against the *Liberties* of one people, with crimes which he urges them to commit against the *lives* of another" (emphasis in original). That section was removed from the Declaration of Independence at the request of representatives from South Carolina.

59. "Testimony Completed Quickly"; Abrams and Gray with Fisher, *Alabama v. King*, 333; Bass, *Taming the Storm*, 110; Lynne, quoted in Yarbrough, *Judge Frank Johnson*, 54.

60. Johnson, quoted in Sikora, *Judge*, 35.

61. Johnson, quoted in Sikora, *Judge*, 36, 35; law clerk for Richard T. Rives, interview by Pat Arneson, February 22, 2017.

62. Abrams and Gray with Fisher, *Alabama v. King*, 333; *Plessy*, 163 US 537 at 552; Rives to Johnson, May 18, 1956; "Judgment: Browder vs. Gayle," RTR Papers; Norman L. Blumenfeld, interview by Pat Arneson, January 26, 2017; *Brown I*, 347 U.S. 483; *Brown II*, 349 U.S. 294; Louis Michael Seidman, "Brown and Miranda," *California Law Review* 80 (1992): 674.

63. "Judgment: Browder vs. Gayle," Perkins v. Endicott Johnson Corp., 128 F.2d 208 (2nd Cir. 1942).

64. John Daniel Reaves, interview by Pat Arneson, April 11, 2023; *Brown I*, 347 US 483; John Michael Spivack, "Race, Civil Rights, and the United States Court of Appeals for the Fifth Judicial Circuit" (PhD diss., University of Florida, 1978), 257; David A. Strauss, *The Living Constitution* (New York: Oxford University Press, 2010), 35.

65. "Judgment: Browder vs. Gayle"; Seybourn H. Lynne to Richard T. Rives, May 29, 1956, RTR Papers; *Brown I*, 347 US 483; *Flemming*, 224 F.2d 752.

66. "Judgment: Browder vs. Gayle"; Timothy Oyen, "Stare Decisis," Legal Information Institute, Cornell Law School (website), last modified March 2017: "stare decisis is not an 'inexorable command.' When prior decisions are 'unworkable or are badly reasoned,' then the Supreme Court may not follow precedent, and this

is 'particularly true in constitutional cases'. . . . As stated in Burnet v. Coronado Oil & Gas Co., 285 US 393 (1932) at 407, in such cases 'correction through legislative action is practically impossible.'"

67. Lynne to Rives, May 29, 1956; Bobby Jack Howard v. United States of America, 232 F.2d 274 (5th Cir. 1956) at 275; Davis v. United States, 165 US 373 (1897); Durham v. United States, 214 F.2d 862 (D.C. Cir. 1954) at 876n21; *Browder*, 142 F. Supp. at 718.

68. *Flemming*, 224 F.2d 752; Legal Information Institute, "Persuasive Authority," Cornell Law School (website), last modified May 2020; Lynne to Rives, May 29, 1956; "Judgment: Browder vs. Gayle."

69. "Judgment: Browder vs. Gayle"; Browder, 142 F. Supp. at 717.

70. *Browder*, 142 F. Supp.; Euel Screws Jr., quoted in "Richard T. Rives, Judge on Court That Helped Integrate the South," *New York Times*, October 30, 1982; Clifford Durr, quoted in Bass, *Taming the Storm*, 116; Abrams and Gray with Fisher, *Alabama v. King*, 302.

71. Seidman, "Brown and Miranda," 678–79; John Daniel Reaves, interview by Pat Arneson, April 11, 2023.

72. Richard T. Rives, quoted in Frank T. Read and Lucy S. McGough, *Let Them Be Judged: The Judicial Integration of the Deep South* (Lanham, MD: Scarecrow Press, 1978), 34; Barrow and Walker, *Court Divided*, 17; William H. McDonald, "Judge Rives Gets Lots of 'Fan Mail,'" *Southern School News* 8, no. 9 (March 1962); Name Withheld to Judge Rives, June 6, 1956, RTR papers; Name Withheld to Richard Taylor Rives, June 22, 1956, RTR Papers; Name Withheld to R. T. Rives, June 5, 1956, RTR Papers; Richard Wright, *Native Son* (New York: Harper and Brothers, 1940); Name Withheld to Richard Rives, June 12, 1956, RTR Papers.

73. Roger Williams to Richard T. Rives, June 6, 1956, RTR Papers; J. E. Pierce to Richard T. Rives, n.d., RTR Papers; Richard T. Rives to Mrs. Mabel G. Harrington, June 13, 1956, RTR Papers.

74. Rives, quoted in Read and McGough, *Let Them Be Judged*, 34.

75. "City Bus Segregation Doomed in Ruling by Federal Court: Judgment Held Up for 2 Weeks on Plea Filing," *Alabama Journal*, June 5, 1956; "Quislings in the South," *Alabama Labor News*, June 19, 1956, RTR Papers; Sparrow, "Case under Study"; Rives, quoted in Spivack, "Richard Taylor Rives and," 233; law clerk for Richard T. Rives, interview by Pat Arneson, February 22, 2017.

76. Law clerk for Richard T. Rives, interview by Pat Arneson, February 22, 2017.

77. R. Carter Pittman to Richard T. Rives, n.d., RTR Papers; Southern Carolina v. United States, 199 US 437 (1905) at 448.

78. "Ben Cameron," Mississippi Encyclopedia (website), accessed April 4, 2022; *Brown I*, 347 US 483; Sheldon Goldman, *Picking Federal Judges: Lower Court Selection from Roosevelt through Reagan* (New Haven, CT: Yale University Press, 1997), 129; Spivack, "Richard Taylor Rives and," 227–30.

79. *Browder*, 142 F. Supp. 707; H. W. Denton and Int'l Union of Elec., Radio and Machine Workers, CIO v. City of Carrollton, Ga., 235 F.2d 481 (5th Cir. 1956) at 487, 491, 497; US Constitution, amend. X.

80. Bass, *Taming the Storm*, 137; *Denton*, 235 F.2d 481; Richard T. Rives to Ben F. Cameron, July 23, 1956, RTR Papers; Richard T. Rives to Ed Wadsworth, July 23, 1956, RTR Papers.

81. Ben F. Cameron to Richard T. Rives, July 25, 1956, RTR Papers; Richard T. Rives to Ed Wadsworth, July 23, 1956, RTR Papers; Ed Wadsworth to Judge Rives, July 31, 1956, RTR Papers.

82. Richard T. Rives to Ben F. Cameron, August 2, 1956, RTR Papers.

83. *Browder*, 142 F. Supp. at 713; *Denton*, 235 F.2d at 490; Douglas v. City of Jeannette, 319 US (1943) at 157, 159.

84. Richard T. Rives to Ben F. Cameron, August 7, 1956, RTR Papers.

85. Joseph C. Hutcheson Jr. to Richard T. Rives, August 7, 1956, RTR Papers; *Denton*, 235 F.2d 481; Ben F. Cameron to Richard T. Rives, August 10, 1956, RTR Papers.

86. *Browder*, 142 F. Supp.; Gayle v. Browder, 352 US 903 (1956); Richard T. Rives to Joe E. Estes, September 10, 1956, RTR Papers.

87. *Browder*, 142 F. Supp.; *Gayle*, 352 US 903 at 903; *Brown II*, 349 U.S. at 301; John Daniel Reaves, email message to Pat Arneson, September 27, 2023; "Browder v. Gayle, 352 US 903," Martin Luther King, Jr. Research and Education Institute at Stanford University (website), accessed October 1, 2024.

88. Freyer and Dixon, *Democracy*, 215.

Chapter 3

1. Plessy v. Ferguson, 163 US 537 (1896) at 544, 552; US Constitution, amend. XIV.

2. Roberts v. City of Boston, 59 Mass. 198 (1849); US Constitution, amend. X.

3. See LDF cases including, e.g., Missouri ex rel. Gaines v. Can., 305 US 337 (1938); Westminster Sch. Dist. of Orange Cty. v. Mendez, 161 F.2d 774 (1947); Webb v. Sch. Dist. No. 90, 167 Kan. 395 (1949); *Brown v. Bd. of Educ.* (*Brown I*), 347 US 483 (1954); *Brown v. Bd. of Educ.* (*Brown II*), 349 US 294 (1955) at 301.

4. Frank T. Read and Lucy S. McGough, *Let Them Be Judged: The Judicial Integration of the Deep South* (Metuchen, NJ: Scarecrow Press, 1978), 619–22; Borders v. Rippy, 247 F.2d 268 (5th Cir. 1957); Shuttlesworth v. Birmingham Bd. of Educ., 162 F. Supp. 372 (N.D. Ala. 1958); Gibson v. Bd. of Pub. Instr., Dade Cty., Fla., 272 F.2d 763 (5th Cir. 1959); Armstrong v. Bd. of Educ. of City of Birmingham, 220 F. Supp 217 (N.D. Ala. 1963); Lee v. Macon, 267 F. Supp. 458 (M.D. Ala. 1967); John Michael Spivack, "Race, Civil Rights, and the United States Court of Appeals for the Fifth Judicial Circuit" (PhD diss., University of Florida, 1978), 131.

5. US Congress, *Civil Rights—1959: Hearings, before the Subcommittee on*

Constitutional Rights of the Committee on the Judiciary 86, pt. 1 (Washington, DC: Government Printing Office, 1959), 90–91. E.g., (1) Alabama Legislature, "The Alabama School Placement Law: Act No. 201," *Race Relations Law Reporter* 1 (1956): 235, (2) Alabama Legislature, "Authority of School Officials: Act no. 82," *Race Relations Law Reporter* 1 (1956): 417, (3) Alabama Legislature, "Interposition Resolution: Act no. 42," *Race Relations Law Reporter* 1 (1956): 437, (4) Alabama Legislature, "School Attendance Law: Act no. 117," *Race Relations Law Reporter* 1 (1956): 717; Alabama Constitution, "Amendment 111," Ballotpedia: Encyclopedia of American Politics (website), accessed November 14, 2024.

6. Pat Boyd Rumore, *From Power to Service: The Story of Lawyers in Alabama* (Montgomery: Alabama State Bar and Alabama Bench and Bar Historical Society, 2010), 34; *Brown I*; *Brown II*; Joseph Mark Bagley, "School Desegregation, Law and Order, and Litigating Social Justice in Alabama, 1954–1973" (PhD diss., Georgia State University, 2014), 81; "The Supreme Court: Presumption of Faith," *Time*, December 8, 1958; Alabama Legislature, "The Alabama School Placement Law."

7. Alabama Constitution, "Amendment 111"; Gordon Harvey, "Public Education in Alabama After Desegregation," Encyclopedia of Alabama (website), last modified January 19, 2022; Alabama Constitution, "Amendment 111 Ratified," Justia (website), accessed January 17, 2022.

8. John R. Brown to Richard T. Rives and Jessie Rives, June 18, 1957, John R. Brown Papers, O'Quinn Law Library at the University of Houston Law Center, Houston, TX; Richard T. Rives to John R. Brown, June 21, 1957, JRB Papers; John R. Brown to Richard T. Rives, June 25, 1957, JRB Papers; Robert F. Miller to Joseph C. Hutcheson Jr., June 18, 1957, JRB Papers.

9. Legal Information Institute, "28 U.S. Code § 453: Oaths of Justices and Judges," Cornell Law School (website), accessed November 14, 2024; *Brown I*, 347 US 483; *Brown II*, 349 U.S. 294; Bell v. Rippy, 133 F. Supp. 811 (N.D. Tex. 1955); Brown v. Rippy, 233 F.2d 796 (5th Cir. 1956); Bell v. Rippy, 146 F. Supp. 485 (N.D. Tex. 1956); Borders v. Rippy, 247 F.2d 268 (5th Cir. 1957); Borders v. Rippy, 195 F. Supp. 732 (N.D. Tex. 1961).

10. Betsy Levin, *The Courts, Social Science, and School Desegregation* (New York: Taylor and Francis, 1977/2018), 14n29; *Rippy*, 247 F.2d at 271, 272.

11. *Shuttleswort*h, 162 F. Supp. 372 (N.D. Ala. 1958).

12. *Shuttlesworth*, 162 F. Supp at 384; *Brown II*, 349 US at 301; Tony Freyer and Timothy Dixon, *Democracy and Judicial Independence: A History of the Federal Courts of Alabama, 1820–1994* (Brooklyn: Carlson, 1995), 238; Shuttlesworth v. Bd. of Educ., 358 US 101 (1958) at 101.

13. *Shuttlesworth*, 358 US 101; *Brown I*; *Brown II*; Spivack, "Race, Civil Rights," 280; Carson v. Warlick, 238 F.2d 724 (4th Cir. 1956) at 728: "School authorities have the primary responsibility for elucidating, assessing, and solving these problems; courts will have to consider whether the action of school authorities constitutes good faith implementation of the governing constitutional principles."

14. *Brown II*, 349 US 294; Gibson v. Bd. of Public Instr. of Dade Cty., Fla., 170 F. Supp. 454 (S.D. Fla. 1958); *Shuttlesworth*, 162 F. Supp. 372.

15. Read and McGough, *Let Them be Judged*, 59; Gibson v. Bd. of Public Instr. of Dade Cty., Fla., 246 F.2d 913 (5th Cir. 1957) at 914.

16. *Gibson*, 170 F. Supp. at 459; Richard T. Rives to Warren L. Jones and John R. Brown, August 23, 1957, Richard T. Rives Papers, Alabama Department of Archives and History, Montgomery, AL.

17. Rives to Jones and Brown, August 23, 1957.

18. *Gibson*, 272 F.2d 763 (5th Cir. 1959) at 764.

19. *Gibson*, 272 F.2d 763 at 766; Spivack "Race, Civil Rights," 121.

20. Spivack, "Race, Civil Rights," 75, 83, 258; *Brown I*; *Brown II*.

21. "U.S. Court of Appeals for the Fifth Circuit—Brief History," US Court of Appeals for the Fifth Circuit (website), accessed December 30, 2023; William L. Whittaker, *Description of the Operating Procedures of the United States Court of Appeals for the Fifth Circuit* (Washington, DC: Federal Judicial Center, 1973), 5–6, quoted in Spivack, "Race, Civil Rights," 33; Anne S. Emanuel,, *Elbert Parr Tuttle: Chief Jurist of the Civil Rights Revolution* (Athens: University of Georgia Press, 2014), 174.

22. Richard T. Rives to the Judges of the Fifth Circuit, December 2, 1960, JRB Papers; Emanuel, *Elbert Parr Tuttle*, 292, 236.

23. John R. Brown, "In Recognition: Proceedings of the Degree Ceremony: The Honorable John R. Brown, Doctor of Laws," *Tulane Law Review* 54, no. 1 (1979–1980): 267; Rives to the Judges of the Fifth Circuit, December 2, 1960; Ginny Granade, email message to Pat Arneson, June 5, 2023; Ray Jenkins, "Of Race Question: Rives Turns Up on Both Sides," *Alabama Journal*, May 10, 1961.

24. Ray Jenkins, "Decade on Bench Has Brought Rives Wide Recognition," *Alabama Journal*, May 8, 1961; Ray Jenkins, "McCord Insisted on Naming Rives When He Retired," *Alabama Journal*, May 9, 1961; Jenkins, "Of Race Question"; Elaine Fowler to Warren L. Jones and John R. Brown, May 3, 1961, JRB Papers.

25. Ray Jenkins to Richard T. Rives, May 18, 1961, JRB Papers.

26. Spivack, "Race, Civil Rights," 259n*; Bagley, "School Desegregation," 474; Read and McGough, *Let Them Be Judged*, 396; postcard, n.d., RTR Papers.

27. "Alabama: Hearings End in Birmingham School Cases," *Southern School News* 9, no. 5 (1962): 11; Read and McGough, *Let Them Be Judged*, 395.

28. "(1963) George Wallace, 'Segregation Now, Segregation Forever,'" BlackPast (website), January 22, 2013; Tomiko Brown-Nagin, *Civil Rights Queen: Constance Baker Motley and the Struggle for Equality* (New York: Pantheon, 2022), 179; Robert J. Cook, "Red Termites and Rebel Yells: The Civil War Centennial in Strife-Torn Alabama, 1961–1965," *Alabama Review* 64, no. 2 (2011): 162.

29. *Brown II*, 349 US 294; Armstrong v. Bd. of Educ. of Birmingham, 220 F. Supp. 217 (N.D. Ala. 1963); *Brown I*, 347 US 483.

30. *Armstrong*, 220 F. Supp. 217.

31. Watson v. City of Memphis, 373 US 526 (1963) at 526–27, 533; *Brown II*

at 301; Armstrong, 220 F. Supp. at 220; Shuttlesworth v. City of Birmingham, 399 F.2d 529 (5th Cir. 1968); Gibson, 272 F.2d 763. The Supreme Court reiterated their thinking in Griffin v. Cty. Sch. Bd. of Prince Edward Cty., 377 U.S. 218 (1964) at 229: "There has been entirely too much deliberation and not enough speed."

32. Davis v. Bd. of Sch. Comm'rs of Mobile Cty., 219 F. Supp. 542 (S.D. Ala. 1963) at 544; Bagley, "School Desegregation," 214; *Brown II* at 301.

33. Davis v. Bd. of Sch. Comm'rs of Mobile Cty., Ala., 322 F.2d 356 (5th Cir. 1963); Stell v. Savannah-Chatham Cty. Bd. of Educ., 318 F.2d 425 (5th Cir. 1963) at 428; Armstrong v. Bd. of Educ. of City of Birmingham, 323 F.2d 333 (5th Cir. 1963).

34. Read and McGough, *Let Them Be Judged*, 186.

35. Armstrong v. Bd. of Educ. of Birmingham, Ala., 220 F. Supp. 217 (N.D. Ala. 1963); *Armstrong*, 323 F.2d at 337, 338; Augustus v. Bd. of Public Instruction, 306 F.2d 862 (5th Cir. 1962) at 869.

36. *Armstrong*, 323 F.2d at 339.

37. *Armstrong*, 323 F.2d at 340, 352 (emphasis in original); US Court of Appeals for the Fourth Circuit, "Federal and Local Rules of Appellate Procedure" (website), accessed November 2, 2024.

38. *Armstrong*, 323 F.2d 333.

39. *Armstrong*, 323 F.2d at 353; H. W. Denton and Int'l Union of Elec., Radio and Machine Workers, CIO v. City of Carrollton, Ga., 235 F.2d 481 (5th Cir. 1956); Browder v. Gayle, 142 F. Supp. 707 (M.D. Ala. 1956).

40. *Armstrong*, 323 F.2d at 353; Ben F. Cameron to Warren L. Jones, Walter P. Gewin, and Griffin B. Bell, August 16, 1963, quoted in J. Robert Brown Jr. and Allison Herren Lee, "Neutral Assignment of Judges at the Court of Appeals," *Texas Law Review* 78, no. 5 (1999–2000): 1050n72; *Davis*, 322 F.2d at 360; "In Racial Cases—US Court Accused of Stacking Panels," *Birmingham News*, July 31, 1963, Birmingham Public Library, Courts-Federal-Southern Clippings File.

41. *Armstrong*, 323 F.2d at 359, 353, 342. Cf. Several authors report that Cameron selectively identified cases to emphasize his point: Jack Bass, *Unlikely Heroes: The Dramatic Story of the Southern Judges of the Fifth Circuit Who Translated the Supreme Court's Brown Decision into a Revolution for Equality* (New York: Simon and Schuster, 1981), 240: "a number of factors skewed Cameron's statistics" such as scheduling assignments, including references to different phases of two cases that came before the Fifth Circuit, leaving some cases out of his count, identifying a time frame that would have the most persuasive effect, and identifying issues already settled by the US Supreme Court; Emanuel, *Elbert Parr Tuttle*, 366n17: "Cameron's list of twenty-five opinions represented only twenty matters, because five arose from James Meredith's attempt to matriculate at the University of Mississippi and two arose from a single voting rights matter"; Jonathan L. Entin, "The Sign of 'The Four': Judicial Assignment and the Rule of Law," *Mississippi Law Journal* 68 (1998–1999): 370–71.

42. *Armstrong*, 323 F.2d at 353, 355; Jack Steele, "Fifth Circuit Has Major Part in Civil Rights Conflicts," *Birmingham Post-Herald*, July 20, 1963; Elbert Parr Tuttle, quoted in Spivack, "Race, Civil Rights," 265; Sharp v. Lucky, 252 F.2d 910 (5th Cir. 1958) at 919, 915, 916.

43. *Armstrong*, 323 F.2d at 349–51, 355; Woods v. Wright, 334 F.2d 369 (5th Cir. 1964).

44. *Armstrong*, 323 F.2d at 353.

45. Richard T. Rives to Judges Elbert Parr Tuttle, Joseph C. Hutcheson, Ben F. Cameron, Warren L. Jones, John R. Brown, John Minor Wisdom, Walter P. Gewin, and Griffin B. Bell, March 8, 1964, quoted in Joel William Friedman, *Champion of Civil Rights: Judge John Minor Wisdom* (Baton Rouge: Louisiana State University Press, 2009), 254; Richard T. Rives to Judges Elbert Parr Tuttle, Joseph C. Hutcheson, Ben F. Cameron, Warren L. Jones, John R. Brown, John Minor Wisdom, Walter P. Gewin, and Griffin B. Bell, March 22, 1963, quoted in Friedman, *Champion*, 255.

46. Bagley, "School Desegregation," 224; "Fifth Appeals Circuit Judge Holds Chief Stacks Deck in Race Cases," *Chattanooga Daily Times*, July 31, 1963; "US Appeals Judge Slams 'Favored Trio' in Cases," *Greenwood Commonwealth* (Greenwood, MS), July 31, 1963; "US Judge Blames 'Crusaders' for Decisions to Desegregate," *Tampa Times*, July 31, 1963; "Federal Judge Criticizes 'Unorthodox Procedures' in Racial Cases by Court," *Daily Advertiser* (Lafayette, LA), July 31, 1963; "Feud over Racial Cases Flares in US Appeals Court in South," *New York Times*, July 31, 1963.

47. "Senator to See if Court Stacked in Integration Cases," *Houston Chronicle*, August 2, 1963; Douglas Keith, "Impeachment and Removal of Judges: An Explainer," Brennan Center for Justice, last modified May 6, 2022; Ted Lippman, "US Probes Panel Picks by Tuttle," *Atlanta Constitution*, August 2, 1963.

48. Saul Friedman, "Appeals Court Facing Revolt," *Houston Chronicle*, August 4, 1963; J. P. Coleman, interview by John M. Spivack, audiotape courtesy of John M. Spivack; Emanuel, *Elbert Parr Tuttle*, 257; Brown and Lee, "Neutral Assignment," 1051–52.

49. Friedman, *Champion*, 255; US Dept. of Justice, *Register of the US Department of Justice and the Federal Courts*, 51st ed. (Washington, DC: US Government Printing Office, 1978), 29.

50. Jones, Diary Memorandum, August 7, 1963, quoted in Friedman, *Champion*, 255–56.

51. Edward W. Wadsworth to Warren L. Jones, August 11, 1963, quoted in Friedman, *Champion*, 257; Edward W. Wadsworth to Elbert P. Tuttle, August 17, 1963, RTR Papers; Jones, Diary Memorandum, August 7, 1963, quoted in Friedman, *Champion*, 256.

52. Griffin B. Bell to All Fifth Circuit Judges, August 9, 1963, quoted in Friedman, *Champion*, 262.

53. Jones, Diary Memorandum, August 10, 1963, quoted in Friedman, *Champion*, 258.

54. Brown and Lee, "Neutral Assignment," 1050n72; "Senator to See"; Jones, Diary Memorandum, August 12, 1963, quoted in Emanuel, *Elbert Parr Tuttle*, 259.

55. Richard T. Rives to John R. Brown, December 13, 1960, JRB Papers; Friedman, *Champion*, 256n28.

56. Edward W. Wadsworth to Elbert P. Tuttle, Joseph C. Hutcheson Jr., Richard T. Rives, Ben F. Cameron, Warren L. Jones, John R. Brown, John M. Wisdom, Walter P. Gewin, and Griffin B. Bell, August 17, 1963, quoted in Friedman, *Champion*, 258n40; John Minor Wisdom, "Notes on the Houston Conference," John Minor Wisdom Collection, Tulane University (website), 1, accessed March 17, 2021.

57. Emanuel, *Elbert Parr Tuttle*, 262; Friedman, *Champion*, 266.

58. Emanuel, *Elbert Parr Tuttle*, 260; Bass, *Unlikely Heroes*, 240.

59. Boman v. Birmingham Transit Co., 292 F.2d 4 (5th Cir. 1961) at 24, 4; Brown and Lee, "Neutral Assignment," 1049n63.

60. Bass, *Unlikely Heroes*, 240; Emanuel, *Elbert Parr Tuttle*, 262, 264; Wisdom, "Notes on the Houston Conference," 13; Brown and Lee, "Neutral Assignment," 1063.

61. Wisdom, "Notes on the Houston Conference," 19; "US Judge Says Court Isn't Rigged," *Atlanta Constitution*, August 24, 1963.

62. James O. Eastland, quoted in Bass, *Unlikely Heroes*, 242; Spivack, "Race, Civil Rights," 256, 256n23.

63. Friedman, *Champion*, 267; *Armstrong*, 323 F.2d 333.

64. Lee v. Macon Cty. Bd. of Educ., 221 F. Supp. 297 (M.D. Ala. 1963) at 460, 300.

65. *Lee*, 267 F. Supp. at 460; Lee v. Macon Cty. Bd. of Educ., 231 F. Supp. 743 (M.D. Ala 1964) at 748.

66. Bagley, "School Desegregation," 338; *Brown II,* 349 US at 301; *Lee*, 231 F. Supp. at 756; *Lee*, 267 F. Supp. 458.

67. *Lee*, 231 F. Supp.; *Lee*, 267 F. Supp. at 461; Southern Education Reporting Service, "Alabama," South Carolina Digital Libraries, "School Desegregation in the Southern and Border States" Collection (website), February 1967, 6, accessed June 22, 2024.

68. *Lee*, 267 F. Supp. at 465, 478, 483, 474; Wallace v. Lee, 387 US 916 (1967).

69. United States, Office of Education, *Revised Statement of Policies for School Desegregation Plans: Under Title VI of the Civil Rights Act of 1964* (Washington, DC: US Department of Health, Education, and Welfare, 1966); Southern Education Reporting Service, "Alabama," 5 (emphasis added); Bagley, "School Desegregation," 382, 342; "Alabama Senate Passes Law to Forbid School Desegregation," EJI (website), accessed September 14, 2025; "Educators Join Resistance to U.S. Guidelines," *Florence Herald*, June 9, 1966.

70. "Act 252," Alabama Laws (and Joint Resolutions) of the Legislature of Alabama (State of Alabama: Skinner Printing, 1966): 372–77; Benjamin Trost, "Persistent Resistance: The Struggle against School Integration in Tuscaloosa, Alabama

(1956–2007)," *Crimson Historical Review* 7 (2021): 85; "Federal Reaction Awaited: Special Session Adjourned; Anti-Guidelines Bill Passed," *Florence Herald*, September 8, 1966; "In Federal Defiance Stand: Wallace Anti-Guideline Bill Now Before State Legislature," *Florence Herald*, "School Desegregation in Alabama," August 25, 1966, Shoals Black History (website), accessed Sept. 14, 2025.

71. Southern Education Reporting Service, "Alabama," 5.

72. Southern Education Reporting Service, "Alabama," 6.

73. Southern Education Reporting Service, "Alabama," 5.

74. Southern Education Reporting Service, "Alabama," 5–6; John R. Brown, quoted in Read and McGough, *Let Them Be Judged*, 54.

75. Briggs v. Elliott, 132 F. Supp. 776 (E.D.S.C. 1955); *Brown I*, 347 U.S. at 487, 496n1; *Brown II*, 349 U.S. at 301; *Browder*, 142 F. Supp. at 711; Spivak, "Richard Taylor Rives and," 232.

76. Richard T. Rives to Warren L. Jones and John R. Brown, December 17, 1957, JRB Papers; Read and McGough, *Let Them Be Judged*, 36, 37; Rives, quoted in Spivack, "Race, Civil Rights," 259n26, 259.

77. *Lee*, 267 F. Supp. at 480; Spivack, "Race, Civil Rights," 136–37; United States v. Jefferson Cty. Bd. of Educ., 372 F.2d 836 (5th Cir. 1966) at 847 cited in United States v. Jefferson County Bd. of Educ., 380 F.2d 385 (5th Cir. 1967) at 408; William P. Hustwit, *Integration Now: Alexander v. Holmes and the End of Jim Crow* (Chapel Hill: University of North Carolina Press, 2019), 95.

78. Alexander v. Holmes Cty. Bd. of Educ., 396 US 19 (1969) at 20; *Brown II*, 349 US at 301.

Chapter 4

1. Murray v. Pearson, 169 Md. 478 (1936); Sweatt v. Painter, 339 US 629 (1950); McLaurin v. Okla. State Regents, 339 US 637 (1950); Plessy v. Ferguson, 163 US 537 (1896) at 552; *Brown v. Bd. of Educ.* (*Brown I*), 347 US 483 (1954); *Brown v. Bd. of Educ.* (*Brown II*), 349 US 294 (1955).

2. Tureaud v. Bd. of Supervisors of La. State Univ. & Agricultural & Mechanical Coll., 116 F. Supp. 248 (E.D. La. 1953); Bd. of Supervisors v. Tureaud, 207 F.2d 807 (5th Cir. 1953) at 810; Bd. of Supervisors, Etc. v. Tureaud, 228 F.2d 895 (5th Cir., 1956).

3. Lucy v. Univ. of Ala., 134 F. Supp. 235 (N.D. Ala. 1955); Legal Information Institute, "Contempt of Court, Civil," Cornell Law School (website), last modified February 2024; Richard T. Rives to Orin S. Thiel, January 20, 1961, John R. Brown Papers, O'Quinn Law Library at the University of Houston Law Center, Houston, TX; Richard T. Rives, quoted in John M. Spivack, "Race, Civil Rights, and the United States Court of Appeals for the Fifth Judicial Circuit" (PhD diss., University of Florida, 1978), 262n33.

4. *Lucy*, 134 F. Supp. 235.

5. Frank Sikora, *The Judge: The Life and Opinions of Alabama's Frank M. Johnson, Jr.* (Montgomery: Black Belt Press, 1992), 278; *Lucy*, 134 F. Supp. at 237.

6. *Lucy*, 134 F. Supp. at 238; *New York Times*, July 13, 1955, qd. in United States Commission on Civil Rights, *Law Enforcement:*, 85; "Alabama: Court Tells University of Alabama to Admit Three Negro Students," *Southern School News* 9, no. 12 (1963): 1, 6; "Delay Granted in Alabama," *New York Times*, September 7, 1955, quoted in United States Commission on Civil Rights, *Law Enforcement:*, 85; Adams v. Lucy, 228 F.2d 619 (5th Cir. 1956); Lucy v. Adams, 350 US 1 (1955).

7. "Overturned," Ballotpedia: Encyclopedia of American Politics (website), accessed December 20, 2022; *Brown II*, 349 US 294; "Alabama: Court Tells," 6.

8. *Brown II*, 349 US 294; Meredith v. Fair, 306 F.2d 374 (5th Cir. 1962); Johann N. Neem, *Democracy's Schools: The Rise of Public Education in America* (Baltimore: Johns Hopkins University Press, 2017), 161.

9. Tomiko Brown-Nagin, *Civil Rights Queen: Constance Baker Motley and the Struggle for Equality* (New York: Pantheon, 2022), 144; Meredith v. Fair, 199 F. Supp. 754 (S.D. Miss. 1961) at 754.

10. "Mize, Sidney Carr," Federal Judicial Center (website), accessed December 29, 2022; Evers v. Jackson Mun. Separate Sch. Dist., 232 F. Supp. 241 (S.D. Miss. 1964) at 251; Howard Smead, *Blood Justice: The Lynching of Mack Charles Parker* (New York: Oxford University Press, 1986), 189.

11. Denny Chin and Kathy Hirata Chin, "Constance Baker Motley, James Meredith, and the University of Mississippi," *Columbia Law Review* 117, no. 7 (2017): 1741; "Elmore Greaves Jr. Obituary," *Clarion-Ledger* (Jackson, MS), June 14, 2010; Elmore Douglass Greaves, *The Blackamoor of Oxford: A Reply to Attorney General Robert Kennedy's Report on How He Is Making Progress in Mississippi* (Jackson, MS: Sovereignty Commission Online, 1963), 5; *Clarion-Ledger* quoted in Charles W. Eagles, *The Price of Defiance: James Meredith and the Integration of Ole Miss* (Chapel Hill: University of North Carolina Press, 2009), 74.

12. *Meredith*, 306 F.2d 374; Dixon v. Ala. State Bd. of Educ., 294 F.2d 150 (5th Cir. 1961) at 157.

13. James W. Silver, *Mississippi: The Closed Society* (New York: Harcourt, Brace, and World, Inc., 1964/1966), 114; Meredith v. Fair, 298 F.2d 696 (5th Cir. 1962) at 702–3, 701, 706.

14. Meredith v. Fair, 202 F. Supp. 224 (S.D. Miss. 1962) at 227.

15. Meredith v. Fair, 305 F.2d 343 (5th Cir. 1962) at 361; Meredith v. Fair, 306 F.2d 374; Brown-Nagin, *Civil Rights Queen*, 147.

16. Court orders issued by Judge Cameron, the Fifth Circuit Court, and Justice Black include: "Judge Cameron's Stay Order, July 18, 1962," *Race Relations Law Reporter* 7 (1962): 741–42; "Judge Cameron's Stay Order, July 28, 1962," *Race Relations Law Reporter* 7 (1962): 742–43; "Judge Cameron's Stay Order, July 31, 1962," *Race Relations Law Reporter* 7 (1962): 743; "Court of Appeals Order, August 4, 1962," *Race Relations Law Reporter* 7 (1962): 743–44; "Judge Cameron's Stay

Order, August 6, 1962," *Race Relations Law Reporter* 7 (1962): 744–45; "State Board of Trustees Order, September 4, 1962," *Race Relations Law Reporter* 7 (1962): 745; "Justice Black's Action, September 10, 1962," *Race Relations Law Reporter* 7 (1962): 745–46; Larry Johnson, Deirdre Cobb-Roberts, and Barbara Shircliffe, "African Americans and the Struggle for Opportunity in Florida Public Higher Education, 1947–1977," *History of Education Quarterly* 47, no. 3 (2007): 345; "Court Orders Ole Miss to Integrate," *Clarion-Ledger* (Jackson, MS), July 18, 1962.

17. Howard M. Feuerstein, interview by Pat Arneson, March 1, 2017; Joseph A. Custer, "Ideological Voting Applied to the School Desegregation Cases in the Federal Courts of Appeals from the 1960s and 1970s," *Scholar* 1 (2013): 23; Chin and Chin, "Constance Baker Motley," 1768; Eagles, *Price of Defiance*, 239.

18. Eagles, *Price of Defiance*, 273; Browder v. Gayle, 142 F. Supp. 707 (M.D. Ala. 1956); US Code (28 USC § 42); "Court Orders Ole Miss."

19. "Justice Black's Action: September 10, 1962," *Race Relations Law Reporter* 7 (1962–1963): 744; Mitchell F. Crusto, "Federalism and Civil Rights: The Meredith Case," *National Black Law Journal* 11, no. 2 (1989): 237; "District Court Injunction, September 13, 1962," *Race Relations Law Reporter* 7 (1962–1963): 746–47.

20. Eagles, *Price of Defiance*, 284; Mari Crabtree, "Elegy and Effigy," *Appendix* 2, no. 2 (2014) (website); Silver, *Mississippi*, 43.

21. Eagles, *Price of Defiance*, 295; Claude Sitton, "Barnett Defiant: Threatens to Jail US Aides if They Seize Officials of State," *New York Times*, September 25, 1962.

22. Wright Thompson, *The Cost of These Dreams: Sports Stories and Other Serious Business* (New York: Penguin Books, 2019), 44; Greaves, *Blackamoor*, 24; Silver, *Mississippi*, 132.

23. United States v. Barnett, 376 US 681 (1964) at 685; "Army of Sheriffs, Police Arrive at Ole Miss: Manpower Barrier Against Meredith Estimated at 400," *Shreveport Journal* (Shreveport, LA), September 27, 1962; "Meredith Turned Away Again at Ole Miss: Lt. Gov. Johnson Blocks Entrance at Campus Gates," *Shreveport Journal* (Shreveport, LA), September 26, 1962.

24. United States v. Barnett, 330 F.2d 369 (5th Cir. 1963).

25. Legal Information Institute, "Amicus Curiae," Cornell Law School (website), accessed December 29, 2022; Eagles, *Price of Defiance*, 328.

26. *Meredith*, 313 F.2d 532 at 533.

27. Elbert P. Tuttle, quoted in Frank T. Read and Lucy S. McGough, *Let Them Be Judged: The Judicial Integration of the Deep South* (Metuchen, NJ: Scarecrow Press, 1978), 236.

28. Silver, *Mississippi*, 116, 119; Kathleen W. Wickham, *We Believed We Were Immortal: Twelve Reporters Who Covered the 1962 Integration Crisis at Ole Miss* (Oxford, MS: Yoknapatawpha Press, 2017), 20; Ross Barnett, "September 29, 1962: Ross Barnett, Governor of Mississippi, Giving His 'I Love Mississippi' Speech," YouTube video, 2:41, uploaded by HelmerReenberg on January 3, 2010.

29. "Painful Decision on Force Faces President," *Delta Democrat-Times*

(Greenville, MS), September 28, 1962; Jack Bass, *Unlikely Heroes: The Dramatic Story of the Southern Judges of the Fifth Circuit Who Translated the Supreme Court's Brown Decision into a Revolution for Equality* (New York: Simon and Schuster, 1981), 137.

30. Robert F. Kennedy to Richard T. Rives, June 3, 1963, Richard T. Rives Papers, Alabama Department of Archives and History, Montgomery, AL; Lawrence R. Levin, interview by Pat Arneson, March 27, 2017.

31. Levin, interview by Pat Arneson, March 27, 2017; Brown-Nagin, *Civil Rights Queen*, 252; Mike Wallace, "Transcript: Interview with Senator James Eastland," Harry Ransom Center, The University of Texas at Austin (website), July 28, 1957.

32. Levin, interview by Pat Arneson, March 27, 2017; Lawrence R. Levin, email message to Pat Arneson, February 24, 2020; Leon Daniel, "Vigilante Groups Bombard Oxford with Offers of Armed Assistance," *Delta Democrat-Times* (Greenville, MS), September 30, 1962; "Painful Decision on Force Faces President," *Delta Democrat-Times* (Greenville, MS), September 28, 1962.

33. Joel William Friedman, *Champion of Civil Rights: Judge John Minor Wisdom* (Baton Rouge: Louisiana State University Press, 2009), 167; James Meredith, *Three Years in Mississippi* (Jackson: University of Mississippi Press, 1966/2019), 201; Silver, *Mississippi*, 120; Greaves, *Blackamoor*, 17. Cf. "At Oxford—Negro at Ole Miss; Campus in Uproar," *Clarion-Ledger* (Jackson, MS), October 1, 1962, incorrectly identifies Dunbar Hall as the dormitory in which James Meredith was housed. Per James Meredith, *Three Years in Mississippi* (Jackson: University of Mississippi Press, 1966/2019), 201, he stayed in Baxter Hall.

34. "Oxford, Mississippi Population 1960," World Population Review (website); "400 Marshals Rushed into Oxford Area," *Clarion-Ledger* (Jackson, MS), October 1, 1962; "At Oxford"; Bob Carpenter, "Bloody Violence on Campus Leaves 2 Dead," *Delta Democrat-Times* (Greenville, MS), October 1, 1962; Levin, email message to Pat Arneson, February 24, 2020; "Governor Releases Statement on Case," *Clarion-Ledger* (Jackson, MS), October 1, 1962.

35. Dick Gentry, *Under Fire at Ole Miss: Tales of a Roving Mississippi Reporter in Far-Off America* (London: Woodlord, 2014), 189; Aram Goudsouzian, "Introduction to the New Edition," in Meredith, *Three Years in Mississippi*, xiii (emphasis in original); John F. Kennedy, "JFK Phone Calls and Speech during the University of Mississippi Crisis (Sept. and Oct. 1962)," YouTube video, 15:04, uploaded by David Von Pein's JFK Channel on September 7, 2013; "We Believed We Were Immortal," Vimeo (website), video, 3:13–3:20, documentary, 8:50.

36. Levin, interview by Pat Arneson, March 27, 2017.

37. "JFK Takes Over Guard as Army Enters Crisis: Schedules Video Address to US," *Clarion-Ledger* (Jackson, MS), September 30, 1962; Levin, interview by Pat Arneson, March 27, 2017.

38. John F. Kennedy, "September 30, 1962, President John F. Kennedy's

Address to the Nation on Radio and Television, 'US vs Mississippi: Campus Riots Mark Integration,'" You Tube video, 0:54 to 1:14, uploaded by HelmerReenberg on June 30, 2009, 2:06.

39. "Campus in Shambles With Light of Dawn," *Delta Democrat-Times* (Greenville, MS), October 1, 1962; "Eastland Orders Probe of Events at Ole Miss: Conduct of Marshals, Troops in Question: Meredith at a Glance," *Clarion-Ledger* (Jackson, MS), October 2, 1962; Frank T. Read, "The Bloodless Revolution: The Role of the Fifth Circuit in the Integration of the Deep South," *Mercer Law Review* 32, no. 4 (1981): 1156–157n21; "Meredith in Classes as Riots Spread to Oxford: 2 Die in All-Night Rioting on Campus," *Delta Democrat-Times* (Greenville, MS), October 1, 1962; Susan M. Weill, "Mississippi's Daily Press in Three Crises," in *The Press and Race: Mississippi Journalists Confront the Movement*, ed. David R. Davies (Jackson: University Press of Mississippi, 2001), 3.

40. Friedman, *Champion*, 169; Crystal R. Gafford Muhammad, "Meredith v. Fair," in *Encyclopedia of African American Education*, vol. 1, ed. Kofi Lomotey (Los Angeles: Sage, 2010), 443–44; "Meredith in Classes."

41. Anne S. Emanuel, *Elbert Parr Tuttle: Chief Jurist of the Civil Rights Revolution* (Athens: University of Georgia Press, 2014), 213; *Barnett*, 376 US 681; "Hearing on Return on Contempt Citations Issued against Governor Ross R. Barnett and Lieutenant Governor Paul B. Johnson," October 2, 1962, US Department of Justice (website).

42. *Barnett*, 330 F.2d 369. The en banc panel included seven judges: Judges Hutcheson and Cameron were both in frail health and did not attend; "Barnett Denies Contempt Guilt: 'Conscience Clear' on Legal Duty," *New York Times*, October 17, 1961; Bass, *Unlikely Heroes*, 195, 196; Meredith v. Fair, 306 F.2d 374; "Interview with Judge John Minor Wisdom," October 31, 1985, 43:23, Washington University in St. Louis, University Libraries (website), accessed December 4, 2024; *Meredith*, 298 F.2d at 701. See Brown-Nagin, *Civil Rights Queen*, 153: "Alluding to *Peter Pan*, the appellate court called the state's version of the facts 'never never land' claims, myths invented solely for purposes of litigation."

43. "Judge Sees Small Chance for Barnett: Angry Jurists Delay Hearing until Monday," *Commonwealth* (Greenwood, MS), October 13, 1962; "Barnett May Defy Some of US Court Orders: Big Fines, Imprisonment Braved by Our Governor," *Clarion-Ledger* (Jackson, MS), October 13, 1962; Carl P. Leubsdorf, "Barnett Case to Resume Next Week," *Hattiesburg American* (Hattiesburg, MS), October 13, 1962; Charles L. Pickett (Jackson, MS) to Richard T. Rives, October 14, 1962, RTR Papers; John B. Mason (Robstown, TX) to Richard T. Rivers [*sic*], October 14, 1963, RTR Papers.

44. Elbert Parr Tuttle, "First Draft of Findings of Fact, Order, and Judgment on Hearing to Afford Ross R. Barnett an Opportunity to Purge Himself of Civil Contempt, Meredith v. Fair," RTR Papers.

45. *Barnett*, 330 F.2d at 379; John R. Brown and Richard T. Rives to Elbert P. Tuttle, Warren L. Jones, John M. Wisdom, Walter P. Gewin, and Griffin Bell,

October 16, 1962, RTR Papers; Walter P. Gewin to Elbert P. Tuttle, Richard T. Rives, Warren L. Jones, John R. Brown, John M. Wisdom, and Griffin Bell, October 17, 1962, RTR Papers; Friedman, *Champion*, 172.

46. "Ole Miss Adopts 'Get Tough' Policy on Students Harasing [*sic*]," *Cullman Times Democrat* (Cullman, AL), October 14, 1962; "Barnett Fears Ole Miss Students' Rights May Have Been Violated," *Cullman Times Democrat* (Cullman, AL), October 14, 1962; "Barnett Standing on Law: Action Right, Says Governor," *Anniston Star* (Anniston, AL), October 17, 1962.

47. Bass, *Unlikely Heroes*, 256.

48. "Soviet Ships Steam toward Test of Cuban Arms Blockade: US Forces Move to Enforce Kennedy Order," *Delta Democrat-Times* (Greenville, MS), October 23, 1962; John F. Kennedy, "JFK Cuban Missile Crisis Speech (10/22/1962)," You Tube video, 8:15, Uploaded by CONELRAD6401240 on October 2, 2011, 0:56 and 1:08.

49. Richard T. Rives to Elbert P. Tuttle, Warren L. Jones, John R. Brown, John M. Wisdom, Walter P. Gewin, and Griffin Bell, October 24, 1962, RTR Papers; Elbert P. Tuttle to Richard T. Rives, Warren L. Jones, John R. Brown, John M. Wisdom, Walter P. Gewin, and Griffin Bell, October 25, 1962, RTR Papers.

50. Richard T. Rives to Elbert P. Tuttle, November 5, 1962, RTR Papers; Poston v. Poston, 331 S.C. 106 (S.C. 1998) at 111.

51. Rives to Tuttle, November 5, 1962.

52. Levin, interview by Pat Arneson, March 27, 2017; Richard T. Rives to Warren L. Jones and John R. Brown, December 28, 1955, JRB Papers; Richard T. Rives to Elbert P. Tuttle and John R. Brown, May 28, 1959, JRB Papers.

53. *Barnett*, 330 F.2d 369; Richard T. Rives, quoted in Bass, *Unlikely Heroes*, 255.

54. *Meredith*, 199 F. Supp. 754; W. J. Mahoney Jr., "Mahoney—'As I See It': A Whole Contemptuous Southern People," *Alabama Journal*, November 19, 1962.

55. Richard T. Rives to James J. Carter, November 20, 1962, RTR Papers; James J. Carter to Richard T. Rives, November 21, 1962, RTR Papers; Joseph C. Hutcheson Jr. to Richard T. Rives, November 27, 1962, RTR Papers.

56. *Barnett*, 376 US at 681.

57. United States v. Barnett, 346 F.2d 99 (5th Cir. 1965); Friedman, *Champion*, 176.

58. Warren L. Jones to Richard T. Rives, March 16, 1965, quoted in Friedman, *Champion*, 177; "About James Meredith," UM History of Integration, University of Mississippi (website), accessed November 16, 2024.

59. Rives, quoted in Bass, *Unlikely Heroes*, 255; *Barnett*, 346 F.2d 99; "Draft Opinion: United States v. Barnett, 346 F.2d 99," RTR Papers; Levin, interview by Pat Arneson, March 27, 2017.

Chapter 5

1. J. Wayne Flynt, *Alabama in the Twentieth Century* (Tuscaloosa: University of Alabama Press, 2004), 15.

2. Alabama constitution, art. IV; Dewey W. English Jr., "Alabama's Population: 1800 to the Modern Era," AL.com (website), December 28, 2019; Student Nonviolent Coordinating Committee, "The General Condition of the Alabama Negro," SNCC Atlanta GA, March 1965, 11; William H. Stewart Jr., "Reapportionment with Census Districts: The Alabama Case," *Alabama Law Review* 24 (1972): 694.

3. Sims v. Frink, 205 F. Supp. 245 (M.D. Ala. 1962); Sims v. Frink, 208 F. Supp. 431 (M.D. Ala. 1962); Reynolds v. Sims, 377 US 533 (1964); Sims v. Baggett, 247 F. Supp. 96 (M.D. Ala. 1965); Sims v. Amos, 336 F. Supp. 924 (M.D. Ala. 1972); *Brown v. Bd. of Educ.* (*Brown I*), 347 US 483 (1954); *Brown v. Bd. of Educ.* (*Brown II*), 349 US 294 (1955).

4. "Hatch Act Overview," U.S. Office of Special Counsel (website), accessed August 22, 2024; Gomillion v. Lightfoot, 364 US 339 (1960).

5. Robert J. Cook, "Red Termites and Rebel Yells: The Civil War Centennial in Strife-Torn Alabama, 1961–1965," *Alabama Review* 64, no. 2 (2011): 157, 160–61.

6. *Brown* I, 347 U.S. 483; *Brown* II, 349 U.S. 294; Browder v. Gayle, 142 F. Supp 707 (M.D. Ala. 1956); H.R. 8601, *Civil Rights Act of 1960*, Public Law no. 86–449, US Statutes at Large 74 (1960), 86–92; Cook, "Red Termites," 161.

7. *Frink*, 205 F. Supp. 245.

8. *Frink*, 205 F. Supp. 245; Tony A. Freyer, "Conclusion," in *Frank M. Johnson: Defending Constitutional Rights*, ed. Tony A. Freyer (Athens: University of Georgia Press, 2001), 150; Baker v. Carr, 179 F. Supp. 824 (M.D. Tenn. 1959).

9. "Introduction," in *Redistricting in the South*, Rose Institute of State and Local Government, Claremont McKenna College (website), accessed December 4, 2024; Colegrove v. Green, 328 US 549 (1946).

10. *Colegrove*, 328 US 549 at 556, 552, 568; Baker v. Carr, 369 US 186 (1962).

11. *Baker*, 369 US 186 (1962) at 201, 210, 200; Gray v. Sanders, 372 US 368 (1963) at 369; Tony A. Freyer, *Hugo L. Black and the Dilemma of American Liberalism* (New York: Pearson, 2008), 149.

12. Ray Jenkins, "June Session Would Be 'Reasonable, Prompt,'" *Montgomery Advertiser*, April 1, 1962; *Baker*, 369 US 186; *Brown I*, 347 U.S. 483; US Constitution, amend. XIV; US Const., amend. X; US Constitution, article VI, § 2.

13. *Baker*, 369 US 186; Jenkins, "June Session"; *Brown II*, 349 U.S. 294; "What They Have Done to Us," *Alabama Journal*, July 23, 1962, Richard T. Rives Papers, Alabama Department of Archives and History, Montgomery, Alabama; Browder, 142 F. Supp 707.

14. "Alabama Editors Are Saying It Must Be Done," *Montgomery Advertiser*, July 1, 1962; John Peavy Wright, "Tell It to Old Grandma," *Montgomery Advertiser*, April 22, 1962.

15. Browder v. Gayle, 142 F. Supp 707 (M.D. Ala. 1956); law clerk for Richard T. Rives, interview by Pat Arneson, February 22, 2017; John Michael Spivack, "Race, Civil Rights, and the United States Court of Appeals for the Fifth Judicial Circuit" (PhD Diss., University of Florida, 1978), 262.

16. Virginia Foster Durr, *Outside the Magic Circle: The Autobiography of Virginia Foster Durr*, ed. Hollinger F. Barnard (New York: Simon and Schuster, 1985/1987), 292, 297; C. Vann Woodward, "Montgomery," in *American Places: Encounters with History: America's Leading Historians Talk about the Sites Where the Past Comes Alive for Them*, ed. William E. Leuchtenburg (New York: Oxford University Press, 2000), 347; Liva Baker, *The Second Battle of New Orleans* (New York: HarperCollins, 1996), 286.

17. "What They Have Done"; *Baker*, 369 US 186; *Gray*, 372 US 368; *Frink*, 205 F. Supp. 245.

18. Lawrence R. Levin, interview by Pat Arneson, March 15, 2022; Frink, 205 F. Supp. 247; Sims v. Frink, Civil Action no. 1744-N, Filed April 14, 1962, 3, Richard T. Rives Papers.

19. *Frink*, 205 F. Supp. at 247, 248.

20. *Frink*, 205 F. Supp. at 248.

21. Tom Gordon, "Former Segregationist Gov. John Patterson Now Supports First Black President," *Birmingham News*, January 20, 2009; "Federal Courts Opened to Reapportion Cases," *Montgomery Advertiser*, March 27, 1962; "Legislators Urged to Beat Deadline," *Birmingham Post Herald*, June 13, 1962, quoted in J. Douglas Smith, *On Democracy's Doorstep: The Inside Story of How the Supreme Court Brought "One Person, One Vote" to the United States* (New York: Hill and Wang, 2014), 127; Bob Ingram, "They Made a Mess and Then Took Off," *Montgomery Advertiser-Journal*, July 1, 1962, RTR Papers.

22. Ingram, "They Made a Mess"; Smith, *On Democracy's Doorstep*, 128.

23. Arthur Osgoode, "Reapportionment Court Suit Hopes to Force Action after 60 Years," *Montgomery Advertiser*, July 8, 1962; Ingram, "They Made a Mess."

24. Doug Linder, "US Supreme Court: Reynolds v. Sims, 377 US 533 (1964)," Exploring Constitutional Law (website), accessed March 14, 2021.

25. *Baker*, 369 US 186; *Frink*, 205 F. Supp 245; law clerk for Richard T. Rives, interview by Pat Arneson, February 22, 2017.

26. *Frink*, 208 F. Supp 431; Arthur Osgoode, "Lawmakers' 'Defiance' of Court Under Attack: Prompt Decision Promised on Reapportion Formula," *Montgomery Advertiser*, July 17, 1962.

27. "No End Seen in Heat Wave," *Anniston Star*, July 21, 1962; Richard T. Rives, quoted in "Judges Delay Ruling on Apportion Plans: Lawyers Offer Arguments," *Anniston Star*, July 16, 1962.

28. Osgoode, "Lawmakers' 'Defiance.'"

29. Osgoode, "Lawmakers' 'Defiance'"; Student Nonviolent Coordinating Committee, "The General Condition," 1, 11, 13: The third county was Greene County. The net change in population of Black citizens in Bibb County from 1950-1960 was -20.2 percent while the net change in population of Black citizens in Shelby County from 1950 to 1960 was +5.8 percent.

30. Osgoode, "Lawmakers' 'Defiance'"; Smith, *On Democracy's Doorstep*, 131.

31. "What They Have Done"; Clarke Stallworth, "After Evidence Is

Studied—Prompt Reapportion Decision Is Promised: Legislature Is Accused of Failing to Do Its Duty," *Birmingham Post-Herald*, July 17, 1962, RTR Papers.

32. Osgoode, "Lawmakers' 'Defiance.'"

33. *Frink*, 205 F. Supp 245; *Baker*, 369 US 186; *Frink*, 208 F. Supp. 431 (M.D. Ala. 1962) at 437, 431; Ray Jenkins, "Federal Judges Order Immediate Reapportioning: New Legislature to Take Office after Nov. Vote," *Alabama Journal*, July 21, 1962.

34. Decree, July 25, 1962, Sims v. Frink, Frank M. Johnson Papers, Library of Congress, quoted in Smith, *On Democracy's Doorstep*, 131; *Frink*, 208 F. Supp. at 442.

35. *Baker*, 369 US 186 (1962); Tom Johnson, "In Alabama—Problem of Reseating Is Not Settled Yet," *Memphis Commercial Appeal*, June 21, 1964, RTR Papers; *Frink*, 208 F. Supp. 431.

36. *Frink*, 208 F. Supp. 431 (M.D. Ala. 1962); Reynolds v. Sims, 374 US 802 (1963). J. Mills Thornton III, email to Pat Arneson, April 22, 2023: The state did not appeal the *Frink* ruling as "the state Attorney General's office feared what would become [Chief Justice Earl] Warren's decision in Reynolds."

37. Smith, *On Democracy's Doorstep*, 190; Irving Bernstein, *Guns or Butter: The Presidency of Lyndon Johnson* (New York: Oxford University Press, 1996), 25; Keith M. Finley, "Lyndon Johnson and the Civil Rights Act of 1957: A Reassessment" (MA thesis, Southeastern Louisiana University, 1999), 6; Jeffrey W. Helsing, *Johnson's War/Johnson's Great Society: The Guns and Butter Trap* (Westport, CT: Praeger, 2000), 8.

38. *Reynolds*, 377 US at 534; Frink, 208 F. Supp. 431; Wesberry v. Sanders, 376 US 1 (1964); "Supreme Court Tells Alabama to Revise Legislative System: Reapportion before 1966 Decree Issued: Decision Affects Other States Also," *Alabama Journal*, June 15, 1965.

39. *Reynolds*, 377 US 533; *Frink*, 208 F. Supp. 431; Daniel H. Thomas to Richard T. Rives and Frank M Johnson Jr., June 30, 1964, RTR Papers.

40. Richard T. Rives to Daniel H. Thomas and Frank M. Johnson Jr., July 3, 1964, RTR Papers.

41. Rives to Thomas and Johnson, July 3, 1964.

42. *Reynolds*, 377 US at 534; *Frink*, 208 F. Supp. 431; Wesberry v. Sanders, 376 US 1 (1964); "Supreme Court Tells Alabama to Revise Legislative System."

43. Richard T. Rives, quoted in Frank T. Read and Lucy S. McGough, *Let Them Be Judged: The Judicial Integration of the Deep South* (Metuchen, NJ: Scarecrow Press, 1978), 35; "1964 Civil Rights Act"; Jeff Woods, *Black Struggle, Red Scare: Segregation and Anti-Communism in the South, 1948–1968* (Baton Rouge: Louisiana State University Press, 2004), 174; "Courts: The Fascinating and Frenetic Fifth," *Time*, December 4, 1964, 46; Richard T. Rives, "Defending Alabamians," *Time*, December 11, 1964, 20; John Daniel Reaves, interview with Pat Arneson, April 11, 2023.

44. Law clerk for Richard T. Rives, interview by Pat Arneson, February 22, 2017; Neil T. Bradley, email message to Pat Arneson, February 5, 2017.

45. Read and McGough, *Let Them Be Judged*, 35

46. Read and McGough, *Let Them Be Judged*, 35; Rives, quoted in Read and McGough, *Let Them Be Judged*, 35–36.

47. Toombs v. Fortson, 241 F. Supp. 65 (N.D. Ga. 1965) at 70; "Fair Apportioning Comes Closer," *Anniston Star*, April 5, 1965; "Unfinished Business in Alabama," *Anniston Star*, July 31, 1965; "Once More in Frustration," *Montgomery Advertiser*, December 20, 1964.

48. "Reshuffle Goes to Court Order," *Selma Times-Journal*, July 28, 1965; Judith Helms, "U.S. Court Orders Hearing in August on Reapportionment Plan for Alabama," *Alabama Journal*, July 27, 1965; *Frink*, 208 F. Supp. 431; *Baggett*, 247 F. Supp. 96; H.R. 6400, Voting Rights Act of 1965, Public Law no. 89–110, U.S. Statutes at Large 79 (1965), 437–46.

49. "Lawmakers Set Night Session, Wallace Booked," *Selma Times-Journal*, September 9, 1965; Bob Ingram, "Like the Mighty Babe, the Governor Tries," *Montgomery Advertiser*, September 5, 1965; "Court Gives Notice: 'Reapportion Both Houses,'" *Anniston Star*, August 25, 1965.

50. Joseph F. Gilliland, "Racial Gerrymandering in the Deep South," *Alabama Law Review* 22, no. 2 (1970): 321; Bob Ingram, "Gov. Wallace Considering Special Call," *Montgomery Advertiser*, September 2, 1965; "Special Session Opens Today on Reshuffle Note," *Selma Times-Journal*, September 13, 1965; Bob Ingram, "Apportionment on Agenda for Panel of U.S. Judges," *Montgomery Advertiser*, August 25, 1965.

51. Rives to Thomas and Johnson, July 3, 1964; Frank M. Johnson to Richard T. Rives and Daniel H. Thomas, September 8, 1965, RTR Papers; Richard T. Rives, Personal Note, n.d., RTR Papers; Rives, Sims: Working Notes, RTR Papers; Jonathan R. Harkavy, interview by Pat Arneson, February 15, 2017; "The Legislature Abdicates," *Alabama Journal*, June 26, 1965, RTR Papers.

52. "Aid, Reapportioning Passed; Congress Near Adjournment," *Montgomery Advertiser*, September 25, 1964; Tom Mackin, "House Reapportions Itself: Measure Voted Tuesday Does Not Alter Senate," *Montgomery Advertiser*, September 15, 1965; Sims v. Frink, "Memorandum in Support of Reapportionment Plans," Civil Action no. 1755-N, RTR Papers; Frank M. Johnson Jr. to Richard T. Rives and Daniel H. Thomas, August 30, 1965, Enclosure: Richmond M. Flowers, Sims v. Frink, Civil Action no. 1744-N, August 23, 1965, RTR Papers; David J. Vann and Robert S. Vance, "An Analysis of Reapportionment Plans Submitted," Filed August 25, 1965, RTR Papers; Sims and Farr v. Frink, Civil Action no. 1744-N, "Richmond M. Flowers, Proposal for the Reapportionment of the Alabama State Legislature," RTR Papers; James E. Folsom, Amicus Curiae, filed August 30, 1965, Sims v. Frink, Case Civil Action 1744-N; Frank M. Johnson to Richard T. Rives and Daniel H. Thomas, September 1, 1965, RTR Papers.

53. *Baggett*, 247 F. Supp. 96 (1965); Rex Thomas, "Court: U.S. Judges Set Review of Reapportionment Law," *Montgomery Advertiser*, September 25, 1965; "Voting Rights Act of 1965."

54. Daniel H. Thomas to Richard T. Rives and Frank M. Johnson, September 28, 1965, RTR Papers; Richard T. Rives to Daniel H. Thomas, September 30, 1965, RTR Papers.

55. *Baggett*, 247 F. Supp. at 109–10; Levin, interview by Pat Arneson, March 15, 2022.

56. Sims v. Baggett Civil Action No. 1744-N, "Opinion," October 2, 1965, RTR Papers; Baggett, 247 F. Supp. at 109; "Court Reapportions House: Battle on Succession Joined in Senate: Says Recent Measure Was Discriminatory," *Montgomery Advertiser*, October 5, 1965; Lane v. Wilson, 307 US 268 (1939) at 275 quoted in *Baggett*, 247 F. Supp. at 109; United States Congress, Committee on the Judiciary, Subcommittee on Civil and Constitutional Rights, "Extension of the Voting Rights Act: Hearings before the Subcommittee on Civil and Constitutional Rights of the Committee on the Judiciary," House of Representatives, 97th Cong., 1st Sess., on Extension of the Voting Rights Act. Washington, DC: US Government Printing Office, 1982: 644–46.

57. Nixon v. Brewer, 49 F.R.D. 122 (M.D. Ala. 1970) at 125, 126; *Baggett*, 247 F. Supp. 96.

58. *Amos*, 336 F. Supp. at 936; Milo Dakin, "Court Orders Reapportionment: New Districts Cross County Lines: November '74 Election Is Compliance Deadline," *Montgomery Advertiser*, January 4, 1972.

59. "It's Simple, the Court Said," *Montgomery Advertiser*, January 5, 1972; Stan Bailey, "Alabama Will Appeal Order on Legislature," *Alabama Journal*, January 6, 1972; Wallace v. Sims, 416 US 902 (1974); "State Reapportionment Is Upheld," *Alabama Journal*, October 24, 1972.

60. John A. Salmond, *The Conscience of a Lawyer: Clifford J. Durr and American Civil Liberties, 1899–1975* (Tuscaloosa: University of Alabama Press, 2020), 179; Tom Johnson, "In Alabama—Problem of Reseating Is Not Settled Yet," *Memphis Commercial Appeal*, June 21, 1964, RTR Papers.

Chapter 6

1. AL Constitution of 1819, art. 3, § 5, Alabama Digital Archives (website), accessed December 31, 2023; US Constitution, amend XV; William H. Stewart, *The Alabama State Constitution*, 2nd ed. (New York: Oxford University Press, 2016), 12.

2. Edwin C. Bridges, *Alabama: The Making of an American State* (Tuscaloosa: University of Alabama Press, 2016), 154; "Gen. Shelley Replies to James Weatherly: He Tells Why Ballot Box Stuffing Was Originated—Ministers of the Gospel, He Says, Approved the Method of Getting Rid of the Carpet Baggers," *Age-Herald*

(Birmingham, AL), October 6, 1901; "Election on April 8: Date of City Primary Fixed Last Night," *Montgomery Advertiser*, March 28, 1901.

3. Bridges, *Alabama*, 154–55; "Proceedings of the DSC," April 26, 1900, quoted in Glenn Feldman, *The Disfranchisement Myth: Poor Whites and Suffrage Restriction in Alabama* (Athens: University of Georgia Press, 2004), 55; Harvey H. Jackson III, "White Supremacy Triumphant: Democracy Undone," in *A Century of Controversy: Constitutional Reforms in Alabama*, ed. H. Bailey Thomas (Tuscaloosa: University of Alabama Press, 2002), 21–22.

4. Stewart, *Alabama State Constitution*, 4; Peyton McCrary et al., "Alabama," in *Quiet Revolution in the South: The Impact of the Voting Rights Act, 1965–1990*, ed. Chandler Davidson and Bernard Grofman (Princeton, NJ: Princeton University Press, 1994), 44; Sarah A. Warren, "Alabama Constitution of 1901," Encyclopedia of Alabama (website), last modified April 16, 2024.

5. "Election on April 8"; "The County Committee: Montgomery Democrats Arrange for Election," *Montgomery Advertiser*, February 3, 1901; Jackson, "White Supremacy Triumphant," 30; "Alabama's Population by Race: 1800–2000," Birmingham Public Library (website). See Jack Bass and Walter DeVries, *The Transformation of Southern Politics: Social Change and Political Consequence since 1945* (Athens: University of Georgia Press, 1995), 82: "After Reconstruction, the number of Black citizens registered in 14 Black Belt counties numbered 78,311 in 1900. Three years later, the number of Black voters in those counties had dropped to 1,081."

6. Giles v. Harris, 189 US 475 (1903); Giles v. Teasley, 193 US 146 (1904); R. Volney Riser, *Defying Disenfranchisement: Black Voting Rights Activism in the Jim Crow South, 1890–1908* (Baton Rouge: Louisiana State University Press, 2010).

7. Jack Bass, *Unlikely Heroes: The Dramatic Story of the Southern Judges of the Fifth Circuit Who Translated the Supreme Court's Brown Decision into a Revolution for Equality* (New York: Simon and Schuster, 1981), 269; "Civil Rights Act of 1963," *Cong. Rec.* 110, no. 58 (Washington, DC: US Government Printing Office, 1964): 6499.

8. "Deaths and Burials Index, 1881–1974, Alabama," Department of Alabama Archives and History, Montgomery, AL; Debra Umberson, *Death of a Parent: Transition to a New Adult Identity* (New York: Cambridge University Press, 2003); "Feelings When Someone Dies," Cruse Bereavement Support (website), accessed October 15, 2024.

9. Franklin Roosevelt, "State of the Union Message to Congress, January 11, 1944," Franklin D. Roosevelt Presidential Library and Museum (website); John Daniel Reaves, interview by Pat Arneson, April 11, 2023.

10. Mitchell v. Wright, 62 F. Supp. 580 (M.D. Ala. 1945) at 581; Mitchell v. Wright, 154 F.2d 924 (5th Cir. 1946) at 927.

11. Smith v. Allwright, Civ. Action no. 645 (S.D. Tex 1942); Smith v. Allwright, 131 F.2d 593 (5th Cir. 1943); Smith v. Allwright, 321 US 649 (1944).

12. Vera Chandler Foster, "'Boswellianism': A Technique in the Restriction of Negro Voting," *Phylon* 10, no. 1 (1949): 27; Yarbrough, *Judge Frank Johnson*, 53, 234–35n18; Anne S. Emanuel, "Forming the Historic Fifth Circuit: The Eisenhower Years," *Texas Forum on Civil Liberties and Civil Rights* 6, no. 2 (2002): 239–40; "Senate Passes Poll Tax Bill: Amendment 'Protects' White Supremacy," *Alabama Journal*, June 27, 1945. The term "prominent Birmingham lawyer" to describe an unnamed Grand Cyclops of the Ku Klux Klan who supported the Boswell amendment comes from Emanuel, *Elbert Parr Tuttle*, 134, and Emanuel in turn quoted it from "R. Rives, 1895–1982," editorial obituary, *Montgomery Advertiser*, October 9, 1982.

13. Tony A. Freyer, "Introduction: Johnson's Unusual Origins and Early Career," in *Frank M. Johnson: Defending Constitutional Rights*, ed. Tony A. Freyer (Athens: University of Georgia Press, 2001), xx; Richard T. Rives, "An Argument against the Adoption of the Boswell Amendment," *Alabama Lawyer* 7, no. 3 (1946): 291.

14. Rives, quoted in Peggy Roberson, "Retired Judge Pleased at Progress," *Birmingham News*, April 9, 1975.

15. "Wilkinson Calls for Amendment Four OK—Rives Denounces It: Debate Sponsored by Florence Jaycees Draws Capacity Audience; Amendment 4 Seen Effort Entrench Special Privilege," *Florence (AL) Herald*, November 1, 1946; Davis v. Schnell, 81 F. Supp. 872 (S.D. Ala. 1949) at 879; Rives, "An Argument," 294; Emanuel, "Forming the Historic Fifth," 240.

16. George E. Sims, *The Little Man's Big Friend: James E. Folsom in Alabama Politics, 1946–1958* (Tuscaloosa: University of Alabama Press, 1985), 163.

17. "R. Rives, 1895–1982," *Montgomery Advertiser*, October 9, 1982, quoted in Anne Emanuel, *Elbert Parr Tuttle: Chief Jurist of the Civil Rights Revolution* (Athens: University of Georgia Press, 2011), 134.

18. "Speech," Richard T. Rives, April 18, 1946, quoted in Steven F. Lawson, *Black Ballots: Voting Rights in the South, 1944–1969* (New York: Lexington Books, 1976/1999), 91; Foster, "Boswellianism," 29; Rives, "An Argument," 295.

19. Scotty E. Kirkland, "Mobile and the Boswell Amendment," *Alabama Review* 65, no. 3 (2012): 221; Wilkinson, "Argument for," 375, 382.

20. Rives, "An Argument," 294; Bass, *Unlikely Heroes*, 73.

21. "Rives Attacks Boswell Plan, Cites Court Appeal System," *Montgomery Advertiser*, April 20, 1946; Sims, *Little Man's Big Friend*, 80; "Boswell Amendment," Alabama Moments (website), accessed August 6, 2014.

22. *Davis*, 81 F. Supp. at 877; *Smith*, 321 US; Schnell v. Davis, 336 US 933 (1949); Richard T. Rives, quoted in Frank T. Read and Lucy S. McGough, *Let Them Be Judged: The Judicial Integration of the Deep South* (Metuchen, NJ: Scarecrow Press, 1978), 33.

23. Wilkinson, "Argument for," 375; Rives, quoted in Read and McGough, *Let Them Be Judged*, 33.

24. Martin Luther King Jr., "'Give Us the Ballot,' Address Delivered at the

Prayer Pilgrimage for Freedom," Martin Luther King, Jr. Research and Education Institute at Stanford University (website), May 17, 1957, accessed June 11, 2022.

25. King, "Give Us the Ballot"; Tomiko Brown-Nagin, *Civil Rights Queen: Constance Baker Motley and the Struggle for Equality* (New York: Pantheon Books, 2022), 233.

26. "Civil Rights Act of 1957," Dwight D. Eisenhower Presidential Library (website).

27. "Negroes Imperil White Vote Rule," *Anniston Star* (Anniston, AL), March 31, 1960; "Voter's List to Be Printed In Journal," *Alabama Journal*, April 9, 1964; Bryan Lyman, "The Believer: Arthur Madison Launched a Montgomery Voter Registration Drive in 1944—and Paid a Price," *Montgomery Advertiser*, February 21, 2021.

28. Dick Hines, "Probers Mum on Plan to Open Vote Records: Officials Set 2-Day Goal for Inquiry," *Montgomery Advertiser*, December 8, 1958; In Re: George C. Wallace, 170 F. Supp 63 (M.D. Ala. 1959).

29. "Ike Hits Probe Silence; Justice Agents Arrive: Legal Steps Here Veiled in Secrecy," *Montgomery Advertiser*, December 11, 1958; "Registrars Appointed for Macon: Move Could Delay Federal Referee from Taking Action," *Montgomery Advertiser*, May 7, 1960.

30. United States v. Ala., 192 F. Supp. 677 (M.D. Ala. 1961) [Macon County]; United States v. Ala., Civil Action No. 1677-N (M.D. Ala., 1961) [Bullock County]; United States v. Penton, 212 F. Supp. 193 (M.D. Ala. 1962) [Montgomery County]; Robert F. Kennedy Jr., *Judge Frank M. Johnson, Jr.: A Biography* (New York: G. P. Putnam's Sons, 1978), 256.

31. United States v. Ala., 192 F. Supp. at 679, 683; Shuttlesworth v. Birmingham Bd. of Educ., 162 F. Supp. 372 (N.D. Ala. 1958); Ala. v. United States, 304 F.2d 583 (5th Cir. 1962); Ala. v. United States, 371 US 37 (1962).

32. Ala. v. United States, 304 F.2d at 584, 589, 588, 595.

33. United States v. Ala., Civil Action No. 1677-N (M.D. Ala., 1961), 5, Amazon Web Services (website).

34. *Penton*, 212 F. Supp. at 202; Bass, *Taming the Storm*, 155.

35. United States v. Atkins, 210 F. Supp. 441 (S.D. Ala. 1962) at 735; "Code of Alabama, Title 17, § 33," cited in *Davis*, 81 F. Supp. at 881n3.

36. Wolfgang Saxon, "Daniel H. Thomas, 93, Federal Judge Known for Maritime Cases," *New York Times*, April 19, 2000; *Atkins*, 210 F. Supp. 441. Regarding three-person board of registrars, per J. Mills Thornton III: "The governor appoints one member, the state auditor one, and the commissioner of agriculture one."

37. United States v. Atkins, 323 F.2d 733 (1963) at 736, 743.

38. Marin K. Levy, "Visiting Judges," *California Law Review* 107, no. 1 (2019): 139.

39. Henry J. Friendly, "Judge Paul R. Hays," *Columbia Law Review* 72, no. 3 (1972): 445.

40. *Atkins*, 323 F.2d at 743, 744; Frank M. Johnson, quoted in Bass, *Taming the Storm*, 155.

41. *Atkins*, 323 F.2d at 744; Howard M. Feuerstein, interview by Pat Arneson, March 1, 2017.

42. Feuerstein, interview by Pat Arneson, March 1, 2017; Neil R. McMillen, *The Citizens' Council: Organized Resistance to the Second Reconstruction, 1954–1964* (Urbana: University of Illinois Press, 1994), 360; Rives, quoted in Read and McGough, *Let Them Be Judged*, 35.

43. Ralph McGill, "The Angry South," *Atlantic Monthly* 197, no. 4 (1956): 34.

44. Stanton, *Journey Toward Justice*, 188; "Dr. Henry Edward 'Jeb' Russell," Find a Grave (website), November 19, 2014, accessed January 1, 2023; J. Mills Thornton III, email to Pat Arneson, July 24, 2024; "Ex-Trinity Pastor Dies: Dr. Robert Strong," *Alabama Journal*, June 18, 1980; John Daniel Reaves, interview by Pat Arneson, April 11, 2023; Virginia Durr, "April 19, 1965: Letter to Dearest Carl and Anne [Braden]," in *Freedom Writer: Virginia Durr: Letters from the Civil Rights Years*, ed. Patricia Sullivan (Athens: University of Georgia Press, 2006), 326. Cf. Mary Stanton, *Journey toward Justice: Juliette Hampton Morgan and the Montgomery Bus Boycott* (Athens: University of Georgia Press, 2006), 188, identifies Rives as a lifelong member of Trinity Presbyterian Church, but Rives actually joined Trinity after marrying his wife. Stanton wrote, "both he and his daughter were married" in Trinity, but per "Judge Richard T. Rives," *Alabama Lawyer*, p. 13: Rives was married to Jessie Dougherty of Macon, Georgia, during his time at Camp Wheeler, and per "Brief Life of Callie Dougherty Rives," Family Search (website), accessed October 15, 2024, his daughter was married "in Election Precinct 29 Alabama City, Etowah, Alabama."

45. "Memorials: Robert Strong," *Journal of the Evangelical Theological Society* 24, no. 1 (1981): 96; Richard T. Rives to Dr. Robert Strong, April 20, 1965, Richard T. Rives Papers, Alabama Department of Archives and History, Montgomery, AL.

46. Rives to Strong, April 20, 1965; Ginny Granade, email message to Pat Arneson, June 5, 2023; "Westminster Confession of Faith," Trinity Presbyterian Church, Montgomery, AL (website), accessed June 6, 2023.

47. Granade, email message to Pat Arneson, June 5, 2023.

48. Norman L. Blumenfeld, interview by Pat Arneson March 1, 2023; E. Lloyd Sutter, interview by Pat Arneson, May 15, 2017.

49. Sutter, interview by Pat Arneson, May 15, 2017; Harvey C. Couch, *A History of the Fifth Circuit, 1891–1981* (Washington, DC: Bicentennial Committee of the Judicial Conference of the United States, 1984), 135n126A; George Wallace, "The Inaugural Address of Governor George C. Wallace," Alabama Digital Archives (website), 2; Lawrence R. Levin, interview by Pat Arneson, March 15, 2022; Frank Sikora, *The Judge: The Life and Opinions of Alabama's Frank M. Johnson, Jr.* (Montgomery: NewSouth Books, 2007), 93.

50. Neil T. Bradley, email message to Pat Arneson, February 5, 2017; Anthony Lewis, "Nation's Conscience: The Supreme Court," *Courier-Journal* (Louisville, KY), June 24, 1962, RTR Papers.

51. Levin, interview by Pat Arnesón, March 15, 2022.

52. Joe Hall, "Equal Employment, Voter Section of Civil Rights Bill Explained," *Alabama Journal*, May 22, 1964; Robert J. Cook, "Red Termites and Rebel Yells: The Civil War Centennial in Strife-Torn Alabama, 1961–1965," *Alabama Review* 64, no. 2 (2011): 146.

53. Spider Martin, "Zion United Methodist Church in Marion, Alabama," Alabama Digital Archives (website), accessed August 16, 2024; Steve Fiffer and Adar Cohen, *Jimmie Lee and James: Two Lives, Two Deaths, and the Movement that Changed America* (New York: Regan Arts, 2015); Christopher M. Richardson and Ralph E. Luker, *Historical Dictionary of the Civil Rights Movement*, 2nd ed. (New York: Rowman and Littlefield, 2014), 355. Cf. Richardson and Luker, *Historical Dictionary*, 239, which states "Vivian led marchers from Zion Chapel Methodist Church," and according to Frye Gaillard, *Cradle of Freedom: Alabama and the Movement That Changed America* (Tuscaloosa: University of Alabama Press, 2004), 236, Vivian spoke at Zion Chapel Church; but per photographs in the Alabama Media Group holdings of the Alabama Department of Archives and History, Montgomery, Alabama, the church at which Vivian spoke was actually called Zion United Methodist Church.

54. Craig Swanson, *The Selma Campaign: Martin Luther King Jr., Jimmie Lee Jackson, and the Defining Struggle of the Civil Rights Era* (Bloomington, IN: Archway, 2014); J. Mills Thornton III, *Dividing Lines: Municipal Politics and the Struggle for Civil Rights in Montgomery, Birmingham, and Selma* (Tuscaloosa: University of Alabama Press, 2002), 486; Townsend Davis, *Weary Feet, Rested Souls: A Guided History of the Civil Rights Movement* (New York: W. W. Norton, 1998), 121–23; "Person: Jimmie Lee Jackson, Selma to Montgomery National Historic Trail," National Park Service (website), accessed October 19, 2024. Cf. John Slaughter, *New Battles Over Dixie: The Campaign for a New South* (Dix Hills, NY: General Hall, 1992), 137: "Clark planned to murder Vivian that night in retribution for daring to confront him two days earlier in front of the Selma courthouse to demand voting rights. Vivian had left the area and the sheriff and his posse found Jackson instead." However, there is no evidence that troopers targeted C. T. Vivian specifically. Per John Fleming, "The Man Who Shot Jimmie Lee Jackson, In His Own Words," Sojourners (website), November 16, 2010, accessed May 28, 2025: After protesters dispersed from the jail under threat of violence from troopers, some troopers proceeded to Mack's Café where any Black person could potentially become a target.

55. Randall Kryn, "James L. Bevel: The Strategist of the 1960s Civil Rights Movement," in *We Shall Overcome: The Civil Rights Movement in the United States in the 1950s and 1960s*, vol. 2, ed. David J. Garrow (New York: Carlson, 1989), 517–35; Thornton, *Dividing Lines*, 487; Student Nonviolent Coordinating Committee,

"Selma and Dallas County, Alabama: A Statistical Roundup," Civil Rights Movement Archive (website), accessed July 23, 2024.

56. Brown-Nagin, *Queen of Civil Rights*, 233; Barbara Arnwine and Marcia Johnson-Bianco, "Voting Rights at a Crossroads: The Supreme Court Decision in Shelby Is the Latest Challenge in the 'Unfinished March' to Full Black Access to the Ballot," Economic Policy Institute (website), October 25, 2013; Steven Otfinoski, *The Selma Marches for Civil Rights: We Shall Overcome* (North Mankato, MN: Capstone Press, 2019), 10; Thornton, *Dividing Lines*, 487.

57. Elizabeth Partridge, *Marching for Freedom: Walk Together Children and Don't You Grow Weary* (New York: Viking, 2009); Thornton, *Dividing Lines*, 137, 488.

58. Brown-Nagin, *Civil Rights Queen*, 233; Williams v. Wallace, 240 F. Supp. 100 (M.D. Ala. 1965) at 102, 103.

59. David J. Garrow, *Bearing the Cross: Martin Luther King Jr. and the Southern Christian Leadership Conference* (New York: HarperCollins, 1986), 401–5; Taylor Branch, *At Canaan's Edge: America in the King Years, 1965–68* (New York: Simon and Schuster, 2006); "Selma to Montgomery March," Martin Luther King, Jr. Research and Education Institute at Stanford University (website), accessed December 31, 2023; James T. Patterson, *The Eve of Destruction: How 1965 Transformed America* (New York: Basic Books, 2012), 81; Richardson and Luker, *Historical Dictionary*, 403.

60. Thornton, *Dividing Lines*, 489.

61. Bass, *Unlikely Heroes*, 259; Blumenfeld, interview by Pat Arneson, May 17, 2017.

62. Cameron v. Johnson, 244 F. Supp. 846 (S.D. Miss. 1964) at 856; "Agents Film Race Trouble," *Montgomery Advertiser*, July 17, 1964.

63. Raymond Arsenault, *Freedom Riders: 1961 and the Struggle for Racial Justice* (New York: Oxford University Press, 2006), 274; *Cameron*, 244 F. Supp. at 849; Bailey v. Patterson, 199 F. Supp. 595 (S.D. Miss. 1961) at 615.

64. Cameron v. Johnson, 381 US 741 (1965); Cameron v. Johnson, 262 F. Supp. 873 (S.D. Miss 1966) at 899; Leslie H. Southwick, "Mississippi Supreme Court Elections: A Historical Perspective, 1916–1996," *Mississippi College Law Review* 18, no. 1 (1998): 255; Legal Information Institute, "With Prejudice," Cornell Law School (website), last modified July 2024.

65. *Cameron*, 244 F. Supp at 857, 858n4; Cameron, 262 F. Supp at 897; *Cameron*, 390 US 611 (1968) at 611.

66. David A. Strauss, *Living Constitution* (New York: Oxford University Press, 2010), 33, 38; Blumenfeld, interview by Pat Arneson, May 17, 2017.

67. "First Big City: US Sends Registrars Here: Negroes Impeded, Katzenbach Says," *Montgomery Advertiser*, October 2, 1965.

68. "The Formula for Coverage under Section 4 of the Voting Rights Act," US Department of Justice: Civil Rights Division (website), accessed March 14, 2021.

69. United States Commission on Civil Rights, *The Voting Rights Act: The First Months* (Washington, DC: United States Commission on Civil Rights), 49; Judith Helms, "More Than 75 Negroes Aided by Examiners: State Preparing Contesting Suit," *Alabama Journal*, October 6, 1965; Joe McFadden, "A Little County Office and Big, Tough Cousins," *Montgomery Advertiser*, January 16, 1966; "23,000 Negroes Placed on Voter Lists by Ruling," *Alabama Journal*, November 24, 1965; Reynolds v. Katzenbach, 248 F. Supp. 593 (S.D. Ala. 1965) at 594.

70. "State Probate Judges to Air Court Pleas," *Alabama Journal*, November 18, 1965; Judith Helms, "Vote Rights Rule Likely Today: Federal Jurists Hear Probate Judges," *Alabama Journal*, November 23, 1965.

71. *Reynolds*, 248 F. Supp. at 594; Jim McGregor, "Court Kills Injunction against Probate Judges: Certified Voters Must Be Enrolled," *Montgomery Advertiser*, November 24, 1965; "One-Third County Voters, Applicants Are Negroes," *Montgomery Advertiser*, December 29, 1965.

72. *Atkins*, 323 F.2d at 742, 745.

73. "Document: Complaint: United States v. Baggett (U.S. District Court for the Middle District of Alabama," Civil Rights Litigation Clearinghouse (website), last modified April 3, 2024; "Judges Appointed to Hear Literacy Test Challenge: State Asks Dismissal of Suit," *Alabama Journal*, January 30, 1965.

74. "First Big City."

75. "In re the Challenge of Jessie Acres by Barbara R. Dent," US Civil Service Commission, November 16, 1965, *Race Relations Law Reporter* 11, no. 3 (1966): 1376; "Federal Court Studies Meaning of Rights Act," *Montgomery Advertiser*, March 17, 1966; Jim McGregor, "County Loses Another Round in Voting Rights Act Suit," *Montgomery Advertiser*, March 30, 1966; Dent v. Duncan, 360 F.2d 333 (5th Cir. 1966) at 333; "Orie L. Phillips: Senior Circuit Judge—Tenth Circuit," *ABA Journal* 32, no. 11 (1946): 737; State of S.C. v. Katzenbach, 383 US 301 (1966).

76. *Dent*, 360 F.2d at 337–38.

77. "The Connecticut Poll Tax," Connecticut History (website), accessed December 31, 2023; "Constitution of 1868," Alabama Digital Archives (website), accessed December 31, 2023; 1901 Alabama State Constitution, art. VIII, § 178, Alabama Digital Archives (website), accessed March 14, 2021; US Constitution, amend. XXIV.

78. "Voting Rights Act (1965)," National Archives (website); "Johnson Pleased by Poll Tax End," *Alabama Journal*, January 24, 1964.

79. Breedlove v. Suttles, 302 US 277 (1937); Harper v. Va. Bd. of Elections, 383 US 663 (1966); United States v. Ala., 252 F. Supp. 95 (M.D. Ala. 1966).

80. "Reversal Door Opened: Poll Tax Not Ruled Invalid by Three-Judge U.S. Panel," *Alabama Journal*, December 23, 1965; Judith R. Helms, "Federal Judges Hear Attack on Poll Tax," *Alabama Journal*, February 14, 1966; "Panel Won't Rule out Tax at Present," *Montgomery Advertiser*, December 24, 1965.

81. "Draft," United States v. Ala., 252 F. Supp. 95 (M.D. Ala. 1966), RTR

Papers; *United States v. Ala.*, 252 F. Supp. at 97, 100; Jim McGregor, "Federal Judges Decide against State Poll Tax," *Montgomery Advertiser*, March 4, 1966; Student Nonviolent Coordinating Committee, "The General Condition of the Alabama Negro, March 1965," 20, Civil Rights Movement Archives (website).

82. *United States v. Ala.*, 252 F. Supp. at 97; "Draft," United States v. Ala., 252 F. Supp.; Judith Helms, "State Poll Tax Ruled Invalid: Johnson, Rives Concur in 2–1 Verdict: Gewin Gives Strong Dissent Opinion," *Alabama Journal*, March 3, 1966.

83. *United States v. Ala.*, 252 F. Supp. at 104, 100, 97, 96; "Draft," United States v. Ala., 252 F. Supp.

84. *United States v. Ala.*, 252 F. Supp. at 106 (emphasis in original); "Draft," United States v. Ala., 252 F. Supp.

85. *United States v. Ala.*, 252 F. Supp. at 104, 100, 97, 96; "Draft," United States v. Ala., 252 F. Supp.; US Constitution, amend. X; US Constitution, amend. XIV; US Constitution, amend. XXIV.

86. Lawrence R. Levin, interview by Pat Arneson, May 1, 2017.

87. *United States v. Ala.*, 252 F. Supp. at 109; *Harper*, 383 US; Howard v. United States, 232 F.2d 274 (5th Cir. 1956) at 275; Browder v. Gayle, 142 F. Supp. 707 (M.D. Ala. 1956) at 718.

88. *United States v. Ala.*, 252 F. Supp.; *Harper*, 383 US; Breedlove, 302 US; Hugo L. Black Jr., "The Final Judgement: Richard Taylor Rives, 1895–1982," *Alabama Lawyer* 44, no. 2 (1983): 59.

89. US Constitution, amend. XV; US Constitution, amend. XVIV; Joel Motley, "Joel Motley Talks About Brown v. Board of Education and the Momentum It Carried to Voting Rights Act," You Tube video, 1:48 and 2:36, uploaded by lagarchivist on October 19, 2011, 2:58.

Chapter 7

1. US Constitution, amend. VI; US Constitution, amend. VII.

2. US Commission on Civil Rights, *Book 5: Justice* (Washington, DC: US Government Printing Office, 1961), 96.

3. James Goodman, *Stories of Scottsboro* (New York: Vintage Books, 1995).

4. J. Mills Thornton III, email message to Pat Arneson, April 22, 2023; Goodman, *Stories of Scottsboro*; Norris v. Ala., 295 U.S. 587 (1935) at 597. The legal cases for the other defendants include Powell v. State, 224 Ala. 540 (1932); Patterson v. State, 224 Ala. 531 (1932); Patterson v. Alabama, 294 US 600 (1935); Weems v. State, 224 Ala. 524 (1932).

5. Strauder v. W. Va., 100 US 303 (1880); Va. v. Rives, 100 US 313 (1880); Ex parte Va., 100 US 339 (1880); US Commission on Civil Rights, *Book 5: Justice*, 89–103, 95.

6. *Illegal Racial Discrimination in Jury Selection: A Continuing Legacy*

(Montgomery: Equal Justice Initiative, 2010), 10; Alabama Rules of Criminal Procedure, "Rule 18. Trial by Jury; Waiver; Selection and Preparation of Petit Jurors" (website), accessed December 31, 2023.

7. United States ex rel. Goldsby v. Harpole, 263 F.2d 71 (5th Cir. 1959); Brown v. Bd. of Educ., 347 US 483 (1954); Brown v. Bd. of Educ. (*Brown II*), 349 US 294 (1955); United States ex rel. Seals v. Wiman, 304 F.2d 53 (5th Cir. 1962); Rabinowitz v. United States, 366 F.2d 34 (5th Cir. 1966); Jackson, Thomas, Wells, King, & Chatmon v. United States, 366 F.2d 34 (5th Cir. 1966); Lawrence R. Levin, interview by Pat Arneson, March 15, 2022; "28 USC § 1861: Declaration of Policy: Title 28: Judiciary and Judicial Procedure, Chapter 121: Juries; Trial by Jury, Section 1861: Declaration of Policy (1948)," GovInfo (website), 457.

8. Mozell McCorkle Nelms was the wife of gas station owner Bryant Nelms. In the *ex rel. Goldsby* decision, her name was misspelled "Moselle," but her gravestone in Vaiden Cemetery, Vaiden, Carroll County, Mississippi, shows "Mozell."

9. "Storekeeper and Negro Exchanged Shots in Vaiden," *Delta Democrat Times* (Greenville, MS), November 19, 1954; "Woman Killed by Negro Motorist," *Delta Democrat Times* (Greenville, MS), September 5, 1954.

10. "Slayer to Face Murder Charge: Companions May Also Be Accused," *Clarion-Ledger* (Jackson, MS), September 6, 1954.

11. "Storekeeper"; "Goldsby Sentenced to Die December 24 in Vaiden Shooting," *Clarion-Ledger* (Jackson, MS), November 20, 1954; Goldsby v. State, 240 Miss. 647 (1960) at 662; "Officers Nab Five Negroes in Slaying of Woman at Vaiden," *Clarion-Ledger* (Jackson, MS), September 5, 1954.

12. Leslie Southwick, "Mississippi Supreme Court Elections: A Historical Perspective, 1916–1996," *Mississippi College Law Review* 18, no. 1 (1998): 157; United States v. Cox, 342 F.2d 167 (5th Cir. 1965) at 171.

13. "Political Opinion Believed Swaying United States Appeals Courts: Extension of Remarks of Hon. John Bell Williams of Mississippi," *Cong. Rec.: Appendix* 103, pt. 22 (August 23, 1957): A6989 to A6993; Claude Hatcher, "Venire Facias for Jurors for First Week—Circuit Court, The State of Mississippi," October 30, 1954, available at Vaiden, Mississippi: The Case of R. L. Goldsby (website). *Ex rel. Goldsby*, 263 F.2d.

14. "George Neves Leighton," rpt. *ISBA* [Illinois State Bar Association] *Bar News* 41, no. 10 (December 15, 2000), available at Vaiden, Mississippi: The Case of Robert Lee Goldsby (website), accessed March 15, 2021.

15. Henry L. Rodgers, "State of Mississippi vs. no. 1641 Robert Lee Goldsby," November 19, 1954, book 6, 113–15, Vaiden, Mississippi: The Case of Robert Lee Goldsby (website); Henry L. Rodgers, "Order," November 1954, Vaiden, Mississippi: The Case of Robert Lee Goldsby (website), accessed March 15, 2021; "Sentence of Death Given Negro Killer: Judge Commends Defense Attorney for Doing Duty," *Winona Times* (Winona, MS), November 26, 1954.

16. Goldsby, 240 Miss. at 657; Execution Date Set for Killer," *Conservative* (Carrollton, MS), April 25, 1958.

17. Goldsby v. State, 233 Miss. 338 (1958); *Ex rel. Goldsby*, 263 F.2d at 75.

18. *Ex rel. Goldsby*, 263 F.2d at 76.

19. *Ex rel. Goldsby*, 263 F.2d at 78–79.

20. *Ex rel. Goldsby*, 263 F.2d at 79n21; Alexis de Tocqueville, *Democracy in America*, 4 vols., trans. Henry Reeve (New York: Colonial Press, 1900), book 1, chapter 15n4.

21. Rives chastised Southern lawyers: "As Judges . . ." is from Ex rel. Goldsby, 263 F.2d at 82; Fortunata Giudice and C. William Kraft, "The Presently Expanding Concept of Judicial Notice," *Villanova Law Review* 13, no. 3 (1968): 530, 530n1.

22. *Ex rel. Goldsby*, 263 F.2d at 82; Shepherd v. State of Fla., 341 U.S. 50 (1951) at 55.

23. *Ex rel. Goldsby*, 263 F.2d at 82.

24. *Ex rel. Goldsby*, 263 F.2d at 84.

25. Howard Smead, *Blood Justice: The Lynching of Mack Charles Parker* (New York: Oxford University Press, 1986), 22.

26. "Sidebar Comments," *Conservative* (Carrollton, MS), April 25, 1958; "Speaking About Rights—What About Our Rights?" *Conservative* (Carrollton, MS), May 30, 1958; "Goldsby Case Begins New Route through Courts," *Conservative* (Carrollton, MS), April 18, 1958.

27. William H. McDonald, "Judge Rives Gets Lots of 'Fan Mail,'" *Southern School News* 8, no. 9 (1962), Richard T. Rives Papers, Alabama Department of Archives and History, Montgomery.

28. McDonald, "Judge Rives Gets"; Richard T. Rives, quoted in Frank T. Read and Lucy S. McGough, *Let Them Be Judged: The Judicial Integration of The Deep South* (Metuchen, NJ: Scarecrow Press, 1978), 46.

29. Richard T. Rives, quoted in John M. Spivack, "Richard Taylor Rives and Benjamin F. Cameron: The Varieties of Southern Judges," *Southern Studies: An Interdisciplinary Journal of the South* 1, no. 3 (1990): 233.

30. US Constitution, art. 6; US Constitution, amend. X.

31. Robert E. Luckett Jr., *Joe T. Patterson and the White South's Dilemma: Evolving Resistance to Black Advancement* (Jackson: University Press of Mississippi, 2015).

32. *Brown I*, 347 US 483; *Brown II*, 349 US 294; Thomas Jefferson and James Madison, "Virginia and Kentucky Resolutions (1798)," Bill of Rights Institute (website), accessed December 17, 2023; Robert Brisbane, "Interposition: Theory and Fact," *Phylon* 17, no. 1 (1956): 12–14; United States v. Peters, 9 US 115 (1809).

33. Bush v. Orleans Parish Sch. Bd., 188 F. Supp. 916 (E.D. La. 1960) at 923, 926 (emphasis in original): endnote 12 includes a list of interposition declarations adopted by various states; Ex rel. Goldsby, 263 F.2d at 84.

34. "State Appeals Goldsby Ruling," *Conservative* (Carrollton, MS), June 19, 1959; "No. 112. William Harpole, Superintendent of the Mississippi State Penitentiary, Etc., petitioner, v. United States of America ex rel. Robert Lee Goldsby,"

Supreme Court of the United States, October 12, 1959, 22, available at Vaiden, Mississippi: The Case of Robert Lee Goldsby (website), accessed March 15, 2021.

35. "The Supreme Court: Jury Trial," *Time*, October 26, 1959 (website), accessed March 15, 2021; "Goldsby Case Begins."

36. "Goldsby Jurors Drawn," *Conservative* (Carrollton, MS), December 3, 1959; "Venue Change Given Goldsby: Goldsby Case Moved to Jackson; Others Plead Guilty; Court Ends," *Conservative* (Carrollton, MS), November 12, 1959; "Deny Hearing of Goldsby by Supreme Court," *Conservative* (Carrollton, MS), March 30, 1961; James Saggus, "Goldsby Due to Die Today," *Clarion-Ledger* (Jackson, MS), May 31, 1961.

37. Richard T. Rives to John R. Brown, February 27, 1957, John R. Brown Papers, O'Quinn Law Library, University of Houston, Houston, Texas (hereafter JRB Papers).

38. *Ex rel. Goldsby*, 263 F.2d; Seals v. State of Ala., 122 So. 2d 513 (1960); *Ex parte Seals*, 126 So. 2d 474 (Ala. 1961).

39. *Ex parte Seals*, 126 So. 2d at 623–24.

40. United States ex rel. Seals v. Wiman, 304 F.2d 53 (5th Cir. 1962) at 53, 56.

41. Richard T. Rives to John R. Brown and John Minor Wisdom, March 26, 1962, JRB Papers; Richard L. Pacelle Jr., "Preferred Position Doctrine," Free Speech Center at Middle Tennessee State University (website), last modified September 19, 2023: "The preferred position doctrine expresses a judicial standard based on a hierarchy of constitutional rights so that some constitutional freedoms are entitled to greater protection than others. In the 20th century, the doctrine represented a preference for individual liberties and civil rights."

42. *Ex rel. Seals*, 304 F.2d at 67.

43. "Richard T. Rives, Judge on Court That Helped Integrate the South," *New York Times*, October 30, 1982.

44. John R. Brown to Richard T. Rives and John Wisdom, April 3, 1962, JRB Papers.

45. Richard T. Rives to Clifford J. Durr, May 31, 1962, Clifford Durr Papers, Alabama Department of Archives and History, Montgomery, Alabama; *Ex rel. Goldsby*, 263 F.2d 71; *Ex rel. Seals*, 304 F.2d 53.

46. *Rabinowitz v. United States*, 366 F.2d 34 (5th Cir. 1966); Jackson, Thomas, Wells, King, and Chatmon v. United States, 366 F.2d 34 (5th Cir. 1966); "28 USC § 1861," 457 (hereafter "Jury Selection and Service Act"); "Albany," New Georgia Encyclopedia (website), last modified May 4, 2020; Victor Rabinowitz, *Unrepentant Leftist: A Lawyer's Memoir* (Urbana: University of Illinois Press, 1996), 255; Vanessa Murphree, *The Selling of Civil Rights: The Student Nonviolent Coordinating Committee and the Use of Public Relations* (New York: Routledge, 2006), 30, 31; Julian Bond, "SNCC: What We Did," Student Nonviolent Coordinating Committee (SNCC) Legacy Project (website), 2000, accessed December 17, 2023.

47. Rabinowitz, *Unrepentant*, 256.

48. Ware v. Johnson (M.D. Ga., Albany Div., #749), Civil Liberties Docket 9, no. 3 (1964); "Conspiracy Indictment for Three," *Desert Sun* (Palm Springs, CA), August 10, 1963, California Digital Newspaper Collection at University of California Riverside (website); "Upside-Down Justice: The Albany Cases," Civil Rights Movement Archive at Duke University (website), accessed December 31, 2023, 5; Rabinowitz, *Unrepentant*, 256.

49. "Upside-Down," 5; Dennis Roberts, "Journal: Southwest Georgia, Summer 1963," Civil Rights Movement Archive at Duke University (website); Rabinowitz, *Unrepentant*, 255; Townsend Davis, *Weary Feet, Rested Souls: A Guided History of the Civil Rights Movement* (New York: W. W. Norton, 1999), 172; "Albany Defendants Convicted: White Jury Sits in Perjury Case," *Detroit Tribune*, December 7, 1963, Library of Congress (website). Cf. per Rabinowitz, *Unrepentant*, 256, the picketing lasted "for a few hours" rather than, as Davis reports, only an hour.

50. "Upside-Down," 5, 9.

51. W. G. Anderson, "Reflections on the Origins of the Albany Movement," *Journal of Southwest Georgia History* 9, no. 3 (1994): 3, quoted in Maurice C. Daniels, *Saving the Soul of Georgia: Donald L. Hollowell and the Struggle for Civil Rights* (Athens: University of Georgia Press, 2013), 241n15; "Negro Leaders Seek Dismissal of Charges against Demonstrators," *Indianapolis Recorder* (Indianapolis, IN), October 10, 1964.

52. Albany Civil Rights Institute, "Request for Proposals: Albany Civil Rights Institute Master Plan," September 15, 2021, City of Albany, Georgia (website), accessed December 31, 2023, 9; Michael Chalfen, "'The Way Out May Lead In': The Albany Movement beyond Martin Luther King, Jr.," *Georgia Historical Quarterly* 79, no. 3 (1995): 583, 584; David Levering Lewis, *King: A Biography*, 3rd ed. (Urbana: University of Illinois Press, 2013), 167.

53. Peter J. Ling, *Martin Luther King, Jr.* 2nd ed. (New York: Routledge, 2002); Russell Lowell Riley, *The Presidency and the Politics of Racial Inequality: Nation-Keeping from 1831 to 1965* (New York: Columbia University Press, 1999), 212.

54. "W. G. Anderson, Elijah Harris, Slater King, and Emanuel Jackson v. The City of Albany, Asa D. Kelley, Jr., Mayor the City of Albany, et al.," National Archives Catalog (website), last modified December 17, 2020; Victor S. Navasky, *Kennedy Justice* (New York: Open Road, 2000); Taylor Branch, *Parting the Waters: America in the King Years 1954–62* (New York: Simon and Schuster, 1988); "Upside-Down," 6–7. Cf. Different sources vary in their estimate of the number of FBI agents dispatched to Albany, Georgia. "Civil Subpoena, United States District Court for the Middle District of Georgia, Albany Division, *W. G. Anderson, Elijah Harris, Slater King, and Emanuel Jackson v. The City of Albany, Asa D. Kelley, Jr., Mayor the City of Albany, et al.* Civ. 730, Civil Rights Digital Library of Georgia (website), last modified December 17, 2020: estimated "30–40 agents." "SNCC Worker Convicted on Perjury Charges," *Student Voice: The Student Nonviolent*

Coordinating Committee 4, No. 5 (November 18, 1963), 1: projected "at least 38" agents. Roberts, "Journal": approximated "75 agents."

55. Leonard S. Rubinowitz, Michelle Shaw, and Michal Crowder, "A 'Notorious Litigant' and 'Frequenter of Jails': Martin Luther King, Jr., His Lawyers, and the Legal System," *Northwestern Journal of Law and Social Policy* 10, no. 3 (2016): 515–16n142; Branch, *Parting the Waters*; Rabinowitz, *Unrepentant*, 259.

56. "Civil Subpoena"; Rabinowitz, *Unrepentant*, 261, 255; "SNCC Worker Convicted"; Charles Euchner, *Nobody Turn Me Around: A People's History of the 1963 March on Washington* (Boston: Beacon Press, 2010); United States Dept of Justice, *Annual Report of the Attorney General of the United States for the Fiscal Year Ended June 30, 1962* (Washington, DC: US Government Printing Office, 1962): 187; Smith v. Student Non-Violent Coor. Comm., 421 F.2d 522 (5th Cir. 1969).

57. Rabinowitz, *Unrepentant*, 261; Navasky, *Kennedy Justice*; Roberts, "Journal"; Joni Rabinowitz, "Joni Rabinowitz papers, 1961–2008," Archivegrid (website); Courtney Pace, *Freedom Faith: The Womanist Vision of Prathia Hall* (Athens: University of Georgia Press, 2019), 80; "Red Scare," History (website), last modified February 28, 2020.

58. David J. Garrow, *Bearing the Cross: Martin Luther King, Jr., and the Southern Christian Leadership Conference* (Open Road Media, 2015); George Doss, "Negro Leaders Freed on Bond," *Macon News*, August 10, 1963.

59. Rabinowitz, *Unrepentant*, 264.

60. Achsah Posey, "NY Girl Granted Albany Case Delay," *Atlanta Constitution*, October 22, 1963.

61. "Rabinowitz Trial First for District Court Trial," *Macon Telegraph*, November 5, 1963; Rabinowitz, *Unrepentant*, 266; "Pair Identifies N.Y. Girl as Talking with Pickets," *Macon Telegraph*, November 14, 1963; "Rabinowitz Trial: 12 Witnesses Testify Girl Missing from Scene of Picketing at Albany," *Macon Telegraph*, November 15, 1963; George Doss, "Perjury Trial Continues: White Girl Says She and Not Suspect Was at Picket Scene," *Macon News*, November 15, 1963; "US Jury Here Convicts N.Y. Student of Perjury," *Macon Telegraph*, November 16, 1963.

62. Manley F. Brown and Edward Lukemire, "An Oral Interview with Judge W. A. Bootle, Part II," *Journal of Southern Legal History* 8 (2000): 120; Charles Salter, "Integrationists Are Sentenced," *Macon News*, December 23, 1963; "Leaders Sentenced on Perjury Charge," *Student Voice: Student Nonviolent Coordinating Committee* 4, no. 10 (December 30, 1963), 2, Civil Rights Movement Archive (website).

63. Ala. v. Wilkins (2d Jud. Cir. Lowndes County, Alabama, No. 155); Earl C. Dudley Jr., "Note: The Congress, the Court and Jury Selection: A Critique of Titles I and II of the Civil Rights Bill of 1966," *Virginia Law Review* 52, no. 6 (1966): 1071; Robert B. Semple Jr., "Johnson Pledges Negroes Jury Aid: Says He Has Ordered Clear Bill Drawn to Prevent Injustices by Whites," *New York Times*, November 17, 1965; United States Commission on Civil Rights, *Law Enforcement: A Report on Equal Protection in the South* (Washington, DC: Government Printing Office, 1965).

64. Civil Rights Act of 1957, H.R. 6127, 85th Cong. (1957); 28 USC § 1861; Glasser v. United States, 315 US 60 (1942); "Jury Selection—Key-Man System Eliminated," *Washington Law Review* 42, no. 1 (1966): 280–81.

65. Levin, interview by Pat Arneson, March 15, 2022; Lawrence R. Levin, email message to Pat Arneson, March 27, 2022; LaBat v. Bennett, 365 F.2d 698 (5th Cir. 1966); Scott v. Walker, 358 F.2d 561 (5th Cir. 1966); Billingsley v. Clayton, 359 F.2d 13 (5th Cir. 1966); Brooks v. Beto, 366 F.2d 1 (5th Cir. 1966); Davis v. Davis, 361 F.2d 770 (5th Cir. 1966); Rabinowitz v. United States, 366 F.2d 34 (5th Cir. 1966).

66. Lawrence R. Levin, interview by Pat Arneson, March 27, 2022.

67. Brown and Lukemire, "Oral Interview," 121; Rabinowitz, *Unrepentant*, 268.

68. *Rabinowitz*, 366 F.2d at 37, 40–41.

69. *Rabinowitz*, 366 F.2d at 34, 45, 48. Rives appended two summary reports to the *Rabinowitz* decision: "Appendix A: Legislative History of the 1948 Judicial Code as it Relates to the Process of Selection of Federal Jurors," and "Appendix B: Legislative History of the 1957 Civil Rights Act as It Relates to the Qualifications for Federal Jurors"; *Glasser*, 315 US 60 at 85–86, quoted in *Rabinowitz*, 366 F.2d at 45.

70. Civil Rights Act of 1957; *Rabinowitz*, 366 F.2d at 49, 50–51, 54.

71. *Rabinowitz*, 366 F.2d at 50–51, 54; Rabinowitz, *Unrepentant*, 270.

72. *Rabinowitz*, 366 F.2d at 57n57; Brown v. Allen, 344 US 443 (1953) at 474.

73. Universal Camera Corp. v. National Labor Relations Board, 340 US 474 (1951); *Rabinowitz*, 366 F.2d at 60n63.

74. *Rabinowitz*, 366 F.2d at 78, 92; Rabinowitz, *Unrepentant*, 271; Faith S. Holsaert, "Resistance U," in *Hands on the Freedom Plow: Personal Accounts by Women in SNCC*, ed. Faith S. Holsaert et al. (Urbana: University of Illinois Press, 2010), 192–93.

75. Jack Bass, "Richard T. Rives," Encyclopedia of Alabama (website), last modified January 16, 2015; Levin, interview by Pat Arneson, March 27, 2022; "Jury Selection and Service Act"; Fred A. Summer, "Voter Registration Lists: Do They Yield a Jury Representative of the Community," *University of Michigan Journal of Law Reform* 5, no. 2 (1972): 386.

76. *Brown I*, 347 US 483; *Brown II*, 349 US 294; Summer, "Voter Registration Lists," 385–86n5; *Rabinowitz*, 366 F.2d; "Jury Selection and Service Act."

Chapter 8

1. Tureaud v. Bd. of Supervisors of La. State Univ. & Agricultural & Mechanical Coll., 116 F. Supp. 248 (E.D. La. 1953); Bd. of Supervisors v. Tureaud, 207 F.2d 807 (5th Cir. 1953); Bd. of Supervisors, Etc. v. Tureaud, 228 F.2d 895 (5th Cir. 1956).

2. Browder v. Gayle, 142 F. Supp. 707 (M.D. Ala. 1956); Brown v. Bd. of Educ. (*Brown I*), 347 US 483 1954); Brown v. Bd. of Educ. (*Brown II*), 349 US 294 (1955); Plessy v. Ferguson, 163 US 537 (1896).

3. Frank T. Read and Lucy S. McGough, *Let Them Be Judged: The Judicial Integration of the Deep South* (Metuchen, NJ: Scarecrow Press, 1978), 619–22; Borders v. Rippy, 247 F.2d 268 (5th Cir. 1957); Shuttlesworth v. Birmingham Bd. of Educ., 162 F. Supp. 372 (N.D. Ala. 1958); Gibson v. Bd. of Pub. Instr., Dade Cty., Fla., 272 F.2d 763 (5th Cir. 1959); Davis v. Bd. of Sch. Comm'rs of Mobile Cty., Ala., 322 F.2d 356 (5th Cir. 1963); Armstrong v. Bd. of Educ. of City of Birmingham, 220 F. Supp 217 (N.D. Ala. 1963); Lee v. Macon Cty. Bd. of Educ., 267 F. Supp. 458 (M.D. Ala. 1967).

4. Lucy v. Univ. of Ala., 134 F. Supp. 235 (N.D. Ala. 1955); Meredith v. Fair, 298 F.2d 696 (5th Cir. 1962); Meredith v. Fair, 313 F.2d 532 (5th Cir. 1962); United States v. Barnett, 346 F.2d 99 (5th Cir. 1965).

5. Gomillion v. Lightfoot, 364 US 339 (1960); Sims v. Frink, 205 F. Supp. 245 (M.D. Ala. 1962); Sims v. Frink, 208 F. Supp. 431 (M.D. Ala. 1962); Reynolds v. Sims, 377 US 533 (1964); Sims v. Baggett, 247 F. Supp. 96 (M.D. Ala. 1965); Sims v. Amos, 336 F. Supp. 924 (M.D. Ala. 1972).

6. Smith v. Allwright, 321 US 649 (1944); United States v. Ala., 192 F. Supp. 677 (M.D. Ala. 1961) [Macon Cty.]; United States v. Ala., Civil Action No. 1677-N (M.D. Ala., 1961) [Babcock Cty.]; United States v. Penton, 212 F. Supp. 193 (M.D. Ala. 1962) [Montgomery Cty.]; United States v. Atkins, 323 F.2d 733 (5th Cir. 1963); Dent v. Duncan, 360 F.2d 333 (5th Cir. 1966); United States v. Ala., 252 F. Supp. 95 (M.D. Ala. 1966).

7. United States ex rel. Goldsby v. Harpole, 263 F.2d 71 (5th Cir. 1959); United States ex rel. Seals v. Wiman, 304 F.2d. 53 (5th Cir. 1962); Rabinowitz v. United States, 366 F.2d 34 (5th Cir. 1966); Boeing Co. v. Shipman, 411 F.2d 365 (5th Cir. 1969) at 378; *Brown I*, 347 US 483; *Brown II*, 349 US 294.

8. US Constitution, art. VI; Richard T. Rives, "Law Day Remarks, Cumberland Law School, April 29, 1976," 13, 11 (emphasis in original), manuscript courtesy of Jonathan R. Harkavy; White v. Crook, 251 F.Supp. 401 (M.D. Ala. 1966) at 408.

9. *Boeing*, 411 F.2d at 367, 378–79, 405.

10. Richard T. Rives to John R. Brown and John Minor Wisdom, November 25, 1960, John R. Brown Papers, O'Quinn Law Library at the University of Houston Law Center, Houston, TX; Jonathan R. Harkavy, email message to Pat Arneson, February 15, 2023.

11. Levi S. Udall, "The Essential Characteristics of a Judge," *Journal of the American Judicature Society* 41, no. 3 (1957): 69; Jonathan R. Harkavy, email message to Pat Arneson, January 6, 2023.

12. Deborah J. Barrow and Thomas G. Walker, *A Court Divided: The Fifth Circuit Court of Appeals and the Politics of Judicial Reform* (New Haven, CT: Yale University Press, 1988), 16.

13. Richard T. Rives, interview by John M. Spivack, July 27, 1977, audiotape courtesy of John M. Spivack.

14. Frank M. Johnson Jr., quoted in Linda Parham, "Keep Up Fight for Freedoms, Rives Cautions," *Montgomery Advertiser*, April 30, 1976, RTR Papers; E. J. Devitt, *Your Honor* (Washington, DC: Federal Judicial Center, 1986), 2.

15. Richard T. Rives to John R. Brown and John Minor Wisdom, November 25, 1960, JRB Papers; Hall v. United States, 286 F.2d 676 (5th Cir., 1961); Harkavy, email message to Pat Arneson, February 15, 2023.

16. Miller v. Amusement Enterprises, Inc., 394 F.2d 342 at 353 (5th Cir. 1968).

17. United States v. Cox, 342 F.2d 167 (5th Cir. 1965) at 60; John Daniel Reaves, interview by Pat Arneson, April 11, 2023.

18. White v. Crook, 251 F. Supp. 401 (M.D. Ala. 1966); Frontiero v. Laird, 341 F. Supp. 201 (M.D. Ala. 1972); Frontiero v. Richardson, 411 U.S. 677 (1973); law clerk for Richard T. Rives, interview by Pat Arneson, February 22, 2017.

19. Harkavy, email message to Pat Arneson, February 15, 2023; Jonathan R. Harkavy, interview by Pat Arneson, February 15, 2017; Lawrence R. Levin, interview by Pat Arneson, May 1, 2017.

20. US Constitution, preamble; John J. Patrick, *Understanding Democracy: A Hip Pocket Guide* (New York: Oxford University Press, 2006), 38; Rives, "Law Day Remarks," 4, 6; Richard T. Rives to Roy Nolan, May 28, 1976, Richard T. Rives Papers, Alabama Department of Archives and History, Montgomery, AL. The letter references a speech on April 29, 1976, at Maxwell Officers' Club and Rives may have also delivered this speech there.

21. Rives, "Law Day Remarks," 4, 6.

22. Norman L. Blumenfeld, interview by Pat Arneson, May 17, 2017; "Richard T. Rives, Judge on Court That Helped Integrate the South," *New York Times*, October 30, 1982; Law clerk for Judge Richard T. Rives, interview by Pat Arneson, February 22, 2017.

23. Telegram from Robert F. Kennedy to Richard T. Rives, January 14, 1965, JRB Papers; "[Lyndon B.] Johnson Lauds Rives's Service," *Alabama Journal*, February 25, 1966; Lyndon B. Johnson to Daniel Reaves, January 10, 1965, Richard T. Rives Correspondence, 1965–1975, Fifth Circuit Court of Appeals Library, New Orleans, Louisiana.

24. Telegram from J. Skelly Wright to Richard T. Rives, January 14, 1965, JRB Papers; "Judge Rives Steps Down," *Birmingham News*, February 28, 1966; John Minor Wisdom to Richard T. Rives, January 15, 1965, Richard T. Rives Correspondence, 1965–1975, Fifth Circuit Court of Appeals Library, New Orleans, Louisiana; John R. Brown to Richard T. Rives, January 13, 1965, RTR Papers; Hugo L. Black Jr., "The Final Judgement: Richard Taylor Rives, 1895–1982," *Alabama Lawyer* 44, no. 1 (1983): 59.

Bibliography

Archival Sources

Judge John R. Brown Papers. O'Quinn Law Library, University of Houston Law Center, Houston, TX.

Clifford J. Durr Papers. Alabama Department of Archives and History, Montgomery, AL.

Frank M. Johnson Papers. Library of Congress, Washington, DC.

"Madison Family Collection." Trenholm State Community College (website). Accessed February 21, 2021.

Joni Rabinowitz Papers, 1961–2008. Archivegrid (website). Accessed December 31, 2023.

Richard T. Rives Papers, Alabama Department of Archives and History, Montgomery, AL.

"Rives, Richard T." Courts-Federal-Alabama Clippings File. Birmingham Public Library, Birmingham, AL.

"Rives, Richard T." Clippings File. Fifth Circuit Library, New Orleans, LA.

"Rives, Richard T." *US City Directories, Montgomery City Directories*. Montgomery: R. L. Polk, 1920.

"Rives, Richard T." Correspondence, 1965–1975. Fifth Circuit Court of Appeals Library, New Orleans, LA.

"Rives, Richard T." *US City Directories: Montgomery City Directories*. Montgomery: R. L. Polk, 1925.

Other Sources

"About the US Courts of Appeals." US Courts (website). Accessed January 5, 2023.

Abrams, Dan, and Fred D. Gray, with David Fisher. *Alabama v. King: Martin Luther King Jr. and the Criminal Trial that Launched the Civil Rights Movement*. Toronto: Hanover Square Press, 2022.

"Agents Film Race Trouble." *Montgomery Advertiser*, July 17, 1964.

"Aid, Reapportioning Passed; Congress Near Adjournment." *Montgomery Advertiser*, September 25, 1964.

"Alabama: Court Tells University of Alabama to Admit Three Negro Students." *Southern School News* 9, no. 12 (1963): 1, 6.

"Alabama Editors Are Saying It Must Be Done." *Montgomery Advertiser*, July 1, 1962.

"Alabama: Hearings End in Birmingham School Cases." *Southern School News* 9, no. 5 (1962): 1, 10, 11.

"Alabama Senate Passes Law to Forbid School Desegregation." Equal Justice Initiative (website). Accessed December 3, 2024.

Albany Civil Rights Institute. "Request for Proposals: Albany Civil Rights Institute Master Plan." City of Albany, Georgia (website). Accessed December 31, 2023.

"Albany Defendants Convicted: White Jury Sits in Perjury Case." *Detroit Tribune*, December 7, 1963.

Anderson, José Felipé. *Genius for Justice: Charles Hamilton Houston and the Reform of American Law*. Durham, NC: Carolina Academic Press, 2022.

"Army of Sheriffs, Police Arrive at Ole Miss: Manpower Barrier against Meredith Estimated at 400." *Shreveport Journal*, September 27, 1962.

Arnwine, Barbara, and Marcia Johnson-Bianco. "Voting Rights at a Crossroads: The Supreme Court Decision in Shelby Is the Latest Challenge in the 'Unfinished March' to Full Black Access to the Ballot." Economic Policy Institute (website). Accessed March 29, 2022.

Arsenault, Raymond. *Freedom Riders: 1961 and the Struggle for Racial Justice*. New York: Oxford University Press, 2006.

ASME A17.1 Safety Code for Elevators and Escalators. New York: American Society of Mechanical Engineers, 1921.

"At Oxford—Negro at Ole Miss; Campus in Uproar." *Clarion-Ledger* (Jackson, MS), October 1, 1962.

"Attorney's Office: Legal Department's Function." City of Montgomery, Alabama (website). Accessed March 12, 2021.

"Auditor Lists $751,880 in Lawyer Fees." *Montgomery Advertiser*, May 27, 1939.

Badger, Tony. "'Closet Moderates': Why White Liberals Failed, 1940–1970." In *The Role of Ideas in the Civil Rights South*, edited by Ted Ownby, 83–112. Jackson: University Press of Mississippi, 2002.

Bagley, Joseph Mark. "School Desegregation, Law and Order, and Litigating Social Justice in Alabama, 1954–1973." PhD diss., Georgia State University, 2014.

Bailey, Stan. "Alabama Will Appeal Order on Legislature." *Alabama Journal*, January 6, 1972.

Baker, Liva. *The Second Battle of New Orleans*. New York: HarperCollins, 1996.

Barnard, William D. *Dixiecrats and Democrats: Alabama Politics, 1942–1950*. Tuscaloosa: University of Alabama Press, 1974.

———. "The Old Order Changes: Graves, Sparks, Folsom, and the Gubernatorial Election of 1942." In *From Civil War to Civil Rights: Alabama, 1860–1960: An Anthology from "The Alabama Review"*, edited by Sarah Woolfolk Wiggins, 415–31. Tuscaloosa: University of Alabama Press, 1987.

"Barnett Denies Contempt Guilt: 'Conscience Clear' on Legal Duty." *New York Times*, October 17, 1961.

"Barnett Fears Ole Miss Students' Rights May Have Been Violated." *Cullman Times Democrat* (Cullman, AL), October 14, 1962.

"Barnett May Defy Some of US Court Orders: Big Fines, Imprisonment Braved by Our Governor." *Clarion-Ledger* (Jackson, MS), October 13, 1962.

"Barnett Standing on Law: Action Right, Says Governor." *Anniston Star* (Anniston, AL), October 17, 1962.

Barnett, Ross. "September 29, 1962: Ross Barnett, Governor of Mississippi, Giving His 'I Love Mississippi' Speech." You Tube video, 2:41. Uploaded by HelmerReenberg on January 3, 2010.

Barrow, Deborah J., and Thomas G. Walker. *A Court Divided: The Fifth Circuit Court of Appeals and the Politics of Judicial Reform*. New Haven, CT: Yale University Press, 1988.

Bass, Jack. *Taming the Storm: The Life and Times of Judge Frank M. Johnson, Jr., and the South's Fight Over Civil Rights*. Athens: University of Georgia Press, 2002.

———. *Unlikely Heroes: The Dramatic Story of the Southern Judges of the Fifth Circuit Who Translated the Supreme Court's Brown Decision into a Revolution for Equality*. New York: Simon and Schuster, 1981.

Bass, Jack, and Walter DeVries. *The Transformation of Southern Politics: Social Change and Political Consequence since 1945*. Athens: University of Georgia Press, 1995.

Benton, Jeffrey C. *Respectable and Disreputable: Leisure Time in Antebellum Montgomery*. Montgomery: NewSouth Books, 2013.

Bernstein, Irving. *Guns or Butter: The Presidency of Lyndon Johnson*. New York: Oxford University Press, 1996.

Black, Hugo L., Jr. "The Final Judgement: Richard Taylor Rives, 1895–1982." *Alabama Lawyer* 44, no. 1 (1983): 59.

Bond, Julian. "SNCC: What We Did." Student Nonviolent Coordinating Committee (SNCC) Legacy Project (website). Accessed December 17, 2023.

"Boswell Amendment." Alabama Moments (website). Accessed August 6, 2014.

Branch, Taylor. *At Canaan's Edge: America in the King Years, 1965–68*. New York: Simon and Schuster, 2006.

———. *Parting the Waters: America in the King Years 1954–63*. New York: Simon and Schuster, 2007.

Bridges, Edwin C. *Alabama: The Making of an American State*. Tuscaloosa: University of Alabama Press, 2016.

Brisbane, Robert. "Interposition: Theory and Fact." *Phylon* 17, no. 1 (1956): 12–16.

"Browder v. Gayle Is Filed." African American Registry (website). Accessed December 29, 2023.

Browder, Butler, Jonathan L. Entin, and Robert O. White II. "Browder v. Gayle: An Example of Legal, Political and Economic Radicalism." In *Highway 80: A Drive through Alabama's Civil Rights Corridor*, 2nd ed., edited by Robert O. White II, 23–53. Ronkonkoma, NY: Linus Learning, 2018.

Browder, Butler, "Butler Browder Reflects on Browder v. Gayle," in Jonathan Gold, "'Browder v. Gayle': The Most Important Civil Rights Case You've Never Heard Of," Learning for Justice 53 (Summer 2016) at 2:23, accessed March 12, 2021.

Brown, John R. "In Recognition: Proceedings of the Degree Ceremony: The Honorable John R. Brown, Doctor of Laws." *Tulane Law Review* 54, no. 1 (1979–80): 263–70.

Brown, Manley F., and Edward Lukemire. "An Oral Interview with Judge W. A. Bootle, Part II." *Journal of Southern Legal History* 8 (2000): 95–171.

Brown, J. Robert, Jr., and Allison Herren Lee, "Neutral Assignment of Judges at the Court of Appeals." *Texas Law Review* 78, no. 5 (1999–2000): 1037–116.

Brown-Nagin, Tomiko. *Civil Rights Queen: Constance Baker Motley and the Struggle for Equality*. New York: Pantheon, 2022.

"Bus Segregation Act Faces Test." *Alabama Journal*, May 10, 1956.

"Callie Dougherty Rives." Family Search (website). Accessed June 7, 2023.

"Campus in Shambles with Light of Dawn." *Delta Democrat-Times* (Greenville, MS), October 1, 1962.

"Capitol Profile." *Montgomery Advertiser*, June 14, 1959.

Cardozo, Benjamin Nathan. *The Nature of the Judicial Process*. New Haven: Yale University Press, 1921.

Carpenter, Bob. "Bloody Violence on Campus Leaves 2 Dead." *Delta Democrat-Times* (Greenville, MS), October 1, 1962.

Caudill, David S. "Judge John R. Brown: Enjoyment of Law as Enjoyment of Life." *Mississippi College Law Review* 14, no. 1 (1993): 19–21.

Chalfen, Michael. "'The Way Out May Lead In': The Albany Movement beyond Martin Luther King, Jr." *Georgia Historical Quarterly* 79, no. 3 (1995): 560–98.

Childs, James Rives. *Reliques of the Rives (Ryves): Being Historical and Genealogical Notes of the Ancient Family of Ryves of County Dorset and of the Rives of Virginia, an Essay: Sociological and Historical, of a Family's Contribution to the Making of a Nation*. Lynchburg, VA: J. P. Bell, 1929.

Chin, Denny, and Kathy Hirata Chin. "Constance Baker Motley, James Meredith, and the University of Mississippi." *Columbia Law Review* 117, no. 7 (2017): 1741–78.

Chism, Kahlil G. "Using Primary Records to Understand Brown et al. v. Board of Education of Topeka et al." In *The Unfinished Agenda of Brown v. Board of Education*, edited by The Editors of *Black Issues in Higher Education* with James Anderson and Dara N. Byrne, 7–22. Hoboken, NJ: John Wiley and Sons, 2004.

"City Bus Segregation Doomed in Ruling by Federal Court: Judgment Held Up for 2 Weeks on Plea Filing." *Alabama Journal*, June 5, 1956.

"The Code of Legal Ethics: Thomas Goode Jones." Supreme Court and State Law Library, Alabama Judicial System (website). Accessed March 12, 2021.

"The Connecticut Poll Tax." Connecticut History (website). Accessed December 31, 2023.

"Conspiracy Indictment for Three." *Desert Sun* (Palm Springs, CA), August 10, 1963.

Cook, Robert J. "Red Termites and Rebel Yells: The Civil War Centennial in Strife-Torn Alabama, 1961–1965." *Alabama Review* 64, no. 2 (2011): 143–67.

Cortner, Richard C. *Civil Rights and Public Accommodations: The "Heart of Atlanta Motel" and "McClung" Cases*. Lawrence: University Press of Kansas, 2001.

Couch, Harvey C. *A History of the Fifth Circuit, 1891–1981*. Washington, DC: Bicentennial Committee of the Judicial Conference of the United States, 1984.

"The County Committee: Montgomery Democrats Arrange for Election." *Montgomery Advertiser*, February 3, 1901.

"Court Gives Notice: 'Reapportion Both Houses.'" *Anniston Star* (Anniston, AL), August 25, 1965.

"Court Orders Ole Miss to Integrate." *Clarion-Ledger* (Jackson, MS), July 18, 1962.

"Court Reapportions House: Battle on Succession Joined in Senate: Says Recent Measure Was Discriminatory." *Montgomery Advertiser*, October 5, 1965.

"Courts: The Fascinating and Frenetic Fifth." *Time*, December 4, 1964.

Crabtree, Mari. "Elegy and Effigy." *Appendix* 2, no. 2 (2014) (website).

Crusto, Mitchell F. "Federalism and Civil Rights: The Meredith Case." *National Black Law Journal* 11, no. 2 (1989): 233–48.

Cunningham, David. *Klansville, U.S.A.: The Rise and Fall of the Civil Rights–Era Ku Klux Klan*. New York: Oxford University Press, 2013.

Currie, Cameron McGowan. "Before Rosa Parks: The Case of Sarah Mae Flemming." In *Matthew J. Perry: The Man, His Times, and His Legacy*, edited by W. Lewis Burke and Belinda F. Gergel, 81–95. Columbia: University of South Carolina Press, 2004.

Custer, Joseph A. "Ideological Voting Applied to the School Desegregation Cases in the Federal Courts of Appeals from the 1960s and 1970s." *Scholar* 16, no. 1 (2013): 1–57.

Dakin, Milo. "Court Orders Reapportionment: New Districts Cross County

Lines: November '74 Election Is Compliance Deadline." *Montgomery Advertiser*, January 4, 1972.

Daniel, Leon. "Vigilante Groups Bombard Oxford with Offers of Armed Assistance." *Delta Democrat-Times* (Greenville, MS), September 30, 1962.

Daniels, Maurice C. *Saving the Soul of Georgia: Donald L. Hollowell and the Struggle for Civil Rights*. Athens: University of Georgia Press, 2013.

"David Bibb Graves." Find a Grave (website). Accessed December 30, 2023.

"David Bibb Graves." Geni (website). Accessed November 8, 2020.

Davis, Townsend. *Weary Feet, Rested Souls: A Guided History of the Civil Rights Movement*. New York: W. W. Norton, 1998.

"Democratic and Conservative Party." *Montgomery Daily Advertiser*, April 3, 1883.

Democratic National Committee. *Campaign Text-Book of the National Democratic Party, 1896*. 2nd ed., rev. Chicago: National Democratic Committee, 1896.

"Deny Hearing of Goldsby by Supreme Court." *Conservative* (Carrollton, MS), March 30, 1961.

Devitt, E. J. *Your Honor*. Washington, DC: Federal Judicial Center, 1986.

"District Court Injunction, September 13, 1962." *Race Relations Law Reporter* 7 (1962–1963): 746–47.

"Dr. Henry Edward 'Jeb' Russell." Find a Grave (website). Accessed January 1, 2023.

Doss, George. "Negro Leaders Freed on Bond." *Macon News*, August 10, 1963.

———. "Perjury Trial Continues: White Girl Says She and Not Suspect Was at Picket Scene." *Macon News*, November 15, 1963.

Dudley, Earl C., Jr. "Note: The Congress, The Court and Jury Selection: A Critique of Titles I and II of the Civil Rights Bill of 1966." *Virginia Law Review* 52, no. 6 (1966): 1069–156.

Durr, Virginia. "April 19, 1965: Letter to Dearest Carl and Anne [Braden]." In *Freedom Writer: Virginia Durr: Letters from the Civil Rights Years*, edited by Patricia Sullivan, 325–27. Athens: University of Georgia Press, 2006.

———. *Outside the Magic Circle: The Autobiography of Virginia Foster Durr*. Edited by Hollinger F. Barnard. New York: Simon and Schuster, 1987.

Eagles, Charles W. *The Price of Defiance: James Meredith and the Integration of Ole Miss*. Chapel Hill: University of North Carolina Press, 2009.

"Eastland Orders Probe of Events at Ole Miss: Conduct of Marshals, Troops in Question: Meredith at a Glance." *Clarion-Ledger* (Jackson, MS), October 2, 1962.

"Educators Join Resistance to U.S. Guidelines." *Florence Herald* (Florence, AL), June 9, 1966.

"Election Notice!" *Montgomery Daily Advertiser*, July 26, 1878.

"Election Notice." *Montgomery Daily Advertiser*, October 11, 1882.

"Election on April 8: Date of City Primary Fixed Last Night." *Montgomery Advertiser*, March 28, 1901.

Ellington, Coke. "The Montgomery Advertiser." Encyclopedia of Alabama (website). Last modified April 11, 2022.

Emanuel, Anne S. *Elbert Parr Tuttle: Chief Jurist of the Civil Rights Revolution*. Athens: University of Georgia Press, 2014.

———. "Forming the Historic Fifth Circuit: The Eisenhower Years." *Texas Forum on Civil Liberties and Civil Rights* 6, no. 2 (2002): 233–60.

English, Dewey W., Jr. "Alabama's Population: 1800 to the Modern Era." AL.com (website), December 28, 2019.

Entin, Jonathan L. "The Sign of 'The Four': Judicial Assignment and the Rule of Law." *Mississippi Law Journal* 68 (1998–1999): 369–89.

Euchner, Charles. *Nobody Turn Me Around: A People's History of the 1963 March on Washington*. Boston: Beacon Press, 2010.

"Ex-Trinity Pastor Dies: Dr. Robert Strong." *Alabama Journal*, June 18, 1980.

"Execution Date Set for Killer." *Conservative* (Carrollton, MS), April 25, 1958.

"Fair Apportioning Comes Closer." *Anniston Star* (Anniston, AL), April 5, 1965.

"Fair Dealing Called Key to Prosperity by Rives at Rally: Hill Cites Progress toward Peace; Huge Parade Marks Labor Day Event." *Alabama Journal*, September 5, 1949.

"Federal and Local Rules of Appellate Procedure." US Court of Appeals for the Fourth Circuit (website). Accessed November 2, 2024.

"Federal Court May Order Solons' Reapportionment." *Montgomery Advertiser*, April 14, 1962.

"Federal Court Studies Meaning of Rights Act." *Montgomery Advertiser*, March 17, 1966.

"Federal Courts Opened to Reapportion Cases: Patterson Weighs Plan to Call Special Session: Race with U.S. Judges." *Montgomery Advertiser*, March 27, 1962.

"Federal Judge Criticizes 'Unorthodox Procedures' in Racial Cases by Court." *Daily Advertiser* (Lafayette, LA), July 31, 1963.

"Federal Reaction Awaited: Special Session Adjourned; Anti-Guidelines Bill Passed." *Florence Herald* (Florence, AL), September 8, 1966.

"Feelings When Someone Dies." Cruse Bereavement Support (website). Accessed October 15, 2024.

Feldman, Glenn. *The Disfranchisement Myth: Poor Whites and Suffrage Restriction in Alabama*. Athens: University of Georgia Press, 2004.

———. *Politics, Society, and the Klan in Alabama, 1915–1949*. Tuscaloosa: University of Alabama Press, 1999.

"Feud over Racial Cases Flares in US Appeals Court in South." *New York Times*, July 31, 1963.

Fiffer, Steve, and Adar Cohen. *Jimmie Lee and James: Two Lives, Two Deaths, and the Movement that Changed America*. New York: Regan Arts, 2015.

"Fifth Appeals Circuit Judge Holds Chief Stacks Deck in Race Cases." *Chattanooga Daily Times*, July 31, 1963.

Finley, Keith M. "Lyndon Johnson and the Civil Rights Act of 1957: A Reassessment." MA thesis, Southeastern Louisiana University, 1999.

"First Big City: US Sends Registrars Here: Negroes Impeded, Katzenbach Says." *Montgomery Advertiser*, October 2, 1965.

Fleming, John. "The Man Who Shot Jimmie Lee Jackson, In His Own Words." Sojourners (website), November 16, 2010, accessed May 28, 2025.

Flynt, J. Wayne. *Alabama in the Twentieth Century*. Tuscaloosa: University of Alabama Press, 2004.

———. "Bibb Graves, 1927–1931, 1935–1939." In *Alabama Governors: A Political History of the State*, edited by Samuel L. Webb and Margaret E. Armbrester, 201–8. Tuscaloosa: University of Alabama Press, 2014.

"Former Publisher R. F. Hudson Dies." *Montgomery Advertiser*, December 16, 1965.

"The Formula for Coverage Under Section 4 of the Voting Rights Act." US Department of Justice, Civil Rights Division (website). Accessed March 14, 2021.

Foster, Vera Chandler. "'Boswellianism': A Technique in the Restriction of Negro Voting." *Phylon* 10, no. 1 (1949): 26–37.

"400 Marshals Rushed into Oxford Area." *Clarion-Ledger* (Jackson, MS), October 1, 1962.

"Frank M. Johnson Jr., Judge Whose Rulings Helped Desegregate the South, Dies at 80." *New York Times*, July 24, 1999.

Frederickson, Kari. *The Dixiecrat Revolt and the End of the Solid South, 1932–1968*. Chapel Hill: University of North Carolina Press, 2001.

Freyer, Tony, and Timothy Dixon. *Democracy and Judicial Independence: A History of the Federal Courts of Alabama, 1820–1994*. Brooklyn: Carlson, 1996.

Freyer, Tony A. "Conclusion." In Johnson, *Defending Constitutional Rights*, 137–68.

———. *Hugo L. Black and the Dilemma of American Liberalism*. New York: Pearson, 2008.

———. "Introduction: Johnson's Unusual Origins and Early Career." In Johnson, *Defending Constitutional Rights*, xi–xxvii.

Friedman, Joel William. *Champion of Civil Rights: Judge John Minor Wisdom*. Baton Rouge: Louisiana State University Press, 2009.

Friedman, Saul. "Appeals Court Facing Revolt." *Houston Chronicle*, August 4, 1963.

Friendly, Henry J. "Judge Paul R. Hays." *Columbia Law Review* 72, no. 3 (1972): 445–46.

Gaillard, Frye. *Cradle of Freedom: Alabama and the Movement that Changed America*. Tuscaloosa: University of Alabama Press, 2004.

Garrow, David J. *Bearing the Cross: Martin Luther King, Jr., and the Southern Christian Leadership Conference*. New York: HarperCollins, 1999.

———. "The Origins of the Montgomery Bus Boycott." *Southern Changes* 7 (October–December 1985): 21–27.

"Gen. Shelley Replies to James Weatherly: He Tells Why Ballot Box Stuffing Was Originated—Ministers of the Gospel, He Says, Approved the Method of

Getting Rid of the Carpet Baggers." *Age-Herald* (Birmingham, AL), October 6, 1901.

Gentry, Dick. *Under Fire at Ole Miss: Tales of a Roving Mississippi Reporter in Far-Off America*. London: Woodlord, 2014.

"George Neves Leighton." *ISBA* [Illinois State Bar Association] *Bar News* 41, no. 10 (December 15, 2000). Available at Vaiden, Mississippi: The Case of Robert Lee Goldsby (website).

Gilliland, Joseph F. "Racial Gerrymandering in the Deep South." *Alabama Law Review* 22, no. 2 (1970): 319–48.

Giudice, Fortunata, and C. William Kraft. "The Presently Expanding Concept of Judicial Notice." *Villanova Law Review* 13, no. 3 (1968): 528–63.

Glennon, Robert Jerome. "The Role of Law in the Civil Rights Movement: The Montgomery Bus Boycott, 1955–1957." *Law and History Review* 9, no. 1 (1991): 59–112.

Goldman, Sheldon. *Picking Federal Judges: Lower Court Selection from Roosevelt through Reagan*. New Haven, CT: Yale University Press, 1997.

"Goldsby Case Begins New Route through Courts." *Conservative* (Carrollton, MS), April 18, 1958.

"Goldsby Jurors Drawn." *Conservative* (Carrollton, MS), December 3, 1959.

"Goldsby Sentenced to Die December 24 in Vaiden Shooting." *Clarion-Ledger* (Jackson, MS), November 20, 1954.

Goodman, James. *Stories of Scottsboro*. New York: Vintage Books, 1995.

Gordon, Linda. *The Second Coming of the KKK: The Ku Klux Klan of the 1920s and the American Political Tradition*. New York: Liveright, 2017.

Gordon, Tom. "Former Segregationist Gov. John Patterson Now Supports First Black President." *Birmingham News*, January 20, 2009.

Goudsouzian, Aram. "Introduction to the New Edition." In Meredith, *Three Years in Mississippi*, ix–xxvi.

"Governor Releases Statement on Case." *Clarion-Ledger* (Jackson, MS), October 1, 1962.

Grafton, Carl, and Anne Permaloff. *Big Mules and Branchheads: James E. Folsom and Political Power in Alabama*. Athens: University of Georgia Press, 1985.

"Graves Administration Paid Lawyers $751,873: Matt Murphy Drew Largest Sum in State: Horace Wilkinson Got $54,000 from Alabama Treasury, Report Shows." *Anniston Star*, May 28, 1939.

Gray, Fred D. "Alabama v. King: The Trial That Launched the Civil Rights Movement." You Tube video, 1:01:58. Uploaded by Alabama Department of Archives and History, February 16, 2023.

———. *Bus Ride to Justice: Changing the System by the System: The Life and Works of Fred D. Gray*. Rev. ed. Montgomery, AL: NewSouth Books, 2013.

Greaves, Elmore Douglass. *The Blackamoor of Oxford: A Reply to Attorney General*

Robert Kennedy's Report on How He Is Making Progress in Mississippi. Jackson, MS: Sovereignty Commission Online, 1963.

Guillory, Ferrel. "On the Temper of the Times: Jack Bass." *Southern Cultures* 18, no. 3 (2012): 25–41.

Hall, Joe. "Equal Employment, Voter Section of Civil Rights Bill Explained." *Alabama Journal*, May 22, 1964.

Hamilton, Virginia Van der Veer. *Lister Hill: Statesman from the South*. Chapel Hill: University of North Carolina Press, 1987.

Hatcher, Claude. "Venire Facias for Jurors for First Week—Circuit Court, The State of Mississippi: October 30, 1954." Available at Vaiden, Mississippi: The Case of Robert Lee Goldsby (website).

Hearn, Jesse B. "William Albert Bellingrath." Alabama Business Hall of Fame (website). Accessed November 10, 2022.

Helms, Judith R. "Federal Judges Hear Attack on Poll Tax." *Alabama Journal*, February 14, 1966.

———. "More Than 75 Negroes Aided by Examiners: State Preparing Contesting Suit." *Alabama Journal*, October 6, 1965.

———. "State Poll Tax Ruled Invalid: Johnson, Rives Concur in 2–1 Verdict: Gewin Gives Strong Dissent Opinion." *Alabama Journal*, March 3, 1966.

———. "U.S. Court Orders Hearing in August on Reapportionment Plan for Alabama." *Alabama Journal*, July 27, 1965.

———. "Vote Rights Rule Likely Today: Federal Jurists Hear Probate Judges." *Alabama Journal*, November 23, 1965.

Helsing, Jeffrey W. *Johnson's War/Johnson's Great Society: The Guns and Butter Trap*. Westport, CT: Praeger, 2000.

Hill, Minna Roth. "A Significant History." Sidney Lanier High School (website). Accessed March 12, 2021.

Hilton, Mark. "Aurelia Eliscera Shines [*sic*] Browder: Civil Rights Pioneer." The Historical Marker Database (website). Last modified August 30, 2020.

Hines, Dick. "Probers Mum on Plan to Open Vote Records: Officials Set 2-Day Goal for Inquiry." *Montgomery Advertiser*, December 8, 1958.

"History of the MCBA." Montgomery County Bar Association (website). Accessed December 30, 2023.

"History of the Montgomery Advertiser." *Montgomery Advertiser* (website). Accessed November 5, 2022.

Holsaert, Faith S. "Resistance U." In *Hands on the Freedom Plow: Personal Accounts by Women in SNCC*, edited by Faith S. Holsaert, Martha Prescod Norman Noonan, Judy Richardson, Betty Garman Robinson, Jean Smith Young, and Dorothy M. Zellner, 181–94. Urbana: University of Illinois Press, 2010.

"Hugo L. Black." Oyez (website). Accessed March 12, 2021.

Hustwit, William P. *Integration Now: Alexander v. Holmes and the End of Jim Crow*. Chapel Hill: University of North Carolina Press, 2019.

"Ike Hits Probe Silence; Justice Agents Arrive: Legal Steps Here Veiled in Secrecy." *Montgomery Advertiser*, December 11, 1958.

Illegal Racial Discrimination in Jury Selection: A Continuing Legacy. Montgomery, AL: Equal Justice Initiative, 2010.

"In Federal Defiance Stand: Wallace Anti-Guideline Bill Now before State Legislature." *Florence Herald* (Florence, AL), August 25, 1966.

"Infant Daughter Rives." Find a Grave (website). Accessed December 30, 2023.

Ingram, Bob. "Apportionment on Agenda for Panel of U.S. Judges." *Montgomery Advertiser*, August 25, 1965.

———. "Gov. Wallace Considering Special Call." *Montgomery Advertiser*, September 2, 1965.

———. "Like the Mighty Babe, the Governor Tries." *Montgomery Advertiser*, September 5, 1964.

"Interview with Judge John Minor Wisdom [October 31, 1985]." Eyes on the Prize series. Video, 47:27. Washington University in St. Louis, University Libraries (website). Accessed December 4, 2024.

"It's Simple, the Court Said." *Montgomery Advertiser*, January 5, 1972.

Jackson, Harvey H., III. "White Supremacy Triumphant: Democracy Undone." In *A Century of Controversy: Constitutional Reforms in Alabama*, edited by H. Bailey Thomson, 17–33. Tuscaloosa: University of Alabama Press, 2002.

Jefferson, Thomas. *The Papers of Thomas Jefferson: 1760–1776*. Edited by Julian P. Boyd. Princeton, NJ: Princeton University Press, 1950.

Jenkins, Ray. "Decade on Bench Has Brought Rives Wide Recognition." *Alabama Journal*, May 8, 1961.

———. "Federal Judges Order Immediate Reapportioning: New Legislature to Take Office after Nov. Vote." *Alabama Journal*, July 21, 1962.

———. "June Session Would Be 'Reasonable, Prompt.'" *Montgomery Advertiser*, April 1, 1962.

———. "McCord Insisted on Naming Rives When He Retired." *Alabama Journal*, May 9, 1961.

———. "On Race Question: Rives Turns Up on Both Sides." *Alabama Journal*, May 10, 1961.

"Jesse Dougherty Rives." Find a Grave (website). Last modified September 29, 2010.

"JFK Takes Over Guard as Army Enters Crisis: Schedules Video Address to US." *Clarion-Ledger* (Jackson, MS), September 30, 1962.

Johnson, Frank M. *Defending Constitutional Rights*. Edited by Tony A. Freyer. Athens: University of Georgia Press, 2001.

"Johnson, Frank Minis, Jr." Federal Judicial Center. Accessed March 12, 2021.

Johnson, Larry, Deirdre Cobb-Roberts, and Barbara Shircliffe. "African Americans and the Struggle for Opportunity in Florida Public Higher Education, 1947–1977." *History of Education Quarterly* 47, no. 3 (2007): 328–58.

"Johnson Lauds Rives's Service." *Alabama Journal*, February 25, 1966.

"Johnson Pleased by Poll Tax End." *Alabama Journal*, January 24, 1964.

Johnson, Ruth. "Anecdotes from Judge Johnson's Wife, Ruth." *Alabama Lawyer* 52, no. 6 (1991): 321–23, 325.

"Judge Sees Small Chance for Barnett: Angry Jurists Delay Hearing Until Monday." *Greenwood Commonwealth* (Greenwood, MS), October 13, 1962.

"Judges Appointed to Hear Literacy Test Challenge: State Asks Dismissal of Suit." *Alabama Journal*, January 30, 1965.

"Judges Delay Ruling on Apportion Plans: Lawyers Offer Arguments." *Anniston Star*, July 16, 1962.

"Justice Black's Action: September 10, 1962." *Race Relations Law Reporter* 7 (1962–1963): 743–44.

Keith, Douglas. "Impeachment and Removal of Judges: An Explainer." Brennan Center for Justice (website). Last modified May 6, 2022.

Kennamer, Ralph. "Richard T. Rives Becomes a Federal Judge." *Alabama Lawyer* 12, no. 3 (1951): 297–99.

Kennedy, John F. "JFK Cuban Missile Crisis Speech (10/22/1962)." You Tube video, 8:15. Uploaded by CONELRAD6401240 on October 2, 2011.

———. "JFK Phone Calls and Speech during the University of Mississippi Crisis (Sept. and Oct. 1962)." You Tube video, 15:04. Uploaded by David Von Pein's JFK Channel on September 7, 2013.

———. "September 30, 1962: President John F. Kennedy's Address to the Nation on Radio and Television, 'US vs Mississippi: Campus Riots Mark Integration.'" You Tube video, 2:06. Uploaded by HelmerReenberg on June 30, 2009.

Kennedy, Robert F., Jr. *Judge Frank M. Johnson, Jr.* New York: G. P. Putnam's, 1978.

King, Martin Luther, Jr. "'Give Us the Ballot,' Address Delivered at the Prayer Pilgrimage for Freedom, May 17, 1957." Martin Luther King Jr. Research and Education Institute at Stanford University (website).

———. *The Papers of Martin Luther King Jr.: Birth of a New Age: December 1955–1956*. Vol. 3. Berkeley: University of California Press, 1997.

Kirkland, Scotty E. "Mobile and the Boswell Amendment." *Alabama Review* 65, no. 3 (2012): 205–49.

Kryn, Randall. "James L. Bevel: The Strategist of the 1960s Civil Rights Movement." In *We Shall Overcome: The Civil Rights Movement in the United States in the 1950s and 1960s*, vol. 2, edited by David J. Garrow, 517–35. New York: Carlson, 1989.

"Lawmakers Set Night Session, Wallace Booked." *Selma Times-Journal*, September 9, 1965.

Lawson, Steven F. *Black Ballots: Voting Rights in the South, 1944–1969*. New York: Lexington Books, 1999.

"The Lawyers Club, 1948–1949." Miscellaneous Law School Publications, University of Michigan Law School (website). Last modified August 17, 2017.

"Leaders Sentenced on Perjury Charge." *Student Voice: Student Nonviolent Coordinating Committee* 4, no. 10 (December 30, 1963): 2.

Legal Information Institute. "28 U.S. Code § 453: Oaths of Justices and Judges." Cornell Law School (website). Accessed December 6, 2024.

———. "28 US Code § 2284—Three-judge Court; When Required; Composition; Procedure." Cornell Law School (website). Accessed December 6, 2024.

———. "Amicus Curiae." Cornell Law School (website). Last modified June 2022.

———. "Contempt of Court, Civil." Cornell Law School (website). Last modified February 2024.

———. "Doctrine." Cornell Law School (website). Accessed January 17, 2023.

———. "With Prejudice." Cornell Law School (website). Accessed February 12, 2023.

"Legal Research: An Overview: Mandatory v. Persuasive Authority." UCLA School of Law, Hugh and Hazel Darling Law Library (website). Last modified October 31, 2023.

"Legislators Who Have Represented Montgomery County." *Montgomery Advertiser*, April 14, 1901.

Lesher, Steve. "U.S. Judges Deliberate Bus Segregation Fate: Race Hearing In Court Here Ends Session." *Montgomery Advertiser*, May 12, 1956.

Leubsdorf, Carl P. "Barnett Case to Resume Next Week." *Hattiesburg American* (Hattiesburg, MS), October 13, 1962.

Levin, Betsy. *The Courts, Social Science, and School Desegregation*. New York: Taylor and Francis, 2018.

Levy, Marin K. "Visiting Judges." *California Law Review* 107, no. 1 (2019): 67–140.

Lewis, David Levering. *King: A Biography*. 3rd ed. Urbana: University of Illinois Press, 2013.

Linder, Doug. "US Supreme Court: *Reynolds v. Sims*, 377 US 533 (1964)." Exploring Constitutional Law (website). Accessed March 14, 2021.

Ling, Peter J. *Martin Luther King, Jr.* 2nd ed. New York: Routledge, 2015. First published in 2002 by Routledge.

Lippman, Ted. "US Probes Panel Picks by Tuttle." *Atlanta Constitution*, August 2, 1963.

Luckett, Robert E. Jr. *Joe T. Patterson and the White South's Dilemma: Evolving Resistance to Black Advancement*. Jackson: University Press of Mississippi, 2015.

Lyman, Bryan. "The Believer: Arthur Madison Launched a Montgomery Voter Registration Drive in 1944—and Paid a Price." *Montgomery Advertiser*, February 21, 2021.

Mackin, Tom. "House Reapportions Itself: Measure Voted Tuesday Does Not Alter Senate." *Montgomery Advertiser*, September 15, 1965.

Mahoney, W. J., Jr. "Mahoney—'As I See It': A Whole Contemptuous Southern People." *Alabama Journal*, November 19, 1962.

Marston, Allison. "Guiding the Profession: The 1887 Code of Ethics of the Alabama State Bar Association." *Alabama Law Review* 49, no. 2 (1997): 471–507.

Martin, Spider. "Zion United Methodist Church in Marion, Alabama." Alabama Department of Archives and History, Montgomery, Alabama (website). Accessed August 16, 2024.

McCrary, Peyton, Jerome A. Gray, Edward Still, and Huey L. Perry. "Alabama." In *Quiet Revolution in the South: The Impact of the Voting Rights Act, 1965–1990*, edited by Chandler Davidson and Bernard Grofman, 38–66. Princeton, NJ: Princeton University Press, 1994.

McDonald, William H. "Judge Rives Gets Lots of 'Fan Mail.'" *Southern School News* 8, no. 9 (March 1962): 13, 15.

McFadden, Joe. "A Little County Office and Big, Tough Cousins." *Montgomery Advertiser*, January 16, 1966.

McGill, Ralph. "The Angry South." *Atlantic Monthly* (April 1956): 31–34.

McGregor, Jim. "County Loses Another Round in Voting Rights Act Suit." *Montgomery Advertiser*, March 30, 1966.

———. "Court Kills Injunction Against Probate Judges: Certified Voters Must Be Enrolled." *Montgomery Advertiser*, November 24, 1965.

———. "Federal Judges Decide Against State Poll Tax." *Montgomery Advertiser*, March 4, 1966.

McMillen, Neil R. *The Citizens' Council: Organized Resistance to the Second Reconstruction, 1954–1964*. Urbana: University of Illinois Press, 1994.

Melton, Oakley, Jr. "President's Message," *Alabama Lawyer* 41, no. 1 (1980): 9–11.

"Memorials: Robert Strong." *Journal of the Evangelical Theological Society* 24, no. 1 (1981): 96.

"Meredith in Classes as Riots Spread to Oxford: 2 Die in All-Night Rioting on Campus." *Delta Democrat-Times* (Greenville, MS), October 1, 1962.

"Meredith Turned Away Again at Ole Miss: Lt. Gov. Johnson Blocks Entrance at Campus Gates." *Shreveport Journal*, September 26, 1962.

Meredith, James. *Three Years in Mississippi*. Jackson: University of Mississippi Press, 1966/2019.

"Mize, Sidney Carr." Federal Judicial Center (website). Accessed December 29, 2022.

Momodu, Samuel. "Baton Rouge Bus Boycott (1953)." BlackPast (website). February 4, 2018.

Motley, Joel. "Joel Motley Talks about Brown v. Board of Education and the Momentum it Carried to Voting Rights Act." You Tube video, 2:58. Uploaded by lagarchivist on October 19, 2011.

Muhammad, Crystal R. Gafford. "Meredith v. Fair." In *Encyclopedia of African American Education*, vol. 1, edited by Kofi Lomotey, 443–44. Los Angeles: Sage, 2010.

Murphee, Vanessa. *The Selling of Civil Rights: The Student Nonviolent Coordinating Committee and the Use of Public Relations*. New York: Routledge, 2006.

Myrdal, Gunnar. *An American Dilemma: The Negro Problem and Modern Democracy*. New York: Harper and Bros., 1944.

National Committee for the Albany Defendants. "Upside-Down Justice: The Albany Cases." Albany, GA. Civil Rights Movement Archive, Duke University (website). Accessed December 31, 2023.

Navasky, Victor S. *Kennedy Justice*. New York: Open Road, 2000.

Neem, Johann N. *Democracy's Schools: The Rise of Public Education in America*. Baltimore: Johns Hopkins University Press, 2017.

"Negro Leaders Seek Dismissal of Charges against Demonstrators." *Indianapolis Recorder*, October 10, 1964.

"Negro Vote Lawyer Put in Jail Here: Arthur H. Madison of New York is Arrested for Violating Statute: Faces $2,500 Fine: Act Forbids an Attorney's Appearing for Person Without Being Retained." *Montgomery Advertiser*, April 9, 1944.

"Negroes Imperil White Vote Rule." *Anniston Star* (Anniston, AL), March 31, 1960.

Newman, Roger K. *Hugo Black: A Biography*. New York: Pantheon Books, 1994.

"Newspaper's Tradition Weighed Heavily on Ambitious, Hard-Working R. F. Hudson." *Montgomery Advertiser*, December 16, 1965.

Newton, Wesley Phillips. *Montgomery in the Good War: Portrait of a Southern City, 1939–1946*. Tuscaloosa: University of Alabama Press, 2000.

"1915 Bulletin of the Alabama Polytechnic Institute State College for the Benefit of Agriculture and Mechanical Arts." Auburn, AL (website). Accessed December 30, 2023.

"1940 United States Federal Census." Alabama Department of Archives and History. Montgomery, AL.

"(1963) George Wallace, 'Segregation Now, Segregation Forever.'" BlackPast (website), January 22, 2013.

"No End Seen in Heat Wave." *Anniston Star* (Anniston, AL), July 21, 1962.

"Officers Nab Five Negroes in Slaying of Woman at Vaiden." *Clarion-Ledger* (Jackson, MS), September 5, 1954.

"Ole Miss Adopts 'Get Tough' Policy on Students Harasing [*sic*]." *Cullman Times Democrat* (Cullman, AL), October 14, 1962.

"Once More in Frustration." *Montgomery Advertiser*, December 20, 1964.

"One Cent a Word." *Montgomery Daily Advertiser*, October 27, 1888.

"One-Third County Voters, Applicants Are Negroes." *Montgomery Advertiser*, December 29, 1965.

"Orie L. Phillips: Senior Circuit Judge—Tenth Circuit." *ABA Journal* 32, no. 11 (1946): 736–40.

Osgoode, Arthur. "Lawmakers' 'Defiance' of Court Under Attack: Prompt Decision Promised on Reapportion Formula." *Montgomery Advertiser*, July 17, 1962.

———. "Reapportionment Court Suit Hopes to Force Action After 60 Years." *Montgomery Advertiser*, July 8, 1962.

Otfinoski, Steven. *The Selma Marches for Civil Rights: We Shall Overcome.* North Mankato, MN: Capstone Press, 2019.

Owen, Marie B. "Twenty-Eighth District: Montgomery County." *Alabama Official and Statistical Register, 1919.* Montgomery: Brown Printing, 1920.

"Oxford, Mississippi Population 1960." World Population Review (website).

Oyen, Timothy. "Stare Decisis." Legal Information Institute, Cornell Law School (website). Last modified March 2017.

Pace, Courtney. *Freedom Faith: The Womanist Vision of Prathia Hall.* Athens: University of Georgia Press, 2019.

Pacelle, Richard L., Jr. "Preferred Position Doctrine." Free Speech Center at Middle Tennessee State University (website). Last modified September 19, 2023.

"Painful Decision on Force Faces President." *Delta Democrat-Times* (Greenville, MS), September 28, 1962.

"Pair Identifies N.Y. Girl as Talking with Pickets." *Macon Telegraph*, November 14, 1963.

"Panel Won't Rule Out Tax at Present." *Montgomery Advertiser*, December 24, 1965.

Partridge, Elizabeth. *Marching for Freedom: Walk Together Children and Don't You Grow Weary.* New York: Viking, 2009.

"Past Presidents." Alabama State Bar (website). Accessed November 10, 2022.

Patrick, John J. *Understanding Democracy: A Hip Pocket Guide.* New York: Oxford University Press, 2006.

Patterson, James T. *The Eve of Destruction: How 1965 Transformed America.* New York: Basic Books, 2012.

Permaloff, Anne. "Black Belt-Big Mule Coalition." Encyclopedia of Alabama (website). Last modified March 30, 2023.

"Person: Jimmie Lee Jackson, Selma to Montgomery National Historic Trail." National Park Service (website). Accessed October 19, 2024.

Posey, Achsah. "NY Girl Granted Albany Case Delay." *Atlanta Constitution*, October 22, 1963.

Posner, Richard A. *The Problems of Jurisprudence.* Cambridge, MA: Harvard University Press, 1990.

"R. T. Rives, Jr., Killed, 5 Hurt in Car Mishap: Vacationists Involved in Three-Way Crash at Jacksonville, Fla." Richard T. Rives, Vertical Names File, Birmingham Public Library, Birmingham, AL.

"Rabinowitz Trial First for District Court Trial." *Macon Telegraph*, November 5, 1963.

"Rabinowitz Trial: 12 Witnesses Testify Girl Missing from Scene of Picketing at Albany." *Macon Telegraph*, November 15, 1963.

Rabinowitz, Victor. *Unrepentant Leftist: A Lawyer's Memoir*. Urbana: University of Illinois Press, 1996.

Rawls, John. *A Theory of Justice*. Cambridge, MA: Belknap Press, 1971.

Read, Frank T. "The Bloodless Revolution: The Role of the Fifth Circuit in the Integration of the Deep South." *Mercer Law Review* 32, no. 4 (1981): 1149–66.

Read, Frank T., and Lucy S. McGough. *Let Them Be Judged: The Judicial Integration of the Deep South*. Metuchen, NJ: Scarecrow Press, 1978.

"Recent Developments: Jury Selection—Key-Man System Eliminated." *Washington Law Review* 42, no. 1 (1966): 280–85.

"Red Cross Unit to Hold Parley." *Alabama Journal*, January 16, 1939.

"Red Scare." History (website). Last modified February 28, 2020.

Redistricting in the South. Rose Institute of State and Local Government at Claremont McKenna College (website). Accessed December 4, 2024.

"Registrars Appointed for Macon: Move Could Delay Federal Referee from Taking Action." *Montgomery Advertiser*, May 7, 1960.

Reichley, A. James. *The Life of the Parties: A History of American Political Parties*. New York: Rowman and Littlefield, 2000.

"Reshuffle Goes to Court Order." *Selma Times-Journal*, July 28, 1965.

"Reversal Door Opened: Poll Tax Not Ruled Invalid by Three-Judge U.S. Panel." *Alabama Journal*, December 23, 1965.

"Richard Rives Heads Enemy Alien Board." *Alabama Journal*, December 24, 1941.

"Richard T. Rives, Judge on Court That Helped Integrate the South." *New York Times*, October 30, 1982.

Richardson, Christopher M., and Ralph E. Luker. *Historical Dictionary of the Civil Rights Movement*. 2nd ed. New York: Rowman and Littlefield, 2014.

Riley, Russell Lowell. *The Presidency and the Politics of Racial Inequality: Nation-Keeping from 1831 to 1965*. New York: Columbia University Press, 1999.

Riser, R. Volney. *Defying Disenfranchisement: Black Voting Rights Activism in the Jim Crow South, 1890–1908*. Baton Rouge: Louisiana State University Press, 2010.

"Rives Attacks Boswell Plan, Cites Court Appeal System." *Montgomery Advertiser*, April 20, 1946.

"Rives Funeral Slated Sunday: Body Being Returned to Montgomery Today." *Alabama Journal*, April 2, 1949.

"Rives Re-Appointed Judge Advocate of State's Legion." *Alabama Journal*, August 3, 1942.

Rives, Richard T. "An Argument against the Adoption of the Boswell Amendment," *Alabama Lawyer* 7, no. 3 (1946): 291–97.

———. "Bureaucracy." *Alabama Lawyer* 5, no. 4 (1944): 420–24.

———. "Defending Alabamians." *Time*, December 11, 1964.

———. "The Scope of Review of Facts by United States Courts of Appeals." *Alabama Law Review* 11, no. 1 (1958): 70–78.

———. "Trying a Case for the Plaintiff." *Alabama Lawyer* 2, no. 4 (1941): 407–18.

Roberson, Peggy, "Retired Judge Pleased at Progress." *Birmingham News*, April 9, 1975.

Roberts, Dennis. "Journal: Southwest Georgia, Summer 1963." Civil Rights Movement Archive, Duke University (website).

Robinson, Jo Ann Gibson. *The Montgomery Bus Boycott and the Women Who Started It: The Memoir of Jo Ann Gibson Robinson*. Knoxville: University of Tennessee Press, 1987.

Roosevelt, Franklin. "State of the Union Message to Congress, January 11, 1944." Franklin D. Roosevelt Presidential Library and Museum, Marist College (website).

Rowe, Stephen J. "Questions and Answers with Judge Frank Johnson." *Alabama Lawyer* 52, no. 6 (1991): 328–31.

Rubinowitz, Leonard S., Michelle Shaw, and Michal Crowder. "A 'Notorious Litigant' and 'Frequenter of Jails': Martin Luther King, Jr., His Lawyers, and the Legal System." *Northwestern Journal of Law and Social Policy* 10, no. 3 (2016): 494–623.

Rumore, Pat Boyd. *From Power to Service: The Story of Lawyers in Alabama*. Montgomery: Alabama State Bar and the Alabama Bench and Bar Historical Society, 2010.

Saggus, James. "Goldsby Due to Die Today." *Clarion-Ledger* (Jackson, MS), May 31, 1961.

Salmond, John A. *The Conscience of a Lawyer: Clifford J. Durr and American Civil Liberties, 1899–1975*. Tuscaloosa: University of Alabama Press, 2020.

Salter, Charles. "Integrationists Are Sentenced." *Macon News*, December 23, 1963.

Saxon, Wolfgang. "Daniel H. Thomas, 93, Federal Judge Known for Maritime Cases." *New York Times*, April 19, 2000.

Schaeffer, Walter V. "Precedent and Policy." *University of Chicago Law Review* 34, no. 1 (1966): 3–25.

Seidman, Louis Michael. "Brown and Miranda." *California Law Review* 80, no. 3 (1992): 673–753.

"Selma to Montgomery March." Martin Luther King Jr. Research and Education Institute at Stanford University (website). Accessed December 31, 2023.

Semple, Robert B., Jr. "Johnson Pledges Negroes Jury Aid: Says He Has Ordered Clear Bill Drawn to Prevent Injustices by Whites." *New York Times*, November 17, 1965.

"Senate Passes Poll Tax Bill: Amendment 'Protects' White Supremacy." *Alabama Journal*, June 27, 1945.

"Senator to See if Court Stacked in Integration Cases." *Houston Chronicle*, August 2, 1963.

"Sentence of Death Given Negro Killer: Judge Commends Defense Attorney for Doing Duty." *Winona Times* (Winona, MS), November 26, 1954.

"Sidebar Comments." *Conservative* (Carrollton, MS), April 25, 1958.

Sikora, Frank. *The Judge: The Life and Opinions of Alabama's Frank M. Johnson, Jr.* Montgomery: NewSouth Books, 2007.

Silver, James W. *Mississippi: The Closed Society*. New York: Harcourt, Brace, and World, 1966.

Sims, George E. *The Little Man's Big Friend: James E. Folsom in Alabama Politics, 1946–1958.* Tuscaloosa: University of Alabama Press, 1985.

Simmons, Joe. "Senior US Judge Rives Dies." *Montgomery Advertiser*, October 28, 1982.

Sitton, Claude. "Barnett Defiant: Threatens to Jail US Aides if They Seize Officials of State." *New York Times*, September 25, 1962.

Slaughter, John. *New Battles Over Dixie: The Campaign for a New South*. Dix Hills, NY: General Hall, 1992.

"Slayer to Face Murder Charge: Companions May Also Be Accused." *Clarion-Ledger* (Jackson, MS), September 6, 1954.

Smead, Howard. *Blood Justice: The Lynching of Mack Charles Parker*. New York: Oxford University Press, 1986.

Smith, J. Douglas. *On Democracy's Doorstep: The Inside Story of How the Supreme Court Brought "One Person, One Vote" to the United States*. New York: Hill and Wang, 2014.

Smithsonian National Museum of African American History and Culture. "An Indomitable Spirit: Autherine Lucy." *Our American Story* (blog), undated. Accessed May 19, 2025.

"SNCC Worker Convicted on Perjury Charges." *Student Voice: The Student Nonviolent Coordinating Committee* 4, no. 5 (November 18, 1963): 1, 3.

Solimine, Michael E. "The Three-Judge District Court in Voting Rights Litigation." *University of Michigan Journal of Law Reform* 30, no. 1 (1996): 79–145.

Southern Education Reporting Service. *School Desegregation in the Southern and Border States, 1966–1967 Statistics*. South Carolina Digital Libraries "School Desegregation in the Southern and Border States" Collection (website), February 1967.

Southwick, Leslie. "Mississippi Supreme Court Elections: A Historical Perspective, 1916–1996." *Mississippi College Law Review* 18, no. 1 (1997–1998): 155–98.

"Soviet Ships Steam toward Test of Cuban Arms Blockade: US Forces Move to Enforce Kennedy Order." *Delta Democrat-Times* (Greenville, MS), October 23, 1962.

Sparrow, Hugh W. "Case under Study—Two of Judges Indicate Bus Laws in Force." *Birmingham News*, May 12, 1956.

"Speaking about Rights—What about Our Rights?" *Conservative* (Carrollton, MS), May 30, 1958.

"Special Session Opens Today on Reshuffle Note." *Selma Times-Journal*, September 13, 1965.

Spivack, John Michael. "Race, Civil Rights, and the United States Court of Appeals for the Fifth Judicial Circuit." PhD diss., University of Florida, 1978.

———. "Richard Taylor Rives and Benjamin F. Cameron: The Varieties of Southern Judges." *Southern Studies: An Interdisciplinary Journal of the South* 1, no. 3 (1990): 225–41.

Stallworth, Clarke. "After Evidence Is Studied—Prompt Reapportion Decision Is Promised: Legislature Is Accused of Failing to Do Its Duty." *Birmingham Post-Herald*, July 17, 1962.

Stanton, Mary. *Journey toward Justice: Juliette Hampton Morgan and the Montgomery Bus Boycott*. Athens: University of Georgia Press, 2006.

"State Appeals Goldsby Ruling." *Conservative* (Carrollton, MS), June 19, 1959.

"State Laws Held Constitutional: Circuit Judge Orders Bus Line to Halt Integration Policy." *Alabama Journal*, May 10, 1956.

"State Military Department: Functional Analysis and Records Disposition Authority, January 27, 2010." Alabama Secretary of State (website).

"State Probate Judges to Air Court Pleas." *Alabama Journal*, November 18, 1965.

"State Reapportionment Is Upheld." *Alabama Journal*, October 24, 1972.

Steele, Jack. "Fifth Circuit Has Major Part in Civil Rights Conflicts." *Birmingham Post-Herald*, July 20, 1963.

Stevenson, Bryan A. "Emphasis and Integrity: Frank Johnson and the Administration of Criminal Justice." *Alabama Lawyer* 52, no. 6 (1991): 338–41.

Stewart, William H. *The Alabama State Constitution*. 2nd ed. New York: Oxford University Press, 2016.

———. "Reapportionment with Census Districts: The Alabama Case." *Alabama Law Review* 24 (1972): 693–713.

"Storekeeper and Negro Exchanged Shots in Vaiden." *Delta Democrat Times* (Greenville, MS), November 19, 1954.

Strauss, David A. "Common Law Constitutional Interpretation." *University of Chicago Law Review* 63, no. 3 (1996): 877–935.

———. "The Common Law Genius of the Warren Court." *William. and Mary Law Review* 49, no. 3 (2007): 845–79.

———. "The Living Constitution." University of Chicago Law School (website). Last modified September 27, 2010.

———. *The Living Constitution*. Oxford: Oxford University Press, 2010.

"Streetcars: Montgomery, Alabama." Hawkins Rails (website). Last modified April 3, 2022.

Student Nonviolent Coordinating Committee. "Selma and Dallas County, Alabama: A Statistical Roundup." Civil Rights Movement Archive, Duke University (website). Accessed July 23, 2024.

Student Nonviolent Coordinating Committee Atlanta GA. "The General Condition of the Alabama Negro: March 1965." Civil Rights Movement Archive, Duke University (website).

Summer, Fred A. "Voter Registration Lists: Do They Yield a Jury Representative of the Community." *University of Michigan Journal of Law Reform* 5, no. 2 (1972): 385–408.

"The Supreme Court: Jury Trial." *Time*, October 26, 1959.

"The Supreme Court: Presumption of Faith." *Time*, December 8, 1958.

"Supreme Court Tells Alabama to Revise Legislative System: Reapportion before 1966 Decree Issued: Decision Affects Other States Also." *Alabama Journal*, June 15, 1965.

Swanson, Craig. *The Selma Campaign: Martin Luther King Jr., Jimmie Lee Jackson, and the Defining Struggle of the Civil Rights Era*. Bloomington, IN: Archway, 2014.

"Testimony Completed Quickly in Segregation Act Attack: No Immediate Ruling Planned by US Court." *Alabama Journal*, May 11, 1956.

"23,000 Negroes Placed on Voter Lists by Ruling." *Alabama Journal*, November 24, 1965.

Thomas, Rex. "Court: U.S. Judges Set Review of Reapportionment Law." *Montgomery Advertiser*, September 25, 1965.

Thompson, Wright. *The Cost of These Dreams: Sports Stories and Other Serious Business*. New York: Penguin Books, 2019.

Thornton, J. Mills, III. "Challenge and Response in the Montgomery Bus Boycott of 1955–1956." *Alabama Review* 67, no. 1 (2014): 40–112.

———. *Dividing Lines: Municipal Politics and the Struggle for Civil Rights in Montgomery, Birmingham, and Selma*. Tuscaloosa: University of Alabama Press, 2002.

———"Hugo Black and the Golden Age." *Alabama Law Review* 36, no. 3 (1984–1985): 899–913.

———. "Selma's Smitherman Affair of 1955." *Alabama Review* 44, no. 2 (1991): 112–31.

Tocqueville, Alexis de. *Democracy in America*. 4 vols. Translated by Henry Reeve. New York: Colonial Press, 1900.

Trost, Benjamin. "Persistent Resistance: The Struggle against School Integration in Tuscaloosa, Alabama (1956–2007)." *Crimson Historical Review* 7 (2021): 77–98.

Tushnet, Mark V. *The NAACP's Legal Strategy against Segregated Education, 1925–1950*. Chapel Hill: University of North Carolina Press, 1987.

Udall, Levi S. "The Essential Characteristics of a Judge." *Journal of the American Judicature Society* 41, no. 3 (1957): 69.

Umberson, Debra. *Death of a Parent: Transition to a New Adult Identity*. New York: Cambridge University Press, 2003.

"Unfinished Business in Alabama." *Anniston Star*, July 31, 1965.

United States Commission on Civil Rights. *Book 5: Justice*. Washington, DC: US Government Printing Office, 1961.

———. *Law Enforcement: A Report on Equal Protection in the South*. Washington, DC: Government Printing Office, 1965.

———. *The Voting Rights Act: The First Months*. Washington, DC: United States Commission on Civil Rights.

"US Appeals Judge Slams 'Favored Trio' in Cases." *Greenwood Commonwealth* (Greenwood, MS), July 31, 1963.

"U.S. Court of Appeals for the Fifth Circuit—Brief History." US Court of Appeals for the Fifth Circuit (website). Accessed December 30, 2023.

"U.S. Court of Appeals for the Fifth Circuit—Legislative History." US Court of Appeals for the Fifth Circuit (website). Accessed December 30, 2023.

"US Judge Blames 'Crusaders' for Decisions to Desegregate." *Tampa Times*, July 31, 1963.

"US Judge Says Court Isn't Rigged." *Atlanta Constitution*, August 24, 1963.

"US Jury Here Convicts N.Y. Student of Perjury." *Macon Telegraph*, November 16, 1963.

"Venue Change Given Goldsby: Goldsby Case Moved to Jackson; Others Plead Guilty; Court Ends." *Conservative* (Carrollton, MS), November 12, 1959.

"Voter's [*sic*] List to Be Printed in Journal." *Alabama Journal*, April 9, 1964.

Wallace, George. "The [January 14, 1963] Inaugural Address of Governor George C. Wallace." Alabama Department of Archives and History Digital Collections (website).

Wallace, Mike. "Transcript: Interview with Senator James Eastland [July 28, 1957]." Harry Ransom Center, University of Texas at Austin (website).

Ware, Leland B. "Setting the Stage for Brown: The Development and Implementation of the NAACP's School Desegregation Campaign, 1930–1950." *Mercer Law Review* 52, no. 2 (2001): 631–73.

"Warren, Earl." Oyez (website). Accessed November 12, 2022.

"Westminster Confession of Faith." Trinity Presbyterian Church (website). Accessed June 6, 2023.

"What They Have Done to Us." *Alabama Journal*, July 23, 1962.

"We Believed We Were Immortal." Vimeo (website), video, 8:51. Uploaded by Larry Wells on January 8, 2018.

Weill, Susan M. "Mississippi's Daily Press in Three Crises." In *The Press and Race: Mississippi Journalists Confront the Movement*, edited by David R. Davies Jackson, 17–54. Jackson: University Press of Mississippi, 2001.

Weiss, Debra Cassens. "Students Try to Avoid Law School Costs with 'Reading Law' Path to Law License." *ABA Journal*, July 30, 2014.

Welz, Steve. "Judge Rives Is Honored." *Pro Confesso* [Cumberland School of Law at Samford University, Birmingham, AL] (April 1975): 1, 4.

Wickham, Kathleen W. *We Believed We Were Immortal: Twelve Reporters Who Covered the 1962 Integration Crisis at Ole Miss.* Oxford, MS: Yoknapatawpha Press, 2017.

"Wilkinson Calls for Amendment Four OK—Rives Denounces It: Debate Sponsored by Florence Jaycees Draws Capacity Audience; Amendment 4 Seen Effort Entrench Special Privilege." *Florence Herald* (Florence, AL), November 1, 1946.

Williams, Donnie, with Wayne Greenhaw. *The Thunder of Angels: The Montgomery Bus Boycott and the People Who Broke the Back of Jim Crow.* Chicago: Lawrence Hill Books, 2006.

Wisdom, John Minor. "Notes on the Houston Conference." John Minor Wisdom Collection, Tulane University (website). Accessed March 17, 2021.

"Woman Killed by Negro Motorist." *Delta Democrat Times* (Greenville, MS). September 5, 1954.

Woods, Jeff. *Black Struggle, Red Scare: Segregation and Anti-Communism in the South, 1948–1968.* Baton Rouge: Louisiana State University Press, 2004.

Woodward, C. Vann. "Montgomery." In *American Places: Encounters with History: America's Leading Historians Talk about the Sites Where the Past Comes Alive for Them*, edited by William E. Leuchtenburg, 339–52. New York: Oxford University Press, 2000.

Wright, John Peavy. "Tell It to Old Grandma." *Montgomery Advertiser*, April 22, 1962.

Wright, Richard. *Native Son*. New York: Harper and Brothers, 1940.

Yarbrough, Tinsley E. *Judge Frank Johnson and Human Rights in Alabama.* Tuscaloosa: University of Alabama Press, 1981.

Index

Page numbers in italics refer to figures and tables.